Guide to Optimal Operational Risk & Basel II

OTHER AUERBACH PUBLICATIONS

Agent-Based Manufacturing and Control Systems: New Agile Manufacturing Solutions for Achieving Peak Performance
Massimo Paolucci and Roberto Sacile
ISBN: 1574443364

Curing the Patch Management Headache
Felicia M. Nicastro
ISBN: 0849328543

Cyber Crime Investigator's Field Guide, Second Edition
Bruce Middleton
ISBN: 0849327687

Disassembly Modeling for Assembly, Maintenance, Reuse and Recycling
A. J. D. Lambert and Surendra M. Gupta
ISBN: 1574443348

The Ethical Hack: A Framework for Business Value Penetration Testing
James S. Tiller
ISBN: 084931609X

Fundamentals of DSL Technology
Philip Golden, Herve Dedieu, and Krista Jacobsen
ISBN: 0849319137

The HIPAA Program Reference Handbook
Ross Leo
ISBN: 0849322111

Implementing the IT Balanced Scorecard: Aligning IT with Corporate Strategy
Jessica Keyes
ISBN: 0849326214

Information Security Fundamentals
Thomas R. Peltier, Justin Peltier, and John A. Blackley
ISBN: 0849319579

Information Security Management Handbook, Fifth Edition, Volume 2
Harold F. Tipton and Micki Krause
ISBN: 0849332109

Introduction to Management of Reverse Logistics and Closed Loop Supply Chain Processes
Donald F. Blumberg
ISBN: 1574443607

Maximizing ROI on Software Development
Vijay Sikka
ISBN: 0849323126

Mobile Computing Handbook
Imad Mahgoub and Mohammad Ilyas
ISBN: 0849319714

MPLS for Metropolitan Area Networks
Nam-Kee Tan
ISBN: 084932212X

Multimedia Security Handbook
Borko Furht and Darko Kirovski
ISBN: 0849327733

Network Design: Management and Technical Perspectives, Second Edition
Teresa C. Piliouras
ISBN: 0849316081

Network Security Technologies, Second Edition
Kwok T. Fung
ISBN: 0849330270

Outsourcing Software Development Offshore: Making It Work
Tandy Gold
ISBN: 0849319439

Quality Management Systems: A Handbook for Product Development Organizations
Vivek Nanda
ISBN: 1574443526

A Practical Guide to Security Assessments
Sudhanshu Kairab
ISBN: 0849317061

The Real-Time Enterprise
Dimitris N. Chorafas
ISBN: 0849327776

Software Testing and Continuous Quality Improvement, Second Edition
William E. Lewis
ISBN: 0849325242

Supply Chain Architecture: A Blueprint for Networking the Flow of Material, Information, and Cash
William T. Walker
ISBN: 1574443577

The Windows Serial Port Programming Handbook
Ying Bai
ISBN: 0849322138

GUIDE TO OPTIMAL OPERATIONAL RISK & BASEL II

Ioannis S. Akkizidis
Vivianne Bouchereau

CRC Press is an imprint of the
Taylor & Francis Group, an **informa** business

CRC Press
Taylor & Francis Group
6000 Broken Sound Parkway NW, Suite 300
Boca Raton, FL 33487-2742

First issued in paperback 2019

ISBN-13: 978-0-8493-3813-7 (hbk)
ISBN-13: 978-0-367-39188-1 (pbk)

Library of Congress Card Number 2005048153

Library of Congress Cataloging-in-Publication Data

Akkizidis, Ioannis S.
Guide to optimal operational risk and Basel II / Ioannis S. Akkizidis and Vivianne Bouchereau.
p. cm.
Includes bibliographical references and index.
ISBN 0-8493-3813-1 (alk. paper)
1. Financial services industry--Risk management. 2. Bank management. 3. Basel Committee on Banking Supervision. I. Bouchereau, Vivianne. II. Title.

HG173.A37 2005
332.1'068--dc22 2005048153

Visit the Informa Web site at
www.informa.com

and the Informa Healthcare Web site at
www.informahealthcare.com

Dedication

This book is dedicated to

My father (Ioannis Akkizidis)

My family (Vivianne Bouchereau)

Contents

Preface

Risk creates value and profits come from taking risks.

—Ulrich Doerig

Businesses are becoming more and more competitive and managing risk continues to be at the heart of financial organizations' activities. Risk management was in its elementary stages until the 1980s. It was not recognized as part of business management processes, but only as a method of taking precautionary measures when business went wrong. In recent years, managerial practices are recognizing the importance of enterprisewide risk management and trying to strategically analyze corporate activities. Organizations are realizing the need to properly understand their risks due to various actions as well as interrelations of the risks within the organization.

New disciplines are emerging for risk management, as well as a new focus on operational risk management. Operational risks have existed as financial organizations evolved. However, as a separate discipline, operational risk management surfaced only in recent years. Compliance regulations, such as Basel II, mandate a focus on operational risks, and have forced the market to evaluate the implications these regulations will have on procedures and strategies in coming years. Of all the different types of risks that can affect financial organizations, operational risks can be among the most devastating and the most difficult to anticipate. Operational risk continues to receive heightened attention among market participants and regulators, prompting dialogues and debates on the best ways to identify, measure, evaluate, control, and manage this important type of risk. This recognition has led to an increased emphasis on the importance of sound operational risk management in financial organizations and, to a greater extent, operational risks in banks' internal capital assessment and allocation processes. Operational risk management is one of the most complex and fastest growing areas in financial organizations today. As one of the most heavily regulated industries, financial organizations are often required to set the ball rolling with regard to rules and guidelines, while other industries follow suit.

As the pace of change inside and outside financial organizations continues to increase exponentially and as the marketplace becomes more and more complex due to technological advancement and innovations, the management of operational change and operational risks has become a critical success factor. For the first time, the Basel Committee has proposed to establish capital charges for operational risks, in exchange for lowering them on market and credit risk. This new accord, aiming for a closer correspondence between the capital that banks hold and the risks they take, should lead to more stable, efficiently run financial organizations. Thus operational risk management has been placed high on the agenda for financial organizations. Incentives to comply with Basel II allow banks that can prove they have effective and sophisticated operational risk management systems to reduce their level of protective capital buffer, freeing potentially millions of dollars for investment in profitable activities. Efficient operational risk management is a decisive competitive advantage. It helps to maintain stability and continuity and supports revenue and earnings, a process for which senior management and boards of directors are increasingly called upon to ensure. Business operations will need to be as efficient as possible to deliver reliable services to customers. Operational risk management frameworks and practices will need to mature to satisfy all stakeholders versus shareholders, employees, government, regulators, and society as a whole. The Basel II Capital Accord marks a significant shift in the philosophy of capital regulation and the supervision of banks. Although numerical minimum capital requirements remain, they are embedded deep within Basel II's mathematical structure, a structure that places much more emphasis on the range of capital that may be required for specific operational risks faced by each bank. Basel II clearly lays down that financial organizations need to focus on loss data collection of three to five years varying according to different lines of business. It also stresses more effective ways to track, monitor, analyze, and report operational risk data.

The Basel II Accord is all about bringing together the world's financial organizations under a common regulatory framework, although the way to manage operational risk is different for each financial organization. Financial organizations could improve their operational risk management in a way that would have a bottom-line impact even without Basel II. Still, there are important reasons to go all the way: financial organizations certified as Basel II compliant could benefit from lower capital charges and the enhanced reputation that would come from the regulators' seal of approval. Applying the Basel II requirements will take financial organizations to, or close to, best practices in operational risk management.

Significant operational losses in recent years in the banking industry have highlighted that operational risks can arise from internal and external fraud, failure to comply with employment laws or meet workplace safety standards, policy breaches, compliance breaches, key personnel risks, damage to physical assets, business disruptions and system failures, transaction processing failures, information security breaches, and so on. Financial organizations such as banks, security companies, and insurance companies have particularly been adversely affected by operational risks in recent years. The list of cases involving catastrophic consequences of procedural and operational momentary failure is long and unfortunately growing. To see the implications of operational risk events, one need only look at the devastating $691 million rogue trading loss at Allfirst Financial, the $484 million settlement due to misleading sales practices at Household Finance, the $1.3 billion loss of Barings Bank as a result of rogue trading operation, and the loss arising from the September 11, 2001, terrorist attack on the World Trade Center, which is estimated to be about $16.9 billion. However, the terrorist attack that took place in Madrid on March 11, 2004 had significantly fewer losses, and the most recent in London on July 7, 2005 found financial organizations worldwide more mature, and thus their financial losses are expected to be respectively less. This is because financial organizations have more knowledge on such risks and are designing and implementing more effective operational risk management frameworks. Concerning the London attack, the market also expects that there will be a big investment for designing and implementing effective operational risk management systems for many operations supporting business sectors that will be part of the upcoming Olympic games in London in the year 2012. Losses such as those that were initiated from the natural disasters of an earthquake and its associated tsunamis that hit the Indian Ocean on December 26, 2004, was one of the most devastating operational risks that are classified in the group of 'external risks' in these last few years. The terrible loss of human lives is estimated at over 200,000. The financial loss is yet unknown. This event illustrates how external calamities can affect and disrupt organizations' normal day-to-day operational activities.

One highly visible operational risk event can suddenly end the life of a financial organization. Moreover, many, almost-invisible individual errors of persistent operational risk events over a period of time can strain the resources of the financial organization. Whereas a fundamentally strong organization can often recover from market risk and credit risk events, it may be almost impossible to recover from certain operational risk events. The extent of potential operational risk losses will increase in the future as global financial organizations specialize in unpredictable new products and services, mergers and acquisitions, and outsourcing, to name just a few.

For effective operational risk assessment, control, and management, it is vital to identify, measure, model, monitor, evaluate, and determine the operational risk profile, but more important to optimize the implications of the operational risks in operational business performances. This ensures an alignment of these operational risks to the business/strategic objectives, planning process, decision making, practices, and quality initiatives. Moreover, strategic and planning policies on when and how to accept, avoid, or mitigate operational risks according to their actual probability, impact, and exposure should be defined. This definition must be consistent with the optimal levels of operational risks. Apart from the underlying approaches, the provision of sound practical tools is essential for efficient operational risk management.

This book presents all the key aspects of operational risk management that are also aligned with the Basel II requirements. More important, it gives detailed guidance for the design and implementation of efficient operational risk management systems. Thus, all the elements of the assessment analysis, including the operational risk identification analysis, measurement, modeling, and monitoring analysis, together with the evaluation analysis and the estimation of capital requirements, make up a great part of this book. Additionally, a significant part of this book addresses managing and controlling operational risks, which includes operational risk profiling, optimization, decision making, and design of optimal risk policies. Several novel approaches that combine aspects of advanced mathematical algorithmic modeling with business intelligent techniques together with total quality management are outlined in the book. Moreover, a forward-looking design of sound practical tools to drive optimal bottom-line results is highlighted. Practical examples of the approaches are presented to support the guidelines of the book. Because one picture is worth a thousand words, this book contains specially designed graphics to help readers visualize as many ideas and concepts as possible. The graphical output results for the case studies illustrated in the book originate from a software tool that the reader can access at www.crcpress.com/e_products/downloads/download.asap?cat_no=AU3813. The software tool supports the applicability of the material of the book. For more details about the software and any feedback related to the subject of this book, please contact the authors or visit http://www.riskoptimisation.com.

Audience

This book is intended for practitioners or those who have an interest in learning about operational risk management and its role in the Basel II

Accord. It is particularly suitable for those seeking to grasp the more advanced approaches of assessing, controlling, and managing operational risk in financial organizations. It also serves as a guide to understand the fundamentals of operational risk management and the Basel II operational risk management principles. More important, it serves as a guide for implementing optimal operational risk management systems. Potential readers of the book include but are not limited to:

- Operational risk managers/chief risk officers/risk analysts
- Operational risk consultants
- Operations and business line managers
- Chief security officers
- Financial risk managers
- Chief information officers
- Actuaries
- Auditors
- Compliance officers
- Insurers
- University lecturers in risk management subjects
- Postgraduate students in financial and banking undertaking subjects related to banking processes, management, and risks
- Financial project managers

Organization of This Book

The book is divided into four parts. The first part introduces the idea of operational risks and how they affect financial organizations. It also focuses on the main aspects of managing operational risks in financial organizations. Part II focuses on the requirements of an operational risk management framework according to the Basel II Accord. Part III and Part IV of this book give overview guidelines on how to design an efficient framework for operational risk management systems in accordance with Basel II requirements. Whereas Part III concentrates notably on the operational risk assessment phase, Part IV focuses on the controlling and managing of these operational risks. All these stages combine to implement efficient and optimal operational risk management systems. The book is organized as shown in Figure 0.1

Chapter 1: Operational Risks in Financial Organizations

This chapter introduces several topics that form the basis of the subsequent chapters. It attempts to show the multifaceted definition of operational risk and highlights some of its major concerns. Examples of operational

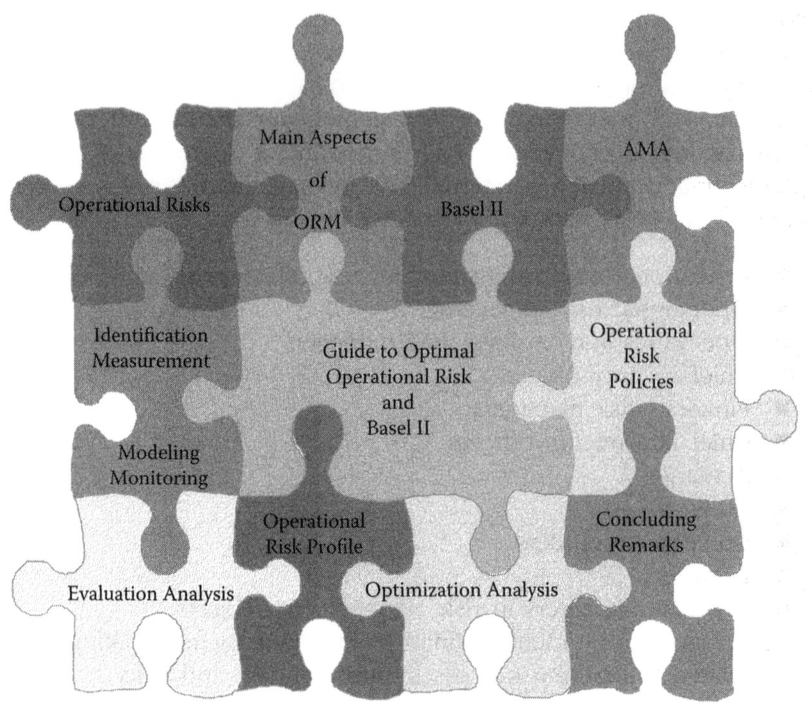

Figure 0.1 Organization of the book.

losses in various organizations around the globe are highlighted to put in perspective the need to manage these risks. The characteristics of operational risks are generally discussed, and then the chapter examines the effect of IT and IT security in the realism of operational risks.

Chapter 2: Main Aspects of Operational Risk Management

This chapter contains a discussion of the main aspects of operational risk management (ORM). Furthermore, effective operational risk management frameworks are outlined. The quantification of operational risks and the testing and verification of the operational risk management framework are then discussed. Enterprisewide risk management, which aims to integrate the management of the different types of risks faced by financial organizations, is introduced, together with some main operational risk management concerns. Finally some key players for implementing effectively operational risk management frameworks are listed.

Chapter 3: Operational Risk in Basel II

This chapter introduces the Basel II Accord, briefly comparing it with its predecessor. The chapter then highlights the meaning of operational risk in Basel II and lists some of the main objectives and targets of the Basel II Accord. A discussion of the three pillars of the accord is also included. The calculation of the minimum capital requirements is subsequently discussed in relation to which of the three proposed Basel II approaches is implemented. The qualifying criteria for operational risk capital calculation are then highlighted with reference to the main factors in selecting an appropriate approach. Finally, Chapter 3 introduces the ten principles of the accord with some action points concerning the three pillars of Basel II, to consider in preparation for an efficient operational risk management framework.

Chapter 4: Advanced Measurement Approach

Chapter 4 focuses on the advanced measurement approach (AMA) proposed by Basel II. It discusses the quantitative standards of the AMA, including the three broad AMA approaches proposed by Basel II. It then discusses the qualifying criteria for operational risk capital calculation using the AMA. In addition, this chapter introduces the supervisory standards for the AMA. Finally, it discusses the use of insurance as an operational risk mitigation strategy under the AMA.

Chapter 5: Operational Risk Identification, Measurement, Modeling, and Monitoring Analysis

This chapter deals with the framework of methodologies for operational risk identification, measurement, modeling, and monitoring analysis. The chapter gives guidelines on when and how to define key performance and risk indicators and how to measure these indicators, for the information data extraction process related to operational risk causes, events, and consequences. It also shows how to model and monitor efficiently both operational risks and affected operations based on correlation analysis defined from multidimensional operational risk parameters. Results that illustrate the mapping of the pattern or contour topography of the operational risks and affected operations are presented. Advanced graphical representation using three-dimensional surface illustrations shows the correlation models for both operational risk and affected operations.

Chapter 6: Operational Risk Assessment via Evaluation Analysis

This chapter focuses on the evaluation process for both operational risks and affected operations. The evaluation is based on significance analysis referring to cause, events, and consequences. Clustering approaches based on fuzzy logic theory are presented to show their implementation for the operational risk evaluation analysis. The identification of the equilibrium points referring to operational risk and affected operations based on two different methods are presented in this chapter. A method called "mountain surface evaluation," which is based on advanced algorithmic analysis and graphical representation, is also discussed extensively in this chapter. Finally, the estimation and evaluation of the economical capital reserves using the operational VaR and the application of extreme value theory are described in this chapter.

Chapter 7: Operational Risk Profiling

This chapter gives guidance on how to estimate the probability and impact based on the analysis of the operational risk causes, events, and consequences. This analysis is mainly focused on the correlations, significances, actual, and loss values of operational risks. Furthermore, the modeling and monitoring of the operational risk profile, based on fuzzy clustering and fuzzy logic techniques and methodologies, are discussed. These advanced approaches for decision making are applied to different case studies of operational risks in banking organizations. Advanced graphical representation of the results are presented and discussed extensively to show the applicability of the approaches.

Chapter 8: Operational Risk Optimization

This chapter presents operational risk optimization by means of optimizing the levels of operational risk parameters to minimize the overall value of risks and their effect on the operations. Moreover, techniques of optimizing the resources that should be allocated to manage these risks are also discussed in this chapter. Different optimization techniques and methodologies that can be used for designing effective and optimal operational risk management systems are introduced with a focus on significance–exposure– correlation optimization. Results coming from the optimization analysis are also presented and discussed.

Chapter 9: Framework for Decision Making and Designing Optimal Risk Policies

This chapter provides guidance on how financial organizations should plan their actions and policies for designing efficient operational risk management frameworks. This includes the policies of when to accept, avoid, or transfer/mitigate operational risks. Scenarios used for risk analysis are also presented. Business impact analysis for designing the "worst-case scenario" is also discussed. Moreover, this chapter gives guidelines for designing business continuity plans to deal with operational risks that are severe. The main guidelines for undertaking internal control, in relation to Basel II's requirements, are also presented. Finally, the importance of reporting tools that banking organizations must have in place to manage the vast amount of information data gathered from operational risk management systems is discussed. All these analyses present a solid platform for effective decision making concerning the assessment, control, and management of operational risks.

Chapter 10: Concluding Remarks

This chapter offers some concluding remarks and discusses future directions of operational risk management.

References are given at the end of every chapter for those interested in strengthening their knowledge beyond the scope of this book. All referenced documents written by the Basel Committee on Banking Supervision are available free of charge from their Web site at http://www.bis.org/bcbs/publ.htm. A list of acronyms is given in the appendix to ease understanding of the terms used throughout the book.

Acknowledgments

The authors would like to especially thank all those who supported them in various ways to enable them to complete this book. These include, first of all, their individual families, Athena Akkizidou and Nikos Akkizidis. Special thanks go to Vasilios Masmanidis and Christos Ventiadis for their support, Helen Sjöberg for her inspiration, and Maja Kotzmuth-Clarke and Stelios Apostolopoulos for their constant encouraging words. They would also like to thank Dr. Lampros Kalyvas for the valuable participation in discussions, feedback, and small contributions for the material of this book. Finally, the authors would like to mention the country of Sweden, always open to new ideas, which gave them the opportunity to first implement their ideas. They would also like to thank CRC Press and Auerbach Publications, members of The Taylor & Francis Group, for giving them the opportunity to publish their work.

About the Authors

Ioannis Akkizidis, Ph.D. is a business and risk analyst and the main architect of the approaches presented in this book. He has been developing and applying advanced mathematical algorithmic theories and practices to identify, model, map, evaluate, and optimize complex operational risks for banking organizations and big enterprises. He has extensive academic knowledge through his master's (M.Sc.) in control systems analysis and Ph.D. in artificial intelligence and applied mathematics. He has published several scientific and working papers from journals to newspapers, has presented at several international conferences, and has given ample talks on the subject of operational risk optimization and management. He has worked worldwide for many years in business and risk analysis and has designed and implemented advanced software tools for large organizations and financial organizations.

Vivianne Bouchereau, Ph.D. is a business and risk analyst. She has undertaken projects in the field of business performance, operational risk analysis, and optimization, as well as quality management. She has contributed to the design of the various methodologies on operational risk assessment, control, and management presented in this book. She has given seminars and talks on operational risk management and Basel II and has several years of working experience in the quality engineering field. She is also a qualified lead quality auditor for ISO 9001: 2000, has written numerous papers on the subject of total quality management, and has been a presenter at numerous international seminars and conferences. She has extensive academic background and working knowledge in this field. She obtained her combined bachelor's and master's degree (M.Eng.) in electronic and electrical engineering and her Ph.D. in quality engineering.

Contacting the Authors

The authors are pleased to have any feedback and are open to any discussion referring to the subject and material presented in this book. Please contact them via e-mail at:

- i.akkizidis@optimisation4business.com (Ioannis S. Akkizidis)
- v.bouchereau@optimisation4business.com (Vivianne Bouchereau)

OPERATIONAL RISK AND ITS MANAGEMENT

This first part of this book, which consists of Chapters 1 and 2, introduces the idea of operational risks and how they affect financial organizations. It also focuses on the main aspects of managing operational risks in financial organizations.

Chapter 1

Operational Risks in Financial Organizations

Where there is money, there is risk.

—Paul Getty

Introduction

Managing risk is an old habit of human beings. In their day-to-day lives, people always seem to be worried about future risks. As a result, they end up investing in insurance or other investment methods to secure themselves against unforeseen risks. Accidents, environmental disasters, bankruptcy, and loss of business are risks that have plagued the human race since time began. Generally, no complete protection exists against every potential risk, but appropriate proactive measures to mitigate certain risks can be adopted. The same concept also applies to financial organizations. Understanding risks has always been a fundamental, if only implicit, management process in financial organizations. What is new is the following:

- The increased explicit awareness and consciousness of managers and senior management of risk issues
- The explicit and analytical approaches

- The greater awareness to direct an organization's risk profile toward those risks for which it has a comparative advantage in managing
- The pressure to allocate resources more consciously

Risk management was in its elementary stages until the 1980s. It was not recognized as part of the business management process but only as a method of taking precautionary measures when business went wrong. The concept was, "Do business and then measure the risks," whereas in today's economy, the concept is, "Measure the risk first, then do business." Thus, during the late 1980s and early 1990s, apart from profit-making goals, organizations were faced with other goals, such as accountability, transparency, and performance, as demanded by their investors. Risk management has always been a fundamental management process in financial organizations. It is a well-known fact that where there is money, a certain amount of risk must be involved. In the realm of the financial domain today, the term "risk" is being used more frequently. It is recommended that operations integrate risk management into decision making in the same way it has already integrated such critical factors as time, money, and labor. Managing risks effectively has become the duty of everyone involved in financial organizations. Nowadays, however, there is more pressure to avoid things going wrong while continuing to improve corporate performance. By monitoring risk more closely, financial organizations can minimize the required amount of reserve capital and maximize their profitability.

Good risk management is a decisive competitive advantage. It helps to maintain stability and continuity, and it supports revenue and earnings, a process for which senior management and boards of directors are increasingly called upon to ensure. The Basel Committee on Banking Supervision created the first Basel Accord in 1988 (as discussed in Chapter 3) to ensure capital allocation by examining market risk and credit risk within banking organizations. The new version, Basel II, finalized in June 2004, is set to modify its evaluation of credit risk and, more importantly, seeks to assess operational risk, an area previously not clearly defined in the financial services marketplace. It will give banks more flexibility in weighing those risks by providing several new options for calculating credit and operational risks. The bottom-line, less-risky loans should require less capital. The Basel Committee itself does not actually have any authority to impose capital-reserve requirements on the world's banks; instead, it formulates broad supervisory standards and recommends best practices, which it then turns over to regulatory authorities in its 13 member countries for implementation. The 13 members include the G10 plus Luxembourg and Spain (G10: Canada, Belgium, Germany, Italy, Japan, the Netherlands,

Sweden, Switzerland, United Kingdom, United States). Many nonmember countries are also seeking to comply with its recommendations.

Operational risk has existed as financial organizations evolved. Operational risk management in financial organizations as discussed throughout this book is preventive rather than reactive. It is based on the philosophy that it is irresponsible and wasteful to wait for an accident to happen and then figure out how to prevent it from happening again. Over the past several years, financial organizations have focused on developing sophisticated tools to measure market risk and credit risk. Today, operational risk has become another critical aspect in risk capital allocation. Unlike with market risk and credit risk, which mainly involve only risks associated with trading and lending, everyone in the organization can be a source of operational risk. The new Basel II Accord instigated by the Bank of International Settlement is undertaking a major effort to fundamentally increase the quantification of operational risk. Operational risk as the most recent area of risk management is therefore all set to face formal quantification through the regulatory process. The Basel Committee has observed through various surveys[1] that the current measurement of operational risk by banks is relatively undefined and qualitative in nature. Comprehensive, enterprisewide strategy and tactics toward risk can no longer be achieved by applying common sense only — although common sense remains crucial. There is a need for credible and relevant methodologies to define, identify, assess, measure, analyze, control, and manage risks. Operational risks are highly multifaceted, complex, and often interlinked. Although not avoidable, operational risks are manageable. Financial organizations and regulators and supervisors should be aware of the cost-benefit relationship of setting in place the quantification of operational risk, which involves data gathering, models, procedures, systems, and staff. The value of financial organizations increasingly lies in its intangible assets, such as data, knowledge, skills, people, network, reputation, and brand. These assets are bundled together in the organization and can also reflect in operational risks.

Although operational risk is not a new risk, deregulation and globalization of financial services, together with the growing sophistication of financial technologies, new business activities, and delivery channels, are making organizations' operational risk profiles (i.e., the level of operational risk's probability, impact, and exposure across an organization's activities and risk categories) more complex.

Regulators are currently examining operational and compliance risks under the Bank Secrecy Act,[2] USA Patriot Act,[3] Gramm–Leach–Bliley Act,[4] Basel II Accord,[27] Sarbanes–Oxley,[31] and Federal Financial Institutions Examination Council (FFIEC) guidelines.[5] The Bank Secrecy Act and the

USA Patriot Act require programs to be in place for anti-money-laundering, reporting of suspicious activity, large cash transactions, customer identification, and more. The Gramm–Leach–Bliley Act requires safeguards for customer information, privacy, and information security. The Federal Deposit Insurance Corporation Improvement Act of 1991 (FDICIA) and Sarbanes–Oxley both require internal controls review across most departments, which are a subset of the bankwide risk assessment process. FFIEC information technology (IT) handbooks direct senior management and the board of directors to manage IT risks, including information security, business continuity, and disaster recovery.

Three excellent reasons for a banking organization to advance its operational risk program are as follows:

1. Regulators are going to require the organization to do so over time.
2. Taking a proactive attitude means doing it according to the organization's own timelines and on its own terms.
3. The organization's shareholders expect the organization to add value to its bank.

Financial organizations should not accept operational risks simply as fate but should deal with them intentionally. Financial organizations are thus challenged to do the following:

- Meet their compliance commitment.
- Employ best practices such as Basel II.
- Build an appropriate and effective operational risk management system.
- Assess, measure, analyze, and report operational risks.
- Design strategies to align and manage operational risks across the organization.
- Have timely and accurate reporting, tracking, and control of operational risks.
- Maximize the potential benefits of freeing up capital charge.

This chapter introduces several topics that form a basis for subsequent chapters. It begins by defining operational risks and why financial organizations should be concerned about them. This leads to a presentation of where operational risks exist in financial organizations, with concrete examples of where operational risks have caused major catastrophes in financial organizations in the past. Next, causes of operational risks in financial organizations are examined. The characteristics of operational risks are generally discussed; then further details are presented of how operational risk affects, or is affected by, IT. Finally, this chapter looks briefly at IT security. The layout of this chapter is presented pictorially in Figure 1.1.

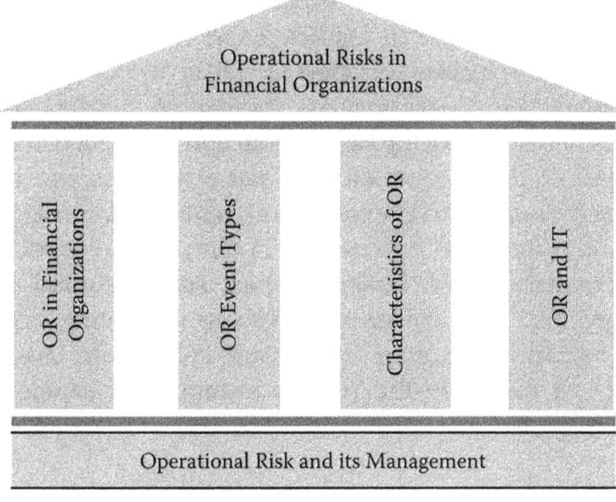

Figure 1.1 Layout of Chapter 1.

Operational Risks in Financial Organizations

Of all the different types of risks that affect financial organizations, operational risks can be among the most destructive and most difficult to foresee. Operational risks continue to receive keen attention among market participants and regulators, triggering dialogues and debates on the best ways to identify, measure, and manage this important risk. This recognition has led to an increased prominence of the importance of sound operational risk management in financial organizations and, to a greater degree, operational risk in banks' internal capital assessment and allocation processes. In fact, the banking industry is currently undergoing a surge of innovation and development in these areas. The extraordinary demands of setting up a robust yet sensible and practical operational risk management system are puzzling risk professionals in every industry, and even more in financial organizations, where the regulators set out very detailed requirements.

The Basel II Accord focuses on bringing together the world's financial organizations under a common regulatory framework, although the way to manage operational risk is different for each financial organization; after all, there are over 30,000 banks and an estimated 20,000 insurance companies worldwide. Basel II will enable banks to align regulatory requirements more closely with their internal risk measurement and to improve operational processes. Forward-thinking organizations recognize that the accord also provides a unique opportunity to modernize and upgrade their overall risk practices and risk infrastructure, specifically for credit and operational risk. For these banks, Basel II means more than compliance; rather, it denotes the opportunity to achieve distinct competitive advantage in a tight global market. Some banking organizations have begun developing processes required by Basel II, but few if any organizations have made the operational risk framework a practical tool to drive bottom-line results by enhancing operational and performance effectiveness.

Management of risk in operations is not a new practice in banking; it has always been essential to prevent fraud, maintain internal controls, and reduce errors in transaction processing. In the past, however, banks relied on internal controls within business lines, supplemented by the audit function, to manage operational risk. By supplementing internal control with monitoring and managing operational risks more closely, financial organizations can minimize the required amount of capital reserve and maximize their profitability.

Defining Operational Risks

So far, this chapter has discussed operational risk without actually defining what it means. A definition of operational risk is thus needed. A common definition of operational risk has to be understood, accepted, and identical across a financial organization. A common practical definition of operational risk does not exist in literature or in the industry. Operational risk encompasses various risks inherent in business activities across an organization, and consequently, its losses have the potential to be of much greater magnitude. Operational risk is a broader risk discipline and recognizes that there are components of operational risks that underlie all other risks.

The term "operational risk" itself has been defined only in the past few years, although this type of risk has been around for hundreds of years. As opposed to the definitions of "market risk" and "credit risk," which are relatively clear, the definition of operational risk has evolved rapidly over the past few years. At first, it was commonly defined as every type of nonquantifiable risk faced by a bank. However, further analysis has refined the definition considerably. Theoretically, there are as many definitions as there are financial organizations. The British Bankers' Association (BBA) survey in 1999[6] showed that, although there is a broad agreement on the general concept of operational risk, diversity in some detailed aspects will continue to exist. Some definitions of operational risks are reproduced here:

- "Operational Risk is the risk of everything other than credit and market risk." (This is the definition of 15 percent of the 55 organizations surveyed.)[6]
- "Operational Risks are events, activities, or circumstances that can affect an organization and the achievement of business/quality objectives."

- "Operational Risk is the risk that deficiencies in information systems or internal controls will result in unexpected loss. The risk is associated with human error, systems failure and inadequate procedures or controls" (Bank for International Settlements [BIS]).[7]
- "Operational Risk is the risk of losses resulting from inadequate or failed processes, people, and system or from external events."[8]

A survey conducted in June 2000 by the Risk Management Group (RMG) of the Basel Committee, through its Other Risks Technical Working Group (ORTWG),[9] indicated that although a range of definitions is presently used, there has been a high degree of convergence during the past one to two years. The following definition of operational risk, or close variants of it, is used by a large number of banks: "the risk of direct or indirect loss resulting from inadequate or failed internal processes, people, and systems or from external events." Although some banks included legal risk in their definitions, almost all organizations reject the idea of including strategic and business risk in a regulatory capital charge (although many allocate economic capital for this).

Operational risks are only eliminated if a bank ceases to exist; and although market and credit risks are revenue driven, operational risks are not. Credit and market risks originate from outside the bank. In contrast, operational risks originate primarily from within the specific bank, except risks in the category "external" as discussed in the subsequent section. Losses from external events, such as a natural disaster that damages an organization's physical assets or electrical or telecommunications failures that disrupt the business, are somewhat easier to define than losses from internal problems, such as employees' fraud and product flaws. Because the risks from internal problems will be closely tied to a bank's specific products and business lines, they should be more organization specific than the risks due to external events.

Because operational risks exist in the natural course of corporate activity, there is a great emphasis on process orientation in the operational risk concept, which positions the definition of operational risk management closer to "total quality management." In the banking sector, operational risk resembles similar risks in industry more closely than it resembles market or credit risks in a bank. Operational risk should be managed whenever the way something is usually done is modified, to make the chances of success as great as possible, while making the chances of failure, injury, or loss as small as possible. It is a common-sense approach to balancing the risks against the benefits to be gained in a situation and then choosing the most effective course of action.

To further understand operational risks, it is important to view this type of risk in the context of the other risks that affect financial organizations. These risks are generally defined as follows:

- Credit risk
- Market risk
- Business risk, which is the risk of losses from business volume changes
- Insurance underwriting risk, which is the risk of losses from unexpected insurance claims volume
- Reputation risk, which is the risk of losses by not meeting stakeholders' expectations
- Strategy risk, which is the risk of losses from not choosing "to do the right thing"

The characteristics of operational risks are clearly different from other risks: market and credit risks are — with relatively objective market prices or ratings — willingly taken for revenue's sake. Operational risks are usually not willingly incurred and not priced in the market. Checks and controls of the market and reputation aspects cause every bank not to sustain operational losses because they increase expenses or affect the share prices.

Operational risk, simply put, is the risk associated with everyday activities of an organization, which involves the management of the performance of its processes, its people, and its systems to reach the expected business performance, targets, and objectives. Banks can tune their processes to reduce human errors and operational failures, and develop contingency plans for problems such as system breakdowns.

Under new regulatory rules, each bank will be allowed to adopt its own definition of operational risk. These individual definitions are subject to the requirement that they provide a clear understanding of what is meant by operational risk, consider the full range of operational risks facing the bank, and capture the most significant causes of severe operational losses. In arriving at the definition, the regulators recognize that the exact approach for operational risk management that a bank chooses "will depend on a range of factors, including its size and sophistication and the nature and complexity of its activities." Notwithstanding individual differences, the new Basel II Accord demands clearly documented strategies and oversight by the board and senior management, a strong operational risk culture, and internal control culture (including, among other things, clear lines of responsibility and segregation of duties), effective internal escalation, reporting, and contingency planning.

Existence of Operational Risks in Financial Organizations

In the financial world, operational risks have always been present, and a newly established bank is confronted with operational risks even before it decides on its first credit transaction or market position. Operational risks are primarily internal risks or "bank made." External risks must be handled differently and are largely insurable, or will increasingly become insurable. Operational risks include breakdowns in internal controls and corporate governance. These kinds of breakdowns can lead to financial losses through slip-ups, frauds, or failure to carry out operations in a timely manner. It might lead to a situation where the interests of the bank are compromised in some ways; for example, its dealers, lending officers, or other staff exceeding their authority or conducting business in an unscrupulous or hazardous manner. Other aspects of operational risks include major failure of IT systems or events such as natural mishaps, major fires, or other disasters. Operational risk surfaced in financial organizations since the 1990s as a chain of operational catastrophes affecting numerous financial organizations around the globe. The entire last decade of the twentieth century and the early part of the twenty-first century witnessed news of banking failures as front-page headlines all around the world.

One such event took place in late January 2003, when a computer worm called Sapphire spread quickly throughout the Internet and overwhelmed business computers with data. It was a nightmare for business operations, shutting down automatic teller machines (ATMs), congesting online ticketing systems, and blacking out an emergency call center in Seattle, Washington. It highlighted a fear of corporate managers and directors everywhere of operational risk. Operational failures such as those caused by Sapphire can result in huge financial losses and a damaged reputation. In 2001, Deutsche Bank and JPMorgan Chase disclosed large economic capital in insurance premiums for operational risks.[10,11] Table 1.4, later in this chapter, highlights further some operational risks that financial organizations have suffered in the past.

The increasing number of high-profile operational risk cases has left no doubt in the minds of bank managers and regulators that risk systems and risk-adjusted performance measures are potentially unreliable if they ignore operational risk. Shareholders, employees, rating agencies, equity analysts, and other stakeholders are demanding more focused operational risk information.

Each financial organization has its own individual and unique operational settings. Thus, being able to manage operational risk might require tailoring its definition to the organization's specific settings. Operational risks may tangibly reveal themselves in the likes of business disruption, control failures, errors, misdeeds, or external events and can be captured in five major operational risk categories, which are depicted in Figure 1.2:

1. Organization
2. Processes and Policies

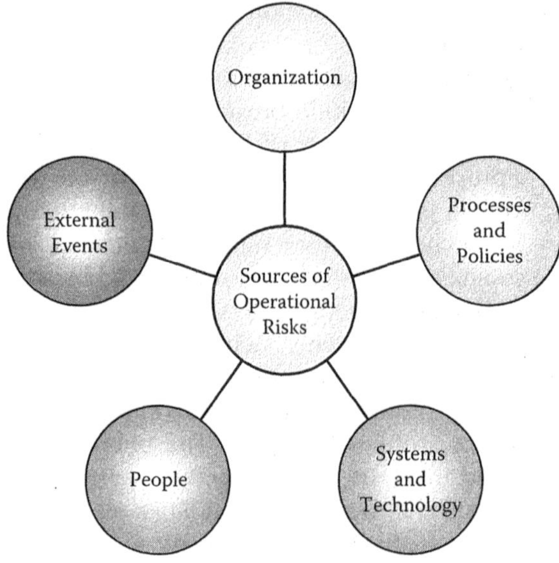

Figure 1.2 Sources of operational risk in financial organizations.

3. Systems and Technology
4. People
5. External Events

These five categories can be further expanded.

1. Organization

Whatever the reason for a change in business strategy, most major operational risk incidents happen during a period of change in the organization of the business. This could result in a change in staffing levels, a significant change in volumes of transactions as a result of a merger, new product or service launches, or the introduction of new computer programs. The banking history is littered with cases where merger strategies have gone horribly wrong and integration problems far exceeded the expected benefits of integration. In the 1980s and early 1990s many European banks sought their fortunes by buying into the U.S. market only to find that the crisis in the residential real estate market and the economy generally forced them to reverse their strategies. These types of risks also arise from such issues as project management, corporate culture and communication, responsibilities, allocation of resources, and business continuity planning. Furthermore, operational risks brought on by the risks embedded in the governance and structure, outsourcing, and security of the organization form part of this type of risk.

2. Processes and Policies

Financial organizations use a huge number of processes to deliver their products and services to their customers. Process and policy risks can arise at any stage in the value chain. For example, marketing material can be mailed to the wrong customers; account opening and transactions can be processed incorrectly. Changes in legislation can render processes that were previously compliant out of compliance. Pension legislation changes in the United Kingdom caused a number of companies to mis-sell pension funds due to a lack of training in new procedures. The total cost to the financial services sector in the United Kingdom to rectify the problem was estimated in excess of £10bn.[13] Unexpected volumes of new businesses can also be a source of operational risk. There are numerous examples of new product and service launches that either failed or were seriously compromised due to the bank not being able to cope with the demands for its new product and services. In the urgency to get to market, key processing requirements can be overlooked. In brief, process and policy risks are related to the execution and maintenance of transactions, and to the various aspects of running a business. This includes risks such as mergers and acquisitions, new products and services risks, errors and omissions, inadequate or problematic security, inadequate quality control, and so forth. These stem from risks arising from such issues as model or methodology errors, design errors, and workflows with ambiguously defined process steps. It also includes risks arising from weaknesses in processes such as settlement and payment, noncompliance with internal policies or external regulations, or failures in products or in dealing with clients. Inconsistent or badly documented processes can put the business at risk even if they are followed perfectly. There are three organizational dimensions of internal processes where operational risks should be assessed, controlled, and managed. These dimensions are interrelated:

1. Business-line processes, including their functions
2. Corporate functions (IT, Human Resources, Finance, Legal, etc.)
3. General management

3. Systems and Technology

The growing dependency of financial organizations on IT systems is a key source of operational risk. Data corruption problems, whether accidental or deliberate, are regular sources of embarrassing and costly operational mistakes. One bank made payments in excess of $150 million before a computer program patch involving a change in decimal points was found to have been incorrectly tested.[13] Another example of a system risk failure was discovered in February 2003 by staff at Provident Financial Group when they were testing the installation of a new financial model. As a result, Provident was forced to subtract $70.3 million from earnings statements released in the previous six years.[13] On November 20, 1985, the clearing operation of the Bank of New York (BNY) handled more than 32,000 Treasury security trades for the first time. This record volume triggered a software problem, preventing the organization from delivering Treasuries to buyers. The next morning was settlement day, and BNY began accumulating undelivered securities, which had to be financed by borrowings at the discount window of the New York Federal Reserve. BNY had to borrow a staggering $23 billion by the end of the day.[13] The following morning, with the software still malfunctioning, dealers were told not to deliver more Treasuries through the affected clearer, which led to a broadening of the disruption. Fortunately, the software was corrected later that day and clearing normalized. Because of a high concentration in the market for clearing services, a single malfunction in a single organization's system led to an expensive crisis.

General technology problems (operational errors that are technology related, unauthorized use or misuse of technology, etc.); hardware (equipment failure, inadequate or unavailable hardware, etc.); security (hacking, firewall failure, external disruption, etc.); software (computer viruses, programming bugs, etc.); systems (system failures, system maintenance, etc.); and telecommunications (telephone, fax, e-mails, etc.) are increasingly great sources of operational risks. The IT staff may precisely follow a perfectly designed process, yet fail to meet business goals because of problems with the hardware or software. Only IT people (who are sometimes far removed from the banking business) understand the technologies behind many new banking systems.

4. People

Risks arising from people are the most dynamic of all sources of operational risks. Internal controls are often blamed for operational breakdowns, whereas the true causes of many operational losses can be traced back to human failure. Every chief executive officer (CEO) has argued that people are the most important resource in their banks, yet the difficulty in measuring and modeling people risks has often led management to shy away from the problem when it comes to evaluating this aspect of operational risk. Operational risk losses can occur due to workers' compensation claims, violation of employee health and safety rules, organized labor activities, and discrimination claims. People risks can also include inadequate training and management, human error, lack of segregation, reliance on key individuals, lack of integrity, and lack of honesty. These operational risks may be intensified by poor training, inadequate controls, poor staffing resources, or other factors. These types of operational risks cover losses intentionally or unintentionally caused by an employee, that is, employee errors (general transaction errors, incorrect routing of transaction, etc.), employee misdeeds, or that involve employees, such as in the area of employment disputes, human resource issues (employee unavailability, hiring or firing, etc.), personal injuries, physical injury (bodily injury, health and safety, etc.), and wrongful acts (fraud, unlawful trading, etc.).

In a people operational risk case, the United Kingdom's Financial Services Authority (FSA) fined ABN Amro £900,000 in April 2003[12] for "serious compliance failures." According to the FSA, the compliance environment within a financial organization is a fundamental protection against the spread of poor standards of conduct. ABN Amro failed to provide adequate resources for its compliance function, which resulted in the absence of robust compliance. In July 2003, JPMorgan Chase agreed to pay €135 million and Citigroup agreed to pay €120 million to the Securities and Exchange Commission for their roles in Enron's manipulation of its financial statements.[13] These are operational risks arising from fraud or incompetence, allowed by control weaknesses in processes or systems, failure of employees or the employer due to conflict of interest or from other internal fraudulent behavior. It is well known in most financial organizations that fraud is initiated from people and is one of the most important risks with unknown further implications. Human processing errors (for example, mishandling of software applications, reports containing incomplete information, payments made to incorrect parties without recovery, unnecessary rejection of a profitable trade or improper trading strategy due to incomplete information) are all examples of operational risk resulting from people. Even if an organization's processes and technology are flawless, human actions (whether accidental or deliberate) can put a business at risk.

5. External Events

Banks tend to have the least control over this source of operational risk, yet it still needs to be managed. External risks can arise from unexpected legislative changes, such as consumer affairs, and from physical threats, such as bank robberies, terrorist attacks, and natural disasters. The most striking example of external operational risk on a financial organization is the effects of the terrorist attack on the Bank of New York in September 2001. In addition to the lost lives, the total lost output to the New York City economy from the World Trade Center attack is estimated at $16.9 billion.[14] These losses included the cost of business disruption, a combination of lost revenues due to market closure, and dislocation expenses. Although the aggregate losses were manageable in this incidence, many individual financial services organizations experienced a devastating loss of life and intellectual capital.

Some factors are beyond the organization's control, but can still affect the infrastructure in a way that harms the business. Natural events such as earthquakes and floods also fall into this category, which can cause damage to physical property or assets. A more recent act of operational risk took place only last year. This time, it was from an external event. On December 26, 2004, an undersea earthquake hit the Indian Ocean. The earthquake generated a tsunami that was among the deadliest disasters in modern history. At a magnitude of 9.0, it was one of the largest earthquakes to hit in modern times. The loss of human lives is estimated at more than 200,000.[15] But some economists believe that damage to the affected countries' economies will be minor because losses in the tourism and fishing industries are a relatively small percentage of the gross domestic product (GDP). Tourism is likely to recover quickly because tourist operators and tourists are largely insured for loss.[16] However, others caution that damage to infrastructure is an overriding factor. In some areas, drinking water supplies and farm fields may have been contaminated for years by saltwater from the ocean.[17] Beyond the heavy toll on human lives, the Indian Ocean earthquake has caused an enormous environmental impact that will affect the region for many years to come. It is important to understand that natural disasters on this scale have less visible, but critically important, economywide (macroeconomic) effects. This is because of the impact of damage to productive sectors (fishing, tourism) that generate jobs, tax revenue, and foreign exchange, but also because government expenditure must be diverted from other uses.

Furthermore, externally generated, man-made problems such as civil unrest, strikes, and demonstrations fall into this category. There can even be strategic risks such as taxation or political risks under this group of operational risks. This category also includes the risk presented by actions of external parties, such as fraud, or in the case of regulators, the execution of change that would alter the organization's ability to continue operating in certain markets. These also include operational risks arising from fraud or legal actions by parties external to the organization, as well as lack of physical security for the organization and its representatives.

The exposure of an organization to operational risk may increase during times of significant changes to its business, infrastructure, and business operating environment (for example, following a corporate restructure or changes in regulatory requirements). Before, during, and after expected changes, an organization should assess and monitor their effect on its operational risk profile.[18] Operational irregularities tend to happen more often in branches or remote subsidiaries than at head offices. Senior management and boards of directors have to take their supervisory function seriously and invest time in it. This often requires a personal follow-up, no hesitation in being more demanding on details, as well as a sharing of the personal assessment of the situation with colleagues.

Interactions between Operational Risks

The categories described thus far are broad, and there is a certain amount of overlap or interaction (Figure 1.3) between the individual components that should form the characteristics of an effective operational risk management system. The intertwined relationship among them may be very complex. This interactive relationship must somehow be understood. From an internal perspective, people and systems and technology interact to produce a successful process (or, sometimes, an unsuccessful one). The organization provides the procedures, standards, rules, and controls that govern the interactions between the other elements.

When an operation is unsuccessful or an incident occurs, the operational risk management system must be analyzed and the inputs and

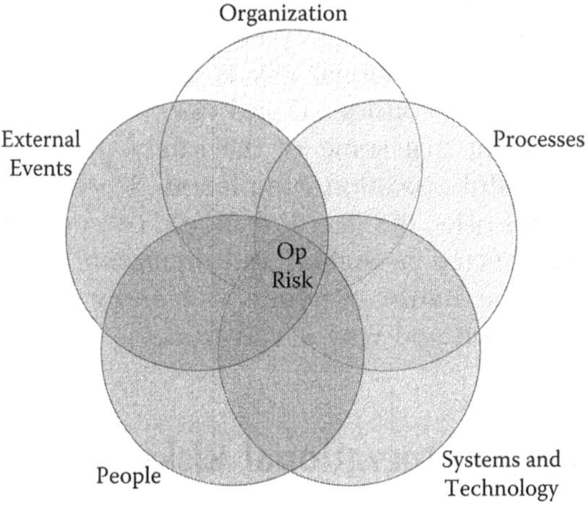

Figure 1.3 Operational risks are related to a certain degree.

interaction among the elements must be thoroughly reassessed. The organization is often the controlling factor in operational success or failure.

People are the area of greatest variability and, as a result, the sources of the majority of operational risks. For example, if a newly hired operator undergoes training on the backup software and a week later makes a mistake that causes the backup to fail, is the source of operational risk "people" or "process"? It is recommended that the organization look for root causes as opposed to effect. When a risk event is formulating, the causes or originating source of it must be identified as well as what consequences it will have and the resulting effect it will have on other risks. The resulting consequences if the risk is to be "accepted," "avoided," or "mitigated" must also be understood. It is important that this categorization relies on a root cause analysis, that is, causes of operational risk loss events, which are captured in the loss event database.

Identifying root causes can help to identify additional, related risks. By linking causation to relevant business activities, through correlation analysis, this structure is intended to be used as a tool with which to act upon operational risks. This provides management with an effective operational risk management framework. The structure also lends itself to quantification of operational risks by drawing on data sources relevant for modeling. Such a structure is discussed more thoroughly in later chapters, but Figure 1.4 shows a brief example of the sequence of events, consequences, and effects of an operational risk such as "Network Connection Failure."

Realistically, some operational risks must be accepted. How much is accepted, or not accepted, mainly depends on the operational risk impact and internal policies of the organization. Operational risks with a high degree of impact should not be accepted even if their probability is low. The decision to accept operational risk is affected by many inputs and policies. As trade-offs are considered and operation planning progresses, it may become evident that some of the safety parameters are forcing higher risk to successful operation completion. When a manager decides to accept operational risks, the decision should be coordinated whenever practical with the affected personnel and organizations, and then documented so that in the future everyone will know and understand the elements of the decision and why it was made.

Characteristics of Operational Risks

Some of the major reasons and concerns why operational risks have recently surfaced in the financial world are outsourcing, deregulation and

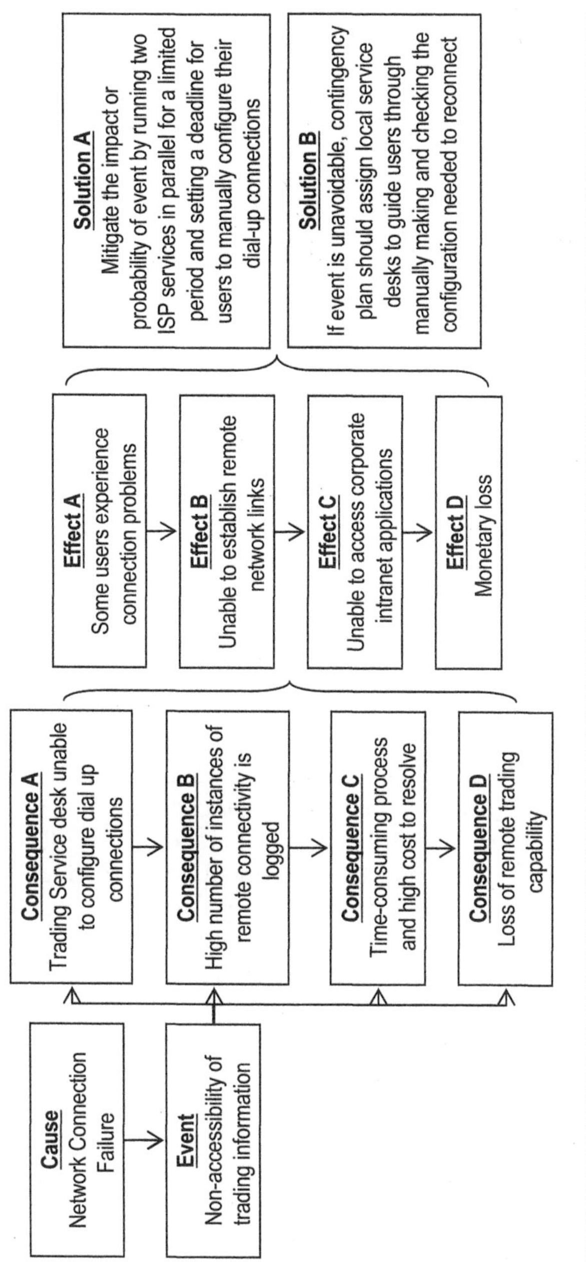

Figure 1.4 A chain of operational risk events.

Figure 1.5 Reasons for increased operational risks.

globalization, regulations, mergers and acquisitions, E-commerce, technological innovations, and terrorism, to name just a few. These are depicted in Figure 1.5.

Developments such as the use of more highly automated technology, the growth of E-commerce, and large-scale mergers and acquisitions test the viability of newly integrated systems. The increased popularity of outsourcing and the greater use of financing techniques that reduce credit and market risk, but that create increased operational risk all suggest that operational risk exposures may be substantial and growing. The emergence of banks acting as large-volume service providers creates the need for continual maintenance of high-grade internal controls and backup systems. Although globalization has many advantages for the stakeholders of a modern organization, it usually adds complexity and diversity of cultures, management, and staff. The growing sophistication of financial technology makes the activities of banks and their risk profiles more complex by operating in different markets, using different operations, different systems, and different laws. Large-scale acquisitions, mergers, and alliances, as well as de-mergers and consolidations, test the capability of new or newly integrated systems, processes, and people.

The two major drivers — globalization and Internet-related technologies — will challenge financial organizations to take on additional and partly new operational risks. Operational risks are primarily driven by the following factors:

- New products
- Product sophistication
- New distribution channels
- New markets
- New technology
- Complexity (IT interdependencies, data structures)
- E-commerce
- Processing speed
- Business volume
- New legislation
- Globalization
- Shareholder and other stakeholder pressure
- Regulatory pressure
- Mergers and acquisitions
- Reorganizations
- Staff turnover
- Cultural diversity of staff and clients
- Faster aging of know-how
- Rating agencies
- Insurance companies
- Capital markets

Operational risks mostly affect business lines that have:

- High-volume transactions
- High turnover (transactions/time)
- A high degree of structural change
- Complex systems

One such business line is trading activities.

Table 1.1 lists certain characteristics of operational risks and their challenges.

Operational risk deficiencies appear in every bank, almost daily. The magnitude of the impact of such risks can be categorized into different levels, such as High, Medium, and Low, as shown in Table 1.2. The table also shows the impact definition in terms of business disturbances and losses.

Operational Risk Event Types

Table 1.3 is an adapted list of the types of operational risk events identified as having the potential to result in substantial losses. A more explicit detail

Table 1.1 Characteristics of Operational Risks and Their Challenges

Operational Risk Characteristics	*Challenges*
Operational risks are mainly defined by internal parameters, i.e., specific to the facts and circumstances of each organization. Thus, they are shaped by the organization's processes, systems, technology, personnel, and culture.	There is a need to gather a wide range of well-distributed and well-structured information data. Although most organizations have large amounts of information data, they are erratically structured. In banking organizations, large amounts of information data are being gathered, but they may not be representative of all processes, systems, and human areas of activities.
Most operational risks that result from external events are uncontrollable or partly controllable. Most organizations do not have any specific evaluation process for estimating the actual implications of such risks to the operations.	Organizations prefer to face such risks as fully uncontrollable and mitigate them usually through insurance coverage. Based on the lack of evaluation for these types of risks, insurance companies may under- or overcharge for the coverage of such operational risks.
Operational risks are constantly and dynamically changing in relation to business strategies, processes, technologies, competitions, cultures, systems updates, etc.	Organizations that have large amounts of well-structured historical information may not have data that is representative enough of current and future risks.
The most cost-effective strategies for mitigating operational risks involve changes/tuning of the organization's processes, systems, technologies, and personnel.	Organizations need identification and modeling approaches that can measure and assess the impact of operational decisions. For example, "How will operational risks change if the organization starts selling and servicing products over the Internet, or if a key function is outsourced?"

of this list can be found in Annex 7 of the "International Convergence of Capital Measurement and Capital Standards."[27] This paper is freely available from the BIS Web site.[19] These risk event types are the ones Basel II recommends that financial organizations map their identified risk types into.

Table 1.2 Magnitude and Impact of Operational Risk

Magnitude of Impact	*Impact Definition*
High	■ May result in highly and costly loss of major tangible assets or resources ■ May significantly violate, harm, or impede an organization's mission, reputation, or interest, or may even result in serious injuries or human death
Medium	■ May result in marginal cost and loss of tangible assets or resources ■ May violate, harm, or impede an organization's mission, reputation, or interest, or may result in human injury
Low	■ May affect the organization's mission, reputation, or interest, but losses are normally insignificant

Operational risks not only are limited to back-office activities, but also include front-office and virtually any aspect of the business process in financial organizations. They are primarily organizational, "bank made," "internal," context dependent, and incredibly multifaceted. Lack of good governance at large and lack or breach of policies and processes are the common issues for increased operational risks. Human inadequacies are not surprisingly relevant in all cases, as shown in Table 1.4. External risks did not play a major role in any of the most severe cases of the past, with the exception of the Bank of Credit and Commerce International (BCCI) case. However, the past is not necessarily an indicator for the future: potential external hazards need appropriate attention.

It is difficult to list operational risks in a way that can help managers see how they connect to one another and connect to business lines, to weigh them in importance, and to manage them. Financial organizations have experienced more than hundreds of operational loss events over the past decade. Examples include the $691 million rogue trading loss at Allfirst Financial[20] and the $484 million settlement due to misleading sales practices at Household Finance.[21]

Some further examples of financial organizations that have experienced large operational losses are listed in Table 1.4. These examples paint a general but grim picture of how operational risks have affected financial organizations in the past. In all cases, people who drive the processes and eventually the organization had a major role to play.

For a more thorough explanation of these cases, see Reference 22. For further details of the BCCI and Barings collapses, see Reference 23. It is safe to say that no financial organization would wish to be the next Barings

Table 1.3 Adapted List of Operational Risk Event Types Defined by Basel II[27]

Risk Event Types	*Examples Include:*
1. Internal fraud	Intentional misreporting of positions, employee theft, and insider trading on an employee's own account
2. External fraud	Robbery, forgery, check kiting, and damage from computer hacking
3. Employment practices and workplace safety	Workers' compensation claims, violation of employee health and safety rules, organized labor activities, discrimination claims, and general liability
4. Clients, products, and business practices	Fiduciary breaches, misuse of confidential customer information, improper trading activities on the bank's account, money laundering, and sale of unauthorized products; includes clients, products, and business transactions; data entry errors; product complexity; document and contract errors; and privacy breaches
5. Damage to physical assets	Terrorism, vandalism, earthquakes, fires, and floods
6. Business disruption and system failures	Hardware and software failures; telecommunication problems; utility outages; programming errors; IT crashes caused by new applications; loss of information data from systems, process, people intentionally or unintentionally
7. Execution, delivery, and process management	Data entry errors, collateral management failures, incomplete legal documentation, unapproved access given to client's accounts, nonclient counterparty poor performance, and vendor disputes

Used with permission.

case, which occurred due to a failure to identify and control operational risks effectively.

Fraud is among the biggest sources of operational risk in financial organizations. The two major categories of fraud (internal and external) result mostly from people in banking organizations. They include internal and external fraud.

Table 1.4 Examples of Financial Organizations Experiencing Major Operational Losses

Organization and Date	Losses in Billion Dollars	Why	Breakdown In: Organization	Process	Systems	People	External
BCCI 1991	10.0	Wide range of illegal activities that included fraudulent loans, fictitious deposits, money laundering	✓	✓		✓	✓
Sumitomo Corporation 1996	2.6	Unauthorized commodity trades (double of firm's annual trading) over 10 years	✓	✓	✓	✓	
Orange County 1994	1.6	Trading in securities not legally approved; nondisclosure of massive potential losses	✓	✓		✓	
Barings 1995	1.3	Unauthorized and concealed trading in options and futures; loss concealment	✓	✓		✓	
Daiwa 1995	1.1	Unauthorized trading; forgery of back-office documentation; losses concealed by management from regulators	✓	✓		✓	
NatWest Markets 1997	0.2	Unauthorized transfers between options books; deliberate option mispricing	✓	✓	✓	✓	

Internal fraud constitutes the following:

- Intentional misreporting of positions and unreported transactions
- Employee theft and smuggling
- Insider and outsider trading
- Check kiting, in which accounts at several banks are used (Money is withdrawn from one bank on the strength of the deposit of a check from a second bank. In-transit or nonexistent cash is recorded in more than one bank account. The crime usually occurs when a bank pays on an unfunded deposit.)

- Bribes, etc.
- Check fraud, which accounts for yearly losses of at least $815 million, more than 12 times the $65 million taken in bank robberies annually[24]

External fraud includes the following:

- Robbery
- Forgery (signatures, etc.)
- Damage from computer hacking

Employee Risks in Banking Organizations

The risk of a loss intentionally or unintentionally caused by an employee, such as employee error or employee misdeeds, or involving employees, such as in the area of employment disputes, is the risk class that covers internal organizational problems, fraud, and losses.

Unfortunately, the largest amount of losses results from intentional activities such as fraud and unauthorized trading. It is people, not businesses or systems, who commit fraud. In today's "connected economy," fraud is on the increase. Fraud permeates every area of businesses. The average size of bank frauds is reported to account for $3.5 million, and internal fraud reported by banks averages to $300,000, whereas external fraud averages to $68,000.[25] Banking and electronic fraud is also on the increase, as reported in one of KPMG surveys in 2003.[26] KPMG also reported that the number of financial and banking frauds increased almost threefold during the first six months of 2003 compared to the last six months of 2002 at an average of £1.1 million per case. Employees using inside knowledge committed many of these frauds. In one example, a former employee of Lloyds TSB in the United Kingdom was charged with stealing £1.2 million from the bank.[26] Cases of fraud are disasters waiting to happen. They often start with a small incident, followed by some sort of "spiral."

Unauthorized trading is also severe in financial organizations. It is difficult to estimate the amount of loss associated with unauthorized trading, however. In many cases, it is included in the losses referring to fraud. Traders and senior managers have access to front-end dealing systems with the focus on pricing, position keeping, and risk management. This gives them a lot of freedom to operate beyond the organization's policy without being noticed by the system. Illegal trading may result in a financial catastrophe.

Table 1.5 lists more explicitly the two types of fraud events according to Basel II.

An example of fraud is highlighted in the following case.

> In the early 1960s, the Chiasso branch manager set up an offshore trustee company (Texon). This was a way for the Chiasso branch manager to "externalize" branch losses and a means for avoiding Credit Suisse (CS) monitoring the loans and investments, hiding losses from their supervisors. By placing customers' saving deposits in high-yield instruments against CS letters of guarantee for Texon, the fraud began. Over time, the fraud extended to transferring nonperforming branch loans for their full value to Texon and converting the guarantees into participations. These practices continued until March 1977.
>
> During this period and until the end of 1976, the head office ignored several internal signals that implied deviations. Senior management also received external hints, but they were minimally investigated. Several competitors' complaints in 1968, 1969, and then again in 1976 about the practices of the Chiasso branch were dismissed or casually investigated, despite documented evidence. Only the concerns of tax authorities on withholding tax evasion initiated an internal investigation. Fact-finding mostly took place on a verbal basis and was satisfied with unclear explanations. The implementation of corrective measures was never verified. In December 1976, the breakdown of Weisscredit Bank — which failed due to similar practices as those practiced by the Chiasso branch — finally triggered concerns about the conditions in Chiasso. Several proposals were launched to investigate the links and exposure of the branch of Texon. A brief press statement about the fraud was issued in March 1977. It contained neither precise information about the amount of risks nor any assurances of a contingency plan. Finally, the wildest assumptions surfaced and produced a major crisis. For a detailed discussion of the Chiasso case, see Reference 28.

The reason for identifying the Chiasso case as an operational risk event is that it occurred solely as a consequence of having conducted business in an improper and inadequate manner. Structural, procedural, and control failures, as well as errors and misdeeds, were all essential in building the Chiasso losses. Although this case took place in the 1970s, its principal aspects are, unfortunately, still around in today's financial organizations.

Table 1.5 Fraud Events According to Basel II[27]

Fraud Event Type Category	*Definition*	*Categories*	*Activities Examples*
Internal fraud	Loss due to acts of a type intended to defraud, misappropriate property or circumvent regulations, the law or company policy, excluding diversity/ discrimination events, which involves at least one internal party	Unauthorized activity	Transactions not reported (intentional) Unauthorized transaction type (with monetary loss) Trading not reported Mis-marking of position (intentional)
		Theft and fraud	Fraud/credit fraud/worthless deposits Theft/extortion/ embezzlement/ robbery Misappropriation of assets Forgery Check kiting Smuggling Account takeover/ impersonation, etc. Tax noncompliance/ evasion (willful) Bribes/kickbacks Insider trading (not on organization's account)
External fraud	Losses due to acts of a type intended to defraud, misappropriate property or circumvent the law, by a third party	Theft and fraud	Theft/robbery Forgery Check kiting
		Systems security	Hacking damage Theft of information (with monetary loss)

Fraud is committed when a motive coincides with an opportunity. Among the main initiating factors for fraud are:

- Pressure to perform, a key factor
- Personal pressure such as debt, excessive lifestyle, or gambling
- Other triggers such as trying to defeat the system, greed, revenge, or boredom
- Oppressive management style; mismatch of personality and status; unquestioning obedience of staff
- Unusual behavior with expensive lifestyle and untaken holidays
- Illegal acts of any sort
- Poor-quality staff with low perceived status
- Low morale with high staff turnover and lack of intellectual challenge
- Results at any cost; compensation tied to nominal performance
- Poor commitment to control and a bad reputation
- Remote locations that are poorly supervised and the existence of several external auditing firms
- Poorly defined business strategy; no "buy-in" by managers and staff
- Continuous profitability in excess of organization and industry standards
- Mismatch between growth and systems development
- Complex organizational structures

In regard to the amount of operational risks caused by the employees, financial organizations should establish and maintain appropriate systems and controls for the management of operational risks that can arise from employees. In doing so, financial organizations should pay particular attention to the following:

- Their operational risk culture, and any variations in this or its human resource management practices, across its operations.
- The way employees are rewarded exposes the organizations to the risk that they will not be able to meet their regulatory obligations. For example, an organization should consider how well compensation and performance indicators reflect the organization's tolerance for operational risk, and the adequacy of these indicators for measuring performances.
- Whether inadequate or inappropriate training of client facing services exposes clients to risk of loss or unfair treatment by not allowing effective communication with the organization.
- The extent of their compliance with applicable regulatory and other requirements that relate to the happiness and conduct of employees.

- Their arrangements for the continuity of operations in the event of an employee's unavailability or resignation.
- The relationship between indicators of "people risk" (such as overtime, sickness, and employee turnover levels) and exposure to operational losses.
- The relevance of all the above to the employees of a third-party supplier who are involved in performing outsourcing activities. As necessary, financial organizations should review and consider the adequacy of the staffing arrangements and policies of a service provider.

Financial organizations should ensure that all employees are capable of performing and aware of their operational risk management responsibilities, including by establishing and maintaining:

- Appropriate separation of employees' duties and appropriate supervision of employees' performances.
- Appropriate recruitment and subsequent processes to review the fitness and appropriateness of employees.
- Clear policy statements and appropriate systems and procedures manuals that are well communicated to employees and available for employees to refer to as required. These should cover, for example, compliance, IT security, and health and safety issues.
- Training processes that enable employees to attain and maintain appropriate competence.
- Appropriate and properly enforced disciplinary and employment termination policies and procedures.

Identifying and assessing risks that result from people are mainly based on qualitative processes that define all the parameters describing how people risks affect operational performances, which are directly or indirectly linked to business targets and objectives. Such measurements could include employees' level of knowledge of the organization's procedures, which are based on qualitative measurements. But there is a need to turn these qualitative measurements into more quantitative measurements. For instance, the frequency of committing the same errors could quantitatively measure the employee's level of knowledge of the organization's procedures. The organization's process map highlights the links between operational processes that can identify and measure operational risks, performances, and business objectives. The identification process defines the key operational risks and performance indicators that measure quantitatively both risks and performances, respectively. Such quantitative measures could include frequency of transactions, recurring transactions from the same employee, approval limit breaches, end-of-day cashier differences, etc. Turning qualitative measurements into quantitative ones is discussed in more depth in the third part of the book.

Operational Risks and IT

Basel II's objective is to instill best-practice, sophisticated, analytically driven risk-management policies based on each bank's experience. This will increase overall IT requirements. Perhaps no part of banking has changed as significantly during the past ten years as the area of IT. For instance, financial organizations have increasingly made their services and data available to customers through ATMs and transactional Web sites.

For most banks, enhanced IT systems and data integration account for more than 75 percent of the investment Basel II requires.[29] In a Gartner survey[30] of large financial services organizations in 2003, Gartner found that 42 percent of respondents spent between $500,000 and $2.5 million that year on risk management solutions, accounting for nearly 10 percent of the average technology budget. The report predicts that building risk-management infrastructures will remain an IT investment priority. Banks with well-integrated IT systems can meet the Basel II requirements relatively easily. Others face limitations from dispersed systems and poor data architectures. Banks should also consider combining the IT programs they undertake for Basel II[27] with those needed to comply with the Sarbanes–Oxley Act of 2002[31] corporate-governance legislation and with international accounting standards.

Computing and Internet-related technologies (IRTs) make every business a data-based business in a new E-economy, especially in financial services. This has the potential to transform operational risks from manual processing errors to system failure risks. Growth of E-commerce, electronic banking, electronic payments, and transactions result in the risk of electronic frauds and system security issues that are not yet fully understood. The pressure from everywhere to invest continuously and dramatically (including in the interest of risk reduction) in modern processes is immense. Integrated IT networks are central, especially for global organizations. IRTs enable much higher and more sophisticated levels of coordination, globality, efficiency, and flexibility. However, they open the door for chaos and risks if they are not consistent, structured, coordinated, and stable over time. New technologies lead to unique opportunities to modify or overhaul business processes. They first and foremost enable business development (e.g., 24/7 availability of E-commerce services with real-time execution of transactions).

Systems that are related to IT failures are significantly increasing in number and severity. The main reasons for this are:

- Business transactions and processes are increasingly dependent on IT, so failures in IT are more likely to impact the business, and that impact is more likely to be severe.
- When an IT failure occurs, its impact on the business is quickly felt.

There are no core systems without backup. Systems, by their nature, are interdependent and complex, with potential conflicts between the interested parties. In addition to having the right infrastructure, technology, service-level agreements, processes, and recoverability, safety management is primarily a matter of operational risk management applying discipline, such as:

- Rigorous password security and changes
- Rigorous control mechanisms for new business activities, involving sign-offs by all concerned parties
- Continuously updated anti-virus software
- Immediate virus notification
- Regular checks and controls of logical security
- Backup
- Rigorous discipline for breaches

The Basel Committee on Banking Supervision expects such operational risks to be recognized, addressed, and managed by banking organizations in a prudent manner according to the fundamental characteristics and challenges of E-banking services. To facilitate these developments, the committee has identified 14 "Risk Management Principles for Electronic Banking" to help banking organizations expand their existing risk oversight policies and processes to cover their E-banking activities.[32] The E-banking risk management principles identified in this report fall into three broad, and often overlapping, categories of issues:

A. Board and Management Oversight (Principles 1 to 3):
   1. Effective management oversight of E-banking activities
   2. Establishment of comprehensive security control processes
   3. Comprehensive due diligence and management oversight process for outsourcing relationships and other third-party dependencies

B. Security Controls (Principles 4 to 10):
   4. Authentication of E-banking customers
   5. Nondisclaimer and accountability for E-banking transactions
   6. Appropriate measures to ensure segregation of duties
   7. Proper authorization controls within E-banking systems, databases, and applications

8. Data integrity of E-banking transactions, records, and information
9. Establishment of clear audit trails for E-banking transactions
10. Confidentiality of key banking information

C. Legal and Reputational Risk Management (Principles 11 to 14):

11. Appropriate disclosures for E-banking services
12. Privacy of customer information
13. Capacity, business continuity, and contingency planning to ensure availability of E-banking systems and services
14. Incidence response planning

These characteristics include the extraordinary speed of change related to technological and customer service innovation, the universal and global nature of open electronic networks, the integration of E-banking applications with inheritance computer systems, and the increasing dependence of banks on third parties that provide the necessary information technology. Each of the above issues is discussed in more depth in "Risk Management Principles for Electronic Banking."[32]

IT migration in banks is another area of IT that has great potential for operational risks. It is basically the process of shifting or adapting an organization's current IT platform to accommodate new products and services or regulatory conditions. In doing so, it may be layering existing software with updates, or brand-new software may be employed altogether. Because IT migration involves the setting up of new methods and systems, the operational risk potential is vast.[33] A poorly performed IT migration can have long-lasting effects on the operation of a business unit, as well as a regulatory impact. Once it has been decided that an existing IT infrastructure is no longer suited to a product line or fails to meet regulatory requirements, the attributes of the new system must be agreed upon. The diversity of the IT infrastructure has also increased. For example, IT groups that formerly maintained the links between several terminals and a handful of hosts now must keep track of local area networks (LANs), wide area networks (WANs), land lines, dial-up access, wireless links, and internal networks, as well as connections to the Internet. In the past, IT dealt with terminals, but today hardware can range from desktops or laptops, to handheld computers, wireless information appliances, or Internet-enabled mobile phones and pagers.

If a service fails, there is a small window of time during which the IT group can attempt to recover the service before the failure directly impacts the business. For example, if an organization uses a billing system that prints and mails monthly statements to its customers showing their outstanding balances, and if that system fails, the window of opportunity to fix the problem might be hours or even days. As long as the statements are received on time to allow customers to pay them before they become overdue, this is sufficient. If IT can recover the service within that time, then the organization's customers will receive their payment reminders on time, and the revenue stream will not be interrupted. The customers of an E-commerce site, however, may expect transactions to complete within ten seconds and to receive e-mail confirmation of each transaction within another five minutes. Quite clearly, in this scenario, any failure would immediately impact the business and may result in customers giving up and going elsewhere. Years ago, IT managers might have wondered, "If a service fails in the data center and no one notices, is it a crisis?" That question has become irrelevant to many IT groups today because IT service failures are immediately noticeable throughout the organization. Five years ago, if an organization's Web site was unavailable for an hour, the only people who noticed were probably the IT staff. Today, the list of people who would notice that failure might include hundreds of customers, a dozen of competitors, and every analyst who tracks that organization's stocks. Visibility is important because not only do people notice failures, but they also react.

Although computing solves many operational risk problems, it also creates new ones such as information control, compliance, security, and privacy protection. Banks may engage in risk-mitigation techniques, minimizing exposure to market and credit risk, but that in turn may induce operational risk and have a significant impact on market and credit risk events. On the other hand, operational risks can induce other credit-related risks. For example, credit-related operational risk occurs in the following:

- Processes: failure in collateral management (e.g., inappropriate or missing documentation, incorrect assignment to trading portfolio, inaccurate valuation).
- People: violation of competence rules in credit-approval processes.
- Systems: unavailability of system support for credit approval processes.
- External events: credit fraud (e.g., credit being granted based on forged balance sheets).

In the past, organizations may have had disaster recovery plans for their IT functions and resources. These plans were typically invoked only in a major disaster situation, when computers and other IT resources were hindered by some significant operational event. These plans now have more of a "business continuity" focus, reflecting the broader context for potential situations in which they could be invoked. Business continuity is discussed in more depth in Chapter 9 of this book.

In short, IT has greater potential to support and enhance business processes than ever before, but in turn, failures in IT have more potential to disrupt business operations and directly affect an organization's profitability and success. Financial organizations are evermore dependent on IT today, and more of the systems that IT manages are critical to successful business operations. For example, ten years ago, communication in many companies was based on such non-IT services as paper memos, an internal mailroom service, an external postal service, and the telephone. Today, IT is responsible for e-mail services, intranets, and Internet sites — communication systems that were not considered business critical a decade ago. The IT environment is more complex. A typical IT environment contains more components today than in the past. There are more desktops, servers, and connections; more end-to-end services; and more integration of systems. Because of this increasing reliance on IT services, the potential failure of these services presents an increasing source of operational risk to the business.

To put in place an effective operational risk management system and thus comply with Basel II, an investment in an appropriate technology solution would require at a minimum:

- Pillar 1 requirements: data, calculation engines, connection with external assessment organizations for real-time data on operational risks.
- Pillar 2 requirements: transparency and the need for a strong management information system to provide operational risk and capital information to the supervisory board in a timely manner.
- Pillar 3 requirements: reporting/disclosure, which requires IT enablement to drive operational risk and capital adequacy information out to the market.

Although Basel II does not mandate automated systems-based processes, such processes may ease the compliance process. Regulators will be looking not only for effective assessment and measurement of operational risks, but also for process consistency. For this reason, regulators may be more critical of manual or paper-based processes. Banks must put the right architecture in place to achieve the information data quality and reliability needed for full Basel II compliance and regulatory disclosure. Those considering best-of-breed systems or ad hoc solutions should recognize that such approaches to compliance do not always deliver the scalability and robustness needed to execute the new minimum capital calculations, let alone those required for more advanced calculations. The good news is that there is a payoff for investing in more sophisticated risk management systems and technologies in the form of potentially lower capital requirements and improved competitiveness. In fact, banks that qualify to monitor their own capital requirements under Basel II's

Advanced Measurement Approaches (AMA), as discussed in Chapter 4, stand to gain the most. It is estimated with analysts estimating that capital requirements for the biggest banks could fall by 25 to 30 percent[34] if the AMA is used.

The important thing is to rethink or even tune processes. New IT systems in conjunction with process tuning have many advantages related to the reduction of operational risks, such as higher automation, quick storage and retrieval time, instant communication, the monitoring of people, processes, and systems, support for quick decision making, better workflows, and support of process work functions.

IT Security

As IT continues to develop at a fast pace, financial organizations come under pressure to understand the security implications of these advances. For competitors, the motivation to take advantage of this time lag is great. A weak security infrastructure increases the number of people gaining access to the skills required to attack a network or data. Because networks are everywhere, access to infrastructure and data becomes a primary concern. IT security has become increasingly challenging for all financial organizations, including banks, with their crucial role in the payments system.

Failures in processing information (whether physical, electronic, or known by employees but not recorded), or of the security of the systems that maintain that information, can lead to significant operational losses. Financial organizations should establish and maintain appropriate systems and controls to manage their information security risks. The growing complexity of the IT environment and the potential for substantial monetary losses has increased the importance of IT security in financial organizations. The complexity of maintaining a secure IT environment will certainly increase as banks continue to improve technological capabilities and delivery means. At the same time, attacks on IT systems are increasing. Exposure to security breaches has increased during the past few years and may have stressed IT budgets. In an effort to cut costs, the outsourcing component of IT budgets may grow the most. However, the decision to outsource brings with it particular concerns. In addition, merger activity augments many IT issues, as complex networks must be coordinated or combined.

Increasing use of the Internet and E-commerce has made security management even more complex. While the basic structure of Internet security is now present, the technology is far from established. Although the board of directors has responsibility for ensuring that appropriate security control processes are in place for E-banking, the substance of these processes needs special management attention because of the enhanced security challenges posed by E-banking. This should include establishing appropriate authorization privileges and authentication measures as well as logical and physical access controls. Furthermore, it should include adequate infrastructure security to maintain appropriate boundaries and restrictions on both internal and external user activities and data integrity of transactions, records, and information. In addition, the existence of clear audit trails for all E-banking transactions should be ensured, and measures to preserve confidentiality of key E-banking information should be appropriate with the sensitivity of such information. For a more in-depth discussion about E-commerce security issues, see Reference 35.

Many technologies, such as smart cards, electronic bill payment, and the migration of traditional banking into the online environment, are bound to further alter how banks do business. Banks may also implement more advanced verification programs, which help prove a user's identity on a computer network. Even if many banking customers can now access account information with an ATM card and a password, biometric technologies, such as retinal or fingerprint scanners, may eventually become the standard. Some organizations may be considering the benefits of more established technologies, such as moving toward online check imaging. Others are considering ways to reconfigure current systems to implement real-time processing.

The central concept that unites all security-related issues is that of a "security awareness culture." Be it the availability of safe networks, adequate staff training, or data storage and backup, the absence of a focused security work ethic will undermine protection efforts. From the perspective of IT-induced operational risk, failure to provide sufficient security is perhaps the greatest threat, because networks virtually define the operations of the business. Comprehensive operational risk management processes for IT security are lacking at some organizations and in general are improving too slowly. Other factors that make IT security more challenging are outsourcing, the increasing sophistication of threat agents, and the heightened demands of national IT security initiatives. The potential damage from security breaches is not only monetary; IT security breaches can cause direct financial losses for banks and can also raise legal and reputational risks if banks are seen as failing to protect confidential customer data. Although the potential for massive fraud exists if adequate controls are not in place, the impact from lost data or a bad reputation is difficult to surmount. Although not easy to quantify, the financial organization's reputation is critical to many customers, who expect their confidential financial information to be secure. There are several sources of regulatory guidance for organizations on safeguarding consumer data and best practices for IT security.[4,36,37]

Perfect security does not exist, and no one solution meets all IT security needs. Persistent and skilled hackers can eventually compromise any security system. Therefore, banking management should not rely on only one security system. By layering IT security, financial organizations can increase the likelihood that should one security system fail, another will prevail. Although each financial organization must ultimately assess the level of its security needs, the following components, if incorporated into an overall IT security strategy, can help minimize disruptions to, or compromises of, a bank's technology infrastructure:

- *Appropriately trained staff and users.* Placing appropriate emphasis on IT security at the senior management and board of directors level is the first step toward minimizing system breaches. By establishing effective policies and procedures, boards of directors can promote an environment that addresses vital security areas and establishes appropriate guidelines and standards for all employees.
- *Integrity.* Safeguarding the accuracy and completeness of information and its processing is critical.
- *Backup systems.* Maintaining appropriate backup systems is important for retrieval of lost information in case it becomes necessary and for keeping data for the legal period of time.
- *Isolation of networks.* Maintaining appropriate isolation among computer networks is vital. For example, data traffic originating from one network segment need not be transmitted to all servers or workstations on the LAN.
- *Firewalls.* A firewall is a set of components consisting of hardware and software that exists between two or more systems to block unauthorized traffic. Firewalls are useful in isolating networks and are the minimum security for organizations that maintain a connection to the Internet.
- *Confidentiality.* Information should be accessible only to persons or systems with appropriate authority, which may require firewalls within a system, as well as entry restrictions.
- *Nondenial and accountability.* This involves ensuring that the person or system that processed the information cannot deny their actions.
- *Virus/worm protection.* IT managers should consider using virus protection methods for data entering bank networks, as well as periodic scanning of files within the network. All hosts, both servers and workstations, should be protected, and should have frequent virus updates.

- *Encryption.* When transmitting sensitive data across the Internet or other nontrusted channels, IT management should ensure that the information is encrypted to prevent unauthorized access.
- *Continuous vulnerability assessments.* All financial organizations should recognize running vulnerability scans of their IT infrastructure as a best security practice.
- *Intrusion detection.* An intrusion detection system (IDS) represents another layer of security, a "burglar alarm" that informs IT management when someone or something may be attacking the network. An IDS typically scans for anomalies in network traffic or data flows that match a known pattern of abuse.
- *External monitoring.* A layered security process requires financial organizations to consider external measures, which enable them to see their network from an outsider's perspective.

The financial organization should ensure the adequacy of the systems and controls used to protect the processing and security of its information and should comply with standards such as ISO17799:2000 Information Security Management.[38] For more information on IT security, refer to "Improved Security Is Vital as Information Technology Grows More Complex"[39] and "Layering Security to Protect Bank Networks."[40]

Summary

Financial organizations today are more dependent on electronic transactions and more inclined to real-time information than ever before. Over and above this, fewer banks have been left in control of more money due to industry consolidation. Banking operations are increasingly complex and sophisticated while, at the same time, significant weaknesses in one of these entities, let alone failure, has the potential for severely adverse macroeconomic consequences. If any bank undertakes a bad deal and loses, the consequences would be felt by the entire industry and the entire global economy could be made vulnerable.

Although operational risks have been around for many years, it has today become a very hot topic in the financial industry. It affects everybody in financial organizations, and the benefits will only increase if there is genuine understanding of it across the business. Defining, measuring, and mitigating operational risks will be difficult. However, developing and documenting processes for dealing with such risks can help minimize what could otherwise be a significant negative effect on the organization.

Operational risks should only be accepted when benefits outweigh the cost.

The Basel Committee has made it clear that operational risk is now a core issue for financial organizations and has set deadlines (depending on which approach is adopted) for financial organizations to allocate capital aimed expressly at reducing exposure to operational risks. This is discussed in Part II of the book.

This chapter introduced the concept of operational risks in financial organizations. It also highlighted the many aspects of operational risks via the various definitions in industry and literature on the subject. Furthermore, it attempted to show where operational risks exist in financial organizations. It then demonstrated types of operational risk events that can affect financial organizations. Particular attention was given to employees' operational risks, one of the most prominent of all the other risks. The characteristics of operational risks were then highlighted. Finally, how operational risks can affect, or be affected by, IT was discussed as well as aspects of IT security.

References

1. Bardoloi, S., Basel II: Measuring the Operational Risk, http://computercops.biz/article2542.html (accessed December 2004).
2. Consumer Compliance Examination, Bank Secrecy Act, Anti-Money Laundering, *Controller's Handbook,* September 2000.
3. Doyle, C., The USA PATRIOT Act: A Sketch, April 2002.
4. Ledig, R.H., Gramm–Leach–Bliley Act, Financial Privacy Provisions: The Federal Government Imposes Broad Requirements to Address Consumer Privacy Concerns, http://www.ffhsj.com/bancmail/bmarts/ecdp_art.htm (accessed December 2004).
5. FFIEC, Guidelines on Contingency Planning and Customer Awareness, May 1998, http://www.ffhsj.com/ (accessed December 2004).
6. British Bankers' Association (BBA), ISDA et al., *Operational Risk, the Next Frontier,* RMA, Philadelphia, pp. 29–38, 1999.
7. Basel Committee on Banking Supervision, Risk Management Group, Other Risks: Operational Risk Discussion Paper, BS/00/27, BIS, April 2000.
8. British Bankers Association, Operational Risk Management Survey, p. 29, 1999.
9. Basel Committee on Banking Supervision, Consultative Document Operational Risk, Supporting Document to the New Basel Capital Accord, Annex 1: Recent Industry Developments, January 2001.
10. Deutsche Bank AG, Annual Financial Statements and Management Report of Deutsche Bank AG for 2001, p. 38, 2001.
11. Jorion, P., Bank Trading Risk and Systemic Risk: Third draft: December 2004.

12. Financial Service Authority (FSA), Press Release 2003, http://www.fsa.gov.uk/pubs/press/2003/053.html (accessed January 2005).
13. Walsh, P., Operational Risk and the New Basel Accord, October 2003.
14. Fiscal Policy Institute, Economic Impact of the September 11 World Trade Center Attack, Preliminary Report, September 2001.
15. Wikipedia, 2004 Indian Ocean Earthquake, http://en.wikipedia.org/wiki/2004_Indian_Ocean_earthquake (accessed January 2005).
16. Benson, C. and Clay, E., Beyond the Damage: Probing the Economic and Financial Consequences of Natural Disasters, Humanitarian Exchange, No. 27, July 2004.
17. Pearce, F., Tsunami's Salt Water May Leave Islands Uninhabitable, *NewScientist.com* news service January 2005, http://www.newscientist.com (accessed January 2005).
18. *FSA Handbook*, Release 037, Operational Risk: Systems and Controls, December 2004.
19. http://www.bis.org/bcbs/publ.htm.
20. Pearson Education Canada Inc., Integrative Case 6: Alleged Rogue Trader at Allfirst Financial, 2004.
21. De Fontnouvelle, P., DeJesus-Rueff, V., et al., Federal Reserve, Using Loss Data to Quantify Operational Risk, Bank of Boston, April 2003.
22. Doerig, H.U., Credit Suisse Group, Operational Risks in Financial Services: An Old Challenge in a New Environment, January 2001, partly adjusted, April 2003.
23. Bank for International Settlements Settlement, Risk in Foreign Exchange Transactions, Basel, March 1996.
24. Bank and Banking Related Fraud, http://www.crimes-of-persuasion.com/Crimes/Business/bank_fraud.htm (accessed November 2004).
25. Currie, C.V., Basel II and Operational Risk: Overview of Key Concerns, *IQPC Operational Risk Forum,* March 2004.
26. Leyden, J., Fraud Cases Up, Financial Losses Down, July 2003. http://www.theregiser.co.uk/2003/07/28/fraud_cases_up_financial_losses/ (accessed November 2004).
27. Basel Committee on Banking Supervision, International Convergence of Capital Measurement and Capital Standards: A Revised Framework, June 2004. This paper is available free from their Web site, http://www.bis.org/bcbs/publ.htm.
28. Jung, J., "Schweizerische Kreditanstalt" to Credit Suisse Group, NZZ Verlag, Zurich, pp. 245–289, 2000.
29. Buehler, K.S., D'Silva, V., et al., The Business Case for Basel II, *The McKinsey Quarterly*, No. 2004.
30. Sun Microsystems, Managing Risk Is Its Own Reward, http://www.sun.com/br/financial_svcs_616/article_risk.html (accessed November 2004).
31. Sarbanes–Oxley Act of 2002, H.R. 3763, 2002.
32. Basel Committee on Banking Supervision, Risk Management Principles for Electronic Banking, July 2003. This article is available free of charge on http://www.bis.org/publ/bcbs98.pdf.

33. Meridien Research Inc., *Time for a New Look at Operational Risk,* p. 3, February 2000.
34. Westlake M., Can Basel II Be Made to Work?, *The Banker,* August 2002, http://www.thebanker.com (accessed January 2005).
35. Security Revolution, International Security Consortium Inc. on http://www.isc2.org (accessed November 2004).
36. *Federal Register,* Standards for Safeguarding Consumer Information (16 CFR 314), Vol. 67, No. 100/May 2002.
37. FDIC FIL-3-2001: Privacy of Consumer Financial Information, Privacy Rule Handbook, January 2001, http://www.fdic.gov (accessed January 2005).
38. Calder, A. and Watkins, S., IT Governance: A Manager's Guide to Data Security and BS 7799/ISO 17799, September 2003.
39. Anas, M., Improved Security Is Vital as Information Technology Grows More Complex, Federal Deposit Insurance Corporation, http://www.fdic.gov (accessed January 2005).
40. *Bank Technology News,* Layering Security to Protect Bank Networks, April 2003.

Chapter 2

Main Aspects of Operational Risk Management

Understand the risk first, then do business.

—Vivianne Bouchereau

Introduction

As a separate discipline, operational risk management only surfaced in recent years. Operational risk management, a subset of risk management, is the systematic application of management and engineering principles, criteria, and tools to optimize all aspects of safety within the constraints of operational effectiveness, time, and cost throughout all operational phases. It is the logical process of weighing the potential costs of risks against the possible benefits of allowing those risks to stand uncontrolled.[1] It is the overall process by which a financial organization accomplishes the following:

- Identifies and understands the full spectrum of its operational risks.
- Defines its appetite for operational risk, based on strategic objectives.

- Assesses the operational risks and means of mitigation on a cost-benefit basis to take informed actions. This reduces the likelihood and impact of loss events and increases the overall performance.
- Reduces the likelihood and impact of loss events.
- Decreases the uncertainty of overall performance.

Operational risk management should be taken seriously and given an appropriate amount of effort and formality. Management at all levels should encourage the view that identifying operational risks is a positive activity that is crucial to an effective operational risk management process. Operational risk management should be performed continuously to ensure that an organization deals with the risks that are relevant today, not just the ones that were relevant last year. Fortunately, formalizing operational risk management practices is an achievable goal. Organizations can enhance the achievement of this goal by fostering an "operational risk management culture." This culture should emphasize at all levels the importance of managing operational risks as part of each person's daily activities. The goal of creating an operational risk management culture is to create a situation where staffs and managers instinctively look for operational risks and consider their impacts when making effective operational decisions.

Financial organizations must find ways to manage operational risks in their daily operations. To properly monitor and manage operational risks, financial organizations must consider the entire scope of the business activities, including every transaction. They should define, measure, and track multiple key risk indicators (KRIs). They should collect, aggregate, and analyze vast amounts of data. Alerts must be sent out quickly so that corrective action can be taken and losses can be minimized.

It should be noted that the underlying concepts of risk management apply to all types of risk (i.e., credit risk, market risk, and operational risk). The model of operational risk management is as important as that of credit risk management. Just as banks have been managing their lending activities, analyzing portfolios, monitoring allowance for loan losses, and varying loan concentrations, a similar idea should be considered for the various aspects of operations and technology. A bank would not think of moving forward without a loan review or credit risk committee, established lending policies, or metrics to follow charge-offs. Operational risk is no different.

Analytical operational risk management approaches are increasingly emerging. The financial services industry as a whole, notwithstanding the major differences among banks, has made considerable progress over the past two to three years in operational risk areas such as definition, aspects of strategy and planning, structure, reporting tools, capital allocation, and operational risk transfer. There is still a gap, however, to reach an effective, credible, and viable operational risk analytical framework. An analytically sophisticated, credible, and accepted approach to operational risk management is one very important attribute of a strong operational risk management effort.

The principles and guidelines set out in this book focus specifically on operational risk management. However, in developing their own frameworks, financial organizations will inevitably need to consider how their procedures and frameworks for managing different types of risk should be integrated to ensure both consistency and completeness in their overall risk management approach. The operational risk management framework should therefore be developed within the parameters of, or to interface with, the organization's existing risk management culture, policies, and practices.

The boards of directors and senior management at each level of a banking organization have an obligation to understand the operational risk profile at that level of the organization and ensure that risks are managed appropriately and that the capital held at each level in respect of those operational risks is adequate. One of the fundamental views of sound corporate governance is that the primary responsibility for a banking organization's overall risk management rests with the organization's board of directors and senior management. Even in instances where a bank may be a wholly owned subsidiary of a larger banking organization, the board and senior management of that subsidiary bank are responsible for conducting their own assessment of the bank's operational risks and operational controls and must ensure that the subsidiary is adequately capitalized for the risks faced by that organization.

The main aspects of operational risk management are among the key issues of Basel II, and this is discussed thoroughly in this chapter, together with best practices in operational risk management. Furthermore, effective operational risk management frameworks are outlined. The quantification of operational risks and the testing and verification of the operational risk management framework is then discussed. Enterprisewide risk management, which aims to integrate the management of the different types of risks, is introduced, together with some main operational risk management concerns. Finally, some key players for implementing effective operational risk management and effective systems and tools that may be required to deploy an effective operational risk management framework are discussed. Figure 2.1 shows the layout of this chapter.

Main Aspects of Operational Risk Management

Operational risk and operational risk management are not only about risks and threats. Both are chances and opportunities as well. Good operational

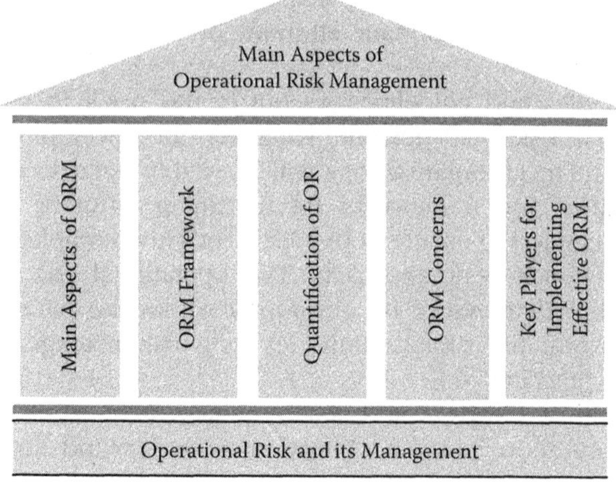

Figure 2.1 Layout of Chapter 2.

risk management improves quality and reduces cost by minimizing individual operational risks. Minimizing individual risks, however, does not always mean that the overall risks are minimized, because risks have a certain degree of interaction between them. For instance, decreasing a particular operational risk may have the potential to increase another. These levels of dependencies must be defined and the optimal level of the overall risk must be sought. This concept is thoroughly discussed in Chapter 8 and forms the core idea of the subject of this book.

Four principles govern all actions associated with operational risk management:

1. *Accept operational risk when benefits outweigh the costs.* All identified benefits should be compared against all identified costs. Even high-risk activities may be undertaken when there is clear knowledge that the sum of the benefits exceeds the sum of the costs.
2. *Accept no unnecessary operational risks.* Unnecessary risks bear no appropriate return in terms of benefits or opportunities. Everything involves risk. The most logical choices for accomplishing an operation are those that meet all requirements with the minimum acceptable operational risk. The opposite of this is to accept the necessary risk required to successfully complete the operation or task.
3. *Make operational risk decisions at the appropriate level.* Anyone can make an operational risk decision. However, the appropriate decision maker is the person or system that can allocate the resources to reduce or eliminate the operational risk and implement

controls. The decision maker must be authorized to accept levels of operational risks typical of the planned operation. Optimally allocating resources is discussed in more depth in Chapter 8.

4. *Integrate operational risk management into planning at all levels.* Operational risks are more easily assessed and managed in the planning stages of an operation. The later changes are made in the process of planning and executing an operation, the more expensive and time-consuming they will become.

Operational risk management is about daily management that supports the stability and continuity of an organization. The management issue, however, concerns human beings in organizations serving other human beings with their actions and reactions. Not surprisingly, therefore, one of the critical operational risk management success factors is the management and staff. Every employee should ideally be a risk or control manager in his or her daily activity. A general pure awareness of risks is already a major step toward successful operational risk management.

The following steps may prove effective in establishing operational risk management as a consistent discipline:

- Obtain management sponsorship.
- Seek advice and mentorship from a risk manager who has personal experiences with and knowledge of potential failures.
- Inform all stakeholders about the importance of managing operational risks and the costs or lost revenues that can result from failure.
- Train a core set of risk managers to act as role models and provide mentorship for others. An effective training approach is to combine a workshop on the theory of operational risk management with real exercises based on day-to-day operational activities.
- Invite all stakeholders to operations management reviews where top operational risks are reviewed.
- Ensure that top operational risks are included in status reports and circulated to service managers and key stakeholders.
- Seek feedback from stakeholders on the effectiveness of the operational risk management process and review the process regularly to ensure that it continues to add value.
- Introduce a recognition scheme for individuals who effectively identify or manage operational risks.
- Ensure that the operations staff considers risk management activities when scheduling and making key decisions.
- Make the systems applied in operational risk management easy to use and accessible. A key requirement is to record risks as soon as they are discovered so they can be analyzed and managed.

Figure 2.2 Operational risk management best practices.

Operational Risk Management Best Practices

Basel II stresses effective ways to track, monitor, analyze, report, and manage operational risk. Under the Basel II three-pillar framework, operational risk management has gained recognition as a separate risk discipline of its own. The general concepts of best practices for operational risk management (ORM) are described here and graphically represented in Figure 2.2:

1. Setting policies
2. Risk identification, which includes people risk (failure to deploy skilled staff)
3. Process risk, which includes execution errors
   a. Technological risk, which includes system failure
   b. Business process, which includes analyzing products and services that each unit or business line offers
4. Measurement method, which includes developing operational risk metrics for quantification of operational risks
5. Operational risk evaluation and optimization analysis, which includes determining the true effect from operational risks after measuring and monitoring them to optimize their levels

6. Economic capital, which includes developing techniques to translate calculation of operational risks into a required amount of economic capital
7. Reporting, which includes how to report operational risk exposures
8. Exposure management, which includes the decision on how to manage operational risk exposure and take action to hedge the risks

1. Setting Policies

The organization must set policies and procedures that clearly describe the major elements of the operational risk management framework, including identifying, measuring, monitoring, and controlling operational risk. The policies should include objectives, which should be integrated into the business strategy; the desired standard for risk measurements; established guidelines and standards for risk measurement; guidelines for reduction of operational risks; policies on off-hour trading, off-premises trading, etc.; and the risk appetite (reflecting the organization's strategic positioning) on when to accept, avoid, or mitigate operational risks. It should also have a scope defining what risks are included, as well as the roles, responsibilities, and accountability.

Operational risk management policies, processes, and procedures should be documented and communicated to appropriate staff. The policies and procedures should outline all aspects of the organization's operational risk management framework, including:

- The roles and responsibilities of the independent organizationwide operational risk management function and line-of-business management
- A definition for operational risk, including the loss event types that will be monitored
- The capture and use of internal and external operational risk loss data, including large potential events (the use of scenario analysis)
- The development and incorporation of business environment and internal control factor assessments into the operational risk framework
- A description of the internally derived analytical framework that quantifies the operational risk exposure of the organization
- An outline of the reporting framework and the type of data/information to be included in line-of-business and organizationwide reporting
- A discussion of qualitative factors and risk mitigants and how they are incorporated into the operational risk framework
- A discussion of the testing and verification processes and procedures

- A discussion of other factors that affect the measurement of operational risk
- Provisions for the review and approval of significant policy and procedural exceptions

These policies should:

- Be designed to govern risk management in all business activities
- Facilitate the monitoring, measurement, and management of such activities
- Reflect the internal and external environment within which the business activities take place
- Be subject to regular reviews and updates

Furthermore, operational risk policies should consider:

- Strategy: whether the appetite for operational risk is consistent with the strategic objectives of the organization
- Scope and application: defining the areas covered by the policy
- Resourcing: the board, subcommittee, and personnel responsible for various aspects of operational risk management

Operational risk management policies should create the mechanisms by which an organization can identify, measure, and monitor all significant operational risks, indicating the tools to be used to measure each category of risk, and as such should be:

- Approved by the board
- Appropriate to the scale of risk and activity undertaken
- Fully understood by the people responsible for managing these risks
- Clearly communicated to all employees within the organization on a regular basis, to ensure that awareness levels are maintained and that they are consistently applied

Areas that operational risk management polices might cover are as follows:

- New product/service development and applications
- Internal control
- Change management
- Human resources (HR)

- Business continuity planning
- Internal audit

A framework for designing the policies of operational risk control and management is described in Chapter 9.

2. Operational Risk Identification

The result of a comprehensive program to identify and measure operational risk is an assessment of the organization's operational risk exposure. Management must establish a process that identifies the nature and types of operational risks and their causes and resulting effects on the organization. Proper operational risk identification supports the reporting and maintenance of capital for operational risk exposure and events, facilitates the establishment of mechanisms to mitigate or control the risks, and ensures that management is fully aware of the sources of emerging operational risk loss events.

An operational risk identification and evaluation process should be established that focuses both on current and future potential operational risks. When identifying operational risks, management should be careful to address the full spectrum of potential operational risks. The operational risk identification process should consider the following:

- The full spectrum of potential operational risks
- The internal and external environment in which the organization operates
- The organization's strategic objectives
- The products and services the organization provides
- Its unique circumstances
- Internal and external change and the pace of that change

In considering operational risks, the full array of potential causes should be considered. These will include but may not be limited to:

- Transaction processing
- Sales practices
- Management processes
- HR
- Vendors and suppliers
- Technology
- External environment

- Disasters
- Unauthorized and criminal activities

A full description of how to identify operational risks is presented in detail in Chapter 5.

3. Business Processes

The means of identifying operational risks is to consider the key operational business processes. An operational process map based on the organizational chart helps to show the links between the various key processes. Proper management and control of operational processes ensures the control and reduction of operational risks. The interactions between these key business processes form a base for understanding the escalating effect of operational risks. This aspect is further explored in Chapters 5 and 6.

4. Operational Risk Measurement

Operational risk is more complicated to be measured than market or credit risk due to the unavailability of objective data, redundant data, lack of knowledge of what to measure, and so forth. The data requirements for measuring market risk are pretty straightforward — prices, volatility, and other external data, packaged with significant history in large databases that are relatively easily accessible and measurable. Similarly, credit risk relies on the assessment and analysis of historic and factual data, which is easily available in most core banking systems. Operational risk, however, is based on "inside measurement," related to the measures of internal performance, such as internal audit ratings; volume; turnover; error rates and income volatility; interaction of people; processes; methodologies; technology systems; business terminology and culture. Uncertainty about which factors are important arises from the absence of a direct relationship between the risk factors. Capturing operational loss experience also raises measurement questions. Further, the costs of investigating and correcting the problems underlying a loss event could be significant and in some cases could exceed the direct costs of operational losses. Measuring operational risk requires both estimating the probability of an operational loss event and the potential size of the loss.

The objectives of measuring operational risks are to:

- Provide an accurate view of the operational risk profile of the business
- Understand the expected losses from operational risks

- Identify the worst-case loss from operational risk and the worst-case loss under stress conditions
- Support the analysis of operational risks
- Identify the most significant operational risks
- Identify how changes to business strategy or control environment will affect the potential of operational risks
- Identify how the potential impact compares with other business units or other banks

Regular measuring and monitoring activities can offer the advantage of quickly detecting and correcting deficiencies in the policies, processes, and procedures for managing and optimizing the levels of operational risk. To fulfill their monitoring managerial responsibilities, directors and top managers must be assisted by a system for continual flow of combined information, in order of significance, and a description of the nature and causes of the losses. Such a system must include management action plans to address areas of performance variation and risk appearances. To design such systems, all information related to risks and performances in operations should be entered into a stochastic system. For more information about performance measurement, see Reference 2. A stochastic system will be able to combine and analyze the key information and measure the degree of significance for each risk and undesired performance. This can be done at an organizationwide level, at a business-line level, at the branch level, and so forth, to produce a ranking list of risks (e.g., from high risk to low risk). This significance analysis can also define the events that need close monitoring. In this book, advanced techniques and methodologies are used to measure operational risks, as described extensively in Chapter 5.

5. Operational Risk Evaluation and Optimization Analysis

Efficient operational risk management includes developing tools for evaluating and optimizing the risks in operations and thus helps to make better decisions. Risk managers and all those who are responsible for managing risks must be able to have the real evaluation of the current and trend of risks in operations within the business lines under study. The operational risk evaluation or analysis process should refer to:

- The overall significance and actual values for each of the operational risk (such as internal frauds) in operations
- Distribution of the operational risks (internal or external) within the operations

- Trend analysis for each of the individual risk within the operations
- Estimation of the capital requirements

Operational risk optimization involves optimizing the acceptable levels of each risk in the affected operations to minimize the overall degree of risks. Moreover, it is necessary to optimize the allocation of resources needed to optimize the operational risks that surface within the business lines. Operational risk evaluation and optimization is further discussed in Chapters 6 and 8.

6. Economic Capital

Another important aspect of measuring losses from operational risks is to estimate the economical capital reserve. Economic capital reserve includes developing techniques to translate calculation of operational risks into a required amount of economic capital. The Basel Committee is trying to develop methodologies for reflecting a bank's operational risk profile. It has three suggestions for determining the amount of capital that should be put aside for managing operational risk:

1. The Basic Indicator Approach links the capital charge simply to a single risk indicator, such as gross income for the whole bank. This relatively simple measure is regarded as suitable only for the smallest financial organizations.
2. The Standardized Approach is slightly more complex, using financial indicators and organizational business lines as a basis for the calculation. Here, the concept of incident reporting is introduced as a basis for assessing loss.
3. The Advanced Measurement Approach bases its calculation on a bank's internal loss data — its operational loss experiences — within a supervisory assessment framework. This allows calculation of the expected loss on each business line and measures the probability of an event occurring and estimates the loss if the event occurs.

Advanced measurement approaches are described more thoroughly in Chapter 4 and further employed and discussed in all the remaining chapters of the book.

7. Reporting

Reporting is a very important tool in the management of operational risks because it ensures timely escalation and senior management overview. The process of monitoring and tracking operational risks should analyze and indicate the current and future operational risks. It should focus on considering measurements based on the large amount of information data already existing in financial organizations. Operational risk monitoring should refer to all those parameters and information related to risk causes, events, consequences, probability, and impact. Moreover, monitoring of the risks ensures that the threshold values are adhered to. If these threshold values are exceeded, then the contingency plans are initiated. Operational risk management has the primary responsibility of establishing and monitoring all aspects of the organization's risk-assessment and prevention activities.

Operational risk management reports must address both organization-wide and line-of-business results. These reports must summarize operational risk exposure, loss experience, relevant business environment, and internal control assessments, and should be produced on a quarterly basis. Operational risk reports must also be provided periodically to senior management and the board of directors, summarizing relevant organizationwide operational risk information. Ongoing monitoring of operational risk exposures is a key aspect of an effective operational risk framework. To facilitate monitoring of operational risks, results from the measurement system should be summarized in reports that can be used by the organizationwide operational risk and line-of-business management functions to understand, manage, and control operational risk and losses. These reports should serve as a basis for assessing operational risks and related mitigation strategies and for creating incentives to improve operational risk management throughout the organization.

Operational risk management reports should summarize:

- Operational risk loss experiences of an organization, line-of-business, and event-type basis
- Operational risk exposures
- Changes in relevant operational risk and control assessments
- Management assessment of early warning factors signaling an increased operational risk of future losses
- Trend analysis, allowing line-of-business and independent organizationwide operational risk management to assess and manage operational risk exposures, universal line-of-business risk issues, and other corporate risk issues
- Significant operational risk exceptions
- Corporate governance exceptions
- Real-time incident reports

A more detailed discussion of the main aspects of the operational risk report is presented in Chapter 9.

8. Exposure Management

Exposure management includes the decision on how to manage operational risk exposure and take action to hedge the risks. This also addresses the cost-benefit of insuring. This step should include a brand-new look at the operation being analyzed to see whether new hazards can be identified.

Each financial organization has its own peculiar history, setup, strategy, structure, values, and challenges — in other words, its unique DNA. Retail banking, asset management, brokerage, trading, investment banking, and insurance all have very different prerequisites. They are all exposed to different types of operational risks. Some of the major questions to pose for all of these financial organizations are:

- Does the organization have an accepted operational risk definition, a formal strategy and policy statement, and a regular review of responsibilities?
- What committee deals with operational risk?
- Who is the owner of an important issue?
- At a functional level, who is responsible for operational risk management?
- Are the policies, structures, and losses documented?
- Is there a clearly defined acceleration process for assessing the impacts of operational risks? Trend analysis?
- How often are there reports on operational risk?
- What is the actual amount of exposure to different types of operational risks?

Chapter 7 discusses operational risk profiling analysis and illustrates in detail the design of decision management systems based on exposure analysis.

Top-Down versus Bottom-Up Operational Risk Management Approaches

In implementing an operational risk management framework, there is a choice of "top-down" versus "bottom-up" solutions. The primary advantages of the top-down approach are its simplicity and low data input requirements. However, it is a rather straightforward way to determine a capital amount for cumulative operational losses that may not be covered by insurance. Nevertheless, top-down operational risk measurement frameworks are appropriate for the determination of overall economic capital levels for financial organizations. However, top-down operational risk solutions tend to be of very little use in designing procedures to reduce operational risk in any particularly exposed area of the organization. That is, they do not comprise any fine-tuning for the execution of operational risk controls, nor do they advise management about specific weak points in the operational process. They merge the organization's processes and procedures and thus serve as inadequate analytical tools. Top-down solutions also use information from the past and cannot integrate dynamic changes in the operational risk surroundings that might affect the operational loss distribution over time.

In contrast to top-down operational risk solutions, more sophisticated approaches utilize a "bottom-up" approach. Bottom-up approaches involve mapping the workflows in which failure may occur. In estimating operational risks, they make use of actual causal relationships between failures and resulting losses. They are sensitive to process improvement, but difficult to implement. The bottom-up approach analyzes operational risks from the point of view of the individual business activities in the business lines. That is, individual processes and procedures are mapped to the risk event types and loss events that are used to produce probabilities of the occurrence of certain scenarios. Potential changes in risk event types and loss events are simulated so as to generate a loss distribution that incorporates correlations between events and processes.

Bottom-up solutions are useful to many parties within the organization, from the internal risk auditor to the business-line managers to the operational staff. Results of the analysis may be employed to correct weaknesses in the organization's operational procedures. Bottom-up models are more forward looking. The primary disadvantages of bottom-up models are their complexity and data requirements. Comprehensive data about precise losses in all areas of the organization must be collected so as to complete the analysis. External industry data may also be substituted to calculate loss events. Moreover, by going into too much detail about the organization's operations, bottom-up solutions may lose sight of some of the interdependencies across business lines and processes. Therefore, neglecting correlations may lead to incorrect results. Thus, bottom-up models are more precise and targeted to the measurement of specific operational risk problems, but at the same time are more complicated and difficult to estimate than are top-down models.

Figure 2.3 shows the differences between adopting top-down and bottom-up approaches.

It is advisable, therefore, to use a combination of the two operational risk measurement approaches. This should allow for easy calculation of the economic capital and the appreciation of correlation that exist among operational processes and business lines using the top-down approach. On the other hand, using bottom-up approaches helps in identifying each

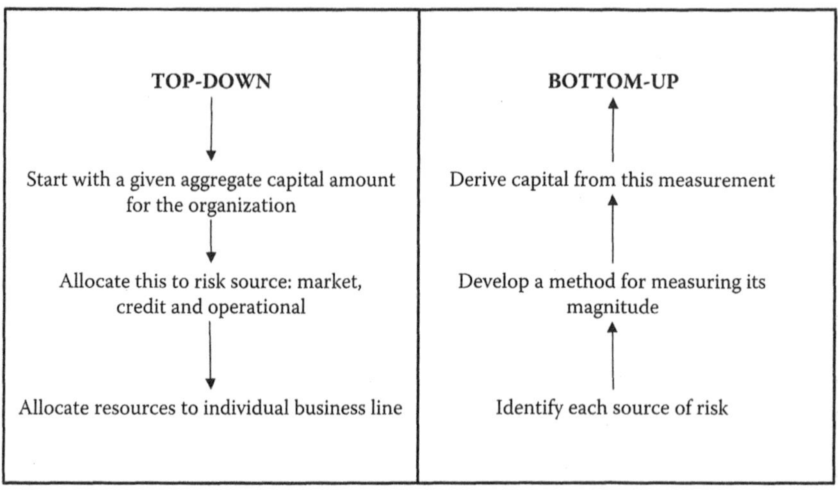

Figure 2.3 Top-down versus bottom-up approaches.

source of operational risk and developing methods for measuring its magnitude and procedures to reduce operational risks.

Bottom-up models use two different approaches to estimate the operational risk of a particular business line or activity: (1) the process approach, and (2) the actuarial approach. The process approach focuses on a step-by-step analysis of the procedures used in any activity. It can be used to identify operational risk exposures at critical stages of the process. The process approach maps the organization's processes to the operational activities. Thus, resources are allocated to causes of operational losses, rather than to where the loss is realized, thereby emphasizing risk prevention. In contrast, the actuarial approach concentrates on the entire distribution of operational losses, comprising the severity of loss events and their frequency. Thus, the actuarial approach does not identify specific operational risk sources, but rather identifies the entire range of possible operational losses, taking into account correlations across risk events. For more discussion about the two approaches, refer to Reference 3.

The framework discussed in this book is based primarily on the bottom-up approach with some essence of the top-down approach. It first attempts to identify sources of operational risk using the process approach and identifies the exposure to operational risks at critical processes. It also makes use of causal relationship between failures and resulting losses. Furthermore, it adopts the idea of the top-down and the actuarial approach as it defines correlations amongst the operations, operational risks, and business lines. To define optimal levels of operational risks and allocation of resources to manage these risks, it always considers the top-level business targets and objectives.

Value Added in Managing Operational Risks

The operational risk management process usually operates on three levels. Although it would be preferable to perform an in-depth application of risk management for every operation or task, the cost, time, and resources may not always be available. The three levels are as follow:

1. *Time-critical.* Time-critical operational risk management is a review of the situation using the basic risk management process without necessarily recording the information. This time-critical process of risk management is employed by personnel to consider risk while making decisions in a time-compressed situation. This level of risk management is used during the execution phase of training or operations, as well as in planning and implementation during crisis responses. It is also the most easily applied level of risk management in off-duty situations. It is particularly helpful for choosing the appropriate course of action when an unplanned event occurs during execution of a planned operation or daily routine.
2. *Deliberate.* Deliberate operational risk management is the application of the complete process. It primarily uses experience and brainstorming to identify risks and hazards, and develops controls; it is therefore most effective when done in a group. Examples of deliberate applications include the planning of upcoming operations; review of standard operations, maintenance, or training procedures; and damage control or disaster-recovery planning.
3. *Strategic.* This is the deliberate process with more thorough hazard identification and risk assessment involving research of available data, use of diagram and analysis tools, formal testing, or long-term tracking of the risks associated with the system or operation (normally with assistance from technical experts). It is used to study the hazards and their associated risks in a complex operation or system, or one in which the hazards are not well understood. Examples of strategic applications include the long-term planning of complex operations; introduction of new equipment, materials, and operations; development of tactics and training curricula; high-risk facility construction; and major system overhaul or repair. Strategic risk management should be used on high-priority or high-visibility risks.

There are a number of reasons why taking a proactive approach to operational risk management is just good business. Developing an operational risk management program ultimately will add value to banks because it:

- Adds control, such as independent risk assessment, compliance, business continuity planning, supervisory requirements, progress reporting, etc. Control basically covers the following: avoiding accidents, capturing noncompliance and illegal actions, complying with rules and regulations, and complying with usual management procedures.
- Creates value for the shareholder, which means efficiency, correct risk evaluation and pricing, rational economic capital allocation, reduction of regulatory capital, product enhancements, competitive strategic advantage, improved reputation, etc.
- Enables banks to meet commitments to customers, employees, and shareholders.
- Differentiates banks favorably to the marketplace during uncertain times when security is a top concern of consumers and the business community.
- Goes beyond the expense of regulatory penalties and fines, because the loss in business momentum and revenue growth after formal agreements could be considerable.
- Strengthens defenses to avoid losses from fraud, hackers, thieves, and natural disasters.
- Avoids reputational risk. This occurs when banks appear on the front page of newspapers.
- Allocates capital based on business unit risk profile to encourage business unit ownership and management of risks.

A good operational risk management framework can significantly enhance an organization's economic performance by linking risk management to the achievement of corporate goals. However, a good operational risk management framework is not just a set of software programs that calculate operational risks and capital. Operational risk management is simply good management and resembles and complements quality management efficiency management and the concept of opportunity cost, thus contributing to client satisfaction, reputation, and shareholder value. Operational risk management in combination with quality management is an effective way of enhancing the reputation of a bank. In this context, reducing operational risks is parallel to improving quality. Good operational risk management relies on proper corporate culture with a thorough risk culture and a positive acceptance of control.

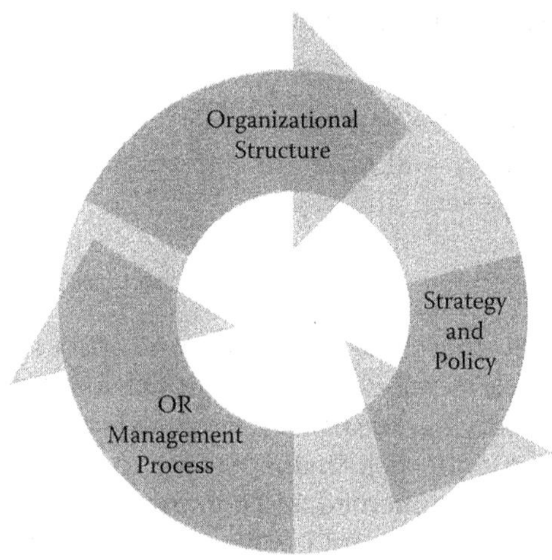

Figure 2.4 The cycle of an operational management risk framework.

Operational Risk Management Framework

An operational risk management framework should be built around an integrated, repeated cycle of operational risk management with three key components (Figure 2.4):

1. Oganizational structure (role of board, corporate governance, operational risk function)
2. Strategy and policy (strategy, policy, procedures)
3. Risk management process (identification, assessment/quantification, mitigation, monitoring, analyzing, optimizing and reporting)

The operational risk management framework provides the overall operational risk strategic direction and ensures that an effective operational risk management and measurement process is adopted throughout the organization. The framework should provide for the consistent application of operational risk policies and procedures throughout the organization and address the roles of both the independent organizationwide operational risk management function and the lines of business. The framework should also provide for the consistent and comprehensive capture of data elements needed to measure and verify the organization's operational risk exposure, as well as appropriate operational risk analytical frameworks, reporting systems, and mitigation strategies. The framework must also include independent testing and verification to assess the effectiveness of implementation of the organization's operational risk framework, including compliance with policies, processes, and procedures.

The key elements in the operational risk management framework are as follows:

- Appropriate policies and procedures
- Efforts to identify and measure operational risk
- Effective monitoring and reporting
- A sound system of internal controls
- Appropriate testing and verification of the operational risk framework

The organization must have policies and procedures that clearly describe the major elements of the operational risk management framework, including identifying, measuring, monitoring, and controlling operational risk. Operational risk management policies, processes, and procedures should be documented and communicated to appropriate staff. The policies and procedures should outline all aspects of the organization's operational risk management framework, including:

- The roles and responsibilities of the independent organizationwide operational risk management function and line-of-business management
- A definition for operational risk, including the loss event types that will be monitored
- The capture and use of internal and external operational risk loss data, including large potential events (such as the use of scenario analysis)
- The development and incorporation of business environment and internal control factor assessments into the operational risk framework
- A description of the internally derived analytical framework that quantifies the operational risk exposure of the organization
- An outline of the reporting framework and the type of data/information to be included in line-of-business and organizationwide reporting
- A discussion of qualitative factors and risk mitigants and how they are incorporated into the operational risk framework
- A discussion of the testing and verification processes and procedures
- A discussion of other factors that affect the measurement of operational risk
- Provisions for the review and approval of significant policy and procedural exceptions

To apply an effective and systematic operational risk management framework, the composite of hardware, procedures, and people that accomplish the objective must be viewed as a system. It is a common-sense approach to balancing the risks against the benefits to be gained in a situation and then choosing the most effective course of action. The framework should include general corporate principles for developing and maintaining a bank's operational risk management environment. For example, a bank's governing board of directors should recognize operational risk as a distinct area of concern and establish internal processes for periodically reviewing operational risk strategy. To foster an effective risk management environment, the strategy and policy should be integral to a bank's regular activities and should involve all levels of bank personnel.

The operational risk management framework would include general procedures for actual operational risk management. For example, banks should implement monitoring systems for operational risk exposures and losses for major business lines. Policies and procedures for controlling or mitigating operational risk should be in place and enforced through regular internal auditing.

An effective operational risk management framework should involve:

- Risk identification and assessment
- Risk measurement, monitoring, and analysis
- Risk profiling
- Risk optimization
- Planning and scheduling of risk actions and policies
- Business continuity or contingency planning
- Risk control and mitigation process
- Risk reporting

Some of these key aspects have been touched upon in the previous sections of this chapter, whereas others will be discussed in more detail in subsequent chapters.

An effective operational risk management framework has the following preconditions for success:

- Strong management support
- Small realistic steps; all at once is impossible
- Respect the constraints; comply also with supervisors' requirements
- Proper structure and governance
- Risk management visibility
- Control and compliance
- Forward-looking internal audit and corresponding follow-ups
- Proper tools and analytical measurement of operational risks
- Quantification of operational risks
- Above all, an attitude of "acceptability of risks"

Quantification of Operational Risks

The quantification of operational risk supports fundamental business needs such as:

- Reduce regulatory capital charge under Basel II
- Allocate operational risk resources to set incentives for the business-line department
- Quantify risk reduction benefits with regard to cost of capital
- Analyze the efficiency of insurances
- Deliver added value — more than just reporting on large losses and issues
- Optimize operational risk to minimize their overall exposure

Organization, policy, and process, however, only permit a quantification based on qualitative assessments. For these elements of operational risk, quantification would allow identifying and tracking changes of the risk level over many years, but not determine the absolute level of this risk. However, there is a need to quantify operational risks as much as possible to collect data on them. It makes sense, for example, to collect internal and external data on losses so that the data can be used to model loss distributions, as Basel II requires, because this is among the few ways to quantify operational risk. Turning qualitative assessments into quantitative ones is discussed in more depth in Chapter 5.

Once identified, operational risks should be evaluated to determine which are of an unacceptable nature and should be targeted for mitigation. This is most commonly accomplished by considering an estimate of the probability that the risk will materialize, namely the likelihood, by considering the drivers or causes of the risk; together with an assessment of its impact, before taking account of the application of control strategies. The potential impact should be assessed not merely in direct financial terms, but more broadly by reference to the potential effect on the realisation of corporate objectives. As an organization aims to become more sophisticated in quantifying operational risks, complete and accurate data on operational loss events (by categories of risk) and potential sources of operational loss must be collected. The organization may then select or develop a model to fit the quantification for each category of risk. The results of the risk assessment and quantification process will enable management to:

- Compare the risks with its operational risk strategy and policies.
- Identify those risk exposures that are unacceptable to the organization, or outside the organization's risk appetite.
- Select and prioritize appropriate mechanisms for mitigation. Business process modeling is the primary mechanism for understanding and supporting the mitigation of operational risks within the business and IT operations of the organization.

To quantify operational risks, it is important to measure them. This can be done by defining and collecting data on key indicators, as discussed in Chapter 5. The market has invented three different names for indicators that are relevant for such measurements:

1. Key performance indicators (KPI), which are normally used for monitoring operational efficiency. Red flags are triggered if the indicators move outside the established range. Examples include failed trades, staff turnover, volume, and system downtime.
2. Key control indicators (KCI), which demonstrate the effectiveness of controls. An example is the number of audit findings.
3. Key risk indicators (KRI), which are primarily a selection of KPIs and KCIs. This selection is made by risk managers from a pool of business data and indicators considered useful for the purpose of risk tracking. A list of such indicators is given in Chapter 5.

Operational risk metrics or KRIs should be established for operational risks to ensure the appreciation of significant risk issues to appropriate management levels. These are intended to:

- Improve the quality of workflow
- Reduce losses caused by process failure
- Change risk culture
- Provide early warning of deterioration in systems or management

Operational risk indicators can be identified on a hybrid level, both top-down for the entire organization and bottom-up for an individual business unit or operational process. The use of hybrid operational risk indicators allows comparisons across different business units and processes, as well as across the entire organization. KRIs are most easily established during the operational risk measurement phase, as discussed in Chapter 5. Each business unit should use approximately 10 to 15 risk indicators to assess its operational risk exposure. It is a matter of judgment, however, which risk indicators are most relevant to the overall operational risk exposure of the organization. Regular reviews of these KRIs should be carried out by internal audit, or other qualified parties, to analyze the control environment and test the effectiveness of implemented controls, thereby ensuring business operations are conducted in a controlled manner. The design aspects of operational performance and risk indicators are discussed more in detail in Chapter 5.

The operational risk quantification faces two major challenges:

1. The high context dependency, which is different in each situation and has many operational risk categories/subcategories. Each organization is different, and its level of operational risk is different, as is the level of risk acceptance to other organizations.
2. The priority for dealing with high-exposure events, for which only very little internal data is available, thereby requiring a credible scenario analysis. For many such risks, insurance coverage is increasingly available.

The industry has made significant progress in recent years in developing analytical frameworks to quantify operational risk. The analytical frameworks, which are a part of the overall operational risk framework, are based on various combinations of an organization's own operational loss experience, the industry's operational loss experience, the size and scope of the organization's activities, the quality of the organization's control environment, and management's expert judgment. Because these models capture specific characteristics of each organization, such models yield unique risk-sensitive estimates of the organization's operational risk exposures. Effective operational risk measurement frameworks are built on both quantitative and qualitative risk assessment techniques. Although the output of the regulatory framework for operational risk is a measure of exposure resulting in a capital number, the integrity of that estimate depends not only on the soundness of the measurement model, but also on the robustness of the organization's underlying operational risk management processes.

A diversity of analytical approaches is emerging in the industry. Most current approaches seek to estimate loss frequency and loss severity to arrive at an aggregate loss distribution. Organizations then use the aggregate loss distribution to determine the appropriate amount of capital to hold for a given standard. Scenario analysis is also being used by many organizations, even if to significantly varying degrees. Scenario analysis requires management to imagine catastrophic operational shocks and estimate the impact on the organization. Some organizations are using scenario analysis as the basis for their analytical framework; others are incorporating scenarios as a means for considering the possible impact of significant operational losses on their overall operational risk exposure. Aspects on scenario analysis are presented in Chapter 9.

The Basel Committee expects that there will be significant variation in analytical frameworks across organizations, with each organization tailoring its framework to leverage existing technology platforms and risk management procedures. The committee expects that there will be some uncertainty and potential error in the analytical frameworks because of the evolving nature of operational risk measurement and data capture. Technology and external risks should allow for database-related quantification of operational risks, similar to the one performed for market or credit risk. Once potential loss events and actual losses are defined, a bank can analyze and model their occurrence. Doing so requires constructing databases for monitoring such losses and creating risk indicators that summarize these data. The Bank for International Settlements has suggested an indicator-based quantification as a possible method for the quantification of operational risk and the corresponding regulatory capital allocation.[4]

Whatever analytical approach an organization chooses, it must document and provide the rationale for all assumptions embedded in its chosen analytical framework, including the choice of inputs, distributional assumptions, and the weighting of qualitative and quantitative elements. Management must document how its chosen analytical framework accounts for dependence (e.g., correlations) among operational losses across and within business lines. The issue of dependence and correlations is discussed explicitly in Chapters 5 and 6. One thing that organizations must keep in mind while selecting operational risk management tools is that they should be flexible enough to accommodate any future regulatory and reporting requirement changes.

Loss Events

Basel II clearly lays down that financial organizations need to focus on loss data collection of three to (ideally) five years, varying according to different lines of business. The committee expects internal loss event data to play an important role in the organization's analytical framework, hence the requirement for five years of internal operational risk loss data. A loss event database captures and gathers individual loss events across business units and risk types. It is a tool that measures, quantifies, and provides financial operational risk losses. An established and complete database can potentially be used for modeling purposes and be applied to external loss events. It is essential to clearly define an "operational risk loss event" and its corresponding "monetary impact." It is extremely costly and time-consuming to develop a historical internal database on operational risk events. More important, the use of historical information data is not very significant in operational risk management because it may not be representative of the actual exposure. Thus, internal data should be supplemented with external data obtained from other organizations. However, external data must be scaled and adjusted to reflect organizational differences in the business unit, activity level, geography, and risk-control mechanisms across organizations. For further reading on the subject, refer to Reference 5.

Operational Risk Data

Operational risks cannot be managed if no information exists about them. According to Edward Deming, one of the most famous quality gurus, "What gets measured and observed gets done."

The operational risk measurement methodology that is chosen is often determined by data availability. Data availability is a precondition to effective operational risk management. Activities only turn into data if they are recorded in a format that can be retrieved at a later stage. The questions operational risk data must answer are: what do the organizations have already, what do they still need, and by which means will they get it?

In particular, two aspects have to be clarified:

1. *The frequency in which operational risk data is available or should be available.* Is it needed on a daily, monthly, quarterly, annual basis? There is a tendency to argue that the more frequent the better, which would call for daily data. This is not realistic and the data may not be relevant. As Albert Einstein stated, "Not everything that can be counted counts, and not everything that counts can be counted."
2. *The level of detail at which operational risk data is or should be available.* Probably many banks can already find operational risk data at the overall level (such as litigation costs) of their organization or for very specific areas (such as transactions or IT). However, operational risk data must be thoroughly collected for all departments and business lines.

Data can be obtained through:

- Collecting internal data
- Collecting external data
- Simulating data using educated estimates
- Extrapolating data based on limited samples

The foundation of any thorough analysis of operational risk is data integrity and quality. If data is sparse, biased, incomplete, or flawed, the outcome of any analysis will not give a true image of the operational risks. Because of this fundamental relationship between data quality and trustworthy results, the process of data gathering must be as diligent as the quantitative analysis. When collecting data, one of the most important issues to address is classification. How data is structured will determine the feasibility of certain analysis and the practicality of obtaining results. Categorization must be done consistently, and it must follow a logical pattern. If losses are grouped randomly, values derived from the data set will reflect its irregularity. When categorizing operational risk loss data, it is advisable to group loss events based on their causes. The collection of all the data can be utilized for other uses as well, such as for economic capital computation, enterprise risk management, hedge accounting, loan pricing analysis, and anti-money laundering.

Presently, useful data with information content is limited. More operational risk data is now being collected on a regular basis and sometimes even down to the business-line level. Relevance must be ensured, however, as banks keep changing and adapting themselves to new environments, new products, and new services. Constant surveys and checks on the type of data being used must be performed to avoid "white noise" or unrealistic indicators. This must be an ongoing process, and organizations must never forget the purpose for which the data is required. More information on data relevance and how to make data comparable can be found in Reference 6.

Operational risk data should be properly managed. In addition to volume, there is the nature of data to be captured, multiple data source systems, user data entry facility, and dynamic data management requirements. A well-developed underlying data model can do the following:

- Model a variety of products and scenarios
- Enable the buildup of historical data, which is essential for compliance reporting
- Manage the collateral information, which is essential for mitigation

Data maintenance is a critical factor in an organization's operational risk management framework. Organizations with advanced data management practices should be able to track operational risk loss events from initial discovery through final resolution. These organizations should also be able to make appropriate adjustments to the data and use the data to identify trends, track problem areas, and identify areas of future risk. Such data should include not only operational risk loss event information, but also information on risk assessments, which is factored into the operational risk exposure calculation. Operational risk data elements captured by the organization must be of sufficient depth, scope, and reliability to:

- Track and identify operational risk loss events across all business lines, including when a loss event impact multiple business lines.
- Calculate capital ratios based on operational risk exposure results. The organization must also be able to factor in adjustments related to risk mitigation, correlations, and risk assessments, and to produce internal and public reports on operational risk measurement and management results, including trends revealed by loss data or risk assessments. The organization must also have sufficient data

to generate exception reports for management. Operational risk reports are discussed more in details in Chapter 9. The types of operational risk reports may include:

- Losses (costs, profiles)
- Issues and near misses
- KRI (trends, forecasts)
- Thresholds and triggers reviews
- Economic/regulatory capital
- Risk management activities

The data warehouse must contain the key data elements needed for operational risk measurement, management, and verification. The precise data elements may vary by organizations and also among business lines within an organization. An important element of ensuring consistent reporting of the data elements is to develop comprehensive definitions for each data element used by the organization for reporting operational risk loss events or for the risk assessment inputs. The data must be stored in an electronic format to allow for timely retrieval for analysis, verification, and testing of the operational risk framework, as well as required disclosures under Pillar 3 of Basel II.

Management will need to identify those responsible for maintaining the data warehouse. In particular, policies and processes must be developed for delivering, storing, retaining, and updating the data warehouse. Policies and procedures must also cover the editing of the data input functions, as well as the requirements for the testing and verification function to validate data integrity. As with other areas of the operational risk framework, it is critical that management ensure accountability for ongoing data maintenance, because this will impact operational risk management and measurement efforts.

Testing and Verification

The operational risk management framework must provide for regular and independent testing and verification of the operational risk management policies, processes, and measurement systems, as well as operational risk data capture systems. The testing and verification function, whether internally or externally performed, should be staffed by qualified individuals who are independent of the operational risk management function and the organization's lines of business. Independent testing and verification should be done to ensure the integrity and applicability of the operational risk framework, operational risk exposure and loss data, and the underlying assumptions driving the regulatory capital measurement process. The verification of the operational risk measurement system should include testing of the following:

- Key operational risk processes and systems
- Data feeds and processes associated with the operational risk measurement system
- Adjustments to pragmatic operational risk capital estimates, including operational risk exposure
- Periodic certification of operational risk models used and their underlying assumptions
- Assumptions underlying operational risk exposure, data decision models, and operational risk capital charge

For most organizations, operational risk verification and testing will primarily be done by the audit function. Internal and external audits can provide an independent assessment of the quality and effectiveness of the control systems' design and performance. However, organizations may use other independent internal units (e.g., quality assurance) or third parties. As well as audits, reviews and stress testing can form part of the testing and verification activity.

Reports summarizing operational risk testing and verification findings for both the independent operational risk management function and lines of business should be provided to management and the board of directors or a designated board committee for appropriate decisions and actions.

Operational Risk Management Audits

Internal and external audits play a very relevant role, especially in the operational risk arena. Forward-looking and diligent audit reports form an excellent basis for operational improvements and reduction or elimination of operational risks. As important as the audit reports themselves are, the corresponding follow-ups and corrective actions by those concerned are critical. The arrival of the operational risk management creates opportunities for internal auditors. Senior management and the board of directors expect internal auditors to ensure that the organization does not encounter any surprises. This expectation implies that internal auditing should be present within the organization. An operational risk management audit process is designed to:

- Understand the responsibilities and operational risks faced by an auditable organization, department, business unit or process.
- Assess the design and operating effectiveness of controls governing key operational processes and business risks.

- Assess the levels of control exercised by management.
- Identify, with management participation, opportunities for improving controls.
- Provide senior management and the board of directors with an understanding of the degree to which management has achieved its responsibilities and mitigated the risks associated with the operation. This includes:
  - Reliability and integrity of operational information
  - Effectiveness and efficiency of operations
- Assist the board in meeting its governance and regulatory responsibilities; compliance with laws, regulations, and contracts.

For more information on operational risk audits, see Reference 7.

Operational Risk Management Reviews

In financial organizations, management, audits, and controls are increasingly tailored to operational risk management aspects. The management and controls must also be periodically reviewed. The review process can be the result of the audit process. Once the optimal resources are allocated to control risks (discussed extensively in Chapter 8), a cost-benefit analysis must be accomplished to see whether risk and cost are in balance. Any changes in the system should be recognized and appropriate risk management controls applied. To accomplish an effective review, supervisors need to identify whether the actual cost is in line with expectations. Also, the supervisor will need to see what effect the control measure has had on operational performances. It will be difficult to evaluate the control measure by itself; therefore, it is important to focus on the aspects of operational performances the control measure was designed to improve.

A review by itself is not enough; a feedback system must be established to ensure that the corrective or preventive action taken was effective and that any newly discovered risks identified during the operation are analyzed. When a decision is made to accept a risk, the factors (cost versus benefit information) involved in this decision should be recorded. When an accident or negative consequences occurs, proper documentation allows for the review of the risk decision process to see where errors might have occurred or if changes in the procedures and tools led to the consequences. It is unlikely that every risk analysis will be perfect the first time. When risk analysis contains errors, it is important that those errors be identified and corrected. Without this feedback loop, there is a lack of the benefit of knowing if the previous forecasts were accurate, contained minor errors, or were completely incorrect.

Operational Risk Management Back Testing and Stress Testing

A key component to the implementation of model-based risk management is model validation, that is, determining whether the model chosen is accurate and performing consistently. This is important both to organizations and their regulators. Back testing and stress testing are key components to model operational risk measurement and management systems. Many tools are available for these purposes. No common criteria have been set as of yet, however; more work using different tools is needed to assist in this choice.

Back testing is done to compare whether observed outcomes with the model are equal to expected outcomes, whereas stress testing is done to examine the model's expected outcomes under extreme conditions. This is basically testing the robustness of the model. Stress tests are tools used by financial organizations to estimate their potential vulnerability to exceptional but possible events. Many of the problems and advantages of stress testing hold true across the different classes of risk in market, credit, and operational.

Banking organizations must be able to stress-test their operations at least once a month, at both corporate and line-of-business levels, using multiple scenario cases. The scenarios used for stress tests should be developed such that the risk environment is duly taken into consideration. The organization's stress-testing methodology assumes that, during a simulated stressed operational event, no action would be taken to change the operations risk profile. This lets the organization capture the decreased liquidity that often occurs when undesirable activities appear.

Stress tests are appropriate tools to use in assessing the risks. It assists the risk manager in making decisions on whether, and what, capital should be reserved to ensure that it will cover all losses in case that operational risk occurs at their extreme levels. It is expected that a part of the operational risk management in banking organizations is to undertake stress testing as a matter of good corporate governance, which should result in better internal controls and risk management. Thus, stress tests should be considered as a fundamental element in an overall operational risk management framework for determining the ordinary reserve capital adequacy or even as a way to monitor performance. The use of such tests should not be seen as a regulatory burden.

Stress tests can help in the following areas:

- Developing and assessing alternative strategies for mitigating an organization's risks
- Addressing significant adverse threats to the future financial condition

Factors to keep in mind concerning frequency and time horizon of operational stress testing include:

- Stress tests should be conducted at least quarterly. In addition, stress tests should be conducted to capture new operational characteristics. The decision on the appropriate frequency will be influenced by factors related to people, system, and process operational change management characteristics together with variations on business targets and objectives.
- Although it is normally appropriate to perform stress testing at least quarterly, less frequent stress testing may be appropriate for operations with a low-risk profile. More frequent stress testing may be appropriate for operations with a high-risk profile, or when operational conditions are changing rapidly. Supervisors may require more frequent stress testing (e.g., monthly), either as a general practice or in response to the particular circumstances of the people, system, and process operational activities. For such nonquarterly stress testing, the supervisory authority may require fewer details than is the case of quarterly stress testing.
- Stress tests should examine the effects and impact that different time horizons for measuring operational risk will have on business plans, strategic risks, and future operating requirements. The time horizon must be long enough for the effects of the stress to be fully evident, for management to act, and for the results to emerge.

Various individuals within the organization, such as risk managers, finance personnel, and business-line managers, should be involved in designing and analyzing the stress tests. In the analysis of the stress-testing results, risk managers and analysts must be able to understand the assumptions underlying the stress testing. They should also receive the results of the most operational stress tests and the critical assumptions underlying them, and have access to the results of all tests. Finally, the results from stress testing should be used for strategic planning and for contingency planning.

Basel II's Pillar 2, which deals with supervisory review, sets out the need for banks to have a clear, robust capital plan. The use of stress testing as part of this capital planning is a good strategy. Stress testing can be based on simple sensitivity tests or events that the organization's risk managers believe may occur in the foreseeable future (scenario analysis). The scenarios are developed either by drawing on a significant event experienced in the past (historical scenarios) or by thinking through the consequences of events that have not yet happened (hypothetical scenarios). Two major goals of stress testing are to evaluate the capacity of the bank's capital to absorb potential large losses and to identify steps the bank can take to reduce its risk and preserve capital.

Although operational Value at Risk (VaR) (discussed in Part II of this book) reflects the risk of operational losses due to undesirable operational activities, stress testing captures the organization's losses to highly unlikely but plausible events in extreme and unexpected operational activities. Stress testing is as equally important as operational VaR to banking organization in identifying the severity and managing operational risk manifestation. Stress testing is discussed more explicitly in Reference 8.

Enterprisewide Risk Management

Traditional risk systems cannot capture the interrelationships among various risk types across geographies, departments, and lines of business. Financial organizations have been realizing the need to correctly understand their risks due to various actions as well as the interrelations within the organization. Since then, the concept of risk management has been evolving, until the late 1990s when enterprisewide risk management entered the business arena. The new Basel Capital Accord is creating even greater pressure for banks to improve their enterprisewide risk management practices. Managing risk individually seems to be less talked about today, while enterprisewide risk management (EWRM), organizationwide risk management, and integrated risk management seem to be the current catchphrases.[9]

There are seven components of EWRM:

1. Corporate governance
2. Line management
3. Portfolio management
4. Risk transfer
5. Risk analytics
6. Data and technology resources
7. Stakeholders management

For more explanation about these components, see Reference 9.

EWRM is much like a green field, likely to be explored by the financial organizations in the near future. It promises to look across organizations to identify all the risks. It also promises to determine how these risks are interrelated and how they affect performance and profitability, thus weaving a direct relationship between processes, products, and profit. It is becoming evident that the ultimate integration of market risk, credit risk, and operational risk for EWRM will be an enormous task, but the following tips may serve useful for organizations willing to try:

- Awareness among employees about risk and its implications
- A clear understanding of the reasons behind most risks and the collection of all significant, appropriate data for an effective strategy to manage those risks
- A clear understanding about the relevant investment in technology to maintain a continuous flow of data across the organization
- A single point of contact in the management board to supervise the risk management process across the enterprise
- The implementation of a single distributed data architecture to collect information from across the organization while feeding a network to strengthen the front, back, and middle office

Other competitive benefits derived from adopting an enterprisewide approach to risk management include:

- *Return on investment.* Companies can leverage their Basel II investments to support other initiatives such as international accounting standards (IAS), risk-adjusted return on capital (RAROC), and value-based management (VBM).
- *Improved performance management.* The ability to align internal performance management with regulatory management for the first time will provide companies with clearer strategic direction and improved decision making.
- *Cost reductions.* Cost reductions can also be achieved through organizational realignment, as well as process and systems efficiencies between and across the finance and risk functions.
- *Better data management.* Improving data quality and use with a single, enterprisewide risk approach to risk management also provides the opportunity to transform information management capabilities. Data controls that ensure availability, consistency, and integrity as part of the overall systems integration approach are crucial.

Operational Risk Management Concerns

Although few financial organizations would argue against managing operational risks, many find it difficult to fully adopt the discipline associated with a proactive risk management process within operations. Often, they might undertake a risk assessment at the start of each project but fail to maintain the process as the project proceeds. Major challenges in operational risk quantification reside in low-probability, high-impact events.

The following reasons are frequently given to explain this failure:

- Pressure of time, combined with the feeling that nothing will be done about reported risks
- Staff who often feels that identifying risks may give the wrong impression to management and may result in vengeance against them
- Concern that a visible focus on risks will present a negative impression to executives and shareholders

The root cause for these beliefs is that managers themselves often do not understand the value that operational risk management delivers. As a result, they are reluctant to assign adequate resources for operational risk management activities. Conversely, where resources are limited, they might sacrifice these activities first if the budget or schedule comes under pressure. It is therefore especially important to ensure that all stakeholders appreciate the importance of managing risks to establish a culture where operational risk management can thrive.

Some of the major concerns banks are faced with, in implementing an operational risk management framework (this is also applicable for credit and market risk) in accordance with Basel II, have been cited as follows:

- High cost of implementing Basel
- Lack of IT flexibility and data collection facilities
- Uncertainty over how regulators will assess the robustness of developed risk management systems
- Disclosure requirements — the amount of information that needs publishing
- Shortage of Basel experts
- Lack of time for data collection
- Storage requirements

The following operational risk management concerns are present for any financial organization, irrespective of size and scope:

- Business continuity planning
- Customer complaints
- IT migration
- IT security
- Outsourcing
- Money laundering
- Fraud
- Settlement
- Communication

Business Continuity Planning

A crucial aspect of operational risk management is having in place effective business continuity planning (BCP) to ensure that the business can function even following a breakdown of a major system or business premises becoming unavailable, due, for example, to industrial action, a terrorist attack, or other major disruptive event. This is an issue that many regulators have been focusing on in recent years. It is now generally recognized by regulators as being crucial that banks, in establishing an effective operational risk management program, have in parallel effective BCP to ensure that they are able to cope effectively with these low-probability but high-impact scenarios. Without effective BCP this could quickly lead to a bank losing business and ultimately being forced into liquidation. Inevitably, focus on BCP has become even more pronounced following September 11, 2001, after the attack on the World Trade Center in New York. BCP is defined as disaster prevention and disaster recovery planning. The goal of disaster prevention is to reduce the threat of a disaster before it takes place. In contrast, disaster recovery seeks to reestablish the critical functions after an interruption or disaster. BCP depends mainly on four resources: people, location, IT, and external services. BCP is also discussed in Chapter 9.

Customer Complaints

Every financial organization vows to have the best customer service and customer satisfaction. But how many really have a proper setup to live up to this promise? Effective customer complaints handling requires good quality and retention management. It can be an operational risk mitigation tool, which again helps to maintain a good reputation. When customers are not satisfied and complain, this may signal an alert to underlying operational risks inside the financial organization. For instance, if a customer complains about unknown transactions on his or her account, this should not be dismissed lightly. It could mean that a fraud is being performed, or that there has been an operational failure somewhere in the system.

Customer satisfaction consists of:

- Soft measures: customer opinions/complaints, perceptions, and feelings (used to predict customer behavior).
- Hard measures: repeat and lost business, market share, customer gains (measures customer satisfaction and reflects customer behavior).

By putting the soft measures and hard measures together, a customer satisfaction index (CSI) can be defined that identifies several good hard and soft measures of customer satisfaction. CSI forms part of a summary report that management can look at every month, or even every week, to determine how well it is satisfying the customer, and may form key inputs to operational risks. For more information of how to compute a CSI, see Reference 10.

Outsourcing

Outsourcing remains an avenue by which a financial organization can attain a competitive edge. Nevertheless, outsourcing is not free of operational risk issues, which must be considered in turn. Primarily, while an operation or service may become outsourced, the ultimate responsibility for it is not. Outsourcing issues are discussed in Reference 11.

Money Laundering

Financial organizations are factually and by perception exposed to money launderers using and abusing the financial system. This is yet another management concern that every financial organization has to take very seriously. Money laundering issues are discussed in Reference 12.

Fraud

It is people, not businesses or systems, who commit fraud. In today's "connected economy," fraud is increasing. Fraud permeates every area of a business. Fraud issues were discussed in Chapter 1 and are further examined in Reference 12.

Settlement Risk

The concept of settlement risk is not anything new to the financial community. Most famously, the Bankhaus Herstatt was rendered insolvent in 1974 due to settlement problems. For a more in-depth explanation of this story, see Reference 13. The term "Herstatt risk" has since been used to describe the risk that involves banks making and receiving payments at different times. It is the risk that a loss might occur in case one counterparty has already fulfilled its obligations while it did not yet receive the corresponding cash flow and security from the other counterparty.

Communication

Communication is the lifeline of any financial organization. The structure, system, processes, and organization in regard to communication is an operational risk in itself. In addition, an ineffective communication setup can escalate any other loss or risk situation, from something small to a full-blown crisis.

Key Players and Elements for Implementing Effective Operational Risk Management

To implement an effective operational risk management framework, many key players should be involved (refer to Figure 2.5). The recommended key internal players from Basel II are boards of directors, senior managers, and internal auditors; key external players are external auditors and supervisors. Other main players should involve the chief executive officer (CEO), chief risk officer (CRO), risk analysts (RA), chief information officer (CIO), chief operations officer (COO), chief security officer (CSO), quality assurance manager (QAM), business continuity officer (BCO), business-line managers, financial managers and controllers, and human resources manager (HRM).

The organization must have an independent operational risk management function that is responsible for overseeing the operational risk framework at the organization level. The roles and responsibilities of the function will vary between organizations, but must be clearly documented. This is to ensure the development and consistent application of operational risk policies, processes, and procedures throughout the organization. The organizationwide operational risk management function must ensure appropriate reporting of operational risk exposures and loss data to the board of directors and senior management. The independent organizationwide operational risk function should have organizational status commensurate with the organization's operational risk profile, while remaining independent of the lines of business and the testing and verification function. At a minimum, the organization's independent organizationwide operational risk management function should ensure the development of policies, processes, and procedures that explicitly manage operational risk as a distinct risk to the organization's safety and soundness. These policies, processes, and procedures should include principles for how operational risk is to be identified, measured, monitored, and controlled across the organization. Additionally, they should provide for the collection of the data needed to calculate the organization's operational risk exposure.

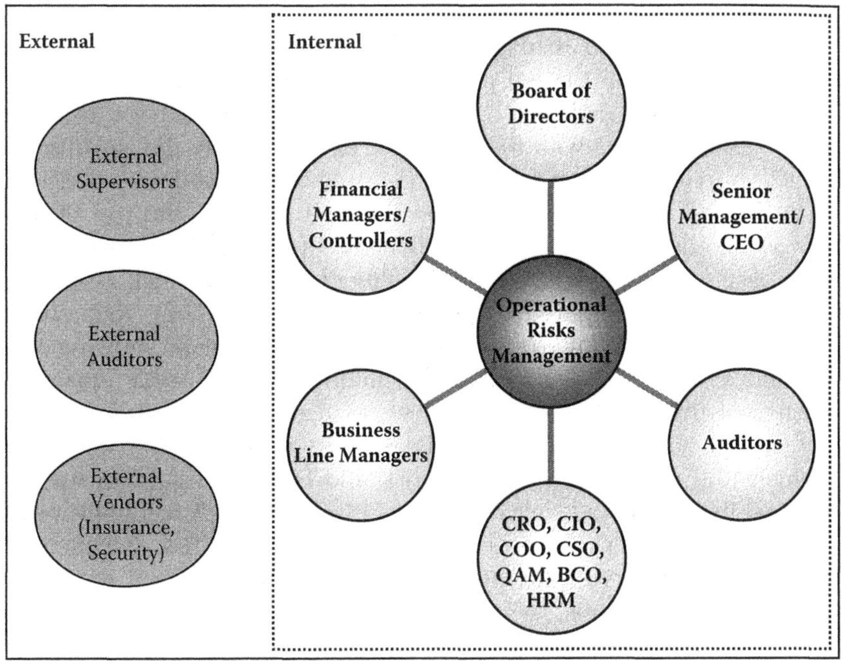

Figure 2.5 Key players for implementing effective operational risk management.

Additional responsibilities of the independent organizationwide operational risk management function include:

- Assist in the implementation of the overall organizationwide operational risk framework.
- Review the organization's progress toward stated operational risk objectives, goals, and risk tolerances.
- Periodically review the organization's operational risk framework to consider the loss experience, effects of external market changes, other environmental factors, and the potential for new or changing operational risks associated with new products, activities, or systems. This review process should include an assessment of industry best practices for the organization's activities, systems, and processes.
- Review and analyze operational risk data and reports.
- Ensure appropriate reporting to senior management and the board.

Boards of directors and senior management are called upon by Basel II to ensure the proper management of operational risks. Their roles are described precisely in the ten principles of the Basel II Accord, and they are highlighted in Chapter 3. They are also responsible for BCP and management, together with the CEO and BCO, to allow the organization to function in as normal a fashion as possible when faced with disasters.

The role of internal auditors is to use and promote the use of tools to measure and quantify operational risks, operational risk status, and quality assurance and report on the quality of operational risk assessment work and reports prepared by management. Furthermore, they should construct and publish enterprisewide operational risk maps showing areas with highest residual risk exposures, including, when possible, quantified estimates of the value at risk and levels of management risk awareness. They should utilize tools and technologies to continuously explore and document the relationship between risk and control designs in use and the actual performance levels and results produced. This will improve the overall global understanding of the principles of good risk management. The QAM, together with the internal auditors, helps to assure the quality of processes, operations, systems, services, and products, which helps minimize operational risks.

The COO and CRO are responsible for effective management of operational risk. They should select from risk reduction options recommended by the staff and accept or reject risk based on the benefit to be derived. They should ensure that interdependency-related risks at the operational level are reported and addressed. Furthermore, they should train and motivate personnel to use operational risk management techniques and raise decisions to a higher level when it is appropriate.

The CIO needs to ensure the consistent and accurate flow of information through IT, whereas the COO needs to measure and monitor the performance of daily operations. The CSO, on the other hand, plays a vital role in assessing and managing the security of the banking operations.

Business-line managers are responsible for the day-to-day management of operational risk within each business unit. They are accountable for operational risk management (identification, assessment, and control) within their business line. They must ensure that internal controls and practices within their line of business are consistent with organizationwide policies and procedures to support the management and measurement of the organization's operational risks. Implementation of the operational risk framework within each line of business should reflect the scope of that business and its inherent operational complexity and operational risk profile. Business-line managers must be independent of both the organizationwide operational risk management and the testing and verification functions. The business-line managers should take the responsibilities for balancing an acceptable level of operational risk against program and project objectives and business opportunities.

The financial manager/controllers and the human resources manager allocate appropriate budget and personnel for the management of operational risks. The financial manager/controllers also deal with ensuring against operational risks, if it has been decided that this is the appropriate mitigation technique. They should also be involved in implementing the risk process to be used at the operational level.

Apart from the more senior staff, it is the duty of every employee in the organization to assess risks and develop risk-reduction alternatives in their everyday operations and integrate risk controls into their operations. They should maintain a constant awareness of the changing risks associated with the operation or task and make supervisors immediately aware of any unrealistic risk-reduction measures or high-risk procedures.

External supervisors and auditors are responsible for the assessment and reporting of the adequacy of the operational risk management framework put in place by the financial organization. Their immediate roles are also described in the ten principles of the Basel II Accord in Chapter 3. External vendors such as insurance companies and security companies are responsible for insuring against operational risks and ensuring adequate security systems are in place if contracted by the banking organization.

Among some of the immediate actions that key players need to take are:

- Define what operational risks means for the particular financial organization.
- Identify key operations of the financial organization.
- Apply business lines as described by Basel II.
- Assess the impact of the three operational risk approaches (Basic, Standard, or Advanced) and define which approach to select.
- Devise a strategy for how operational risks would be identified, assessed, monitored and controlled, or mitigated.
- Develop action plans to implement chosen approach.
- Decide on external help needed for implementation.
- Build a loss event database.

The key to a successful operational risk management deployment is an integration of various best business practices, as shown in Figure 2.6. Among other things, it needs best practices in aspects of IT, data management, and storage; a sound methodological and systematic way of managing and controlling operational risks; the ability and systems to

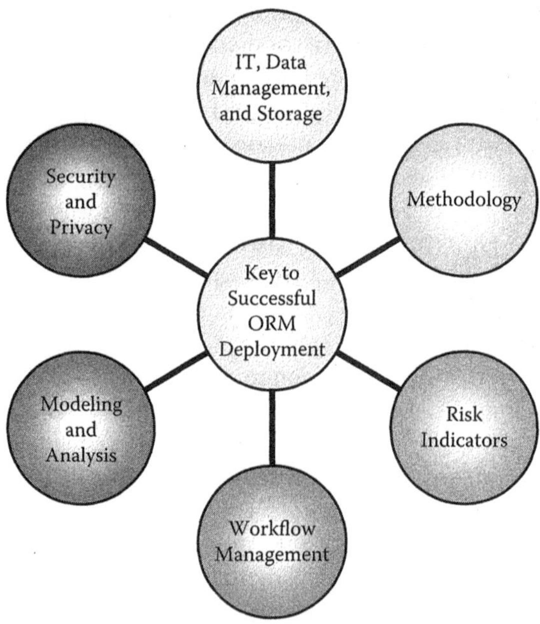

Figure 2.6 Key to successful operational risk management deployment.

identify, measure, monitor, and analyze operational risk indicators; sound workflow and process management; tools for modeling and analyzing operational risks; and best practices in security and privacy management, such as the use of ISO 17799.[14] Full compliance with the Basel II agenda will require revisions to operational risk management processes (if they already exist), as well as upgrades to existing risk resources. Basel II compliance requires banks to upgrade their risk management processes, technology, and corporate governance. Preparing for Basel II compliance will increase overall IT requirements and will require significant resource investments. To effectively support the business model transformation required by Basel II, many banks will have to selectively and strategically improve their IT architecture, data standards, IT governance, and legacy application infrastructure. The role and influence of IT on operational risk is discussed thoroughly in Chapter 1.

Examples of operational risk management procedures required to comply with Basel II may include:

- Technology to identify and measure key operational risk indicators
- Databases for both internal and external current and historical information data
- Tools and processes for gathering and analyzing loss event data

- Tools to conduct probability, impact, and exposure analysis
- Tools to evaluate correlations between operational risk types
- Tools to prioritize operational risks
- Methodologies to identify and estimate the significance, frequency, and severity of losses
- Management information reporting technologies

On the technology side, Basel II compliance will trigger changes in these areas:

- IT architecture
- Data management
- Data storage processes
- The use of workflow technology
- The way transaction processing application systems are designed

Basel II projects can be linked to other valuable business initiatives in customer relationship management (CRM), workflow automation, financial reporting integration, and system upgrades.

Banks that view the transition to Basel II compliance as an opportunity to fundamentally change their management processes and corporate infrastructure will be able to transform their risk to thrive in a Basel II-compliant world. The key to success is looking at the practical opportunities for operations and IT improvements that align with the business agenda. Full compliance with Basel II may require that organizations revise or tune their operational risk management processes together with operational processes and upgrade their existing risk resources and the allocation of these resources.

Summary

The challenge of implementing an effective operational risk management framework is becoming increasingly significant. With the advent of the Basel II Accord and Sarbanes–Oxley, increasing attention is being given, and rightly so, to the management and control of operational risks. Good operational risk management improves quality and reduces cost. Better operational risk management means that banks are less likely to have major losses through error, fraud, or failure to deliver quality service. As a consequence, good operational risk management amounts to a competitive advantage and is reflected in the shareholder value.

As one of the most heavily regulated industries, financial services are often required to set the ball rolling with regard to rules and guidelines, while other industries follow suit. Stringent regulations and market pressures are likely to force every organization to adopt some essence of these operational risk management policies in the near future. As BITS CEO Catherine Allen points out in a report, "This isn't just about Basel. This is about everyone."[15]

Operational risk is intrinsic to financial organizations and thus should be an important component of their organizationwide risk management frameworks. In practice, an organization's operational risk framework must reflect the scope and complexity of business lines, as well as the corporate organizational structure. Each organization's operational risk profile is unique and requires a tailored risk management approach appropriate for the scale and materiality of the risks present, and the size of the organization. There is no single framework that would suit every organization; different approaches may be needed for different organizations. The basic components of an effective operational risk management framework are identifying and defining the risks organizations are exposed to, assessing their magnitude, mitigating them using a variety of procedures, and setting aside capital for potential losses. The range of banking activities and areas affected by operational risk must be fully identified and considered in the development of the organization's operational risk management and measurement framework. Because operational risk is not confined to particular business lines, product types, or organizational units, it should be managed in a consistent and comprehensive manner across the organization. Consequently, risk management mechanisms must encompass the full range of risks, as well as strategies that help to identify, measure, monitor, and control those risks.

The benefits of addressing operational risk management are many. Being able to identify potential problems earlier and faster, and being able to better communicate them through more well-defined linked channels, will show demonstrable reductions in losses, errors, and incidents, as well as improvements in core processes to repair recurring problems. Training on operational risk exposures and priorities produces improved understanding and awareness, as well as better decision making.

This chapter has addressed managing operational risks and identified the elements of effective operational risk management frameworks, best practices for operational risk management, the added value of managing operational risks, and how important it is to quantify operational risks. Quantification is not an end in itself, but a step toward better management, and for some time to come, the greatest gains will be found in setting and improving the organization's core workflows. The top-down approaches are contrasted with bottom-up approaches of operational risk. Top-down approaches measure the overall operational risk exposure using macro-level operational risk indicators such as earnings volatility, cost volatility, and the number of customer complaints. Top-down approaches tend to be easy to implement, but they are unable to diagnose weaknesses in the organization's risk control mechanisms and tend to be backward looking. More forward-looking bottom-up approaches map each process individually, concentrating on potential operational errors at each stage of the process. This enables the organization to diagnose potential weaknesses, but requires large amounts of data that are typically unavailable within the organization. Industrywide data should be used to supplement internal data, although there are problems of consistency and relevance.

Furthermore, this chapter discussed loss events and operational risk data management, and how testing and verification is an important step in an effective operational risk management framework. It then went on to discuss enterprisewide risk management and what financial organizations should be concerned about in implementing such frameworks. In addition, the chapter highlighted some tangible and intangible benefits of complying with Basel II and the key people needed to implement an effective operational risk management system, together with some immediate actions that should be taken to put them on the right path to effectively managing and controlling their inherent operational risks.

References

1. *FAA System Safety Handbook,* Types of Risk Defined, Operational Risk Management, p. 15 –17, December 2000.
2. Harbour, J.L., *The Basics of Performance Measurement*, Productivity Press, 1997.
3. Marshall, C., *Measuring and Managing Operational Risk in Financial Institutions: Tools, Techniques and Other Resources*, John Wiley and Sons, Singapore, 2001.
4. Basel Committee on Banking Supervision, A New Capital Adequacy Framework, Basel, p. 50f., June 1999.
5. De Fontnouvelle, P., DeJesus-Rueff, V., et al., Using Loss Data to Quantify Operational Risk, Federal Reserve Bank of Boston, April 2003.
6. Baud, N., Frachot, A., and Roncalli, T., Groupe de Recherche Operationnelle, Credit Lyonnais, Francey, How to Avoid Over-Estimating Capital Charge for Operational Risk, December 2002.
7. Basel Committee on Banking Supervision, Framework for Internal Control Systems in Banking Organizations, September 1998.
8. Bank for International Settlements Committee: The Global Financial System, Stress Testing by Large Financial Organizations: Current Practice and Aggregation Issues, April 2000.
9. Lam, J., Enterprise-wide Risk Management and the Role of the Chief Risk Officer, March 2000.

10. Brown, M.G., *Keeping Score: Using the Right Metrics to Drive World-Class Performance,* Quality Resources, New York, 1996.
11. Basel Committee on Banking Supervision, The Joint Forum: Outsourcing in Financial Services, Consultative document, August 2004.
12. Ulrich Doerig, H., Credit Suisse Group, Operational Risks in Financial Services: An Old Challenge in a New Environment, January 2001.
13. Bank for International Settlements Committee, Risk in Foreign Exchange Transactions, Basel, March 1996.
14. Calder, A. and Watkins, S., *IT Governance: A Manager's Guide to Data Security and BS 7799/ISO 17799,* Kogan Page, Ltd., London, September 2003.
15. Colkin Cuneo, E., Accepting the Risk, Information Week, September 2003, http://www.financetech.com (accessed January 2005).

OPERATIONAL RISK AND BASEL II

Chapter 3, Operational Risk in Basel II

Chapter 4, Advanced Measurement Approach

This second part of the book consists of Chapters 3 and 4. Chapter 3 discusses the meaning of operational risk according to the Basel II Accord. It then outlines operational risk management under the new accord. It describes the three pillars and the economic capital reserve calculations using the three approaches. It then highlights the ten principles of the accord. Chapter 4 concentrates mainly on the advanced measurement approaches proposed by Basel II. This chapter discusses the Basel II measuring system, Basel II's framework, and Basel II's supervisory standards. It further discusses the use of insurance under the Advanced Measurement Approach (AMA). The AMA forms the basis of the assessment, control, and management of operational risks discussed in Parts III and IV of this book.

Chapter 3

Operational Risk in Basel II

We can't solve problems by using the same kind of thinking we used when we created them.

—Albert Einstein

Introduction

Basel enforces that financial organizations have a risk management strategy. Basel's main focus is on creating regulation guidelines on "Standardization of Risk Management" for financial organizations, which are valid worldwide. These standards, aiming for a closer correspondence between the capital that banks hold and the risks they take, should lead to more stable, efficiently run financial organizations. Harmonization across all sectors in the financial industry is the focus of the Basel Committee on Banking Supervision, which aims to implement detailed disclosure requirements across all sectors. The Basel II Accord focuses on the goals of "Identify-Assess-Monitor-Control/Mitigate" and thus manage:

- Credit risk
- Market risk
- Operational risk

Figure 3.1 The Basel II risk management concept.

These risks, as shown in Figure 3.1, affect all banks and other financial organizations, including insurance and brokers.

One of the most notable changes in Basel II is the introduction of a capital charge for operational risk. Just as in the case of market and credit risk, the financial industry is being pushed in the direction of better controls of operational risk by bank regulators. For the first time, the Basel Committee is proposing to establish capital charges for operational risk, in exchange for lowering them on market and credit risk. The proposed charge would represent approximately 12 percent of the total capital requirement.[1] This charge is focusing the attention of financial organizations on operational risk. Basel II mostly prescribes good banking and business practices. Waiting to implement it at the last moment postpones the benefits and creates the possibility of missing the deadline for compliance. Financial organizations could improve their risk management in a way that would have a bottom-line impact even without Basel II. Still, there are important reasons to go all the way: financial organizations certified as Basel II compliant could benefit from lower capital charges and the enhanced reputation that would come from the regulators' seal of approval. Applying the Basel II requirements will take financial organizations to, or close to, best practice in risk management, particularly in risk measurement and processes.

This chapter introduces the Basel II Accord, giving a brief comparison to its predecessor, the 1988 Basel Capital Accord. It then goes on to talk about what operational risk means in Basel II and highlights some of the main objectives and targets of the Basel II Accord. It then discusses the three pillars of the Basel II Accord: calculation of the minimum capital

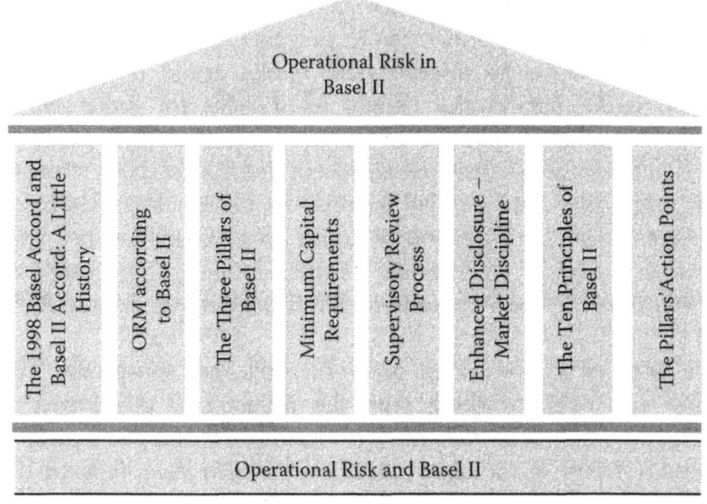

Figure 3.2 Layout of Chapter 3.

requirements, the supervisory review process, and enhanced disclosure (market discipline). The Basel Committee has proposed three approaches to calculate the minimum capital requirements, which are subsequently discussed. The qualifying criteria for risk capital calculation are then highlighted with reference to the main factors in selecting an appropriate approach. Finally, the ten principles of the accord are discussed, and some action points that need to be taken into consideration are suggested. Figure 3.2 shows the layout of Chapter 3.

The 1988 Basel Accord versus the Basel II Accord

The Basel Committee in the year 1988 decided to introduce a new capital measurement system that came to be popularly known as the Basel Capital Accord. Basel, Switzerland, is the place where this committee holds its meetings. This first Basel Capital Accord was introduced to coordinate global regulatory efforts and set up minimum capital requirements to eliminate the threats posed by undercapitalized banks. The 1988 Accord set a capital requirement simply in terms of credit risk (the principal risk for banks), although the overall capital requirement (i.e., the 8 percent minimum ratio) was intended to cover other risks as well. The 1988 Capital Accord prescribed a single, one-size-fits-all credit risk measurement framework. For example, under the 1988 Basel Accord rules, which have been in place since the committee implemented its original Basel Capital Accord in 1988, banks must hold at least the same amount of capital against loans to AAA-rated commercial borrowers (8 percent) as they do against loans to BBB-rated borrowers. Meanwhile, the banks argue that they are not allowed to make meaningful capital allowances for loans secured by collateral versus loans that are not secured. In the 1988 Basel Accord, boards of directors and senior management did not establish strong control cultures, and some banks failed to observe certain key internal control principles, especially segregation of duties. In 1996, market risk exposures were removed and given separate capital charges. For a more detailed discussion on the deficiencies of the 1988 Basel Accord, refer to References 2 and 3.

In its attempt to introduce greater credit risk sensitivity, the Basel Committee has been working with the industry to develop a suitable capital charge for operational risk. This framework has been progressively introduced not only in member countries, but also in more than 100 other countries that have active international banks.

In June 1999, the Basel Committee issued a proposal for a new capital adequacy framework to replace the 1988 Accord. This happened because of certain issues (Figure 3.3) faced by the 1988 Basel Accord.

This framework is known as the second Basel Accord or, as it is more commonly known, Basel II. Basel II is shorthand for the second capital accord proposed by the Basel Committee on Banking Supervision, a subgroup of the Bank of International Settlements, the central bank. In its attempt to introduce greater credit risk sensitivity, the Committee has been working with the industry to develop a suitable capital charge for operational risk (for example, the risk of loss from computer failures, poor documentation, or fraud). Basel II is designed to be more flexible and

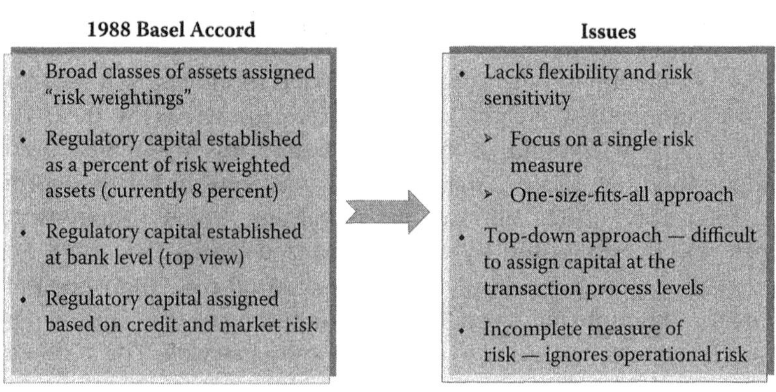

Figure 3.3 Issues with the 1988 Basel Accord.

Table 3.1 Differences between the 1998 Basel Accord and Basel II Accord

1988 Basel Capital Accord	*Basel II Capital Accord*
Focus on single risk measure	More emphasis on bank's own internal risk management methodologies, supervisory review, and market discipline
One size fits all	Flexibility in the types of approaches, capital incentives for better risk management, and differences between the types of business lines and in the risk profiles of their systems and operations
General structure	Multidimensional focus on all operational components of a bank

Source: "The New Basel Capital Accord: An Explanatory Note."[4]

risk sensitive than its predecessor (refer to Table 3.1) and hence provides more complex measurement techniques. It affects all banks and other financial organizations, including bankers, insurers, custodians, fund managers, and brokers.

The new Basel II Accord provides a set of standards that are set to modify the way that banks are capitalized. The new framework is set to improve the trustworthiness of the financial organizations by aligning capital adequacy assessment more closely with the fundamental risks in such organizations. Moreover, it also provides motivation for financial organizations to enhance their risk measurement and management capabilities. Therefore it augments market discipline.

For example, a commercial bank's greatest risk 15 years ago was its loan portfolio, but, due to innovative financial systems today such as derivatives, a bank's capital is exposed to credit risk, interest, and market risk, as well as operational risk. Once Basel II is implemented, operational risk will feature directly in the assessment of capital adequacy for the first time.

Many major banks now allocate 20 percent or more of their internal capital to operational risks.[4] The work on operational risk is in a developmental stage, but three different approaches of increasing sophistication (basic indicator, standardized, and advanced measurement) have been identified in Basel II. The basic indicator approach utilizes one indicator of operational risk for a bank's total activity. The standardized approach specifies different indicators for different business lines. The advanced measurement approach requires banks to utilize their internal loss data in the estimation of required capital. All three approaches are discussed in depth in this chapter.

The committee (G10), formed in 1975, is in charge of creating guidelines for national regulators with regard to capital that banks must set aside against risk. The committee, representing central banks of Belgium, Canada, France, Germany, Italy, Japan, Luxembourg, the Netherlands, Spain, Sweden, Switzerland, the United Kingdom, and the United States, notes that many banks hold capital in excess of the regulatory minimums and some already allocate economic capital for other risks. It also notes that the more risk-sensitive framework of the new accord reflects the advances in the banking industry since the previous accord in 1988. The 1988 Basel Accord only covered internationally active banks; Basel II affects most financial organizations in the following ways:

- All banks in the 110 countries that have signed Basel II will be affected.
- All banks, securities firms, asset managers, and insurance companies with any involvement in banking, fund/asset management, and capital markets in the G-20 (Group of 20) countries will be affected.
- All banks, security firms, fund managers, and enterprises involved in securitization and with long-term equity holdings, such as private equity/venture capital, will be affected.

Basel II will directly cover bank-owned or controlled insurance entities. Moreover, insurance companies that own or control banks and noninsurance financial services functions will be covered by the new rules.

Although the primary focuses are banks that are active internationally, the G-20 central banks and the regulatory authorities of most of the countries that are signatories to Basel II are applying the policies to all the financial service organizations in their specific jurisdictions and are expecting the other countries to follow suit. In some countries, such as Germany, all public companies are required by law to set up a risk management framework, but there are few guidelines on how they should do so. As a result, many companies are searching for proactive risk management solutions. In the United Kingdom, the Cadbury Commission has recommended a similar risk management focus, as has the U.S. Treasury's Committee of Sponsoring Organizations. Either way, it is wise business practice and part of a company's responsibility to all its stakeholders to cover itself against operational risk.

Because compliance with Basel II is mandatory for financial services firms located in European Union (EU) member nations, European regulators and organizations are gearing up faster for it than any other region. In fact, a December 2002 survey of European organizations showed that 61 percent consider themselves to be on schedule for Basel II compliance.[5]

The situation in the United States is less encouraging. In a September 2002 survey of the top 100 financial organizations in North America, Gartner/G2 found that only 25 percent had established a Basel II steering committee.[6]

The Basel Committee expects supervisors to start applying the new framework to internationally active banks from 2004. Those banks that choose its simpler options, however, may continue to calculate capital requirements in a way broadly similar to the 1988 Accord, as explained in the paper "Annex 1 of the New Basel Capital Accord: An Explanatory Note."[4] "Annex 3: History of the Basel Capital Standards," also gives a comprehensive historical aspect of the Basel Accord.

Operational Risk Management According to Basel II

The 1988 Basel Accord examined mainly market risk and credit risk within financial organizations. Basel II modifies its evaluation of credit and market risks and, more importantly, seeks to assess and allocate capital for operational risk, rendering it more risk sensitive and more focused on the management and control of risk. The Basel II standards are specific about what must be measured, but does not set any rules about how to do so.

Basel II defines operational risks as "the risk of losses resulting from inadequate or failed internal processes, people and systems, or from external events."[7] This definition includes legal risks that are exposed to fines, penalties, damages resulting from private settlements, etc., but strategic and reputational risks are not included in this definition for the purpose of a minimum regulatory operational risk capital charge.[8]

A more rigorous, consistent, and quantified approach to operational risk management according to Basel II includes operational risk identification, assessment, monitoring, control, and mitigation, as seen in Figure 3.4. These steps are discussed in Principles 4, 5, and 6 of the Basel II Accord[9] and discussed briefly in the subsequent sections, and more in depth in subsequent chapters.

Among the possible tools that can be used by financial organizations for assessing operational risks are:

- *Self or risk assessment.* A bank assesses its operations and activities against a menu of potential operational risk vulnerabilities. This process is internally driven and often incorporates checklists and or workshops to identify the strengths and weaknesses of the operational risk environment. Scorecards (discussed in the next chapter), for example, provide a means of translating qualitative assessments into quantitative metrics. The assessment process can take the form of:

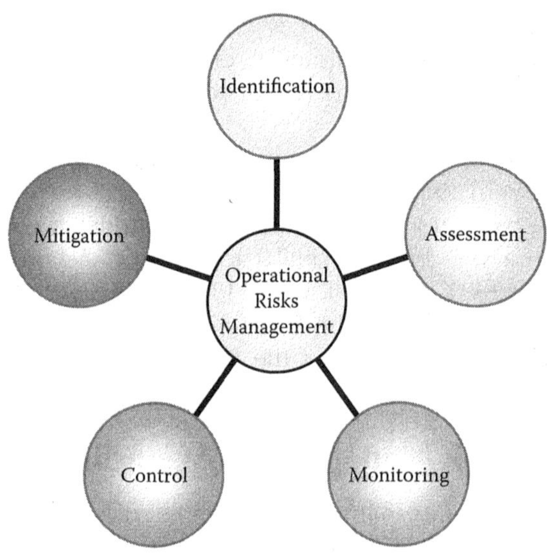

Figure 3.4 A quantified approach to operational risk management according to Basel II.

- Step 1: System characterization. What is there (or what is planned)? How is IT integrated into mission accomplishment?
- Step 2: Threat identification. What threat sources are of concern? (Internal/external, accidental/intentional, malicious/nonmalicious).
- Step 3: Vulnerability identification. What flaws/weakness might be exercised?
- Step 4: Control analysis. What are the current and planned controls?
- Step 5: Likelihood determination. What is the likelihood that an operational risk will occur?
- Step 6: Impact analysis. What impact will this operational risk have on the business?
- Step 7: Risk determination. What operational risks are really significant?
- Step 8: Control recommendations. What controls should be put in place for the identified operational risks?
- Step 9: Documentation. What information about the operational risks should be documented?

- *Risk mapping*. In this process, various business units, organizational functions (defined by an organizational chart), or process flows are mapped by risk type. This exercise can reveal areas of weaknesses and help prioritize subsequent management action.

- *Risk indicators.* Risk indicators are statistics or metrics that can provide insight into a bank's risk position. These indicators tend to be reviewed on a periodic basis (such as monthly or quarterly) to alert banks to changes that may be indicative of risk concerns.
- *Risk measurement.* Some firms have begun to quantify their exposure to operational risk using a variety of approaches. For example, data on a bank's historical loss experience could provide meaningful information for assessing the bank's exposure to operational risk and developing a policy to mitigate and control the risk. An effective way of making good use of this information is to establish a framework for systematically tracking and recording the frequency, severity, and other relevant information on individual loss events. Some organizations have also combined internal loss data with external loss data, scenario analysis, and risk assessment factors. This helps identify over- and undermanaged risks.

All the above aspects are discussed further in Part III of this book.

Main Objectives, Key Drivers, and Benefits of Basel II

The main objectives and goals of Basel II are to:

- Instill best-practices, sophisticated, analytically driven risk management policies based on each financial organization's experience.
- Increase overall information data integration and consolidation across the whole business to manage operational, market, and credit risks.
- Increase the quantification of operational risk.
- Increase the need to focus on loss data collection.
- Define more effective ways to track, calculate, monitor, analyze, and report risk measures.
- Ensure information data integrity and timeliness of measurements.
- Ensure appropriate documentation of risk management systems.
- Effectively integrate different risk types.
- Promote safety and soundness in the financial system; the new framework should at least maintain the current overall level of capital in the system.
- Enhance competitive equality.
- Establish a more comprehensive approach addressing operational risks.
- Refocus orientation toward internationally active banks; underlying principles taking into account the varying levels of complexity and sophistication.

- Promote a strong national supervisory and regulatory process to ensure the maintenance of adequate capital. Supervisors expect that banks will exceed the regulatory minimum requirements, but they have the authority to require from banks to hold more than the minimum capital.

Further information on the objectives of Basel II can be found in Reference 10.

The key drivers and targets of Basel II are based on:

- *Information data and IT systems.* Aligning and upgrading information data and existing IT systems for consistency and integrity across the organization and providing suitable reporting facilities.
- *Organizationwide scope.* Ranging from business processes and operations to organizational structure and strategy, the focus is on the proper integration of the enterprisewide risk management principles. Properly implemented, integrated enterprisewide risk management covers all areas of an organization, highlighting the interrelationships between different business functions and processes and their impact on the organization's success and overall risk profile. It is a proactive process that becomes a key part of the strategy and planning process. It is intended to help the organization detect and respond to changes in the business environment. The Basel II initiative should align with the bank's business, risk management, quality management, and IT strategies, enabling the bank to profitably grow market share.
- *Program governance.* The role and responsibilities of each individual and department must be clearly defined.

Some tangible benefits of complying with Basel II if done effectively are depicted in Figure 3.5, whereas some intangible benefits are depicted in Figure 3.6.

Some other tangible benefits include better market valuation, lower cost of liabilities, and reduction in provisioning requirements. The benefits clearly create a competitive advantage. The investments in technology will also pay itself many times over as:

- The reduced deviation between regulatory and economic capital frees up the excess funds tied to maintain capital adequacy. This improves leverage.
- A robust reporting system captures the possibility of default early to prevent loss.
- The cost of liabilities drop as compliant banks can raise funds at lower costs.

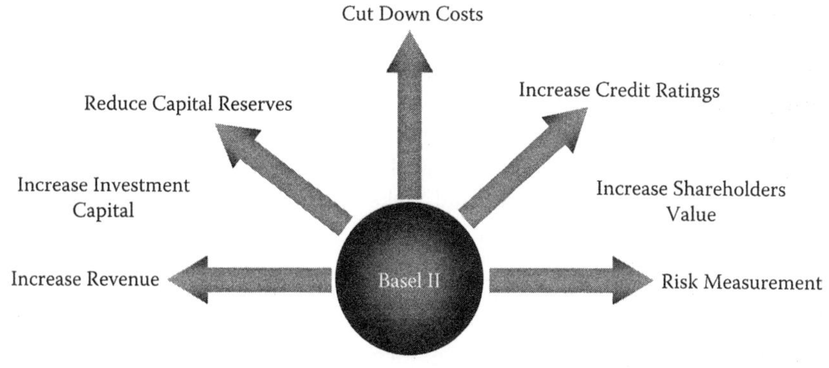

Figure 3.5 Some tangible benefits of Basel II.

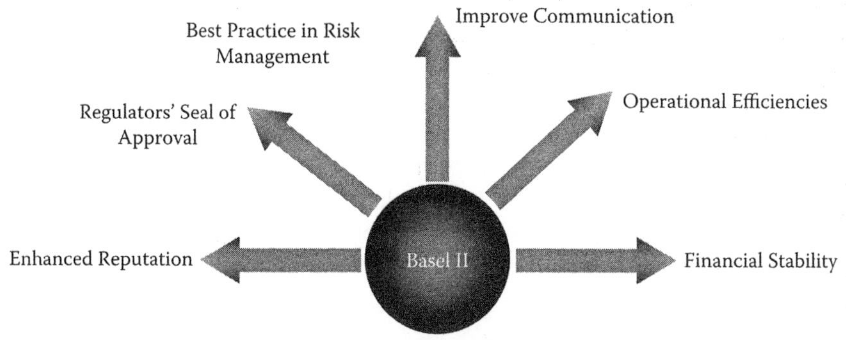

Figure 3.6 Some intangible benefits of Basel II.

Basel II standards are not mandatory for all banks, but this is no comfort. Regulation may not force compliance but the market will. In an interconnected market that allows free flow of funds, Basel-compliant banks stand a better chance of winning. Noncompliant banks will steadily lose their competitive edge as:

- Customers move funds to safer compliant banks
- Cost of meeting an asset-liability difference increases
- Margins fall

What Basel II will do, if done correctly, is to create a more risk-sensitive framework for lenders, with the result that products and services that are less risky should become cheaper. This could result in cheaper credit. The amount of capital that banks are required to set aside can have a profound effect on their lending behavior.

The Three Pillars of Basel II

The ingredients for an effective operational risk management system are comprehensively detailed in the three pillars[4] of Basel II and its standard comprising ten principles. All three pillars play an important and integrated role in the operational risk capital framework. The three pillars are applicable not only to operational risks, but also to credit and market risks. The three pillars of Basel II are as follows:

Pillar 1: Minimum capital requirements, internal view
Pillar 2: Supervisory review process, supervisors view
Pillar 3: Market discipline, external view

and are shown in Figure 3.7.

The three pillars are to be integrated; therefore, the Basel II Accord cannot be considered fully implemented if all three pillars are not in place. Minimum (or partial) implementation of one or two of the pillars will not deliver an adequate level of soundness.

Pillar 1 sets minimum capital requirement and a series of qualitative and quantitative requirements for risk measurement and management. It is used to determine eligibility to use a particular capital assessment approach. The aim of Pillar 1 is to calculate the total minimum capital requirements. The Basel Committee is offering a range of options for assessing the Pillar 1 capital charge for operational risk, and an organization's ability to meet specific criteria will determine the specific capital

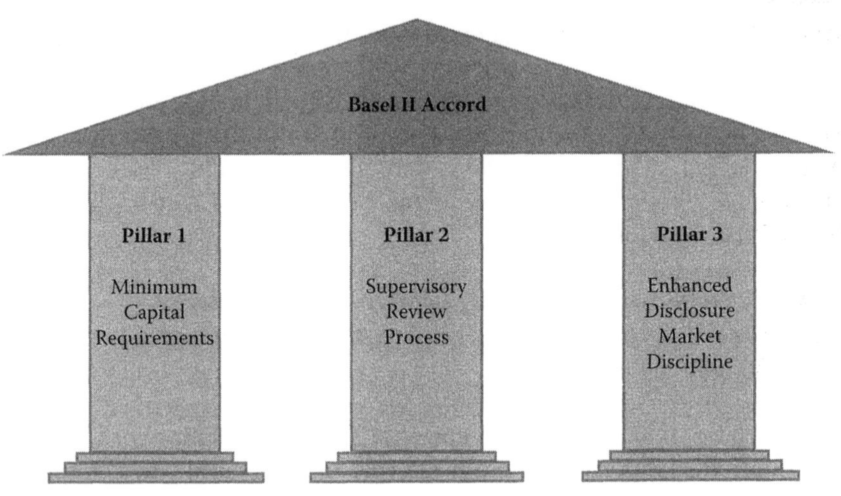

Figure 3.7 The three pillars of Basel II.

framework for its operational risk calculation. To the extent that financial organizations can demonstrate to supervisors increased sophistication and precision in their measurement, management, and control of operational risk, organizations are expected to move into more advanced approaches. This will result in a reduction of the operational risk capital requirement. The new framework maintains both the current definition of capital and the minimum requirement of 8 percent of capital to risk weighted assets. Minimum capital requirements are thoroughly discussed in the following subsections.

Pillar 2 sets out a framework in which banks are required to assess the economic capital they need as defined in Pillar 1 to support their risks, and then this process of assessment is reviewed by supervisors. The Basel Committee proposes that supervisors should also apply qualitative judgment based on their assessment of the adequacy of the control environment in each financial organization. The supervisory review process is discussed in greater detail later in this chapter.

Market discipline (Pillar 3) has the potential to reinforce capital regulation and other supervisory efforts to promote safety and soundness in banks and financial organizations. The Basel Committee believes that, to promote market discipline, banks should publicly, and in a timely fashion, disclose detailed information about the process used to manage and control their operational risks and the regulatory capital allocation approach they use.[18] This encourages monitoring of banks by professional investors and financial analysts as a complement to banking supervision in Pillar 2. Market discipline is reviewed later in this chapter.

Pillar 1: Minimum Capital Requirements

The minimum capital requirements for operational risk under Pillar 1 are calculated using one of the measurement approaches defined by the Basel Committee. These are discussed extensively in the following sections. Banks will be permitted to use different approaches for different parts of their operations. The Committee acknowledges the relationship that exists between the amount of capital held by the bank against its risks and the strength and effectiveness of the bank's risk management and internal control processes.[7] However, increased capital should not be viewed as the only option for addressing increased risks confronting the bank. Other means for addressing risk, such as strengthening risk management, applying internal thresholds, strengthening the level of reserves, and improving internal controls, must also be considered. Furthermore, capital should not be regarded as a substitute for addressing fundamentally inadequate control or risk management processes.

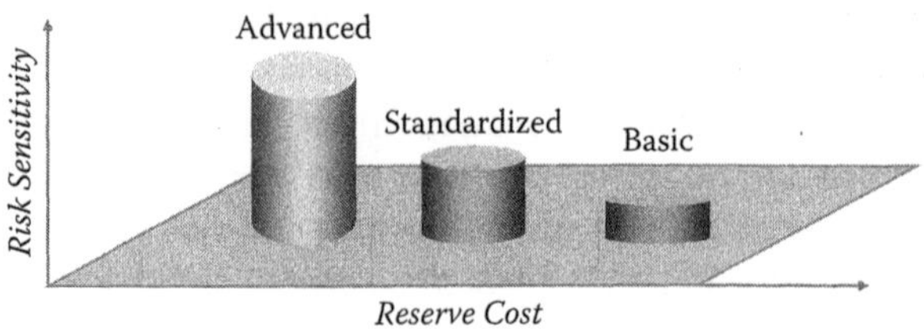

Figure 3.8 The three measurement approaches: risk sensitivity versus capital reserve.

Measurement Approaches for Operational Risks

The framework from the committee presents three methods for calculating minimum capital charge for operational risk under Pillar 1:[7]

1. The basic indicator approach
2. The standardized approach
3. The advanced measurement approach (AMA)

The basic indicator approach is the simplest, but it will charge the most capital because it is less risk sensitive. Refer to Figure 3.8.

The standardized approach (standardized and alternative standardized) calls for an organization to break down its operations into eight business lines. Less capital reserves are required for organizations choosing these approaches, and they are also more risk sensitive than the basic indicator approach.

The advanced measurement approach (AMA) charges the least amount of capital and is more sophisticated and much more risk sensitive than the former two approaches. The AMA offers maximum elasticity for banks to measure risk. The AMA is discussed more extensively in the next chapter.

Banks are encouraged to move along the spectrum of approaches and will be allowed to use a combination of approaches for different business lines. Once an approach is chosen, a bank will not be permitted to revert to a less sophisticated approach. More sophisticated approaches permit greater benefits.

The Basic Indicator Approach

The basic indicator approach uses a single indicator to calculate the capital reserve:

- Average annual gross income (Net Interest Income + Net Non-Interest Income). The capital charge is 15 percent of the average gross income for the last three years.
- Fixed percentage α:

$$K_{BIA} = \left[\sum \left(GI_{1.n} * \alpha\right)\right] \Big/ n \tag{3.1}$$

where

K_{BIA} = The capital charge under the basic indicator approach
GI = Annual gross income for the whole organization over the previous three years
n = Number of the previous three years for which gross income was positive
α = Fixed percentage, set by the Basel Committee. Current level is set to 15 percent.

If negative gross income distorts a bank's Pillar 1 capital charge, supervisors will consider appropriate supervisory actions under Pillar 2.[7]

The advantages of this approach are that it is simple and transparent, and that it uses readily available data. It is easy to implement and universally applicable across financial organizations to arrive at a charge for operational risk. Its simplicity, however, comes at the price of only limited responsiveness to firm-specific needs and characteristics. The capital charge would continue to be set by the supervisors. The problem is that it does not account for the quality of controls. As a result, this approach is expected to be mainly used by small banks with only a few business lines. Although the basic indicator approach might be suitable for smaller banks with a simple range of business activities, the Basel Committee expects internationally active banks and banks with significant operational risks to use a more sophisticated approach within the overall operational risk management framework.

The Standardized Approach

The standardized approach is a more complex variant of the basic indicator approach that uses a combination of financial indicators and organizational business lines to determine the capital charge. Again, gross income is a proxy measure, but in this case it is broken down into eight standard business lines, each with a different beta factor to calculate the minimum capital (refer to Table 3.2). For information on how the beta factor is calculated, refer to Annex 3 of the "Consultative Document Operational

Table 3.2 The Eight Banking Business Lines and Beta Factors Defined by Basel II

Business Unit	*Business Line*	*Indicator*	*Beta Factors Percent*
Investment banking	Corporate finance	Gross income	β_1 18
	Trading and sales	Gross income	β_2 18
Banking	Retail banking	Gross income	β_3 12
	Commercial banking	Gross income	β_4 15
	Payment and settlement	Gross income	β_5 18
	Agency services and custody	Gross income	β_6 15
Other financial services	Asset management	Gross income	β_7 12
	Retail brokerage	Gross income	β_8 12

Source: "Consultative Document Operational Risk Supporting Document to the New Basel Capital Accord."[8]

Risk Supporting Document to the New Basel Capital Accord,"[8] available free of charge at http://www.bis.org/bcbs/publ.htm.

The Risk Management Group (RMG) of the Basel Committee has provided eight standardized business lines and several loss event types as a general means of classifying operational events. The eight business lines are corporate finance; trading and sales; retail banking; payment and settlement; agency services; commercial banking; asset management; and retail brokerage. The loss event types are internal fraud; external fraud; employment practices and workplace safety; clients, products, and business practices; damage to physical assets; business disruption and system failure; and execution, delivery, and process management, as previously discussed. Refer to Annex 7 of "International Convergence of Capital Measurement and Capital Standards"[7] for further explanation of the loss event type classification. The eight business lines are more explicitly described in Annex 2 of the "Consultative Document Operational Risk Supporting Document to the New Basel Capital Accord."[8] The principles for the business line mapping can be found in Annex 6 of the "International Convergence of Capital Measurement and Capital Standards."[7]

The standardized approach calls for an organization to break up its operations into the eight business lines (refer to Table 3.2). Each business line is assigned to an exposure indicator (EI) or annual gross income (GI) in reference to the magnitude of the bank's operation in that particular area. Hence, each of the EIs is multiplied by a percentage, which reflects a business line's operational risk and thus determines the overall capital requirement of the organization. Within each business line, the capital charge is calculated by multiplying the indicator by a factor (denoted beta) assigned to that business line. Beta is set by the Basel Committee. It should be noted that the indicator relates to the data reported for that business line, not the whole organization; that is, in retail banking, the indicator is the GI generated in the retail banking business line.

An insurance business line may also be included in both the standardized and advanced measurement approach, where insurance is included in a consolidated group for capital purposes. The choice of business lines and indicators is discussed further in Section VI of the "Consultative Document on Operational Risk."[8] If a bank is unable to allocate an activity to a particular business line, it is proposed that income relating to that activity should be subject to the highest beta factor for which the bank reports activity[12] or to the activity for the business line it supports. The primary incentive for the standardized approach is that most banks are in the early stages of developing firmwide data on internal loss by business lines and risk types.

For the standardized approach, the capital reserve is thus calculated using:

- Annual gross income per business line
- Several indicators — size or volume of banks activities in a business line, where banks activities are divided into eight business lines:

$$K_{TSA} = \left\{ \sum\nolimits_{years(1-3)} \max\left[\sum \left(GI_{(1-8)} * \beta_{(1-8)} \right), 0 \right] \right\} \Big/ 3 \qquad (3.2)$$

where

K_{TSA} = Total capital charge under the standardized approach

$GI_{(1-8)}$ = Annual gross income for each of the eight business lines in a given year over a period of three years

$\beta_{(1-8)}$ = A fixed percentage, set by the Basel Committee, related to the business line

The total capital charge is calculated as the three-year average of the simple summation of the regulatory capital charges across each business line in each year.

As before, the beta factors are set by supervisors. This approach is still simple but better reflects varying risks across business lines. It can be used only if the bank demonstrates effective management and control of operational risk. To qualify for the standard approach, a set of minimum entry standards is required, which will be highlighted later in this chapter.

Banks, at the national supervisor's discretion, may be permitted to substitute an alternative measure known as the alternative standardized approach (ASA) in the case of retail and commercial banking. In this case, the volume of outstanding loans will be multiplied by the beta factor and the result multiplied by 3.5 percent. This alternative approach is discussed in the next section.

The Alternative Standardized Approach (ASA)

The operational risk capital charge and methodology for the alternative standardized approach (ASA)[7] is the same as for the standardized approach except for two business lines: retail banking and commercial banking. For these business lines, loans and advances, multiplied by a fixed factor *m*, replace *GI* as the EI. The betas for retail and commercial banking are unchanged from the standardized approach. For example, the capital charge for retail banking would take the form of:

$$K_{RB} = \beta_{RB} * m * LA_{RB} \tag{3.3}$$

where

K_{RB} = Total capital charge under ASA for retail banking
β_{EB} = A fixed percentage (Table 3.2), set by the Basel Committee, for retail banking business line
LA_{RB} = Total outstanding retail loans and advances averaged over the past three years
m = 0.035 = Exposure indicator

A supervisor can choose to allow a bank to use the ASA provided the bank is able to satisfy its supervisor that this alternative approach provides an improved basis by, for example, avoiding double counting of risks.[7] Once a bank has been allowed to use the ASA, it will not be allowed to revert to use of the standardized approach without the permission of its supervisor. The ASA is discussed in Reference 7.

Advanced Measurement Approach

The advanced measurement approach (AMA) will allow banks to develop their own methodologies in measuring operational risk and the capital they will have to set aside in accordance with certain guidelines proposed in Basel II. Such approaches are intended to be the most risk sensitive and to relate to the experience of each organization. These approaches form the subject of the next chapter.

Qualifying Criteria for Operational Risk Capital Calculation

An organization's ability to meet specific criteria would determine the framework adopted for its regulatory operational risk capital calculation. An initial set of guidelines for using the approaches is given below. More detailed guidelines are given in Section 560 of the "Consultative Document: The New Basel Capital Accord";[4] Section 41 of the "Operational Risk, Supporting Document to the New Basel Capital Accord";[11] and Annex 1 of the "Working Paper on the Regulatory Treatment of Operational Risk."[12] All these documents are available free of charge at http://www.bis.org/bcbs/publ.htm.

Basic Indicator Approach

The basic indicator approach is the easiest approach to adopt. The criteria to use it are:

- Applicable to any bank regardless of complexity and sophistication
- Need to comply with the guidance document "Sound Practices for Management and Supervision of Operational Risk"[9]

Standardized Approach

To qualify for the use of the standardized approach, a bank must convince its supervisor that, at a minimum, it can:

- Comply with the guidance document "Sound Practices for Management and Supervision of Operational Risk" [9]
- Demonstrate the existence of an independent risk control and audit function
- Demonstrate effective use of risk reporting systems
- Demonstrate clear responsibilities assigned to operational risk management functions
- Demonstrate that its board of directors and senior management are actively involved in the oversight of the operational risk management framework
- Have an operational risk management system that is conceptually robust and is implemented with integrity
- Have sufficient resources for using the approach in the major business lines as well as in the control and audit areas

Supervisors will have the right to insist on a period of initial monitoring of a bank's standardized approach before it is used for regulatory capital purposes.

Advanced Measurement Approach

More details on the qualifying criteria for using the AMA are given in the next chapter.

Factors in Selecting an Approach

Selection of a measurement approach requires careful consideration to balance cost with accuracy, transparency, and potential benefits in minimum regulatory capital. Assuming satisfaction with the relevant criteria, the approach that an organization selects to calculate operational risk capital charges should be a free choice of management, subject to the requirement that should be appropriate to the nature and complexities of the business. Some key considerations are:

- *Data availability.* Advanced models are data intensive. The loss distribution approach models discussed in the next chapter require an organizational commitment for thorough, ongoing data collection.
- *Commitment* to implement an operational risk framework. All advanced measurement approaches require a comprehensive risk management framework with assessments, indicators, data collection, and reporting.
- The framework and capital methodology require *technology*, primarily to support the data collection efforts, the risk analytics, and reporting. An appropriate budget needs to be planned.
- *Size of firm.* Larger firms tend to be able to justify the investment. Smaller firms may have fewer benefits for employing advanced approaches; however, it is more flexible to employ these types of approaches.
- *Degree of sophistication* in relation to economic capital. Firms committed to economic capital and its use as a management tool will be driven to accurate models and ones that are risk sensitive. They should consider the AMA.
- *Level of complexity.* Firms with complex products, services, and operations will have exposure to more extreme events (tail risks). Advanced models will provide more insight into the true risk profile for such firms.

Supervisory Review Process

The supervisory review process under Pillar 2 applies to all risks that a bank is facing, regardless of whether there is a minimum capital requirement. The supervisory review process of the framework is intended to ensure that financial organizations have adequate capital to support all the risks in their business. It also encourages these organizations to develop and use better risk management techniques in monitoring and managing their risks. The Basel Committee has identified four key concepts of the supervisory review, which are elaborated below. For further details of these concepts, refer to Reference 7.

- Concept 1: Banks should have a process for assessing their overall capital in relation to their risk profile and a strategy for maintaining their capital levels. The five main features of a rigorous process are as follows: board and senior management oversight, sound capital assessment, comprehensive assessment of risks, monitoring and reporting, and internal control review.
- Concept 2: Supervisors should review and evaluate banks' internal capital adequacy assessments and strategies, as well as their ability to monitor and ensure their compliance with regulatory capital ratios. Supervisors should take appropriate supervisory action if they are not satisfied with the results of this process.
- Concept 3: Supervisors should expect banks to operate above the minimum regulatory capital ratios and should have the ability to require banks to hold capital in excess of the minimum.
- Concept 4: Supervisors should seek to intervene at an early stage to prevent capital from falling below the minimum levels required to support the risk characteristics of a particular bank. They should require rapid remedial action if capital is not maintained or restored.

A further important concept of Pillar 2 is the assessment of compliance with the minimum standards and disclosure requirements of the more advanced methods in Pillar 1, in particular the AMAs for operational risk. Supervisors must ensure that these requirements are being met, both as qualifying criteria and on a continuing basis. The qualitative judgments by supervisors inherent in Pillar 1 increase the relative importance of the supervisory assessment of a bank's strategies, policies, practices, and procedures considered under Pillar 2. Pillar 2 is discussed explicitly in Reference 13. Many guidance documents related to the supervisory review process are published by the Basel Committee on Banking Supervision. The papers are available from the BIS[14] Web site.

The Supervisory Assessment

This independent assessment of operational risks by supervisors should incorporate a review of the following:

- The bank's particular capital framework for determining its Pillar 1 operational risk capital charge (i.e., basic indicator, standardized approach, or AMA). This is the process that associates capital to the levels of operational risk.
- The bank's process for assessing overall capital adequacy for operational risk in relation to its risk profile and its internal capital targets, including whether banks are appropriately addressing the relationship between different types of risks. This process should define capital adequacy goals with respect to risk, taking into account the bank's strategic focus and business plan.
- The effectiveness of the bank's risk management process and overall control environment with respect to operational risk. This involves the policies and procedures designed to ensure that the bank identifies, measures, and reports all measurable risks.
- The bank's methods for monitoring and reporting its operational risk profile, including data on operational losses and other indicators of potential operational risk.
- The bank's procedures for the timely and effective solution of operational risk events and vulnerabilities.
- The bank's process of internal controls, reviews, and audit to ensure the reliability of the overall operational risk management process.
- The effectiveness of the bank's operational risk mitigation efforts, such as the use of insurance.
- The quality and comprehensiveness of the bank's disaster recovery and business continuity plans.

Supervisors must also explore issues surrounding cross-border risk transfer.[15] If supervisors become concerned that a bank either is not meeting its requirements or is at significant risk of not meeting them in the future, the Basel Committee expects some kind of supervisory response. Deficiencies identified during the supervisory assessment may be addressed through a range of actions. Supervisors should use the tools most suited to the particular circumstances of the bank and its operating environment. Possible supervisory responses can include:

- Increased monitoring of the bank's overall operational risk management and assessment process
- Requiring enhancements to internal measurement techniques
- Requiring improvements in the operational risk control systems or personnel
- Requiring the bank to raise additional capital immediately
- Requiring changes in responsible senior management
- Requiring the bank to hold capital in excess of the Pillar 1 minimum

- Requiring the bank to prepare and implement a satisfactory capital restoration plan, which might involve plans to raise additional capital, restricting asset growth or reducing the level of assets, withdrawal from certain lines of business, and restricting the payment of dividends or executive bonuses

For a comprehensive listing of suggestions as to what actions supervisors should take into consideration, see References 16 and 18.

The supervision of banks is not an exact science, and therefore, cautionary elements within the supervisory review process are expected. Supervisors must take care to carry out their obligations in a transparent and accountable manner. Supervisors should make publicly available the criteria to be used in the review of banks' internal capital assessments. Banking supervision cannot function effectively and efficiently if sound corporate governance is not in place, and consequently, banking supervisors have a strong interest in ensuring that there is effective corporate governance at every banking organization. Supervisory experience emphasizes the necessity of having the appropriate levels of accountability and checks within each bank. Put plainly, sound corporate governance makes the work of supervisors infinitely easier.[17]

"Corporate governance" is the general term used to describe the manner in which the business and affairs of an organization are governed by their board of directors and senior management. This includes how a financial organization accomplishes the following:

- Sets (establishes and communicates) corporate objectives (including generating economic returns to owners)
- Oversees the day-to-day operations of the business
- Considers the interests of stakeholders (employees, customers, suppliers, and the community)
- Aligns corporate activities and behavior with the expectation that the organization will act in a safe and sound manner and in compliance with applicable laws and regulations
- Protects the interests of depositors, customers, and other interested parties; the corporate values; codes of conduct and other standards of appropriate behavior; and the system used to ensure compliance with them
- Derives a well-articulated corporate strategy against which the success of the overall organization and the contribution of individuals can be measured
- Defines clear assignment of responsibilities and decision-making authorities, incorporating a hierarchy of required approvals from individuals to the board of directors

- Establishes a mechanism for the interaction and cooperation among the board of directors, senior management, and the auditors
- Establishes strong internal control systems, including internal and external audit functions, risk management functions independent of business lines, and other checks and balances
- Monitors risk exposures where conflicts of interest are likely to be particularly great, including business relationships with borrowers associated with the bank, large shareholders, senior management, or key decision makers within the organization (e.g., traders)
- Forms financial and managerial incentives to offer to senior management, business-line management, and employees in the form of compensation, promotion, and other recognition
- Supervises appropriate information flows internally and to the public

Enhanced Disclosure — Market Discipline

The aim of Pillar 3, enhanced disclosure — market discipline, is to help financial organizations conduct business in a safe, sound, and efficient manner. Furthermore, it aims to complement the minimum capital requirements (Pillar 1) and the supervisory review process (Pillar 2). The Basel Committee seeks to encourage market discipline by a set of disclosure requirements that will allow market participants to assess key pieces of information on the scope of application, capital, risk exposures, risk assessment processes, and hence the capital adequacy of the organization. Frequent public disclosure of relevant information by banks can lead to enhanced market discipline and, therefore, more effective risk management. Market participants —creditors, shareholders, and analysts — can be key allies of the regulators by penalizing organizations that perform poorly or take excessive risks. For market discipline to be effective, however, market participants must be adequately informed about the operational risks these banks are taking, and hence the important role played by financial transparency in Basel II.

The Basel Committee recognizes the need for a Pillar 3 disclosure framework that does not conflict with requirements under accounting standards, which are broader in scope. The committee believes it is desirable that the disclosures should be made on a semiannual basis, as cited in Section 211 of the "New Basel Capital Accord: An Explanatory Note."[13] In recognition of the increased risk sensitivity of the framework and the general trend toward more frequent reporting in capital markets, large internationally active banks must disclose their total capital adequacy ratios on a quarterly basis. Qualitative disclosures that provide a general summary of a bank's risk management objectives and policies, reporting system, and definitions may be published on an annual basis. Furthermore, if information on risk exposure or other items is subject to rapid change, then banks should also disclose information on a quarterly basis. In all cases, banks should publish material information as soon as practicable as and not later than deadlines set by similar requirements in national laws. For further information on frequency of disclosure, refer to Section 818 of the "International Convergence of Capital Measurement and Capital Standards."[7]

The committee is aware that supervisors have different powers available to them to achieve the disclosure requirements. Market discipline can contribute to a safe and sound banking environment, and supervisors require organizations to operate in a safe and sound manner. On safety and soundness grounds, supervisors could require banks to disclose information. Alternatively, supervisors have the authority to require banks to provide information in regulatory reports. Some supervisors could make some or all of the information in these reports publicly available. Further, there are a number of existing mechanisms by which supervisors can enforce requirements. These vary from country to country, and include warnings or fines. The nature of the exact measures used will depend on the legal powers of the supervisor and the seriousness of the disclosure deficiency.

In brief, banks should have:

- A formal disclosure policy approved by the board of directors that addresses the bank's approach for determining what disclosures it will make and the internal controls over the disclosure process
- A process for assessing the appropriateness of their disclosures, including validation and their frequency

The enhanced disclosure, which leads to market discipline under Pillar 3, is discussed extensively in Section 199 of the "Consultative Document: Pillar 3 (Market Discipline) Supporting Document to the New Basel Capital Accord."[18]

In addition, the Basel Committee will further explore qualitative and quantitative disclosures of both the processes used by banks to manage and control their operational risks, and banks' methods of calculating minimum capital requirements.

Qualitative and Quantitative Disclosures

The Basel Committee has developed a set of specific qualitative and quantitative disclosures in four key areas:

- Scope of application
- Composition of capital
- Risk exposure assessment and management processes
- Capital adequacy

Some of the main qualitative and quantitative aspects that financial organizations need to disclose are listed in Table 3.3:

1. *Qualitative disclosures (core aspects).* This discloses approach(es) that the bank qualifies for (per business line). Banks can apply the standardized and advanced measurement approaches to different business lines at the same time. Therefore, they should disclose the approach used for each business line, and a bank using the basic indicator approach should also disclose this fact. This information is important because a level of risk management and internal control is attached to the use of each methodology. Furthermore, banks should provide information about its risk management framework for managing operational risk. Such information could include discussions on operational risk policies and measurement methodologies, organizational roles and responsibilities for managing operational risk, and operational risk mitigation techniques employed.
2. *Quantitative disclosures (core and supplementary).* Banks should publish information on their operational risk exposures. In many cases banks will not be measuring their exposure directly, and an alternative will be used. To further facilitate comparison, the operational risk capital charge as a percentage of minimum regulatory

Table 3.3 Operational Risk Qualitative and Quantitative Disclosures

	Core Aspects	*Supplementary Aspects*
1. Qualitative Disclosures	(1) Approach(es) the bank qualifies for (2) Operational risk management framework	
2. Quantitative Disclosures	(1) Operational risk exposure (by business line if available) (2) The operational risk capital charge as a percent of minimum regulatory capital	Actual annual operational losses (in total or by business line if available)

Source: Appendix 5 of the "Consultative Document: Pillar 3 (Market Discipline)."[18]

> capital should also be disclosed. One way would be to disclose the indictor used. An alternative way is to publish the total actual annual operational losses, but this would only apply to banks using the AMA (although some banks in the standardized approach may have such data). As more work is conducted on the AMA, then a more useful indicator may be available.[18] This is likely to include loss data. At this stage, the Basel Committee is concerned that a requirement to publish loss data might serve as a discouragement to develop more sophisticated approaches to operational risk. It is therefore recommending that loss data be a supplementary disclosure.

According to reliable signals given by the market under the disclosure requirements of Pillar 3, supervisors under Pillar 2 could intervene and decide on a course of action at any particular time if there is a sign that banks are falling below the threshold levels. More details about the core banking disclosures can be found in Appendix 5 of the "Consultative Document Pillar 3 (Market Discipline)"[18] and in "The New Capital Accord."[19]

The Ten Principles of Basel II

This framework for the Operational Risk Management Standard of the Basel II Accord is based on ten sound principles for the management and supervision of operational risk.[9] These ten principles are depicted in Figure 3.9.

The Ten Sound Principles for the Management and Supervision of Operational Risk (developed by the Bank of International Settlements)[9] are summarized below. For a more comprehensive explanation of the principles, refer to the "Sound Practices for the Management and Supervision of Operational Risk."[9] In brief, the ten principles are captured and grouped under four headings: Appropriate Risk Management Environment, Risk Management, Role of Supervisors, and Role of Disclosure, as highlighted in Figure 3.10.

Appropriate Risk Management Environment

1. Operational risk is a distinct category of risk, so there should be a board-level framework and operational risk strategy.
2. Operational risk is subject to a comprehensive audit and trail.
3. Senior management needs to implement the framework.

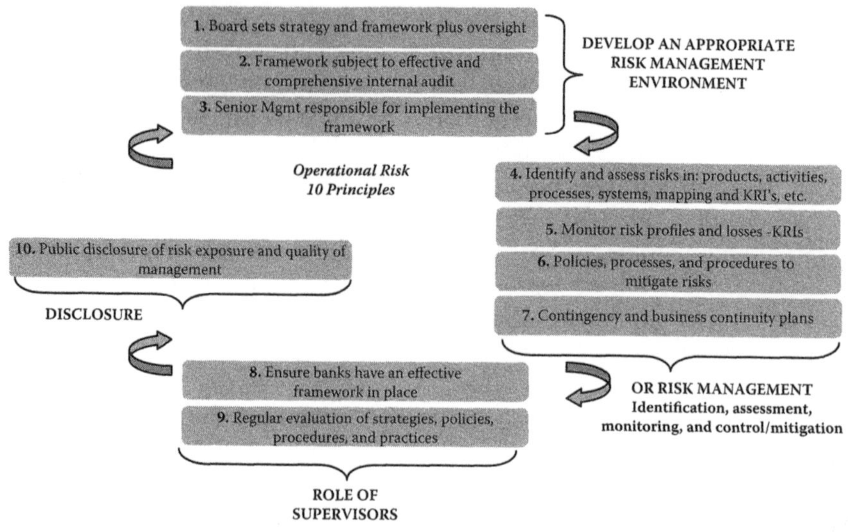

Figure 3.9 The ten principles of effective operational risk management.

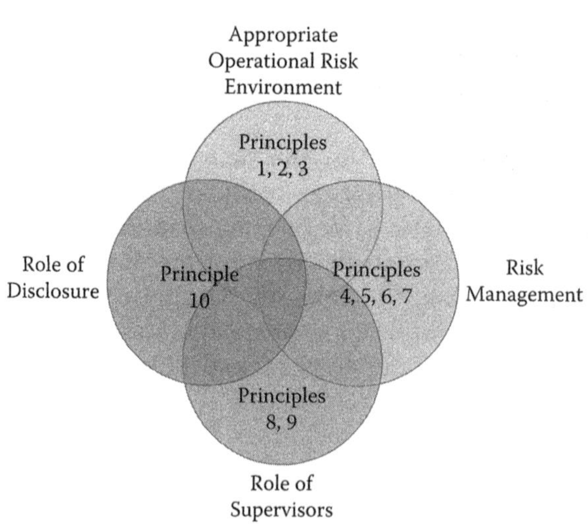

Figure 3.10 The ten principles grouped under four headings.

Risk Management

4. Identity and assess operational risk in new and existing products, activities, processes, and systems. Includes self-assessment, risk indicators, and risk mapping.
5. Define processes to monitor operational risk or losses.
6. Determine policies and procedures to control and mitigate risks; operational risk advancement toward stated objectives.
7. Design contingency and business continuity plans.

Role of Supervisors

8. Ensure effective operational risk framework.
9. Independent evaluation of policies and procedures on an ongoing basis.

Role of Disclosure

10. Sufficient disclosure to permit market participants to assess banks' operational risk.

Principles 1, 2, and 3 support Pillars 1 and 2 and are concerned about developing an appropriate risk management environment, including the roles of the board of directors and senior management.

Principle 1

The board of directors should be aware of the major aspects of the bank's operational risks as a distinct risk category that should be managed, and it should approve and periodically review the bank's operational risk management framework. The framework should provide a firmwide definition of operational risk and lay down the principles of how operational risk is to be identified, assessed, monitored, and controlled/mitigated. The board is responsible for overseeing the establishment of the operational risk framework, but may delegate the responsibility for implementing the framework to management with the authority necessary to allow for its effective implementation. Other key responsibilities of the board include:

- Ensuring appropriate management responsibility, accountability, and reporting
- Understanding the major aspects of the organization's operational risk as a distinct risk category that should be managed
- Reviewing periodic high-level reports on the organization's overall operational risk profile, which identify material risks and strategic implications for the organization
- Overseeing significant changes to the operational risk framework
- Ensuring compliance with regulatory disclosure requirements

What does this mean to financial organizations?

- The board is to approve the implementation of operational risk framework.
- The board is to give clear guidance on operational risk management framework to senior managers.
- Approve relevant policies developed by management.
- Have clear internal appropriate definition of operational risk.
- Define operational risk appetite, including extent of risk transfer.
- Develop policies to identify, assess, monitor, and control/mitigate operational risk.
- Ensure an appropriate management structure is in place.
- Have a framework to define key processes to manage operational risk.
- Ensure that the framework is regularly reviewed in line with best practices.

The responsibility for operational risk management ultimately rests with the board of directors and senior management, or its equivalent. Although the board may delegate the management of this process, it must ensure that its requirements are being executed. This responsibility requires directors to have a thorough understanding of the organization's full spectrum of products, processes, and associated risks.

What does this mean to financial organizations?

- There should be an individual director who is responsible for operational risk and is independent.
- The board may also establish a committee (or other appropriate mechanism) to authorize and manage the day-to-day decisions for implementing the organization's operational risk strategy and for ensuring that there are processes in place to manage and escalate operational risk issues from all sources within the organization.
- The board should review operational risk reports on a regular basis to ensure that its requirements for operational risk management are being met.

Principle 2

The board of directors should ensure that the bank's operational risk management framework is subject to effective and comprehensive internal audit by operationally independent, appropriately trained, and competent staff. The internal audit function should not be directly responsible for operational risk management. Key management responsibilities include ensuring that:

- Operational risk management activities are conducted by qualified staff with the necessary experience, technical capabilities, and access to adequate resources.
- Sufficient resources have been allocated to operational risk management, in the business lines, as well as the independent firmwide operational risk management function and verification areas, so as to sufficiently monitor and enforce compliance with the organization's operational risk policy and procedures.
- Operational risk issues are effectively communicated with staff responsible for managing credit, market, and other risks, as well as those responsible for purchasing insurance and managing third-party outsourcing arrangements.

What does this mean to financial organizations?

- There should be an independent audit function, separate from the operational risk management function.
- Audits must be conducted to periodically verify the effectiveness of operational risk management framework.
- The audit function should not have direct operational risk management responsibilities.

Principle 3

Senior management should have responsibility for implementing the operational risk management framework approved by the board of directors. The framework should be consistently implemented throughout the whole banking organization, and all levels of staff should understand their responsibilities with respect to operational risk management. Senior management should also have responsibilities for developing policies, processes, and procedures for managing operational risk in all of the bank's products, activities, processes, and systems. The board of directors and senior management must ensure that appropriate resources are allocated to support the operational risk management framework.

Effective board and management oversight forms the cornerstone of an effective operational risk management process. The board and management have several broad responsibilities with respect to operational risk:

- To establish a framework for assessing operational risk exposure and identify the organization's tolerance for operational risk
- To identify the senior managers who have the authority for managing operational risk
- To monitor the organization's performance and overall operational risk profile, ensuring that it is maintained at prudent levels and is supported by adequate capital
- To implement sound fundamental risk governance principles that facilitate the identification, measurement, monitoring, and control of operational risk
- To devote adequate human and technical resources to operational risk management
- To set up compensation policies that are consistent with the organization's appetite for risk and are sufficient to attract qualified operational risk management and staff

The organization must have an independent firmwide operational risk management function. The roles and responsibilities of the function will vary between organizations, but this must be clearly documented. The independent firmwide operational risk function should have organizational importance appropriate with the organization's operational risk profile, while remaining independent of the lines of business and the testing and verification function. At a minimum, the organization's independent firmwide operational risk management function should ensure the development of policies, processes, and procedures that explicitly manage operational risk as a distinct risk to the organization's safety and soundness. These policies, processes, and procedures should include principles for how operational risk is to be identified, measured, monitored, and controlled across the organization. Additionally, they should provide for the collection of the data needed to calculate the organization's operational risk exposure.

Additional responsibilities of the independent firmwide operational risk management function include:

- Assist in the implementation of the overall firmwide operational risk framework.
- Review the organization's progress toward stated operational risk objectives, goals, and risk tolerances.

- Periodically review the organization's operational risk framework to consider the loss experience, effects of external market changes, other environmental factors, and the potential for new or changing operational risks associated with new products, activities, or systems. This review process should include an assessment of industry best practices for the organization's activities, systems, and processes.
- Review and analyze operational risk data and reports.
- Ensure appropriate reporting to senior management and the board.

What does this mean to financial organizations?

- Management should translate the framework into verifiable policies and procedures.
- Senior management must assess appropriateness of management oversight.
- Operational risk/audit functions must be resourced with qualified technical staff.
- The operational risk policy is to be clearly communicated to all levels.
- Operational risk staff should communicate with credit risk and market risk staff.
- The compensation policy should be consistent with risk appetite.
- There must be well-documented procedures for high-volume processes.

Principles 4, 5, 6, and 7 support Pillar 1, and relate to the "Operational Risk Management Framework: Identification, Assessment, Monitoring, and Mitigation/Control."

Principle 4

Banks should identify and assess the operational risk inherent in all material products, activities, processes, and systems. Banks should also ensure that before new products, activities, processes, and systems are introduced or undertaken, the operational risks inherent in them are subject to adequate assessment procedures.

What does this mean to financial organizations?

- Risk identification should consider internal and external factors.
- In addition to assessing risks, banks need to assess vulnerability to risks.
- Self-assessment tools can be used in conjunction with workshops.

- The significance of inherent risks should be ranked before and after controls are exercised.
- Scorecards can be used to quantify risks and allocate capital.
- Risk maps can be used to map risk by types.
- Risk indicators should be defined and collected on a frequent basis.
- Loss events should be collected and stored by frequency and severity.
- Loss events should include external data as well as internal data.

Principle 5

Banks should implement a process to regularly monitor operational risk profiles and exposures to losses. There should be regular reporting of significant information to senior management and the board of directors that supports the proactive management of operational risk. These reports should allow senior management to:

- Evaluate the level and trend of operational risks and their effect on capital levels
- Evaluate the sensitivity and rationality of key assumptions used in the capital assessment measurement system
- Determine if the bank holds sufficient capital against the various risks and that it is in compliance with established capital adequacy goals
- Assess the bank's future capital requirements based on the reported risk profile
- Make necessary adjustments to the bank's strategic plan accordingly

What does this mean to financial organizations?

- Regular and prompt monitoring of events is required to prevent intensification of the operational risks.
- Early warning indicators of future losses (the "stress points" where weaknesses are known), such as high growth rates, should be identified and tracked. Thresholds should be set for early warning indicators or key risk indicators.
- Regular internal reporting should contain internal and external data as well as compliance data.
- Reports should fully reflect identified problem areas and prompt corrective and preventive actions.
- Boards must receive high-level information to assess operational risk profile.

Principle 6

Banks should have policies, processes, and procedures to control and mitigate operational risks. Banks should periodically review their risk limitation and control strategies and should adjust their operational risk profile accordingly using appropriate strategies, in light of their overall risk appetite and profile. Both the board of directors and senior management are responsible for establishing a strong internal control culture in which control activities are an integral part of the regular activities of a bank. Internal practices are in place as appropriate to control operational risk such as:

- Closely monitoring assigned risk limits or thresholds
- Maintaining safeguards for access to, and use of, bank assets and records
- Ensuring that staff have appropriate expertise and training
- Ensuring regular verification and settlement of transactions and accounts
- Managing risks associated with outsourcing activities

An organization's internal control structure must meet or exceed minimum regulatory standards established by the Basel Committee. Sound internal controls are essential to an organization's management of operational risk and are one of the foundations of safe and sound banking. When properly designed and consistently enforced, a sound system of internal controls will help management safeguard the organization's resources, produce reliable financial reports, and comply with laws and regulations. Sound internal controls will also reduce the possibility of significant human errors and irregularities in internal processes and systems, and will assist in their timely detection when they do occur.

A system that can mitigate operational risks would have:

- One illustration of each data item, such as a security definition
- No needless movement of data
- No reconciliation of data
- Data treated in a stable manner
- A stable user interface
- Data stored in one database, thereby condensing reporting for both clients and internal auditing processes
- One technology, thus avoiding the need for multiple operations

What does this mean to financial organizations?

- Make intelligent decisions on whether to mitigate and control risks or bear them.
- If risks cannot be controlled, accept risk or reduce or withdraw from the particular business activity.
- Review progress toward objectives.
- Implement compliance checking using management controls.
- Update policies, processes, and procedures to resolve noncompliance issues.
- Approvals must be documented to ensure management accountability.
- Policies must be reinforced via strong internal risk culture.
- Ensure appropriate segregation of duties with no conflicts of interest.
- Implement close monitoring, strong access controls, appropriate staff training/expertise.
- Ensure regular settlement of transactions and accounts.
- Place special emphasis on new activities, products, and markets, and geographically remote branches.
- Examine risk mitigation tools such as insurance.
- Create disaster recovery plans for critical processes.
- Examine potential deficiencies in third-party vendor or outsourced products and services.

Principle 7

Banks should have in place contingency and business continuity plans to ensure their ability to operate on an ongoing basis and limit losses in the event of severe business disruption.

What does this mean to financial organizations?

- Identify critical business processes.
- Identify alternative mechanism for service continuation.
- The business continuity plan should be tested regularly.

The contingency challenge has shifted from disaster recovery — cleaning up and getting back to work after a catastrophic event — to operational robustness — designing your organization to operate effectively right through a disruption. Business continuity planning is addressed further in Chapter 9.

Principles 8 and 9 support Pillar 2 and define the role of supervisors.

Principle 8

Banking supervisors should require that all banks, regardless of size, have an effective framework in place to identify, assess, monitor, and control/mitigate material operational risks as part of an overall approach to risk management.

What does this mean to financial supervisors?

- Ensure operational risk management frameworks are consistent with complexity of the individual bank.
- Encourage noncomplying banks to take appropriate action.

Principle 9

Supervisors should conduct, directly or indirectly, regular independent evaluation of a bank's policies, procedures, and practices related to operational risks. Supervisors should ensure that appropriate mechanisms are in place that allow them to remain informed of developments at banks.

What does this mean to financial supervisors?

- Determine the effectiveness of processes and control mechanisms.
- Evaluate the methods for monitoring and reporting operational risk profile.
- Evaluate the way of ensuring the integrity of operational risk processes.
- Determine the effectiveness of risk mitigation.
- Evaluate the quality of the business continuity and disaster recovery plans.
- Evaluate the process for assessing operational risk capital adequacy versus risk and capital targets.
- Determine if relevant internal bank reports are being circulated to the supervisors.

Principle 10 supports Pillar 3, which enforces the role of disclosure.

Principle 10

Banks should make sufficient public disclosure to allow market participants to assess their approach to operational risk management.

What does this mean to financial organizations?

- Disclosure policy should be agreed upon by the board.
- Timely and frequent public disclosure is required.

In developing an efficient and optimal risk management system as discussed in the second part of this book, all the aspects of the above ten principles are taken into consideration.

The Pillars' Action Points

Some action points are suggested for each of the three pillars of Basel II. They are as follows.

Pillar 1: Capital Requirement — Action Points

- Ensure the definition of operational risk enables sufficient collection of loss data.
- Apply business line as described by Basel II. Determine how loss data arising from shared services should be allocated back to business lines.
- Assess the impact of the three operational risk approaches and define which approach to select.
- Calculate the capital charge based on the basic indicator approach, the standardized approach, and the AMA.
- Develop action plans to implement the chosen approach.
- Perform gap analysis against Basel II requirement of the chosen approach.
- Develop a project plan to ensure compliance.
- Identify resources and budget required.
- Write a report to the board of directors for approval of the proposed approach.

The principles of supervisory review are primarily addressed to the supervisory community. However, banks will be on the receiving end of actions taken under Pillar II and so will need to understand what it means and the motives behind actions taken by their regulators.

Pillar 2: Supervisory Review — Action Points

- The board of directors and senior management need to ensure banks have a strategic plan that outlines economic capital needs.
- The board of directors and senior management need to ensure that proper risk measurement systems and strong internal controls are in place and communicated.
- Ensure document compliance with the operational risk standards (ten principles), documentation, and audit trail requirements.
- A process for assessing overall capital adequacy in relation to its risk profile must be implemented. Regular reports should be issued to the board of directors and senior management.
- A strategy should be implemented for maintaining capital levels that can be communicated to regulators.

Pillar 3: Market Discipline — Action Points

- Reassess or develop policy for public disclosure.
- Identify gaps between current disclosures (including frequency) and those required by Basel II.
- Determine data sources and system requirements to deal with new issues identified in gap analysis.
- Evaluate the impact of additional disclosures on the business and competitive positions.
- Identify other laws and regulations that will be taken into account when disclosing such information (such as accounting rules, stock exchange rules, etc.).
- Develop procedures for disclosure.

Summary

The risk management community is going through exponential growth fueled by new regulatory requirements and best practices for managing risks within financial organizations. In the past, companies have concentrated their risk management efforts on credit and market risk. However, the Basel Committee has made it clear that operational risk is now a core issue for financial organizations and has set a deadline to allocate capital aimed expressly at reducing exposure to operational risks. Fundamentally, the message is this: the greater the effort an organization adopts to understand, mitigate, and manage operational risk, the safer its business is considered to be, and the capital charge lowers accordingly.

Banks that have already started risk management programs view Basel II as a change agent. They use the new accord to focus bankwide attention on efforts to achieve risk management leadership. Basel II is also good news for banks whose risk management efforts began with the best of intentions, but have disappeared gradually through lack of attention. Chief executive officers should recognize that moving so many parts of a bank — most business units as well as the treasury and other corporate-center functions — to best practice involves a huge effort. If top management does not take the lead and ensure that benefits from a well-developed business case are captured, then the effort to put together an effective operational risk management program will fail.

Whatever financial organizations do, they must ensure that they fulfill regulatory requirements and observe all laws, financial or other. A bank's reputation is its most valuable asset and is an issue of confidence and trust for which aspects of safety and security play such a crucial role.

Financial organizations will need to put in considerable effort to ensure that their processes for gathering operational risk data are up to the standards required by Basel II. Financial organizations need to collect at minimum two years of data. Apart from the data-gathering processes, banks must also undertake a review of their disclosure policy, as Basel II recommends significantly greater public disclosure obligations for all banks, and banks will also need to assess how disclosure about their risks and their management will affect market and stakeholder perceptions. Time is running out, and banks should start thinking about operational risk management and Basel II compliance, and approach Basel II as a major project with several distinct phases (diagnostic, design, implementation, and testing), which may take several years.

The Basel Committee on Banking Supervision has proposed a New Basel Capital Accord (Basel II) that seeks to implement a more risk-sensitive, flexible, and sophisticated approach to financial risk management. This chapter introduced the concept of the accord with its key objectives and drivers, with particular reference to operational risk management, which is the newer concept in Basel II. The accord consists of three mutually reinforcing pillars, which together contribute to increasing the safety and soundness of the financial system. These three pillars were discussed, examining their underlying measurement approaches and what criteria must be passed to use the approaches. Factors in selecting a particular approach were emphasized. Boards of directors and senior management of financial organizations as well as auditors are responsible for the integrity of operational risk management systems and processes, and this is stressed in the ten principles that form the standard of operational risk management. This chapter suggested some immediate actions under each of the three pillars.

References

1. Sebton, E., The New Capital Accord, International Swaps and Derivatives Association, September 2002 http://www.isda.org/educat/ppt/Emmanuelle-Sebton-Capital-Accord.ppt#43 (accessed January 2005).
2. Basel Committee on Banking Supervision, Supervisory Lessons Learned from Internal Control Failures, Appendix II, Framework for Internal Control Systems in Banking Organizations, Basel, September 1998. This paper is available free from their Web site: http://www.bis.org/publ/bcbs40.htm.
3. Burhouse, S. and Feid, J., et al., Basel and the Evolution of Capital Regulation: Moving Forward, Looking Back, Federal Deposit Insurance Corporation, January 2003.
4. Basel Committee on Banking Supervision, The New Basel Capital Accord: An Explanatory Note, January 2001.
5. Kasprowicz, T., The Road to Basel II, IBM Corporation, December 2002.
6. Furlonger, D., North American Banks Are Too Passive on New Capital Accord, Gartner/G2, p. 1, September 2002.

7. Basel Committee on Banking Supervision, International Convergence of Capital Measurement and Capital Standards: A Revised Framework, June 2004. This paper is available free from their Web site: http://www.bis.org/bcbs/publ.htm.
8. Basel Committee on Banking Supervision, Consultative Document Operational Risk, Supporting Document to the New Basel Capital Accord, January 2001.
9. Basel Committee on Banking Supervision, Sound Practices for the Management and Supervision of Operational Risk, Feb. 2003. This paper is available free from their Web site: http://www.bis.org/publ/bcbs86.htm.
10. Basel Committee on Banking Supervision, Overview of the New Basel Capital Accord, Consultative Document, January 2001.
11. Basel Committee on Banking Supervision, Operational Risk, Supporting Document to the New Basel Capital Accord, January 2001.
12. Basel Committee on Banking Supervision, Working Paper on the Regulatory Treatment of Operational Risk, September 2001.
13. Basel Committee on Banking Supervision, New Basel Capital Accord: An Explanatory Note, January 2001.
14. http://www.bis.org/bcbs/publ.htm.
15. Basel Committee on Banking Supervision, The Joint Forum: Operational Risk Transfer Across Financial Sectors, August 2003.
16. Ulrich Doerig, H., Credit Suisse Group, Operational Risks in Financial Services: An Old Challenge in a New Environment, pp. 110–113, April 2003.
17. Basel Committee on Banking Supervision, Enhancing Corporate Governance for Banking Organizations, Basel, September 1999.
18. Basel Committee on Banking Supervision, Consultative Document, Pillar 3 (Market Discipline), Supporting Document to the New Basel Capital Accord, January 2001.
19. Basel Committee on Banking Supervision, The New Basel Capital Accord, April 2003.

Chapter 4

Advanced Measurement Approach

It is good to keep it simple, but not simpler.

—Albert Einstein

Introduction

The purpose of the Basel II Accord is to provide the foundation for a sound operational risk framework, while allowing organizations to identify the most appropriate means to meet the requirements. Each organization will need to consider its complexity, range of products and services, organizational structure, and risk management culture as it decides which approach to use to calculate its minimum capital requirements. To encourage banks to improve their operational risk management frameworks, the new Basel Accord has also set criteria for implementing more advanced approaches to operational risk. Such approaches are based on banks' internal calculations of the probabilities of operational risk events occurring and the average losses from those events. Of the three approaches available for calculating operational risk, the advanced measurement approach (AMA) is likely to have the most appeal because of its flexibility and the amount of self-discipline it provides. Using an AMA allows banks to develop their own methodologies in measuring operational risk and the capital they will set aside in accordance with certain guidelines proposed in Basel II. With an AMA, banks may use their own method for assessing their exposure to operational risk, as long as it is sufficiently comprehensive and systematic. Moving beyond the averaging of the other methods, the bank is allowed to collect the history of its losses, analyze that history, and use multiple risk factors to derive a probability of loss. The use of these approaches will reduce the operational risk capital requirement, as is currently done for market risk capital requirements and is proposed for credit risk capital requirements. These approaches, however, will be subjected to audit and regulatory oversight. The result should be that banks that invest to reduce their risks would ultimately get the financial return of lower capital requirements. More importantly, banks will achieve operational risk management that will warranty better business operational stability and performances. Under the AMA, if a bank invests in improved contingency procedures and systems, the investment will be reflected in a reduction in the need for operational risk capital, which is inevitably higher in the less advanced approaches. As a result, there is an incentive for organizations to use the more advanced and sophisticated approaches.

The Basel Committee does not prescribe exact capital required methodology under the advanced measurement approaches. Banks are encouraged to develop their own methods, provided the measure calculates capital that covers both expected loss and unexpected loss. Capital charges will not be required against unexpected operational losses in the AMA where banks show they have adequately budgeted for such losses. More rigorous quantitative and qualitative entry standards are required before a bank is permitted to qualify for the advanced measurement approaches. These are set out in Annex 1 of the "Working Paper on the Regulatory Treatment of Operational Risk"[1] and are also highlighted in this chapter.

This chapter introduces the AMA proposed by Basel II. It examines the quantitative standards of the AMA, including the three broad AMA approaches proposed by Basel II. It then discusses the qualifying criteria for operational risk capital calculation using the AMA. In addition, it introduces the supervisory standards for the AMA. Finally, it discusses the use of insurance under the AMA. Figure 4.1 shows the layout of Chapter 4.

Advanced Measurement Approach

Under the advanced measurement approach (AMA), a bank will have to show that its operational risk measurement system is closely integrated into the day-to-day risk management processes of the bank. Its output must be an integral part of the process of monitoring and controlling the

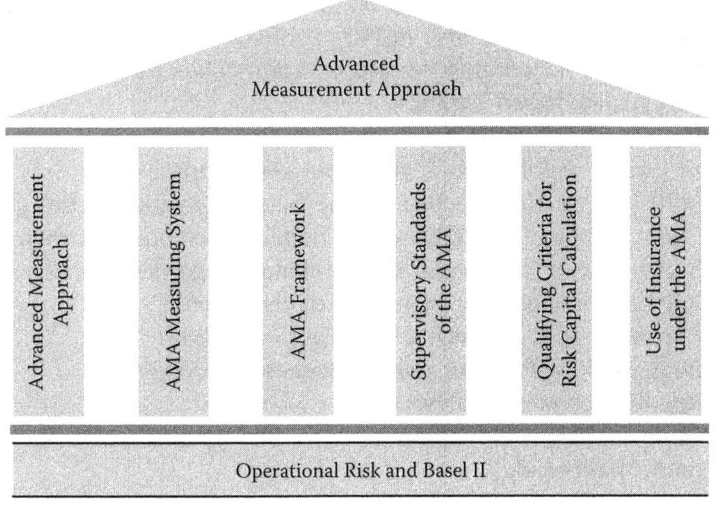

Figure 4.1 Layout of Chapter 4.

bank's operational risk profile. For a bank to qualify for AMA, validation of the operational risk management framework by external auditors or supervisory authorities is required to verify that internal validation processes are satisfactory and to ensure that data flows and processes associated with the risk measurement system are transparent and accessible. In particular, auditors and supervisors must have easy access to the system's specifications and parameters.

Incentives to comply with Basel II allow banks that can prove they have effective and sophisticated risk management systems to reduce their level of protective buffer capital, freeing up potentially millions of dollars for investment in profitable activities. The Basel Committee has stated that the level of capital required under the AMA will be lower than under the simpler approaches to encourage banks to make the improvements in risk management and measurement needed to move toward the AMA.[1] The development also suggests that, once a bank convinces regulators it has an effective and disciplined approach to operational risk management, it should attract less regulatory oversight.

The AMA promotes the following:

- The quantification of operational risks, which supports fundamental business needs
- The focus on measurement, control, and management of operational risk

- Supervisory approval based on qualitative and quantitative standards
- Consistently sound and rapidly evolving industry practices
- Sensitivity (in contrast to simple approaches for calculating operational risk-based capital)
- Improved operational risk management
- Innovation (ability to design your own approach)
- Reflection of the specifics of the bank's operational risk profile
- Encouragement and rewards for better operational risk management
- Active role of the board and senior management
- Regular management reporting of risk profile
- Bankwide and consistent loss data collection
- Integration with other risk management processes
- Regular scenario analysis
- Comprehensive documentation for the operational risk measurement framework
- Regular reviews of operational risk management framework by internal or external audit
- Robust and representative internal operational risk data
- Minimum historical observation period of three years
- Use of external risk data when deemed necessary
- Regular validation of complete operational risk measurement process
- Appropriate systems information infrastructure capable of identifying and gathering data and of supporting analytics
- Preventative, reactive, and detective management processes
- Identification of risk concentrations
- Loss avoidance and risk mitigation
- Operational risk assessment for key risk indicators
- Causal analysis
- Day-to-day efficient process management
- Operational risk monitoring, reporting, and profiling
- Business continuity planning
- Management follow-up and action

The Basel Committee believes that a standard definition of business lines, risk indicators, and loss events should apply in the stages of developing the AMA. A certain degree of standardization will promote the development of industrywide loss data and facilitate the supervisory validation process of banks' internal methodologies. The committee's provisional mapping of business lines, risk types, and exposure indicators, which reflects considerable discussion with the industry, is discussed in "International Convergence of Capital Measurement and Capital Standards: A Revised Framework."[2]

AMA Measuring System

A bank's AMA operational risk measurement system must take into account the following elements:

- Internal data
- External data
- Scenario analysis
- Internal control and business environment factors (organizations will be expected to at least meet the minimum standards relating to internal controls as a criterion for AMA qualification)

The measurement system should also consider the following elements:

- Risk mitigation (e.g., insurance)
- Correlations between types of risks

These elements can be combined in different ways to quantify the exposure to operational risk.

To make possible the adoption by large internationally active banks and banks with significant operational risk exposures of the more risk-sensitive AMA, the Basel Committee is prepared to allow for its partial adoption. Banks may use either the basic indicator approach or the standardized approaches to operational risk for some parts of its operations and an AMA for others, provided that all operational risks are captured within the banking organization on a global consolidated basis. A bank, however, will not be allowed to revert to the simpler approaches once it has been approved to use one of the more advanced operational risk approaches, unless advised to do so by its supervisor. Just as an organization should be able to choose its overall approach, it should be able to apply different approaches to different business units. This presents several advantages:

- It encourages improvements to be made as they become possible — progress is not dependent on the speed of the slowest portion of the organization.
- It allows organizations to focus their efforts.
- It allows tailored solutions for individual business units.

Quantitative Standards of the AMA

According to the quantitative standards of the Basel Committee for the AMA,[2] the risk categories should be broken down into the seven loss

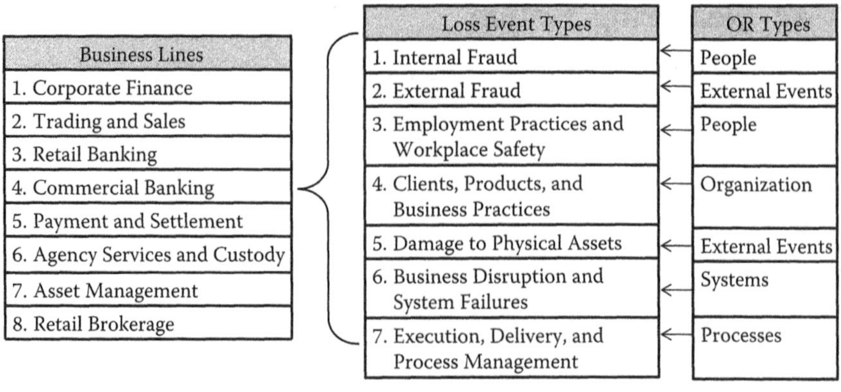

Figure 4.2 Mapping the operational risk types to the seven loss event types and to the eight business lines.

event types and into the business line(s) that most suit the activity of the organization (Figure 4.2). A mapping of these business lines is given in Annex 6 of the "International Convergence of Capital Measurement and Capital Standards."[2]

Operational risks should be broken down into a number of sub-risks using business lines and risk categories per loss event types defined by the bank. For each sub-risk, data should be collected and robust techniques should be developed. This allows the capital charge to be driven by the bank's own operational loss experiences, within a supervisory assessment framework. As is the case under the standardized approach, the total capital charge for operational risk is the sum of the capital requirements for each business line.

Although the AMA offers flexibility on the types of approaches used, it has been observed that there are three broad types of approaches currently under development:[5]

1. Internal measurement approaches (IMAs)
2. Loss distribution approaches (LDAs)
3. Scorecard approaches

It does not imply that this is the final form of these approaches, or that these will necessarily be approved under the AMA. Furthermore, there is explicit recognition by the committee that alternative approaches may emerge. In developing their methodologies, organizations may combine different elements of the three approaches.

Internal Measurement Approaches (IMAs)

In the first step, banks classify their business units along the same lines as the standardized approach; that is, separate into the eight business lines. Based on their own internal loss data, and based on similar methodologies to credit risk Internal Ratings Based (IRB) approaches, banks then measure and collect data inputs for a specified set of business lines and risk types:

- An operational risk exposure indicator (EI) within each business line — the amount of risk for different business lines
- A parameter representing the probability that a loss event (PE) occurs
- A parameter representing the losses given such events (LGE)

In this type of approach, banks generate estimates of operational risk capital based on measurements of expected operational risk losses. That is, the approach assumes a fixed and stable relationship between expected losses (the mean of the loss distribution) and unexpected losses (the tail of the loss distribution). The expected loss (EL) is given as the product of the EI, PE, and LGE.

$$\text{EI} * \text{PE} * \text{LGE} = \text{Expected Loss (EL) for each business line/loss type combination}$$

To calculate the capital charge, the bank will apply to the data it has collected a fixed percentage ("gamma factor") for each business line. Thus, the capital charge is obtained as the summation of expected loss multiplied by gamma across business lines. The overall capital charge for a particular bank is the simple sum of all the resulting products. This can be expressed as in Equation 4.1:

$$\begin{aligned}\text{Required capital} &= \sum_i \sum_j \left[\gamma_{(i,j)} * \text{EI}_{(i,j)} * \text{PE}_{(i,j)} * \text{LGE}_{(i,j)}\right] \\ &= \gamma_{(i,j)} * \text{EL}_{(i,j)}\end{aligned} \tag{4.1}$$

where i is the business line and j is the risk type.

To facilitate the process of supervisory validation, banks supply their supervisors with the individual components of the expected loss calculation, that is, EI, PE, and LGE, instead of just the product EL. Based on this information, supervisors calculate EL.

PE could be expressed either in "number" or "value" terms, as long as the definitions of EI, PE, and LGE are consistent with one another. For instance, PE could be expressed as "the number of loss events per the number of transactions" and LGE parameters can be defined as "the average loss amount per transaction amount." Although it is proposed that the definitions of PE and LGE are determined and fixed by the Basel Committee, these parameters are calculated and supplied by individual banks.

However, the risk profile of a bank's loss distribution may not always be the same as that of the industrywide loss distribution. One way to address this issue is to adjust the capital charge by a risk profile index (RPI), which reflects the differences between the bank's specific risk profile compared to the industry as a whole. The Basel Committee plans to examine the extent to which an individual bank's risk profile will deviate significantly from that of the types of portfolios used to arrive at the regulatory specified gamma term, and the cost-benefits of introducing an RPI to adjust for such differences. A more detailed explanation of RPI is given in Annex 5 of the "Consultative Document Operational Risk."[3]

Loss Distribution Approaches (LDAs)

Under the loss distribution approaches (LDAs), banks need to calculate two distributions: one for frequency and one for event severity:

- Frequency distributions are usually binomial, negative binomial, or Poisson.
- Event severity distributions are wider in choice: log normal, Pareto, Weibull, or inverse Gaussian.
- Estimate the mean and the 99.9 percentile from the resulting distribution (1 year value at risk); mean is the expected loss.
- Difference between 99.9 percentile value at risk and expected loss equals to unexpected loss, equals to capital charge.

For a description of each of these statistical distributions, see Reference 4.

Under LDAs, banks estimate, for each business line and risk type combination, the likely distribution of operational risk losses over some future horizon (for instance, one year). It models the distribution tails, as shown in Figure 4.3.

The capital charge resulting from these calculations is based on a high percentile of the loss distribution. The LDA follows an actuarial methodology (math, statistics, and financial theories) where distributions are constructed based on historical internal and external loss data. This method differs from internal measurement approaches in one important respect:

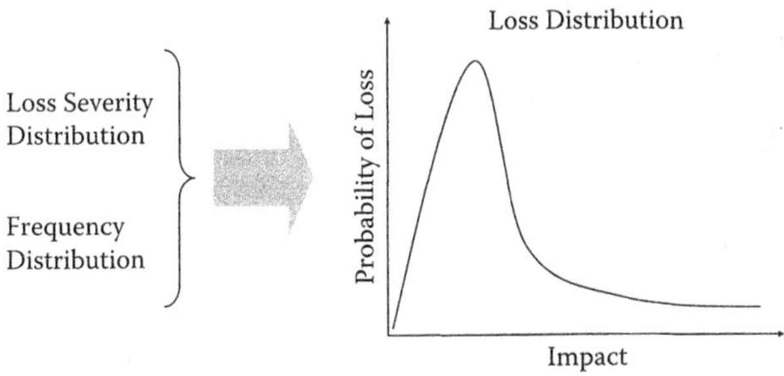

Figure 4.3 Loss distribution under the LDA.

it aims to assess unexpected losses directly rather than via an assumption about the relationship between expected loss and unexpected loss. Thus, there is no need for the determination of a multiplication (gamma) factor under this approach. More details about the LDA are given in Annex 6 of the "Consultative Document Operational Risk Supporting Document to the New Basel Capital Accord."[5] Also see Reference 6. Moreover, Chapter 7 discusses how the loss distribution is used during the decision making analysis.

Scorecard Approaches

In these approaches, banks determine an initial level of operational risk capital at the organization or business-line level, and then modify these amounts over time on the basis of risk indicators. The scorecard approach combines loss data with risk indicators and performs a self-assessment of the potential operational risks on the business lines, as shown in Figure 4.4.

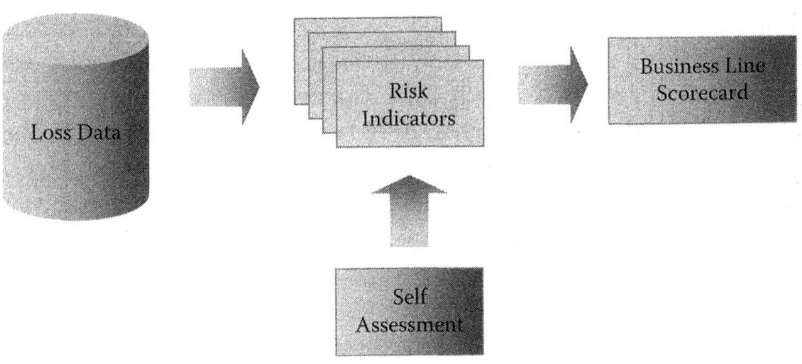

Figure 4.4 Scorecard approach.

The scorecard approach relies less exclusively on historical loss data in determining capital amounts. Nevertheless, historical loss data must be used to validate the results of scorecards. To qualify for the AMA, a scorecard approach must have a sound quantitative basis with rigorous analysis of internal and external data. Supplementing internal data with external loss data on extremely large rare events could significantly improve the bank's models of operational risk. Adoption of the Basel II standards will help to enhance the consistency of data collection both within and between banking organizations. Such consistency will make it possible for banks to compare their loss experiences across business lines, and for supervisors to compare loss experiences across banks. These scorecards are intended to bring a forward-looking component to the capital calculations, that is, to reflect improvements in the risk control environment that will reduce both the frequency and severity of future operational risk losses.

In fact, the LDA and scorecard approaches have complementary strengths and weaknesses. Many leading organizations are combining the two approaches to build methodologies with the bottom-up, objective benefits of LDA and the forward-looking responsiveness of scorecards.

Although the Basel Committee has acknowledged the need for flexibility in implementing the accord, it is also concerned that such flexibility may weaken the accord's fundamental objective of ensuring banks are sufficiently capitalized. Accordingly, the committee is pursuing a "hybrid" approach for AMA banks. This means that a banking group would be permitted, subject to supervisory approval, to use a combination of stand-alone AMA calculations for significant internationally active banking subsidiaries and an allocated portion of the groupwide AMA capital requirement for its other internationally active banking subsidiaries.[7] Under this hybrid approach, a significant internationally active banking subsidiary wishing to implement an AMA and able to meet the qualifying criteria would have to calculate its AMA capital requirements on a stand-alone basis. In calculating stand-alone AMA capital requirements, significant internationally active banking subsidiaries may incorporate a well-reasoned estimate of diversification benefits of its own operations, but may not consider groupwide diversification benefits. Where such subsidiaries are part of a group that wishes to implement an AMA on a groupwide basis, they would be permitted to utilize the resources of their parent or other appropriate entities within the group. This means that they could rely on data and parameters calculated at the group level, for example, provided that those variables were adjusted as necessary to be consistent with the subsidiary's operations. Other internationally active subsidiaries that are not determined to be significant in the context of the overall group would be permitted, subject to supervisory approval, to use as their Pillar 1 charge for operational risk, an amount that has been allocated to them from the groupwide AMA calculation.[7]

In this book, the concepts of the LDA and scorecard approaches are used to form underlying support for the more advanced approaches developed and presented in Parts III and IV.

AMA Framework

Organizations will be expected to develop an AMA framework that measures and quantifies operational risk for regulatory capital purposes. To do this, organizations will need a systematic process for collecting operational risk loss data, assessing the risks within the organization, and adopting an analytical framework that translates the data and risk assessments into an operational risk exposure. The analytical framework must be appropriate for the overall robustness of the quantification process. Because organizations will be permitted to calculate their minimum regulatory capital on the basis of internal processes, the requirements for data capture, risk assessment, and the analytical framework should be detailed and specific. Banks may develop a range of approaches, which, if consistent with the common criteria, may be approved by supervisors.

Organizations will be required to meet, and remain in compliance with, all the supervisory standards to use an AMA framework. However, evaluating an organization's qualification with each of the individual supervisory standards will not be sufficient to determine an organization's overall readiness for AMA. Instead, supervisors and organizations must also evaluate how well the various components of an organization's AMA framework complement and reinforce one another to achieve the overall objectives of an accurate measure and effective management of operational risk.

Important definitions that organizations must incorporate into an AMA framework[8] include:

- *Operational risk:* the risk of loss resulting from inadequate or failed internal processes, people, and systems, or from external events. The definition includes legal risk, which is the risk of loss resulting from failure to comply with laws as well as prudent ethical standards and contractual obligations. It also includes the exposure to lawsuit from all aspects of an organization's activities. The definition does not include strategic or reputational risks. The organization must include the regulatory definition of operational risk as the baseline for capturing the elements of the AMA framework and determining its operational risk exposure. An organization's definition of operational risk may encompass other risk elements as long as the supervisory definition is met.

- *Operational risk loss:* the financial impact associated with an operational event that is recorded in the organization's financial statements consistent with generally accepted accounting principles (GAAP). Financial impact includes all out-of-pocket expenses associated with an operational event, but does not include opportunity costs, or costs related to investment programs implemented to prevent subsequent operational risk losses. Operational risk losses are characterized by seven event types as discussed in Table 1.1, Chapter 1.
- *Operational risk exposure:* an estimate of the potential operational losses that the banking organization faces at a soundness standard consistent with a 99.9 percent confidence level over a one-year period. The organization will multiply the exposure by 12.5 percent to obtain risk-weighted assets for operational risk. This is added to the risk-weighted assets for credit and market risk to arrive at the denominator of the regulatory capital ratio.
- *Business environment and internal control factor assessments:* the range of tools that provides a meaningful assessment of the level and trends in operational risk across the organization. Although the organization may use multiple tools in an AMA framework, they must all have the same objective of identifying key risks. A number of existing tools, such as audit scores and performance indicators, may be acceptable under this definition.

The above definition of operational risk gives a sense of the breadth of exposure to operational risk that exists in banking today as well the many interdependencies among risk factors that may result in an operational risk loss. A critical point of any AMA framework is the treatment of correlations between operations, operational risk, and operational risk events. Thinking of operational risk categories as "operational risk processes," it is clear that there are functionally defined sequential dependencies between individual processes, which together enable a big organization to work.

In actual fact, operational risk can occur in any activity, function, or unit of the organization. The management structure underlying an AMA operational risk framework may vary between organizations. However, within all AMA organizations, three key functional roles must be present:

1. The organizationwide operational risk management function
2. Lines of business management
3. The testing and verification function, as discussed in Chapter 2

These three elements are functionally independent organizational components, but should work in cooperation to ensure a robust and efficient operational risk management framework.

To qualify for the AMA, the bank must track its internal loss experiences in a manner consistent with the regulatory framework set out in Annex 2 of the "Working Paper on the Regulatory Treatment of Operational Risk."[1] As part of this process, banks must track operational risk losses related to its market and credit activities (e.g., fraud in credit cards). There must be regular reporting of operational risk exposures and loss experiences to business unit management, senior management, and to the board of directors.

Elements of an AMA Framework

The organization must have clear standards for the collection and modifications of the elements of the operational risk AMA framework. It must demonstrate that it has appropriate elements to support its operational risk management and measurement framework. These elements resemble those of the measuring system described in preceding sections of this chapter.

Internal Operational Risk Loss Event Data

For the basic and standardized approaches, there is no need to collect loss data events; whereas for the AMA, collecting loss data is at the heart of the approach. The organization must have at least five years of internal operational risk loss data captured across all material business lines, events, product types, and geographic locations.

Organizations will not be required to produce reports or perform analysis for internal purposes on the basis of the loss event type categories, but will be expected to use the information about the loss event type categories as a check on the comprehensiveness of the organization's data set. A common theme in the AMA is that the approaches are rooted in loss data collection and verification in a form that is consistent with the frameworks set out in Annex 2 of the "Working Paper on the Regulatory Treatment of Operational Risk."[2]

The key to internal data integrity is the consistency and completeness with which loss event data capture processes are implemented across the organization. Management must ensure that operational risk loss event information captured is consistent across the business lines and incorporates any corporate functions that may also experience operational risk events. The organization must have a policy that identifies when an operational risk loss becomes a loss event and must be added to the loss event database. The policy must provide for consistent treatment across the organization. In addition, the organization must establish appropriate operational risk data thresholds. Policies and procedures should be addressed to the appropriate staff to ensure that there is satisfactory understanding of operational risk and the data capture requirements under the AMA operational risk management framework.

Furthermore, the independent operational risk management function must ensure that the loss data is captured across all operational business lines, product types, and event types, and from all significant geographic locations. The organization must be able to capture and aggregate internal losses across multiple business lines or event types. If data is not captured across all business lines or from all geographic locations, the organization must document and explain the exceptions.

Aside from information on the gross loss amount, the organization should collect information about the date of the event, any recoveries, and descriptive information about the drivers or causes of the loss event. The level of details of any descriptive information should be proportional to the size of the gross loss amount. Some examples of the type of information collected may include:

- Loss amount
- Description of loss event
- Where the loss is reported
- Loss event type category
- Date of the loss
- Discovery date of the loss
- Event end date
- Management actions
- Insurance recoveries
- Other recoveries
- Adjustments to the loss estimate

A number of additional data elements may be captured. It may be appropriate, for example, to capture data on "near-miss" events, where no financial loss was incurred. These near misses will not feature into the regulatory capital calculation, but may be useful for the operational risk management process.

The organization must have a clear policy that allows for the consistent treatment of loss event classifications (e.g., credit, market, or operational risk) across the organization. Losses that have any characteristics of credit risk, including fraud-related credit losses, must be treated as credit risk for regulatory capital purposes. Organizations will also be permitted and encouraged to capture loss events in their operational risk databases that are treated as credit risk for regulatory capital purposes, but have an underlying element of operational risk failure. These types of events, although not incorporated into the regulatory capital calculation, may have implications for operational risk management. It will be essential for organizations that capture loss events, which are treated differently for regulatory capital and management purposes, to demonstrate that:

1. Loss events are being captured consistently across the organization.
2. The data systems are sufficiently advanced to allow for this differential treatment of loss events.
3. Credit, market, and operational risk losses are being allocated in the correct manner for regulatory capital purposes.

For a more detailed view of how to deal with loss event data, see Reference 9.

The organization must hold five years of internal loss data, although a shorter range (three years) of historical data may be allowed, subject to supervisory approval. The extent to which an organization collects operational risk loss event data will, in part, depend on the data thresholds that the organization establishes. An organization may use a number of standards to establish the thresholds. They may be based on product and service types, business lines, geographic location, or other appropriate factors. The organization must capture comprehensive data on all loss events above its established threshold level. The supervisors will allow flexibility in this area, provided the organization can demonstrate that the thresholds are reasonable, do not exclude important loss events, and capture a significant proportion of the organization's operational risk losses.

Relevant External Operational Risk Loss Event Data

Where internal loss data is limited, external data may be useful in determining the organization's level of operational risk exposure as long as the data is relevant (i.e., from similar organizations, with similar types of operational risks faced, etc.). Even where external loss data is not an explicit input to an organization's data set, such data provides a means for the organization to understand industry experience and, in turn, provides a means for assessing the adequacy of its internal data. The organization should have policies and procedures that provide for the use of external loss data in the operational risk framework. Management should systematically review external data to ensure an understanding of industry experiences. External data may serve a number of different purposes in the operational risk framework.

To incorporate external loss information into an organization's framework, the organization should collect the following information:

- External loss amount
- External loss description
- Loss event type category
- External loss event date
- Adjustments to the loss amount (i.e., recoveries, insurance settlements, etc.) to the extent that they are known
- Sufficient information about the reporting organization to facilitate comparison to its own organization

Organizations may obtain external loss data in any reasonable manner. There are many ways to do so; some organizations are using data acquired through membership with industry consortia, and others are using data obtained from vendor databases or public sources such as court records or media reports. An established and complete database can potentially be used for modeling purposes and be applied to external loss events. Several initiatives have been formed for this, such as the Global Operational Loss Database managed by the British Bankers Association (BBA)[10] and the Operational Risk Data Exchange Association (ORX).[11] OpVantage[12] is a vendor that gathers information on operational losses. It collects data from public sources such as news reports and court filings. As well as classifying losses by Basel business line and causal type, the databases include descriptive information concerning each loss. In all cases, management will need to carefully evaluate the data source to ensure that they are comfortable that the information being reported is relevant and reasonably accurate.

Organizations using the AMA for regulatory capital purposes must use advanced data management practices to produce credible and reliable operational risk estimates. In general, organizations using the AMA should have the same data maintenance standards for operational risk as those set forth for the IRB organizations under the credit risk guidance. External data may also prove useful to undertake scenario analysis, fit severity distributions, or benchmark the overall operational risk exposure results.

Scenario Analysis

Although quantitative analysis of operational risk is an important input to bank risk management systems, these risks cannot be reduced to pure statistical analysis. Hence, qualitative assessments, such as scenario analysis, could be an integral part of measuring a bank's operational risks. Algorithmic analysis that combines all measurements should be used in such situations. Elements of scenario analysis are discussed further in Chapters 7 and 9.

Scenario analysis is a systematic process of obtaining expert opinions from business managers and risk management experts to derive reasoned assessments of the likelihood and impact of credible operational losses consistent with the regulatory soundness standard. Within an organization's operational risk framework, scenario analysis may be used as an input or may form the basis of an operational risk analytical framework.

As an input to the organization's framework, scenario analysis is especially relevant for business lines or loss event types where internal data, external data, and assessments of the business environment and internal control factors do not provide a sufficiently robust estimate of the organization's exposure to operational risk. In some cases, an organization's internal loss history may be sufficient to provide a reasonable estimate of exposure to future operational losses. In other cases, the use of well-reasoned, scaled external data may itself be a form of scenario analysis. Because financial organizations are moving at such an acute technological pace, operational risks and losses that were relevant in the past may not be relevant in the present nor in the future. Therefore, basing the analysis only on past data may give a false indication of the real present and future operational risks.

The organization must have policies and procedures that define scenario analysis and identify its role in the operational risk framework. The policy should cover key elements of scenario analysis, such as the manner in which the scenarios are generated, the frequency with which they are updated, and the scope and coverage of operational loss events they are intended to reflect. Scenario analyses are especially useful to evaluate high severity events.

Supervisory Standards of the AMA

Organizations will be required to meet, and remain in compliance with, all the supervisory standards to use an AMA framework. However, evaluating an organization's qualification with each of the individual supervisory standards will not be sufficient to determine an organization's overall readiness for AMA. Instead, supervisors and organizations must also evaluate how well the various components of an organization's AMA framework complement and reinforce one another to achieve the overall objectives of an accurate measure and effective management of operational risk. In performing their evaluation, supervisors will exercise considerable supervisory judgment, both in evaluating the individual components and the overall operational risk framework.

Figure 4.5 depicts a general view of the supervisory standards for the AMA. For the complete supervisory standards of the AMA, refer to "Supervisory Guidance on Operational Risk Advanced Measurement Approaches for Regulatory Capital."[8]

Qualifying Criteria for Risk Capital Calculation

An organization's ability to meet specific criteria would determine the framework adopted for its regulatory operational risk capital calculation. An initial set of guidelines for using the AMA is described below. A more detailed guideline is given in the "Consultative Document: The New Basel Capital Accord, Section 560;"[13] the "Consultative Document: Operational Risk, Supporting Document to the New Basel Capital Accord, Section 41;"[5] Annex 1 of the "Working Paper on the Regulatory Treatment of Operational Risk;"[1] and the "International Convergence of Capital Measurement and Capital Standards."[2] A bank's AMA will be subject to a period of initial monitoring by its supervisor before it can be used for regulatory purposes. This period will allow the supervisor to determine whether the approach is credible and appropriate.

Four broad areas will be monitored and assessed:

1. Operational risk corporate governance
2. Operational risk loss data
3. Risk quantification
4. Risk mitigation

For the operational risk corporate governance, the evaluation will include such areas as:

- Board and senior management oversight
- Independent enterprisewide operational risk framework and function
- Policies and procedures for all aspects of the operational risk framework
- Independent testing and verification (e.g., audit)
- Lines of business responsible for day-to-day operational risk management
- Reporting of operational risk exposures, losses, risk indicators, etc. to board and senior management
- Sound internal operational risk control environment

S1. ORM: independent firmwide ORM function, line of business management oversight and independent testing and verification functions

S2. Board oversees development of firmwide ORM function. Management roles and accountability identified

S3. Board and management ensure adequate allocation of resources for ORM

S4. Organization ensure independent ORM function

S5. Ensure appropriate reporting of operational risk exposures and loss data

S6. Business line management responsible for the day-to-day management of OR in business units

S7. Business line management must ensure internal controls and practices in line of business are consistent with firmwide policies

S8. Organization needs policies and procedures that clearly describe the major elements of the ORM framework

S9. ORM reports must address both firmwide and line of business results

S10. ORM reports must be provided periodically to senior management and the board of directors

S11. Organization's internal control structure must meet or exceed minimum regulatory standards

S12. Capture relevantinternal/external loss event data, assessments of business environment, internal control factors and scenario analysis results

S13. Include regulatory definition of operational risk as the baseline for capturing elements of the AMA

S14. Clear standards for the collection and modification of the elements of the OR AMA framework

S15. Have at least five years of internal operational risk loss data captured

S16. Map internal OR losses to the loss-event type categories

S17. Must have policy that identifies when an operational risk loss becomes a loss event and must be added to the loss event database

S18. Must establish appropriate operational risk data thresholds

S19. Clear policy that allows for the consistent treatment of loss event classifications (e.g., credit, market, or operational risk)

S20. Have policies and procedures that provide for the use of external loss data in the ORM framework

S21. Management must systematically review external data to ensure an understanding of industry experience

S22. Have a system to identify and assess business environment and internal control factors

S23. Compareresults of business environment and internal control factor assessments versus actual OR loss experience

S24. Have policies and procedures that identify how scenario analysis will be incorporated into the OR framework

S25. OR analytical framework to estimate organization's OR exposure, aggregate operational loss over 1 year, with 99.9 percent confidence level

S26. Must document the reason for all assumptions underlying its chosen analytical OR framework

S27. Combine internal/external operational loss event data, business environment, internal control factor and scenario analysis

S28. Organization'scapital requirement for OR is the sum of expected and unexpected losses

S29. Management must document how its chosen analytical framework accounts for dependence (e.g., correlations) among operational losses

S30. Organizationsmay reduce their OR exposure results by no more than 20% to reflect the impact of risk mitigants

S31. If using AMA for regulatory capital purposes, use advanced data management practices to produce credible and reliable OR estimates

S32. Organizationsmust test and verify the accuracy and appropriateness of the ORM framework

S33. Testing and verification must be done independently of the firmwide ORM function

Figure 4.5 Supervisory standards for the AMA.

For the operational risk loss data, the evaluation may include such areas as:

- Collection of internal operational loss data
- Reference to relevant external loss data to understand industry experiences with respect to large losses
- Mapping to the seven event types
- Identifying drivers of operational risk and how changes in the risk management or control environments affect operational risk profile

For the operational risk quantification, the evaluation may include such areas as:

- Data elements that were combined to quantify operational risk exposures at a designated confidence level
- Assessment of the likelihood and severity of "tail events"
- Whether scenario analysis was incorporated into quantification
- Whether correlations had sound foundation

For the operational risk mitigation, the evaluation may take into account the risk-mitigating effect of insurance. Insurance under the AMA is discussed more thoroughly later in this chapter.

A bank must meet certain qualitative and quantitative standards before it is permitted to use an AMA for operational risk capital. In the AMA, business lines, risk types, and exposure indicators are standardized by supervisors, and individual banks are able to use internal and external loss data. In addition to the standards required for banks using the basic indicator approach (comply with guidance "Sound Practices for Management and Supervision of Operational Risk"[14]), the criteria for the standardized approach as described in Chapter 3, banks should also meet the qualitative and quantitative qualifying criteria listed in Table 4.1 and Table 4.2, respectively, to use the AMA. A more comprehensive explanation of these criteria can be found in "International Convergence of Capital Measurement and Capital Standards: A Revised Framework."[2]

In general, banks must have the ability to fully integrate an internal measurement methodology into the day-to-day activities and major business decisions. It must also recognize in a forward-looking manner possible improvements or deteriorations in the organization's operational risk exposure or control environment.

The contents of these tables have been adopted from "International Convergence of Capital Measurement and Capital Standards: A Revised Framework,"[2] which is available[15] free of charge, and are used with permission.

Table 4.1 Qualitative Qualifying Criteria for the AMA

The bank must have an independent operational risk management function that is responsible for the design and implementation of the bank's operational risk management framework.
The bank's internal operational risk measurement system must be closely integrated into the day-to-day risk management processes of the bank.
There must be regular reporting of operational risk exposures and loss experiences to business unit management, senior management, and the board of directors.
The bank's operational risk management system must be well documented.
Internal or external auditors must perform regular reviews of the operational risk management processes and measurement systems.
The bank must verify that the internal validation processes are operating in a satisfactory manner and ensure that data flows and processes associated with the risk measurement system are transparent and accessible.

Supervisory authorities, whether national or home country, will have the right to insist on a period of initial monitoring of a bank's AMA before it is used for supervisory capital purposes. In addition, supervisors view the introduction of the AMA as an important tool to further promote improvements in operational risk controls and management at large banking organizations. Supervisors and organizations must also evaluate how well the various components of an organization's AMA framework complement and reinforce one another to achieve the overall objectives of an accurate measure and effective management of operational risk. In performing their evaluation, supervisors will exercise considerable supervisory judgment, both in evaluating the individual parts and the overall operational risk management framework.

Use of Insurance under the AMA

Although there is a variety of possible ways for transferring operational risk, much of this section will focus specifically on insurance coverage. Insurance contracts can be purchased to transfer some of the organization's operational risk to an insurance company. Insurance is not the only form of operational risk transfer; but because it is so widely used and accepted as a form of mitigating operational risk in Basel II, it deserves some extra attention. The Risk Management Group (RMG) of the Basel Committee also recognizes that arguments have been put forward for the explicit

Table 4.2 Quantitative Qualifying Criteria for the AMA

Bank must be able to demonstrate that its approach captures potentially severe "tail" loss events. It must have accuracy of loss data, plus confidence (99.9 percent) in the results of the calculations using that data. Banks must review and understand the assumptions used in the collection and assignment of loss events.
Banks must have and maintain rigorous procedures for operational risk model development and independent model validation. Banks must regularly conduct validation of their loss rates, risk indicators, and size estimations to ensure the proper inputs to the regulatory capital charge.
The AMA must be consistent with the scope of operational risk defined by the Basel Committee and the loss event types defined.
Supervisors will require banks to calculate their regulatory capital requirement as the sum of expected loss (EL) and unexpected loss (UL), unless the bank can demonstrate that it is adequately capturing EL in its internal business practices.
The bank's operational risk measurement system must be sufficiently detailed to capture the major drivers of operational risk affecting the shape of the tail of the loss estimates. They must have the ability to capture infrequent but severe events.
A bank may be permitted to use internally determined correlations in operational risk losses across individual operational risk estimates, provided it can demonstrate that its systems for determining correlations are sound, implemented with integrity. The bank must validate its correlation assumptions using appropriate quantitative and qualitative techniques.
Any operational risk measurement system must have certain key features to meet the supervisory soundness standard. These features must include the use of: ■ Internal data ■ Relevant external data ■ Scenario analysis ■ Factors reflecting the business environment and internal control systems
The bank needs to have a credible, transparent, well-documented, and verifiable approach for giving weights to these fundamental features described above in its overall operational risk measurement system. In all cases, the bank's approach for weighing the four fundamental features should be internally consistent and avoid double-counting of qualitative assessments or operational risk mitigants already recognized in other elements of the framework.

Table 4.2 (continued) Quantitative Qualifying Criteria for the AMA

Banks must track internal loss data and must develop specific criteria for assigning loss data to a particular business-line and risk types. They must have systems capable of collecting data from all appropriate subsystems and geographic locations. They must develop sound internal loss reporting practices, supported by an infrastructure of loss database systems extending back for a number of years (3–5 years). They must have the ability to use the collected data and the resulting measures for risk reporting, management reporting, internal capital allocation purposes, operational risk analysis, etc.
Banks must have the ability to identify which historical loss experiences are appropriate.
The bank's operational risk measurement system must use relevant external data (either public data or pooled industry data), especially when there is reason to believe that the bank is exposed to infrequent, yet potentially severe, losses.
Banks must use scenario analysis of expert opinion in conjunction with external data to evaluate its exposure to high-severity events.
Banks must develop rigorous conditions under which internal loss data would be supplemented with external data, as well as a process for ensuring the relevance of this data for their business environment. They must have the ability to explicitly identify and track relevant missing data, and have documented an approval process to ensure objectivity of results.
In addition to using loss data, whether actual or scenariobased, a bank's organizationwide risk assessment methodology must capture key business environment and internal control factors that can change its operational risk profile.
Banks must have an operational risk measurement methodology, knowledgeable staff, and appropriate systems and infrastructure capable of identifying and gathering comprehensive operational risk loss data necessary to create a loss database.
Banks must identify clearly those exceptional situations in which judgment overrides may be used, to what extent they are used, and who is authorized to make such decisions.

recognition of robust and comprehensive insurance of operational risk, and it is currently of the view that if such recognition of insurance is permitted, it should be limited to those banks that use AMAs. Under the AMA, a bank will be allowed to recognize the risk-mitigating impact of insurance in the measures of operational risk used for regulatory minimum capital requirements. The recognition of insurance mitigation will be limited to 20 percent of the total operational risk capital charge calculated under the AMA.[2]

This reflects the quality of risk identification, measurement, monitoring, and control inherent in the AMA and the difficulties in establishing a rigorous mechanism for recognizing insurance where banks use a simpler regulatory capital calculation approach. The RMG does not at this stage intend to specify the exact technique by which insurance is captured under the AMA; to do so would contradict the flexibility inherent in the AMA concept. However, a number of issues do deserve consideration, including:[1]

- If an explicit, rigid action is developed, what standards should be in place for qualifying insurance companies and insurance products, and what is an appropriate formula for recognition of insurance that is risk sensitive but not excessively complex?
- How is it possible to differentiate between commonly used insurance products, with which both banks and supervisors have extensive experience, and innovative, new products that may be developed to provide coverage for emerging operational risks?

The RMG feels that whatever ways banks in the AMA capture insurance, there should be a limit to the overall impact of insurance risk mitigation on the final capital amount. The limit is set to recognize that in some cases, insurance may provide less-than-perfect coverage of operational risks, due to such factors as delays in payment or legal challenges of contractual terms. In addition, the limit helps ensure that the remaining capital charge provides an adequate protection for operational risks. For these reasons, the RMG proposes that the capital reduction stemming from the impact of insurance be included within the floor of 75 percent of the standardized capital charge.[1]

Recognition of any insurance contract would be subject to a set of qualifying criteria intended to ensure that the policy will provide coverage of operational risk losses with a high degree of certainty. Although the RMG has yet to develop specific criteria, these would likely cover issues such as:

- Ability or willingness of insurer to pay; the timeliness of payment following loss events
- The certainty of coverage (that is, contingencies in the terms of the contract that might open the possibility that certain losses would not be covered); third-party risk transfer
- Maps to actual operational risk loss events
- Issues surrounding length of contract and policy renewal, minimum cancellation, and nonrenewal periods

Qualifying criteria might also establish standards concerning the insurance companies issuing the policies, such as minimum acceptable credit or claims payment ratings, use of and policies surrounding reinsurance, or regulatory oversight. The RMG plans to consult with the banking and insurance industries as work on developing these qualifying criteria progresses. Work remains to be done to refine a potential treatment for insurance under the operational risk capital charges. The RMG plans to study the various alternatives and to consult further with banking and insurance industry representatives.[1]

For an organization that wishes to adjust its regulatory capital requirement as a result of the risk-mitigating impact of insurance, management must demonstrate that the insurance policy is sufficiently capital-like to provide the protection that is necessary. A product that would fall in this category must have the following characteristics:

- The policy is provided through a third party that has a minimum claims-paying ability rating of A7.
- The policy has an initial term of one year.
- The policy has no exclusions or limitations based on regulatory action or for the receiver or liquidator of a failed bank.
- The policy has clear cancellation and nonrenewal notice periods.
- The policy coverage has been explicitly mapped to actual operational risk exposure of the organization.

Insurance policies that meet these standards may be incorporated into an organization's adjustment for risk mitigation. An organization should be conventional in its recognition of such policies. For example, the organization must also demonstrate that insurance policies used as the basis for the adjustment have a history of timely payouts. If claims have not been paid on a timely basis, the organization must exclude that policy from the operational risk capital adjustment. Insurance companies spread risks by holding large portfolios of policies. Moreover, insurance companies have access to actuarial information and data obtained from past loss experiences to better assess operational risk exposures. This expertise can also be used to advise their clients about internal risk management procedures to prevent operational losses.

Derivatives can be viewed as a form of insurance that is available directly through financial markets rather than through specialized insurance companies. Swaps, forwards, and options can all be designed to transfer operational risks as well as other sources of operational risks (e.g., interest rate, exchange rate, and credit risk exposures). In recent years, there has been immense growth in the use of derivatives for insurance purposes.

All insurance contracts suffer from the problem of moral hazard. That is, the mere presence of an insurance policy may induce the insured to engage in risky behaviors because the insured does not have to bear the financial consequences of that risky behavior. Thus, the organization's overall insurance program must be carefully monitored to target the areas in which the organization is most exposed to operational risks so as to economize on insurance premium payments. Therefore, insurance contracts must be taken out with due care and constantly reviewed for adequacy. The impact of insurance, therefore, is to protect the organization from catastrophic losses that would cause the organization to become bankrupt, not to protect the organization from all operational risks.

Summary

The AMA allows financial organizations to develop their own methodologies in measuring operational risks and the capital they need to set aside in accordance with certain guidelines proposed in Basel II. This approach is intended to be the most risk sensitive and to relate to the experiences of each organization. It offers the most refined measurement of operational risks and is expected to be used by more sophisticated financial organizations. Supervisors predict that the advanced measurement approaches will provide the incentives to invest in new systems and practices that will reduce the potential for serious losses from operational risks.

Management needs to evaluate the adequacy of countermeasures, both in terms of their effectiveness in reducing the probability of a given operational risk, and of their effectiveness in reducing the impact should it occur. Where necessary, steps should be taken to design and implement cost-effective solutions to reduce the operational risk to an acceptable and optimum level. It is essential that ownership for these actions be assigned to ensure that they are acted upon. In addition to developing calibration of the operational risk charge, the Basel Committee will continue to explore ways of improving the risk sensitivity of the operational risk framework. This will include work on a risk profile index in the AMA internal measurement approach, loss distribution approach, and the recognition of risk-mitigation techniques, all of which are discussed in the supporting document.

This chapter has introduced the advanced measurement approach, with its measuring system. It then went on to discuss the quantitative standards of the AMA. Furthermore, it discussed the elements of an AMA framework with emphasis on the internal operational risk loss event data and relevant external operational risk loss event data. It then went on to highlight the supervisory standards of the AMA and highlighted the qualifying criteria for risk capital calculation for banks wanting to apply an AMA framework. Finally, it discussed the use of insurance under the AMA.

References

1. Basel Committee on Banking Supervision, Working Paper on the Regulatory Treatment of Operational Risk, September 2001. This paper is available free from their Web site: http://www.bis.org/bcbs/publ.htm.
2. Basel Committee on Banking Supervision, International Convergence of Capital Measurement and Capital Standards: A Revised Framework, June 2004. This paper is available free from their Web site: http://www.bis.org/bcbs/publ.htm.
3. Basel Committee on Banking Supervision: Consultative Document Operational Risk: Supporting Document to the New Basel Capital Accord, January 2001. This paper is available free from their Web site: http://www.bis.org/bcbs/publ.htm.
4. Marshall, C., *Measuring and Managing Operational Risk in Financial Institutions: Tools, Techniques and Other Resources*, John Wiley & Sons, Singapore, 2001.
5. Basel Committee on Banking Supervision, Consultative Document on Operational Risk. Supporting Document to the New Basel Capital Accord, January 2001. This paper is available free from their Web site: http://www.bis.org/bcbs/publ.htm.
6. Georges, P. and Frachot A., et al., The Loss Distribution Approach for Operational Risk, Working Paper, Credit Lyonnais, 2000.
7. Basel Committee on Banking Supervision, Principles for the Home Host Recognition of AMA Operational Risk Capital, January 2004. This paper is available free from their Web site: http://www.bis.org/bcbs/publ.htm.
8. Federal Deposit Insurance Corporation, Supervisory Guidance on Operational Risk Advanced Measurement Approaches for Regulatory Capital, July 2003.
9. Güllich, H.P., Manser, R.F., and Wegmann, P., Operational Risk Management: How to Deal with Loss Data Correctly, December 2001.
10. See http://www.bba.org.uk/bba/jsp/polopoly.jsp?d=134&a=587 (accessed January 2005).
11. See http://www.orx.org (accessed January 2005).
12. See http://www.fitchrisk.com/frm/opvantage/products/ov_lossdata.cfm?pageId=OpVantage&bodyId=products&productId=ovLossData (accessed January 2005).
13. Basel Committee on Banking Supervision, Consultative Document: The New Basel Capital Accord, January 2001.
14. Basel Committee on Banking Supervision, Sound Practices for the Management and Supervision of Operational Risk, Feb. 2003. This paper is available free from their Web site: http://www.bis.org/publ/bcbs86.htm.
15. See http://www.bis.org/bcbs/publ.htm.

FRAMEWORKS FOR DESIGNING EFFICIENT OPERATIONAL RISK ASSESSMENT

Efficient Operational Risk Assessment, Control, and Management

For efficient operational risk assessment, control, and management, it is vital to identify, measure, model, monitor, evaluate, and map the operational risk profile. More important is optimizing the implications of the operational risks for the operational business performances. This helps to align the operational risks to the business/strategic objectives, planning process, decisions making, business practices, and quality initiatives. Moreover, reporting strategies and planning policies on when and how to accept, avoid," or mitigate risks according to their actual probability, impact, and exposure in relation to the optimal levels of operational risks are the main emphasis for efficient and optimal operational risk management. Part III and Part IV of this book give overview guidelines on how to design an efficient framework for operational risk management systems in accordance with Basel II requirements. Whereas Part III concentrates notably on the operational risk assessment phase, Part IV focuses on the controlling and managing these operational risks.

The key elements in designing efficient operational risk management systems for Basel II, discussed in previous chapters, combine operational risk assessment and operational risk control and management. The fundamental steps of the assessment phase involve identifying, measuring, modeling, monitoring, and evaluating the operational risks. Correlation analysis plays an effective role in many of these steps. Furthermore, the risk profiling in terms of operational risk probability impact and their exposure needs to be identified. The primary steps of the operational risk control and management phase involves operational risk profiling, optimizing the levels of the operational risks to minimize their implications to business performances with minimal costs, reviewing and reporting on the management of the operational risks, decision management, and risk policies. In addition, the estimation of the optimal allocation of resources needed to be distributed within the operational activities render the risk management more cost effective. The operational risk profiling and optimization analysis are used as a basis for defining and managing the policies for risk reporting, decision making, and setting risk policies. All the above elements are combined to construct the risk pyramid to dynamically manage operational risks, as illustrated in Figure III.1.

In this part of the book, a methodology for designing efficient operational risk management systems is presented. Based on the operational risk pyramid, the main steps of the methodology include risk assessment analysis, which combines the following:

- Operational risk identification analysis, which includes process, business line, and operational risk mapping
- Operational risk measurement
- Operational risk modeling analysis
- Operational risk monitoring
- Evaluation analysis (including the estimation of capital requirements)

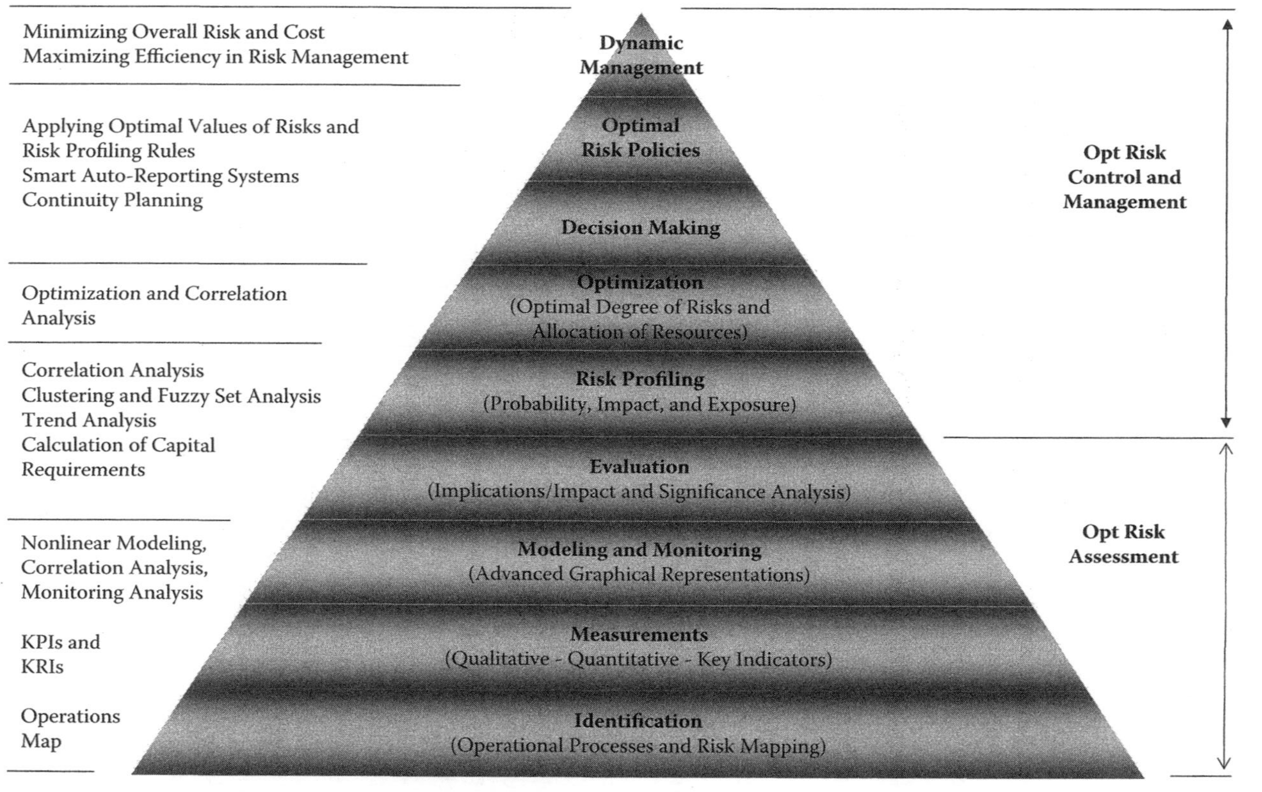

Figure III.1 The risk pyramid.

The operational risk control and management, which will be discussed in Part IV of this book, consists of:

- Operational risk profiling
- Operational risk optimization
- Operational risk reporting and decision management, including the setting of future operational risk policies

The proceeding chapters present methodologies that are used to support each of the above operational risk management elements that construct the operational risk pyramid.

Key Elements of Efficient Operational Risk Assessment

The operational risk assessment phase includes operational risk identification, measurement, modeling, and monitoring analysis as well as the operational risk evaluation analysis. The first step in the operational risk pyramid is the identification phase, which entails the mapping of the business lines and operational processes, the mapping of the operational risks, and the capturing of the strategic business objectives. The business lines of the banking organization should be mapped into those identified by Basel II, as discussed in Chapter 3. Then there is a need to identify and map the operations within the business lines. Furthermore, the identified operational risks associated with the operations should be mapped into the risk event types defined by Basel II. It is important to identify and capture the operational business objectives as well. On the other hand, the measurement phase includes the identification of qualitative and quantitative indicators and defines the parameters of measurements. By analyzing the operations defined through the operation process map, key qualitative operational risks can be identified. There is a need to transfer their qualitative attributes to quantitative measurement indicators by measuring and tracking them using key risks and key performance indicators. The next step is to measure, extract, and record the information data related to all multifactorial parameters that characterize the risks in operations. This results in a multidimensional tracking system of all those operational risks that affect, with different degrees, the operations within all business lines. To understand the actual amount of the operational risk effect on the operations, with other operational risks and on operational performances, a nonlinear modeling analysis must be performed. This analysis involves modeling, monitoring, and evaluating the implications of both internal and external operational risks on operational performances. The impact and degree of significance of each of the operational risks in operations and their implications on business lines and strategic objectives are defined in the operational risk evaluation step. Furthermore, in the evaluation step, the capital requirement that should be reserved for banking organizations is calculated. Because this approach is geared for the AMA, the capital reserve calculations are based on the AMA. Operational value at risk (operational VaR) is used for this calculation.

Chapter 5

Operational Risk Identification, Measurement, Modeling, and Monitoring Analysis

First weigh the considerations, then take the risks.

—Helmuth von Moltke

Introduction

In this chapter, a framework of methodologies for assessing operational risks is discussed, a framework used for designing an effective and optimal operational risk management system. During the identification phase, the use of the operational risk and operations process mapping is highlighted, together with the identification of the qualitative and quantitative parameters of both operational performances and risks. Guidance on when and how to define the key performance and risk indicators is also presented. The measurement of these indicators, for the information data extraction process related to operational risk causes, events, and consequences, is illustrated. The construction of the matrices that include the operational

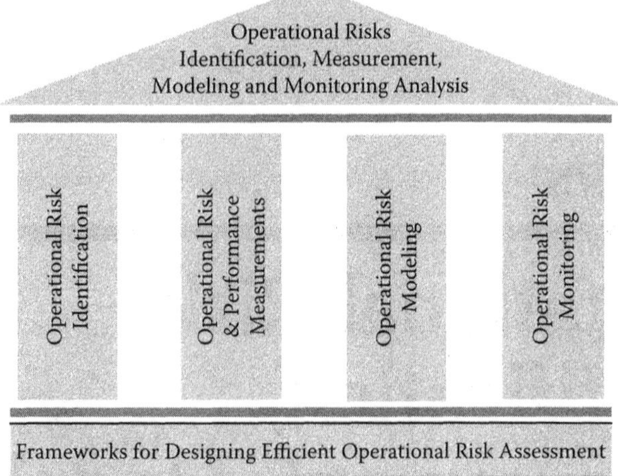

Figure 5.1 Main elements of Chapter 5.

risk measurement values obtained from the key risk indicators (KRIs) and the loss event database associated with risk causes, events, and consequences is also defined. Based on the above information, the design of modeling and monitoring strategies for both operational risks and affected operations is duly discussed in this chapter. Correlation analysis defined from multidimensional operational risk parameters is used as one of the main techniques for implementing the modeling and monitoring framework. The chapter presents advanced ways for monitoring efficiently the operational risks as well as the affected operations. The results illustrate the mapping of the pattern or contour topography of the operational risks and operations. Moreover, the correlations between the operational risks are defined using bar chart representation and mosaic mapping. Finally, surface illustrations using three-dimensional correlation models are presented for both operational risk and affected operations. This gives an indication of what risk management teams should look for to monitor operational risks. The integration of all the above phases is used for the operational risk assessment analysis.

Figure 5.1 illustrates the main elements of this chapter.

Operational Risk Identification

A main assessment function in designing an effective optimal operational risk management system is the identification of both internal and external operational risks. Principle 4 of Basel II[1] states that financial organizations should identify and assess the operational risk inherent in all products, activities, processes, and systems. Financial organizations should also ensure that before new products, activities, processes, and systems are introduced or undertaken, the operational risk inherent in them is subject to adequate assessment procedures. It further states that risk identification is vital for the subsequent development of a viable operational risk monitoring and control system. Effective risk identification considers both internal factors (such as the bank's structure, the nature of the bank's activities, the quality of the bank's human resources, organizational changes, and employee turnover) and external factors (such as changes in the industry and technological advances) that could negatively or positively affect achievement of the bank's objectives. The operational risk identification process needs to focus both on current and future potential operational risks and identify the vulnerability to these risks. Effective operational risk identification, as part of the assessment process, allows the bank to better understand its operational risk profile (discussed in Part IV of this book) and more effectively target operational risk management resources. When identifying operational risks, management should be careful to address the full spectrum of potential operational risks. Thus, the operational risk identification process should consider:

- The full spectrum of potential operational risks
- The internal and external environment in which the banking organization operates
- The organization's strategic objectives
- The products and services the banking organization provides
- The unique circumstances
- The internal and external change, and the pace of that change

The operational risk identification process involves:

- *Risk and operations process mapping*. The first step of operational risk identification is based on defining all the parameters that describe the relation of how risks affect operational performances, which are directly or indirectly linked to business targets and objectives. The operations process map is used here to define the key operational processes, the various business units, organizational functions, and process flows and links between them.
- *Operational risk indicators*. On the basis of this map, key operational risks and performance indicators that measure quantitatively both risks and performances, respectively, can be identified for each of the key operations. These indicators are metrics, which can provide insight into a bank's risk position. These indicators tend to be reviewed on a periodic basis (such as monthly or

quarterly) to alert banks to changes that may be indicative of operational risk concerns.

The identification step through the assessment process must take place to monitor "what is going wrong," and try to identify "what could go wrong" at each step in the process and systems within all business lines. Operational risk identification system must be closely integrated into the risk management processes of the financial organization. Its output must be an integral part of the process of measuring, modeling, monitoring, evaluating, optimizing, and controlling the operational risk profile of financial organizations. Thus, this information plays a prominent role in risk reporting.

Operational Risk and Operations Process Mapping

One of the fundamental steps in designing optimal operational risk management systems is to identify the process map of operations and the risks that influence them. An operational process mapping exercise would help banks identify key operations and design a roadmap of the combined key operations. The result will take the form of an "operations process map," defining inputs and outputs and linkage between operations. In the risk mapping process, all possible risks that might affect the main processes, people, and operational systems must be identified and linked to the operations process map. Basel II has also identified seven operational risk event types, as discussed in Chapter 1, that the financial organization should try and map their identified risks to. These risk event types include internal fraud; external fraud; employment practices and workplace safety; clients, products, and business practices; damage to physical assets; business disruption and system failures; and execution, delivery, and process management.

In the design of the optimal operational risk management system, it is important to define and measure all the operational performances, within all business lines, and the risks that influence them. The operational risk mapping is used as the basis for the identification of the key operations and key risks and thus key performance and risk indicators.

Operational Risk and Performance Measurements

Operational performances focus on the actual accomplishment or produced output. Thus, for each operation in a financial organization, either at business-line levels or at a more corporate level, the output performance of the operations that may be associated with any internal or external operational risks must be clearly defined and measured. However, the definition of performances in operations is both quantitative and qualitative and therefore they can be measured directly or indirectly, as described in the next sections.

Operational risks need to be defined and measured at any stage of manifestation and can either be defined as a risk cause, a risk event, or a risk consequence. These operational risks include but are not limited to:

- Transaction processing
- Sales practices
- Management processes
- Human resources
- Vendors and suppliers
- Technology
- External environment
- Disasters
- Unauthorized and criminal activities

Some organizations have begun to quantify and measure their exposure to operational risks using a variety of approaches. For example, data on a bank's historical loss experience could provide meaningful information for assessing the bank's exposure to operational risk and developing a policy to mitigate and control the risk. An effective way of making good use of this information is to establish a framework for systematically tracking and recording the frequency, severity, and other relevant information on individual loss events. Some organizations have also combined internal loss data with external loss data, scenario analyses, and risk assessment factors. Financial organizations must have a comprehensive operational risk analytical framework that provides an estimate of the banking organization's operational risk exposure, which is the combined operational loss it faces over a certain time period. The organization's operational risk analytical framework should use a combination of internal operational loss event data, relevant external operational loss event data, business environment and internal control assessments, and scenario analysis. The organization should combine these elements in a manner that most effectively enables it to quantify and measure its operational risk exposure. The organization can choose the analytical framework that is most appropriate to its business model. The banking organization's capital requirement for operational risk will be the sum of expected and unexpected losses unless the organization can demonstrate, consistent with supervisory standards, the expected loss offset.

Financial organizations are in very early stages of measuring operational risk, with only a few having formal measurement systems. However, in most cases, the measurement methodologies that are being used are rather simple and experimental, with no systematic and crisp ways to identify and categorize what, how, and when to measure. Nevertheless, few banking organizations seem to have made considerable progress in developing more advanced techniques for allocating capital with regard to operational risk.

The experimental approaches of existing operational risk measures reflect several issues. The risk and performance indicators, discussed later on, usually identified by the organization are typically measures of internal risks and performances, such as error rates and income volatility, volume, and turnover. However, external indicators are rarely used to measure operational issues. Uncertainty about what are the most significant indicators arises from the absence of direct relationships between the risk factors and parameters usually identified and the size and frequency of losses.

There is a rather clear contrast between operational risk and market risk. In market risk, changes in prices have an easily computed impact on the value of the bank's trading portfolio. Furthermore, a contrast also exists between operational risk and credit risks, where changes in the borrower's credit quality are often associated with changes in the interest rate spread of the borrower's obligations over a risk-free rate. These are easily measured. On the contrary, operational risks are not so easily identified or measured. Today, there is inadequate and minimal research available for identifying and measuring the degree of correlation between the operational risks as well as with their resulting operational losses. Capturing operational loss experience also raises measurement questions. Financial organizations noted that in several cases the costs of investigating and correcting the problems underlying a loss event were significant and, in many cases, exceeded the direct costs of the operational losses.

Measuring operational risk requires both estimating the probability of an operational risk and its potential impact. Most approaches use interviews that are biased in nature and rely to some extent on risk indicators that provide some indication of the likelihood of an operational risk occurring. Risk indicators are sometimes described qualitatively and subjective assessments translated into grades (such as an audit assessment). These qualitative assessments should be translated into quantitative ones if a viable measuring system is to be found. The set of indicators used can include variables that measure risk in each business unit, for instance, grades from qualitative assessments such as internal audit ratings; generic operational data such as volume, turnover, and complexity; and data on quality of operations such as error rate or measures of business "riskiness," for example, revenue volatility. The risk indicators are usually related to historical losses to come up with a comprehensive measurement methodology. However, two main issues should be considered when using such measurement approaches: (1) few banks have started to collect data on their historical loss experiences, and (2) past data does always give a good indication of future occurrences of risks in operations. Finally, because there are many indicators and sources for defining and measuring the values of operational risks, the challenge is to combine all these measurements within the existing operational stratification and identify their meanings in terms of current and future trend status.

The pace of business today requires, at *requested* time, access to data and metrics related to business performances and operational effectiveness. The key issue, however, is not only to access the data and matrices, but to access them at the "right time" to give value to the collected information. Another important issue in setting measurement systems is the frequency of collecting this information data. This could be:

- *Constant.* Many risks in operations are monitored constantly in real-time or near-real-time or at least many times each day. Those are mainly risks that have high degree of significance value. An example of constant monitoring is the cash flow on cash-points machines in certain geographical areas.
- *Periodic.* This could review periodically the information data that refers to the top operational risks list. This list is always updated, where the top risks are reviewed on a periodic basis.
- *As needed.* In cases of major operational risk occurrences, its value must be tracked and recorded. Moreover, in some other cases, particular operational risk measurements need to be recorded and evaluated as they are needed.

The risk indicators that give measurement and information data related to operational risks must have comprehensive but reasonable depth and bandwidth. The depth and bandwidth are in terms of historical information as well as in terms of different operational parameters and activities within the business lines. The main rule referring to operational risk measurement and evaluation analysis is: try to keep the "depth" of time short and the "width" of operations involved in operational risk analysis large. The expression "short depth" indicates use of short-term historical data, and the expression "large width" indicates that all affected operations should be considered. That is because past information referring to operational risks does not have such significant information that could indicate enough knowledge for evaluating and managing the current and candidate risks. This is because operations are dynamically changing or updating in financial organizations. However, in big and multi-operational organizations such as banks where the dependencies between the operations are very high, it is more important to consider the affected operations, and identify their intercorrelations, within different business lines.

The definitions of most operational risks are initially described qualitatively; however, a process to transfer these definitions to quantitative values is desirable to convert all these operational risks into measurable ones. These quantitative values defined as risk indicators should be established for operational risks to ensure the escalation of significant risk issues to appropriate management levels. Operational risks affect to a certain degree, directly or indirectly, some of the operational business performances. Such performances are required to be defined, and their variations should be measured quantitatively.

Qualitative Performance

Qualitative performance in banking organizations, such as customer complaints that may be initiated from operational failures, are based on perceptions and feelings to predict customer satisfaction, are indirectly measurable. On the other hand, repeat and lost business and market share are directly measuring the customer satisfaction that reflects the customer behavior. The quality of a service (or product) is also a qualitative performance measure. However, it is quantified when measures that refer to the service time, number of on-time billing payments, etc. are considered.

Quantitative Performance

Quantitative operational performances are easily measured through key performance indicators (KPIs), where their parameters are defined from the outcome of the operations. In banking organizations, KPIs measure the performance of all operational activities within all business lines. Operational metrics are proactive or preventive in nature, and focus on work activity as it occurs; that is, not only is the output performance being measured, but also the activities that drive and determine these outputs. Quantitatively measuring performances of operations and their associated activities helps to drive desired results, because you cannot improve what you cannot measure.

Defining Key Performance Indicators for Operations

The identification of an organization's performance is a vital way to show how well it is doing, understand its weak and strong areas and thus areas for further improvement, and identify what performance generates true value. Executives and decision makers need at-a-glance access to key business metrics so they can quickly assess the health of the business and take charge when conditions change. With KPIs, banking organizations define and help deliver instant access to personalized views of key business information. KPIs can be used to show the current situation for each performance dimension, where their stochastic combination is used to assess the business performance globally as well as to identify areas and ways of improvements. Although specific performance indicators will vary by industry and company, they generally fall into a few key areas:

- Customer, which includes customer satisfaction index, average customer profitability, and market share
- Corporate, which includes labor costs, employee productivity, and return on equity
- Products and services, which include revenue, shares, operating profit, and competitive advantage
- Human resources, which includes cost to hire, training costs versus budget, number of new hires, and average benefit (employer)
- Supplier, which includes on-time delivery, quality services, and cost of operations
- Financial, which includes sales, costs, gross profit margin, net profit margin, return on assets, economic value added, and cash flow
- Safety/environmental, which includes number and seriousness of accidents, loss time incident rate, and insurance claims

Under these key areas there are different types of performance measures that include:

- Timeliness measures (e.g., 90 percent of documents completed on time)
- Cycle time measures (e.g., average 3.5 days to process invoices)
- Productivity measures (e.g., 50 applications processed per day)
- Quality measures (e.g., 4.2 defects per 100 units)
- Cost measures (e.g., processing cost of €10/document)
- Baseline measures (the current performance level)
- Trending measures (for evaluating performance changes over time)
- Control measures (which determine whether performance is staying within predetermined boundaries)
- Diagnostic measures (which identify the cause or location of a problem)
- Planning measures (which look at past and current performance to predict the future)

In defining KPIs, it is important to possess a clear view of either the business or the departmental objectives because these are "what is needed" to be achieved at the end of the day. Therefore, KPIs are ways to measure the banking organization and department objectives and are linked with the objectives through the operations or processes they are measuring.

Qualitative Operational Risks

Risks that are indirectly measurable, normally driven by external factors, are qualitative in nature. Some events affect financial organization infrequently and are of a nonuniform nature, such as terrorism, natural disasters, and trader fraud. It is evident that the result of natural disasters impacts every aspect of an organization: its people, its systems, and its process/infrastructure. The most common course of action for such events is to insure against these risks. But even when such risk impacts are mitigated, it is important to evaluate their real business effect and financial costs as well as to define their real degree of exposure based on probability and impact analysis. To truly understand operational risks' probability and impact, it is important to try and estimate them and turn these qualitative risks into quantitative ones. Probability and impact analysis is discussed in subsequent chapters.

Quantitative Operational Risks

Risks that are directly measurable and are normally internal to the organization are quantitative in nature. For operational risk, certain incidents are particularly agreeable to quantitative techniques. For example, settlement errors in a trading operation's back office happen with sufficient regularity that they can be measured quantitatively. KRIs are used to measure such risks; they are metrics that can provide insight into a bank's risk position. Such indicators may include the number of failed trades, staff turnover rates, and the frequency or severity of errors and omissions. The fourth principle of Basel II highlights the use of risk indicators as a key assessment technique.

Defining Key Operational Risk Indicators

Operational risk indicators are used to identify the elevated operational risks. Key risk indicators (KRIs) are one of the most common ways of measuring the actual values of risk causes, the risk events, and their risk consequences. A KRI is a variable that provides a reliable basis for estimating the loss corresponding to risk. A KRI can be a specific causal variable or a proxy for the drivers of the loss attributed to risks. The challenge for defining KRIs is to quantify the qualified risks by identifying their mathematical functions.

KRIs are becoming an increasingly important tool in the framework of operational risk management systems. As organizations further understand the complex relationships between cause and effect, KRIs can be used as predictive indicators of arising risks, risk events, and potential losses. Key performance and risk indicators in all operational business lines define the metrics that can provide insight into a financial organization's risk position. KRIs can be measured using both loss event and performance databases. Loss events collect data such as settlement errors, systems failures, petty fraud, customer lawsuits, and so forth. The use of risk indicators to measure the disturbances of operational performances differs from loss event approaches. KRIs are not associated with specific losses, but indicate the deviation of the operational performances within different business lines.

There are three types of data that may refer to a *cause*, to an *event*, and to a *consequence*, where KRIs are used to measure their values. A good way is to measure the volatility of the operational performances and the declination of the business targets when an operational risk occurs. The volatility in operational performance within the business lines can also be characterized as a risk event or a cause to a new event or even a consequence. Operational risk events are associated with internal control weaknesses or lack of compliance with existing internal procedures. They are found in all areas of an organization and are mainly caused by the intertwined actions of people, technological systems, processes, and some unpredictable external events. As a result, most operational risks are measured directly or indirectly through the key performance indicators.

KRIs refer to:

$$KRIs\begin{Bmatrix} Systems \\ Processes \\ People \end{Bmatrix}\begin{Bmatrix} Cause \\ Events \\ Consequences \rightarrow impact \end{Bmatrix} Performance\_Volatility$$

Table 5.1 is a list of sources of operational risks, together with some of their underlining types of risks and some associated KRIs. Because financial organizations are faced with these sources of operational risks on a daily basis, organizations should identify KRIs in each of these elements and, more important, how they affect one another. Ideally, the KRIs would be easily quantifiable measures currently available to management. The more familiar management is with the data elements and

Table 5.1 Sources of Operational Risks and Related KRIs

Sources of OR	*Types of Risks*	*Some Key Risk Indicators*
People	Internal control and corporate governance breakdown leading to financial losses, slip-ups, incompetence, internal/external fraud, theft. *Internal fraud:* Intentional misreporting of positions and unreported transactions, employee theft and smuggling, insider and outsider trading, bribes, etc. *External fraud:* Robbery, forgery, damage from computer hacking, etc. *Transactions:* Document/contract error, privacy breaches, misuse of confidential customer information, money laundering, sale of unauthorized products, data entry errors, etc.	■ Frequency or severity of transactions errors and omissions ■ Number of failed trades ■ Staff turnover rates ■ Number of documentation errors ■ Staff training and experience levels ■ Transaction and trades volume ■ Income instability
Technological systems	System failures caused by internal and external events: *Internal:* Programming errors, IT crash caused by new applications, loss of Information data, incompatibility with existing systems, internal telecommunication failures, failure of system to meet business requirements, etc. *External:* Utility outages such as power cut, business disruption caused by system failures, telecommunication problems, information risks and losses, external security breaches, etc.	■ Number of instances of network or systems downtime ■ Maintenance fail-over rate ■ Systems failure rate ■ Data integrity after outage ■ System failure retrieval time ■ Backup failure rate

Table 5.1 (continued) Sources of Operational Risks and Related KRIs

Sources of OR	*Types of Risks*	*Some Key Risk Indicators*
Processes	*Process execution:* Delivery and process management, product service complexity, management failures, security failures, incomplete/missing legal documentation, unapproved access given to client accounts, delivery failure and vendor disputes, payment/settlement delivery risk, employment practices and workplace safety, workers' compensation claims, violation of employee health and safety rules, organized labor activities (strikes, etc.), discrimination claims and general liability	■ Number of contracts noncompliant with organization's policy ■ Settlement failure rate ■ Accounting losses' rate ■ Number of issues raised by regulators/auditors ■ Payment failure rate
External events	*Political uncertainties:* War (global effect), damage to physical assets, fires, viruses/mass diseases, terrorism, vandalism, etc. *Natural disasters:* Earthquakes, floods, hurricanes, volcanoes, etc. Breach of environmental management, bankruptcy of supplier, transportation failures, etc.	■ Amount of physical losses (financial, people, systems) ■ Loss data rate

measures selected, the more likely they are to trust and use the measures in an effective risk management system.

Financial organizations incorporating risk indicators into their measurement approach are using them to clearly identify, measure, and alert the business lines when a higher degree of operational risks prevails.

In some cases it is difficult to justify the differences between causes, events, and consequences. This is because a cause may be characterized also as an event or an event as a consequence, and vice versa. A theft, for example, may be characterized as a "cause" of an event such as misleading trade in the financial organizations. Furthermore, it may be characterized as an "event," which may be caused by employees' attitudes, and may have as a consequence the loss of reputation of the financial organization. Finally, it may be characterized as a consequence of an event such as systems failure that could have been caused by a security breach. Risk analysts and managers must clarify what to characterize and define as a cause, an event, or a consequence. In this matter, the analyst should consider two main rules:

1. What is characterized as a "cause" must result into one or more events. What is characterized as an "event" must have at least one cause and it must result in one or more consequences. And finally, what is characterized as a "consequence" must come from one or more events and may result in new cause(s).
2. No matter what has initially been characterized as a "cause," "event," or "consequence," the organization should stick to that definition. However, any changes from the initial definition must be documented, and all those that are involved in the operational risk management process and systems must be informed.

Table 5.2 shows some of the main types of cause, events, and consequences in financial organizations. Table 5.3 illustrates some typical causes, events, consequences, and business impacts of operational risks.

Table 5.2 Types of Causes, Events, and Consequences

Cause Types	*Event Types*	*Consequence Types*
Deception of individual's behavior Organizational and corporate behavior Faults from information technology External banking environment Nonbanking external environment	Internal fraud External fraud Employment practices and workplace safety Business disruption Systems failures Execution, delivery, and process management Damage to physical assets Clients, products, and business practices	Regulatory and compliance Legal liability Loss/damage to assets Loss of reputation Restitution Loss of resources Loss of opportunities Loss of market share

Table 5.3 Examples of Causes, Events, Consequences, and Business Impacts of Operational Risks

Causes	*Events*	*Consequences*	*Business Impacts*
Inadequate staffing	Inability of the help service desk to handle the number of calls that it receives per day	■ The service level agreement (SLA) will not be met and customers will have to wait longer for support ■ Reduced customer satisfaction ■ Bad organization's reputation Reduced number of future new customers	Reduced future cash income flow and business growth
Technology modifications	The CRM vendor plans to withdraw or limit the support for the current product's version.	■ Limited supporting of the existing CRM system ■ Inability to set/update sale enhancements ■ Reduced salesforce capabilities	Reduced rate of sales
New regulatory requirement	Web banking transactions needed to be stored and linked in a database for 10 years Current system does not fully support the link process	■ Backup and archiving is not capable and thus reliable to accommodate this need ■ Business trading restrictions may be imposed	Negative effect on the organization's position and image in the market

Constructing Functions for KRIs

Key risk indicators are mathematical functions that include all those parameters that describe the operational variation of specific operations within specific business lines. The value of a key risk indicator $KRI_{(1,\ \ldots,\ op)BL}$ within a business line refers to functional values of causes, events, and consequences, as well as of the performance deviations. Equation 5.1 shows the general function of a KRI.

$$KRI_{\{1,\ldots,p\}} = f\begin{pmatrix} z^{\delta}_{pr} & z^{\gamma}_{pr} & z^{c}_{pr} & dP_{pr} \\ z^{\delta}_{pl} & z^{\gamma}_{pl} & z^{c}_{pl} & dP_{pl} \\ z^{\delta}_{st} & z^{\gamma}_{st} & z^{c}_{st} & dP_{st} \end{pmatrix}, f(t) \tag{5.1}$$

$p \in \{1, \ldots, op\}$, op is the number of the operations

where

δ indicates the value of a cause.
γ indicates the value of an event.
c indicates the value of the consequential financial impact.
dP indicates the unexpected performance variation within the trading business line. Note that the term "unexpected performance" is explained further on in this book.
The pointers *pr*, *pl*, and *st* point out the origination of the cause, that is, process, people, or systems, respectively.
$f(t)$ indicates that all measurement should include a time parameter.

Moreover, in the identification of the quantifying parameters of the risk indicators, the following aspects are also considered:

- The size, severity, or intensity
- The frequency
- The context dependency, which may be different in different situations
- The possible relation with other indicators

The size describes the observed extent of presence of operational risk. The frequency describes the number of times a risk of a given size occurs within a given time period or a given organizational unit. The context dependency describes whether the size of the risk is dissimilar in different causes, events, or consequences. The possible relation with other indicators defines the common parameters between all indicators.

KRIs should be chosen so that they are measured on an ongoing basis so that data can easily be gathered. Moreover, a main guidance for designing KRI functions is to keep them simple (i.e., not very complex) by including a large number of parameters. It is preferable to have a larger number of simple and easy-to-understand KRIs than a smaller number of complex functions. Moreover, it is inefficient in the KRI design process to repeat the same measurement of operational risk using slightly different functions. Finally, an index for explaining all parameters could be very useful for future users and operational risk analysts.

Constructing the Matrix of KRIs

Each banking organization is subject to its own types of operational risks. Thus, its risk appetite is different from other banking organizations. Therefore, KRIs that refer to its particular operational risk parameters must be defined in light of the operational risks in the particular organization. The matrix referring to the definition of the "organization key risk indicators" is a fundamental step in the designing process of operational risk management systems.

Using the definition and measurement parameters of the KRIs for the operational risks under study, a multidimensional data matrix is constructed. This matrix of the measurement data is used for the operational risk evaluation in the next chapter. Figure 5.2 represents the construction of such a matrix.

The dimension of the columns refers to the performances and risks indicators. The dimension of the rows refers to operational activities.

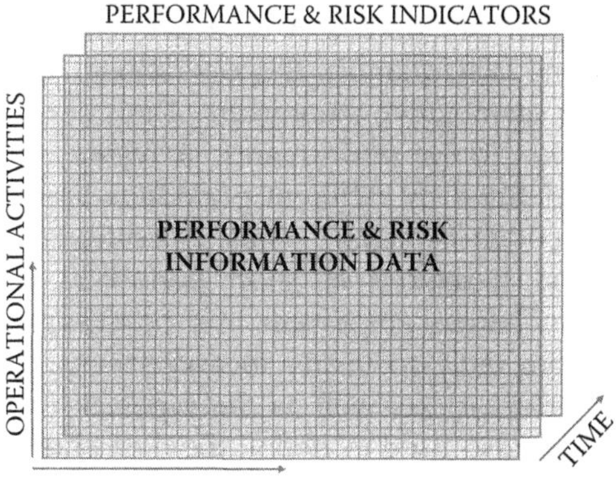

Figure 5.2 Matrix defining the performance and risk indicators within operational activities.

Finally, each cell of the matrix represents the data information extracted for each time period. Thus, the depth of time periods referring to the information data indicates the dimension of time.

In the matrix illustrated in Figure 5.2, there are two main ways of viewing the risks and operations:

1. By looking at the columns, the "operational risks" are illustrated.
2. By looking at the rows, the "affected operations" are illustrated.

The optimal operational risk level of each of these KRIs is determined as explained in Chapter 8. The operational activities that are affected by the risks may refer to people, processes, or systems. In the examples and results of the following chapters of this book, operational activities that are referring to people such as bank tellers, traders, loan and account administrators, and managers are presented. Moreover, operational activities for deposits, withdrawals, check clearance, loan payments, credit card operations, and billings refer to banking business processes. Finally, IT systems that are supporting activities for trading, loans, credit and debit cards, insurances, ATMs, Web banking, telephone banking, and accounting refer to banking systems.

A case study concerning the "back and front office for banking tellers" in corporate banking business lines will help illustrate the many concepts discussed in this chapter. In this case study, the operational risks refer to some of the main activities for the "capital transactions," "check transactions," and "payment transactions" within the banking organization's branches. Such activities are linked to managers, capital transfers, and deposits. Moreover, they include some customers' activities that are related to the management of their accounts. Additionally, the KRI descriptions such as "capital transfer per period of time per teller" must be defined. The transfer functions that quantify the operational risks must also be clearly defined using quantitative parameters. Their definition is driven by measuring the variation in the performance activities. Note that the measuring frequency is defined by different periodical times (i.e., from periodical degree of seconds to years). Thus, operational risks in systems performances can be measured in short periodical frequencies, from seconds to minutes, whereas employees and processes operational risks can be identified from daily to yearly measurements. The identification for which the risk refers to, as well as the types of risks, the loss, and the possible impact, is also used to define the elements that construct the matrix of the KRIs. The construction of this matrix is defined by the elements such as those shown in Table 5.4.

Both operations and KRIs should be described and allocated a unique code. It is useful to group and label these indicators according to where they come from, that is, process, people, systems, or external events, or in relation to if they refer to "causes" of risks, risk "events," or "consequences" of risks. This grouping identification helps in the process of monitoring and operational risk assessment analysis.

The affected operational activities can be these ones that are referring to people (i.e., tellers, loan and accounts administrators, traders, managers, etc.), or to processes (i.e., those that are referring to capital transfers, deposits, withdrawals, check clearance, loan payments, credit cards, bills etc.), or to systems (i.e., those that refer to IT systems and are supporting the accounts, loans, debit cards, ATMs, and Web banking, telephone banking, trading, etc.) On the other hand, the indicators that are describing the operational risks are identifying and measuring failures or any undesirable performances such as the ones that refer to total number of capital transactions, activity time, accounts verification time, check transfers, check verification time, billing transactions, bill verification time, new services, recorded loss, unauthorized access, number of violation access, etc.

Tracking and Monitoring Operational Risk and Performance Information

An effective way of making good use of the extracted information data that may relate to risks in operations is to establish a framework for a systematically tracking, monitoring, and recording mechanism for both KRIs and KPIs. This tracking is based on the frequency, severity, and other relevant information of individual loss events. The tracking process should be based on current or short-time measurements to analyze and indicate the current and future performance and operational risk statements. It should be based on and therefore focus on considering measurements out of the existing large amount of current or in short depth-of-time information data. This proposed data reflection and analysis provides a global view and management analysis by considering as many views and control angles as possible. The practice of trying to identify and extract data for a small number of indicators that will describe the reality concerning operational risk statements and then manage only those indicators does not always give successful results.

Operational risk tracking should refer to all those parameters and information related to risk "causes," "events," "consequences," "probability," and "impact." Moreover, it is responsible for extracting the "threshold values" needed in contingency planning. In some cases, banking organizations are combining internal and external loss data, scenario analysis, and risk assessment factors for tracking operational risks. In the operational risk tracking process, the risk management system is gathering information about how risks are changing. This information supports the decisions and actions that will be made in the processes of risk control. In addition, the operational risk tracking step monitors three main changes, as follows:

1. *Threshold values.* If a set threshold becomes true, the contingency plan needs to be executed, as discussed in Chapter 9.
2. *The operational risk's condition, consequences, probability, and impact,* as discussed in Chapter 7 referring to risk profiling.
3. *The progress of a mitigation plan,* discussed in the section referring to risk mitigation process. If the plan is behind schedule or is not giving the desired result, it needs to be reevaluated.

The majority of performance and operational risk information is mainly collected through IT systems and management tools that support all the processes in operations within all business lines. These direct measurements are used to demonstrate factually the risk in operations. However, in the tracking process it should also consider the "confidentiality," "integrity," and "availability" of data. Confidentiality means that only authorized individuals and systems must be able to have access at different levels. Integrity means that all authorized users and systems must have confidence that the information data is accurate and properly modified. Finally, availability refers to access of data at any requested time.

Minimizing Assumptions

Management must document the rationale for all assumptions underpinning its chosen analytical framework, including the choice of inputs, and distributional assumptions across qualitative and quantitative elements. Financial organizations must review and understand the assumptions[2] used in the collection and measurements referring to operational risks. During the design of operational risk management systems, assumptions may be made that have to be assessed and challenged by suitably qualified parties independently of the development process. Minimizing assumptions, mainly during the risk analysis, by using factual information approaches, gives greater integrity to the developed operational risk management system.

The Matrix of Measurements

The measurement information data resulting from the tracking process of risks and performances consists of typical observations or record values of processes, or people, or system actions and operational activities. Each observation or record value is defined by the associated N number of key indicators. These indicators consist of measured parametric variables that are related to the risk cause, risk events, consequences of risks, and unexpected performance variations, as discussed earlier in this chapter in the section on the construction of KRIs and KPIs. The set of N operational risks and undesired performance observations or records is denoted by $Z = \{\mathbf{z}_k | k = 1, 2, \ldots, N\}$. On the other hand, the operations are also grouped and listed accordingly. The taxonomy can be based on several subjective criteria such as business lines or processes to which they refer.

The data values are grouped into an n-dimensional Euclidean space $\Re^n$ column vector. Its dimension represents an operation that is affected by risks within particular business lines and is defined as $\mathbf{z}_k$, where

$$\mathbf{z}_k = \begin{bmatrix} z_{1k} \\ z_{2k} \\ - \\ z_{nk} \end{bmatrix}, \quad z_k \in \Re^n$$

The resultant matrix is constructed by the operations and the indicators that measures the risks from and construct an $n \times N$-dimensional matrix as defined in Equation 5.2. Thus, the N columns of the matrix represent the indicators that define the measuring parameters, whereas the n rows define the operations under study.

$$\mathbf{Z} = \begin{bmatrix} \mathbf{z}_{11} & \mathbf{z}_{12} & \cdots & \mathbf{z}_{1N} \\ \mathbf{z}_{21} & \mathbf{z}_{22} & \cdots & \mathbf{z}_{2N} \\ \cdot & \cdot & \cdot & \cdot \\ \cdot & \cdot & \cdot & \cdot \\ \cdot & \cdot & \cdot & \cdot \\ \mathbf{z}_{n1} & \mathbf{z}_{n2} & \cdots & \mathbf{z}_{nN} \end{bmatrix} \tag{5.2}$$

Each element $\mathbf{z}$ is an array $\mathbf{z} = [z(t) \;\; z(t-1) \;\; z(t-2) \; \ldots \; z(t-d)]^T$ that defines the measurements in a depth d space.

Such a matrix of measurement is very useful because it includes all the data that is accessible and can be used for further analysis. The taxonomy of the data that constructs the matrix should be based on how to characterize and thus categorize these indicators. This is based on where they originate in terms of causes, events, or consequences of operational risks.

The Matrix of Causes, Events, and Consequences

Another way for defining the operational risk matrix is based on the definition of causes, events, or consequences. Such construction defines a multidimensional matrix as illustrated in Equation 5.3. Its element z of the matrix is an array with measurements mainly based on a time series, i.e., $[z^{\gamma}, z^{\delta}, z^{c}] \in \{z(1), z(2), \ldots, z(t)\}$. By using the elements of this matrix, banking organizations can identify which and how certain causes $\mathbf{z}^{\gamma}$, events $\mathbf{z}^{\delta}$, and consequences $\mathbf{z}^{c}$ are associated with one another as presented in Chapter 6.

$$\mathbf{Z}^{\delta} = \begin{bmatrix} z_{11}^{\delta} & z_{12}^{\delta} & \cdots & z_{1d}^{\delta} \\ z_{21}^{\delta} & z_{22}^{\delta} & \cdots & z_{2d}^{\delta} \\ \cdot & \cdot & \cdot & \cdot \\ \cdot & \cdot & \cdot & \cdot \\ \cdot & \cdot & \cdot & \cdot \\ z_{m1}^{\delta} & z_{m2}^{\delta} & \cdots & z_{md}^{\delta} \end{bmatrix} \mathbf{Z}^{\gamma} = \begin{bmatrix} z_{11}^{\gamma} & z_{12}^{\gamma} & \cdots & z_{1g}^{\gamma} \\ z_{21}^{\gamma} & z_{22}^{\gamma} & \cdots & z_{2g}^{\gamma} \\ \cdot & \cdot & \cdot & \cdot \\ \cdot & \cdot & \cdot & \cdot \\ \cdot & \cdot & \cdot & \cdot \\ z_{m1}^{\gamma} & z_{m2}^{\gamma} & \cdots & z_{mg}^{\gamma} \end{bmatrix} \mathbf{Z}^{c} = \begin{bmatrix} z_{11}^{c} & z_{12}^{c} & \cdots & z_{1q}^{c} \\ z_{21}^{c} & z_{22}^{c} & \cdots & z_{2q}^{c} \\ \cdot & \cdot & \cdot & \cdot \\ \cdot & \cdot & \cdot & \cdot \\ \cdot & \cdot & \cdot & \cdot \\ z_{m1}^{c} & z_{m2}^{c} & \cdots & z_{mq}^{c} \end{bmatrix} \tag{5.3}$$

where:

d, g, and q is the number of the corresponding operational risks (each column of the matrices is defined by a KRI) that refers to risk causes, events and consequences

m is the number of the operations influenced by the risk under study (i.e. affected operations)

The analysis of such matrices is used to further understand and manage the risks in operations and align them to performance and business objectives. This analysis must define the degree and frequency with which certain causes, events, and consequences are associated with one another. The degree of the matrix dimensions indicates the complexity of the risk management process. Their analysis can be achieved using advanced mathematical approaches, as explained in subsequent chapters of this book.

Losses from Causes, Events, and Consequences

According to the Basel Committee, all financial organizations qualified to use the AMA are expected to include all operational risk losses in a database matrix as well as the losses that are initiated from them in a database called a "loss event database" and have clear policies implemented for the management of these risks.[3] A key issue in the area of operational risk management, as well as in the development of regulatory capital requirements, is the collection and analysis of losses. Such data collection is important for the assessment of operational risks. There is also increasing recognition among financial organizations and supervisors that the sharing of loss data, based on consistent definitions and metrics, is necessary to arrive at a comprehensive assessment of operational risks.

A well-constructed loss event database is one of the fundamental elements in designing efficient operational risk management systems. A loss event database includes all the losses that are initiated from the causes of risks, risk events, and consequences of risks. Note that any causes, events, and consequences may result in financial losses. The definition of all possible causes–events–consequences and the relations between them are the key elements for designing an effective loss event database.

It is important to note that:

- A cause or causes of risks results in one or more unexpected or adverse events to processes, people, or systems.
- An event(s) results in one or more consequences and may generate new causes of risks.
- A consequence(s) refers to business impacts that have different degree and level of significance (from minor to catastrophic) and may generate new causes of operational risk(s).

Thus, any cause may result in a series of events, any consequence may result from many events, and any event may have multiple causes or consequences. One challenge is to identify when, what, and how the causes, events, and consequences are initiated. More important is to identify the degree of correlations between causes, events, and consequences. This will help to measure and to understand their value of significance and will form the basis for defining the actual probability and impact of their resulting losses as well as for designing an optimal operational risk management system. The general relation between causes, events, and consequences is defined in the arrows, illustrated in Figure 5.3.

For example, an event might be a misentered trading. The causes might be a system problem, lack of employee's training, or even an employee's fatigue or deception. Consequences might include a market loss, fees paid to counterparty, a lawsuit, or damage to the organization's reputation. Another example could be an operational loss event such as a late payment, that could be caused by a staff error, late confirmation, or telecommunications failure, as seen in Figure 5.4. Consequences of this event might include a lawsuit or damage to the organization's reputation that usually translates into business impact, normally in financial terms such as penalties, a market loss, and so forth.

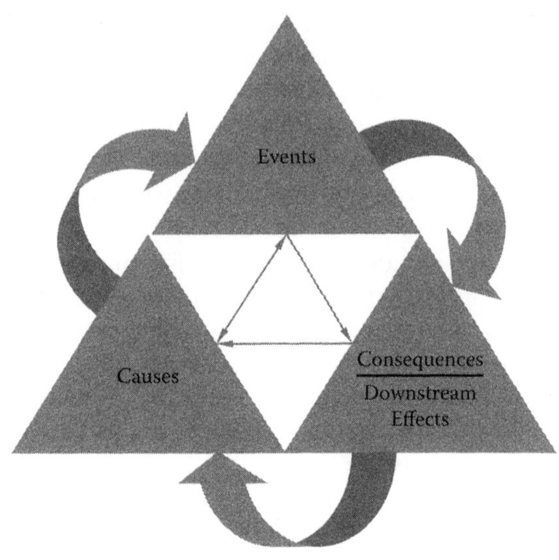

Figure 5.3 Relations between causes of risks, risk events, and consequences/downstream effects.

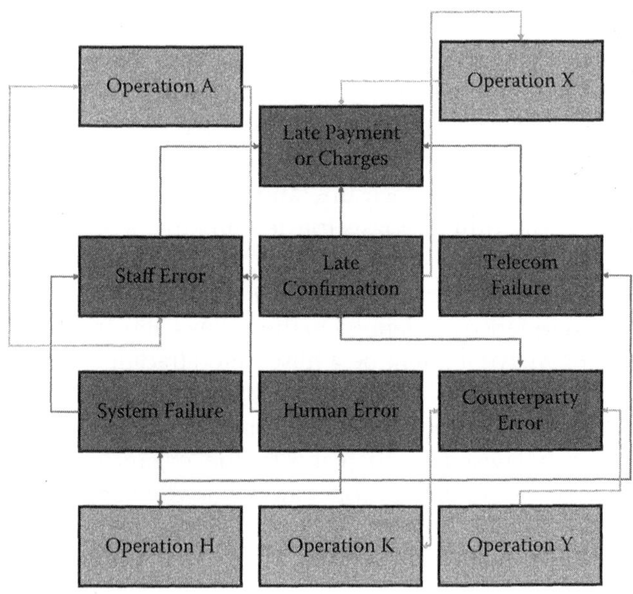

Figure 5.4 Causes of a late payment.

Operational Risk Modeling

The identification analysis discussed in the previous sections is used as the basis for designing the model that defines the operational risks behavior as well as the model that defines the "health" level of the affected operations. The resulting models are used in the monitoring analysis, in the evaluation process, the optimization and risk profiling, and, in general, almost in every process for designing efficient operational risk management systems. The modeling steps are based on correlation analysis (as explained in subsequent sections) for both operational risks and their affected operations. Their significance value is based on this correlation analysis.

Operational risk indicators complement performance tracking and gauge potential negative outcome, weaving a direct relationship between key risk and performance indicators. Utilizing the measurement of one indicator on its own can give misleading or biased information. Key indicators that define and measure risks in operations are related to each other. This relational combination of measurement offers information capture, retrieval, and interpretation to give a clearer picture of the organization's performance and risks levels. Therefore, a need to understand these relationships is very significant. From a modeling of risks and performance standpoint, the goal is to find correlations between specific risks and performance indicators and corresponding rates of loss events, i.e., how many times the same event occurs over a period of time. On the other hand, viewing the identification of modeling from a different corner, the affected operations can be modeled based on their operational risks. In this case the analysis of correlations between operations is defined in terms of their common operational risk values. For instance, if two operations are affected by three common risks, the degree of correlation between the operations under study is defined by considering the relationships between the three risks.

Efficient Operational Risk Modeling through Correlation Analysis

In this book, in an approach for designing optimal operational risk management system, correlation analysis plays a fundamental role in most steps of the risk pyramid, starting primarily with the modeling phase. The dependencies and interactions among risks within operations are considered as fundamental for designing efficient risk management systems. Thus, correlation analysis is used in the analysis for identifying how the operational risk implications are aligned to business processes, people,

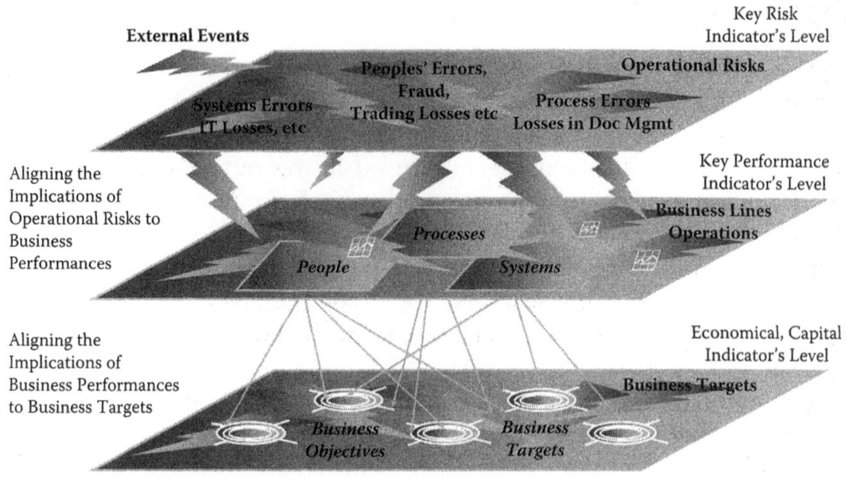

Figure 5.5 Aligning risks to operations and business targets and objectives.

and systems performances within all business lines. In addition, there is a need to align operational risks to strategic business targets and objectives, as illustrated in Figure 5.5. Furthermore, operational risk modeling is used in the analysis of how to calculate the most economical impact of operational risk management.

In this analysis the degree (in defined scale) and type (general, positive, and negative) of relations and correlations are defined between:

- Each operational risk with itself (in depth of time)
- Each operational risk with each other's risks
- Each operational risk with all other risks
- Each operational risk with each affected operation within its business lines
- Each operational risk with all affected operations within its business lines
- Each operational risk with a set (or "beta") risk (internal or external)
- Each affected operation with itself (in depth of time)
- Each affected operation with internal or external business operational activities
- Each affected operation with each other's operations
- Each affected operation with all operations
- Each affected operation with particular set (or "beta") referring to internal or external business operational activities
- Each operation with each or all objectives and economical target values

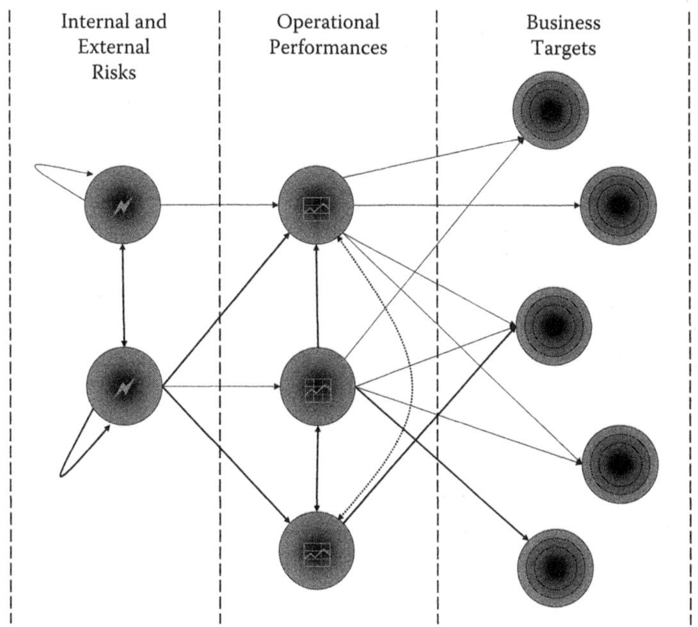

Figure 5.6 Graphical representation of the correlation between internal risks, operational performances, business targets, and objectives.

Figure 5.6 represents graphically the correlation between internal risks, affected operational activities within the business lines, as well as with their alignment to business targets and objectives. The degree and type of the above correlations are defined by considering all those homogeneous and inhomogeneous parameters that characterize the risks, operational performances, business objectives, and economical/financial target values. The problem becomes complicated because a large number of operational risks, business targets, and complex operations must be considered.

The number of risks in operations is defined by Equation 5.4:

$$R_O = \sum_{i=1}^{b} \sum_{j=1}^{\lambda} O_{i,j} \tag{5.4}$$

and the number of business targets and objectives that are influenced by risks in operations is defined by Equation 5.5:

$$R_T = \sum_{i=1}^{b} \sum_{j=1}^{\lambda} \sum_{k=1}^{\sigma} O_{i,j} \cdot T_{j,k} \tag{5.5}$$

where

R_O = Number of risks in operations O within all business lines
b = Number of business lines
λ = Number of the operations that are linked to the risks
R_T = Number of risks that are influencing the business targets
T = Business targets
σ = Number of targets linked to the operations

A complex multidimensional correlation analysis is applied in the identification process.

In the design of the framework of the operational risk management, the models referring to the operational risks and the affected operations are defined by the correlations matrix as in Equation 5.6:

$$OpRisks = \begin{bmatrix} cor(\mathbf{z}_1\mathbf{z}_1) & cor(\mathbf{z}_1\mathbf{z}_2) & \cdots & cor(\mathbf{z}_1\mathbf{z}_r) \\ cor(\mathbf{z}_2\mathbf{z}_1) & cor(\mathbf{z}_2\mathbf{z}_2) & \cdots & cor(\mathbf{z}_2\mathbf{z}_r) \\ \cdots & \cdots & \cdots & \cdots \\ cor(\mathbf{z}_r\mathbf{z}_1) & cor(\mathbf{z}_r\mathbf{z}_2) & \cdots & cor(\mathbf{z}_r\mathbf{z}_r) \end{bmatrix} \tag{5.6}$$

where *cor* defines the correlations between the operational risks or affected operations according to the model under study, and r is the number of operational risks or affected operations.

Figure 5.7 and Figure 5.8 illustrate surface representations for both operational risks and affected operations' models, respectively. The surface is constructed based on the correlation interaction analysis between operational risks and affected operations accordingly. Note that as illustrated in Figure 5.8, there is a correlation to a certain degree between operational activities referring to processes, people, and systems. Such representations show the degree of nonlinearity that exists. High peaks on the surface indicate a high degree of correlation, and vice versa.

By analyzing the value of the above correlations, any dynamic changes in operational risks and performance are noted as they happen. Using these correlation models, referring to operations, banking organizations are able to identify how operations are linked in terms of their risks. Operational risk correlation models are used to identify how operational risks are linked through the affected operations. This analysis is implemented extensively, in the monitoring and evaluation processes.

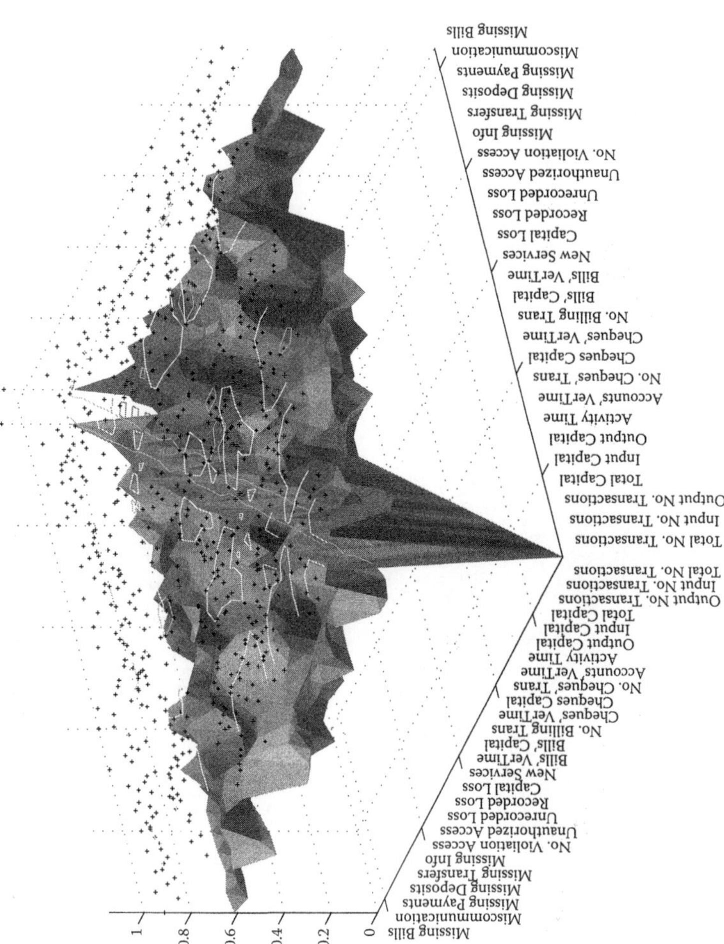

Figure 5.7 Surface illustration of operational risks in a three-dimensional correlation model. The contour and the dot clusters represent the "clouds" and "storms" initiated by these risks.

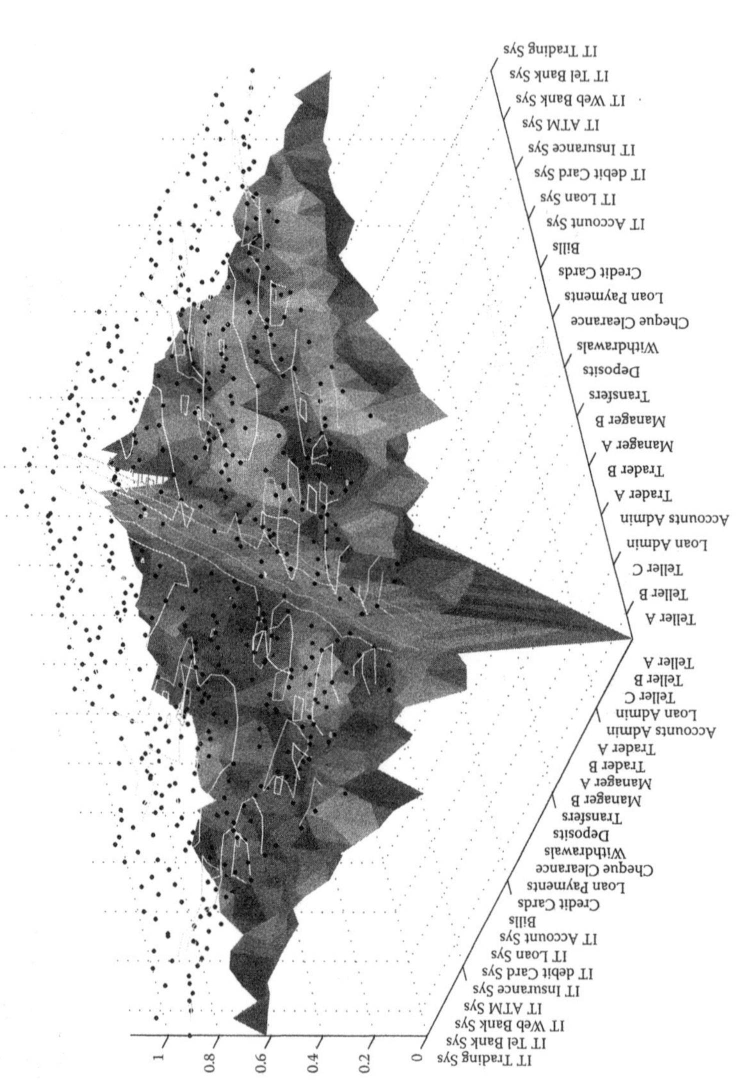

Figure 5.8 Surface illustration of affected operations in a three-dimensional correlation model. The contour and the dot clusters above the operational surfaces represent the "clouds" and "storms" in the affected operations.

Operational Risk Monitoring

Banking organizations have a more formal way of monitoring operational risks than they have for formally measuring operational risks. Most of these organizations monitor operational performances such as volume, turnover, settlement fails, delays, and errors. They develop online systems that record and monitor statistical indices. It is significantly important for banking organizations to be able to analyze the collected information to make effective decisions. Advanced systems need to accommodate and analyze the measurements and reporting of operational risks. Directors and operational risk managers, to fulfill their monitoring managerial responsibilities, must be assisted with systems for continual flow of combined information, in priority order of significance and a description of the nature and causes of the losses. Such systems must include management action plans to address areas of performance variations and emergence of operational risks, as defined in the fourth section of this book referring to operational risk management and control. To design such systems, all information related to risks and performances in operations needs to form the input of a stochastic monitoring system. These systems are able to combine and analyze the key information and measure the degree of correlation and significance for each operational risk. The results of the monitoring analyses should be presented using illustrations that give clear pictures of the current status and future trends for both operational risks and affected operations.

Efficient Operational Risks Monitoring through Correlation Analysis

Monitoring is one of the most difficult processes in operational risk management because there are large numbers of both operational risks and affected operations where the trend in operational risks should be indicated and justified at any requested time. By understanding the interrelations between the operational risks and between the affected operations, it is easier to drill down and around to discover underlying causes of problems, variances, alarms, noncompliance, and unsatisfactory trends. As discussed in the previous section, an operational risk such as "late payment" can be caused by different operational actions (such as staff error, late confirmation, or a telecommunications failure), which in turn have their routes in many underlying operational actions. The monitoring system should be employed to alert supervisors about "problematic areas" before they become threatening or even catastrophic. An efficient operational risk management system that takes into account the relation between operational risks and the use of correlation analysis is most appropriate to aid in this matter. Mapping the topography and the correlations between both operational risks and affected operations gives a clear picture of their status, as illustrated in the following subsections.

Mapping the Operational and Operational Risks Topography

One of the first steps in the process of designing monitoring operational risks systems is to get a "picture" of the operations that are at risk and how significant these risks are. In financial organizations, the number of operations is rather substantial and even larger is the number of operational risks that influence them. It is, therefore, essential and valuable when designing risk monitoring systems to represent the affected operations and operational risks on a single graph. Such visual representation includes all levels of operational risks within all operations, giving an overview picture of the "topography" of risks in operations. Figure 5.9 and Figure 5.10 illustrate such topographies of some of the operations and their risks

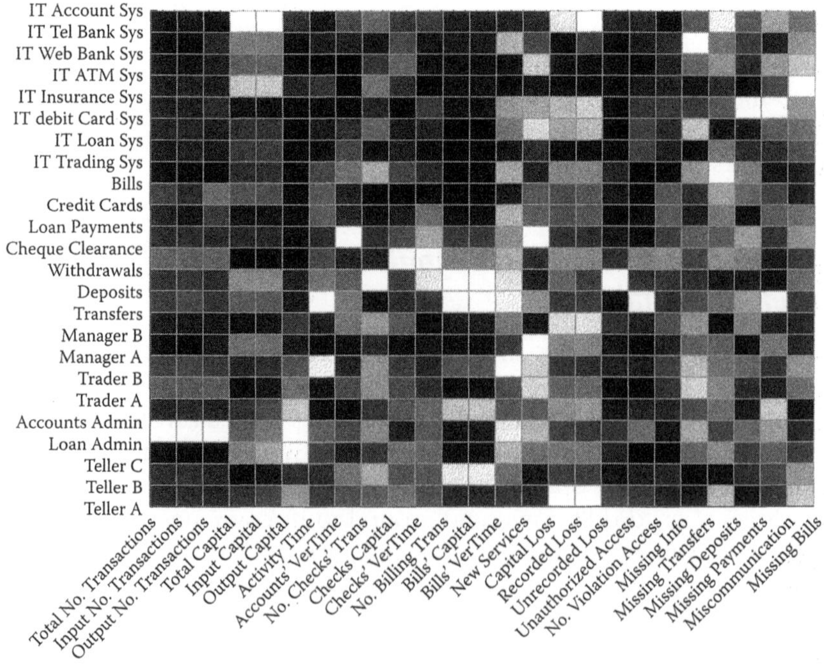

Figure 5.9 Pattern "topographic" mapping of risks and operations that illustrate their relations. Dark areas indicate high correlations and light areas indicate low correlations.

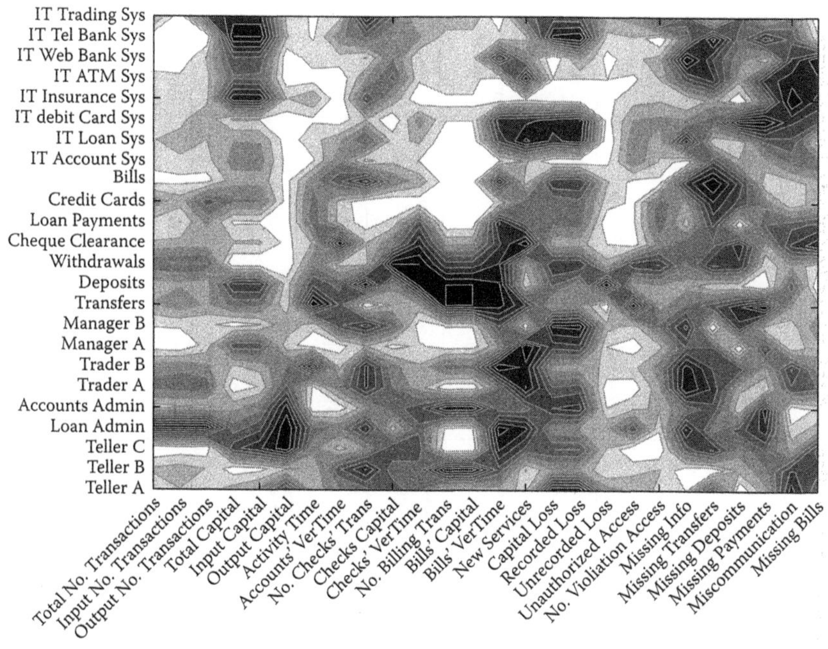

Figure 5.10 Contour "topographic" mapping of risks and operations. The contour indicates the relational area between risks and their associated operations.

defined in Table 5.4. There are two different ways of representing such mapping topographies:

1. Pattern topography
2. Contour topography

In both pattern and contour topography, illustrated in Figure 5.9 and Figure 5.10, respectively, the operations and risks are portrayed in graphs of two axes. The pallet in the gray scale defines the correlations between the operational risks and their affected operations. Dark-gray tones represent high correlations, whereas light-gray tones indicate lower correlation values. These values are extracted from the measurement values of key performance and risk indicators that are grouped, labeled, and stored in the matrix referring to risk measurement. Note that, as discussed in the previous section on the process for constructing the "matrix of measurements," the columns and rows of the matrix should be categorized according to the group key indicators and operations. This group can be defined in relation to the causes, events, and consequences when referring to operational risks. The group is defined in relation to processes, people, and systems when referring to operations. Note also that the risk indicators

Table 5.4 Identification of Key Risk Indicators (referring to their characteristics in terms of performance variation, transfer functions, type of risks, loss and impact)

Business Area	*Operation's Code*	*Operational Activity*	*KRI Code*	*KRI Description Variations on …*	*Function of KRI*	*Risk Referring to …*	*Type of Risk on …*	*Type of Risk Loss*	*Possible Impact to …*
Back and front office in banking branches	OA-BFT-01	Transactions/ capital within a banking branch	KRI-OA-01-AC-1	Transfers per period* of time per teller*	F(1) = d((NoTR)/Per/TL)	"""IN-OUT"" traffic variation"	People's performance	Risk on loss transfers	Bank — customer
			KRI-OA-01-AC-2	Deposits per period of time per teller	F(2) = d((NoDP)/Per/TL)	" ""IN"" traffic variation"	People's performance	Risk on loss deposits	Customer
			KRI-OA-01-AC-3	Withdrawals per period of time per teller	F(3) = d((NoWD)/Per/TL)	"""OUT"" traffic variation"	People's performance	Risk on loss withdrawals	Bank
			KRI-OA-01-AC-4	Transfers' capital per period of time per teller	F(4) = d(TCap/Per/TL)	"Variation for ""IN-OUT"" capital transfer"	People's performance	Risk on capital loss	Bank — customer
			KRI-OA-01-AC-5	Deposit's capital per period of time per teller	F(5) = d(DCap/Per/TL)	"Variation of ""IN"" capital transfer"	People's performance	Risk on capital loss	Customer
			KRI-OA-01-AC-6	Withdrawal's capital per period of time per teller	F(6) = d(WCap/Per/TL)	"Variation for ""OUT"" capital transfer"	People's performance	Risk on capital loss	Bank
			KRI-OA-01-AC-7	Time spent for each transfer-deposit-withdrawal	F(7) = Time(TDW)	Variation of time spent for each transfer-deposit-withdrawal	People's activity time distribution/ system's performance	Risk on time and capital loss	Bank — customer
	OA-BFT-02	Capital transactions/ customer	KRI-OA-02-AC-1	Capital transfers' per customer per period of time per teller	F(8) = d(TCap/Cstmr/ Per/TL)	"Variation of traffic for each customer's ""IN-OUT"" capital transfers"	People's performance	Risk on customer's or bank's capital loss	Bank — customer
			KRI-OA-02-AC-2	Capital deposits per customer per period of time per teller	F(9) = d(DCap/Cstmr/ Per/TL)	Variation of traffic for each customers' deposits capital transfers	People's performance	Risk on bank's capital loss	Customer

			KRI-OA-02-AC-3	Withdrawal's capital per customer per period of time per teller	F(10) = d(WCap/Cstmr/Per/TL)	Variation for each customer's withdrawals	People's performance	Risk on customer's capital loss	Bank
			KRI-OA-02-AC-4	Transfers' capital per customer's account* per period of time per teller	F(11) = d(Cap/CstmrAcnt/Per/TL)	Variation within different accounts per customer managed by each teller	"People, process, and systems performance"	Risk on customer's capital loss	Bank — customer
			KRI-OA-02-AC-5	Time spent for account ID verification for transfers-deposits-withdrawals per capital per customer per period of time per teller	F(12) = d(Vtime/TDW_Cap/Cstmr/Per/TL)	Customer's account id verification	People and systems performance	Risk on customer's or bank's capital loss	Bank — customer
	OA-BFT-03	Cheque transactions	KRI-OA-03-AC-1	Amount of checks received per period per teller	F(13) = d(CHK)/Per/TL	Checks clearance management	People's performance	Risk on customers' or bank's capital loss	Bank — customer
			KRI-OA-03-AC-2	Checks' capital received per period per teller	F(14) = d(CapitalCHK)/Per/TL	Capital checks clearance management	People — process performances	Risk on customers' or bank's capital loss	Bank — customer
			KRI-OA-03-AC-3	Checks' capital received per customer per period per teller	F(15) = d(CapitalCHK)/Cstmr/Per/TL	Customer's checks capital Management	People's performance	Risk on particular customer's or bank's capital loss	Bank — customer

Table 5.4 (continued) Identification of Key Risk Indicators (referring to their characteristics in terms of performance variation, transfer functions, type of risks, loss and impact)

Business Area	*Operation's Code*	*Operational Activity*	*KRI Code*	*KRI Description Variations on …*	*Function of KRI*	*Risk Referring to ..*	*Type of Risk on …*	*Type of Risk Loss*	*Possible Impact to …*
			KRI-OA-03-AC-4	Verification time per check per capital per customer per period per teller	F(16) = d(VTimeCHK)/Captl/Cstmr/Per/TL	Cheques' verification	People's performance	Risk on customer's or bank's capital loss	Bank — customer
	OA-BFT-04	Payment transactions	KRI-OA-04-AC-1	Amount of bills received per customer per period per teller	F(17) = d(BLs)/Per/TL	Payment management	Account process management	Risk on customers' or bank's capital loss	Bank — customer
			KRI-OA-04-AC-2	Bills/payments capital per customer per period per teller	F(18) = d(CaptlBLs)/Cstmr/Per/TL	Capital payment management	People's performance	Risk on customer's or bank's capital loss	Bank — customer
			KRI-OA-04-AC-3	Verification time per bill/payment per capital per customer per period per teller	F(21) = d(VTimeBill)/Captl/Cstmr/Per/TL	Billing authenticity	Account management process performance	Risk on customer's or bank's capital loss	Bank — customer
	OA-BFT-05	Customers' activities	KRI-OA-05-AC-1	Activity rate for customers per time period	F(22) = d(IC)/Per	Activity customers traffic	Customer management	Risk on customer's or bank's capital loss	Bank — customer
			KRI-OA-05-AC-2	Rate of new accounts and customers per time period per number of new services	F(23) = d(NA_C)/Per/No(Serv)	New customers accounts	"Customer management — process, systems performance"	Risk on customer's or bank's capital loss	Bank — customer
			KRI-OA-05-AC-3	New customers per time period per number of services per new accounts	F(24) = d(C)/D/No(Serv)/N_Ac	New services and accounts	"Service management — process, systems performance"	Risk on customer's or bank's capital loss	Bank — customer

Source: O_4B^5

define the columns and the operations are defined in the rows of the above matrix. The values of the measurements should be normalized so they can easily be used in the risk correlation and comparative analysis. In operational risk management, all risks that stem from different sources referring to people, system, processes, or external events should use the same measuring scale, or data should be normalized. Note that data normalization is discussed later in this book.

In the topographical representations illustrated in Figures 5.9 and 5.10, the measurements of the operational risks as well as business operations are grouped and sorted in the x and y axes, respectively. In such representations, there is a clear picture of the connections between the operations and their risks. In these figures, the operations refer to employee operations (i.e., tellers, managers, etc.), to processes (i.e., billing, transfers, withdrawals, etc.), as well as systems operations. The contours indicate the relational areas between the operational risks measured through KRIs and the affected operations under study. For instance, in both figures, it can be seen that there is a dark patch between the affected operations referring to withdrawal, deposit, and transfers with the operational risks referring to capital, transfer, and verification time of bills. This means that there is a high degree of correlation between these affected operations and operational risks.

Both pattern and contour topographic maps are used in monitoring systems and can give a good indication as to how the risks are distributed within the operations. With this monitoring representation, the areas or contours are at certain times changing quite frequently. The modification of these contours indicates the trend of the operational risks under study.

It is very effective to build such "monitoring windows" to be used by the technical staffs involved in daily operational risk management process. They are usually monitoring experts who should be also involved in further analysis of the design process of the risk management system. Monitoring systems are used as high-level visual radars, where an observation can be used as a basis of an alarm signaling system. Moreover, in case of presetting specific and well-defined operational risks, alarms may also ring when a threshold is exceeded. It is important to use these monitoring aspects to view the very top level and observe the general effect on the operations and the degree of operational risks. Additionally, it may be used to zoom in and view the details of the affected operations and operational risks.

Thresholds in Monitoring Systems

Financial organizations must establish appropriate operational risk data thresholds that, when combined with the appropriate KRIs, can provide early warnings of increased levels of operational risks of future losses. When thresholds are directly linked to these indicators, an effective monitoring process can help identify key operational risks in a transparent manner and enable the financial organization to act on these risks appropriately. Thresholds and limits typically tied to risk indicators must not be set arbitrarily. In setting threshold levels, it is important to know the significant levels of the risks in operations and their relation to other operational risks. A monitoring and reporting alarm system should provide instant warning signals if combinations of the operational risk thresholds are exceeded. Such systems should be used by management and boards of directors who are mainly responsible for monitoring and managing operational risks and must be continually reacting to changes in the operational risk environment. Thresholds play vital roles and are used extensively in contingency planning processes, which are discussed in Part IV of this book.

Mapping the Correlations between the Operations and Risks

In large organizations, operations are linked to each other with different degrees. Therefore, the operational risks are also related in terms of how they influence the operations. Thus, in designing operational risk monitoring systems, it is valuable to know and have the ability to view the correlations between:

- The operational risks
- The affected operations

In the first case, the multidimensional correlation analysis defines the degree of correlation between the operational risks by considering their actual values, all the links between their operations, as well as their level of significance in each of the affected operations. Accordingly, in the second case, the correlations between all affected operations are defined based on their actual values, all the links between their associated risks, as well as the levels of significance in each of the operational risks that affects each operation. This representation and analysis was initiated because in the operational risk analysis there is a need to know:

- Which operational risks appear together
- Which operations are affected in parallel and to a similar degree
- What the relative degree (general, positive, or negative) is for both operational risks and their affected operations

The level of correlations between operational risks is defined in terms of how much they influence the operations. In many cases, when an operational risk occurs in one or more operations, some other operational risks may also arise. For example, when a risk of external hacking for unauthorized trading appears, it is important to know when and what other risks are also initiated, directly or indirectly, in the functionality of the processes, people, or systems. Note that the generated risks influence the operations to different degrees.

In operational risk monitoring analysis, the values of the correlations between operations are defined in terms of their risk effects. When such correlations exist, it means that, when an operation within a banking organization is affected by internal or external operational risks, some other operations are also affected. However, the level of effect varies. For instance, a major system failure in a particular IT operation means that there is an automatic malfunction in a number of processes and operations.

One of the main observations in monitoring operational risks is the correlations between the operations and their associated risks. In monitoring analysis, three main types of correlations between operations and risks need to be identified and observed:

1. The "general" one, G_{cor}, considers both positive and negative correlations.
2. The "positive" one, P_{cor}, considers only the correlations with similar directional tendency.
3. The "negative" one, N_{cor}, considers only the correlations with dissimilar directional tendency.

The general degree of correlation indicates the overall relational picture between the operations or between the risks. The positive degree of correlation indicates the tendency for two or more operations to have similar effects or the operational risks to appear simultaneously. The negative degree of correlation indicates an opposite tendency. The mapping and monitoring of all the types of the above correlations are needed.

In Figure 5.11, the bar charts represent the degree of correlations between the operational risks, which refers to "failures in new services," with all other operational risks. This means that when this particular operational risk appears, the other related operational risks will be affected to a certain degree (positively or negatively). By examining this figure, it can be seen that the highest degree of correlation that "failures in new services" has with the operational risk referring to "amount of missing information." In this case, this means that the risk of missing information is the main culprit for failures of new services. Note that the first bar indicates the degree of general correlation, and the second and third bars, the degree of positive and negative correlations, respectively. Figure 5.12 illustrates the degrees of correlation between the operational risk that

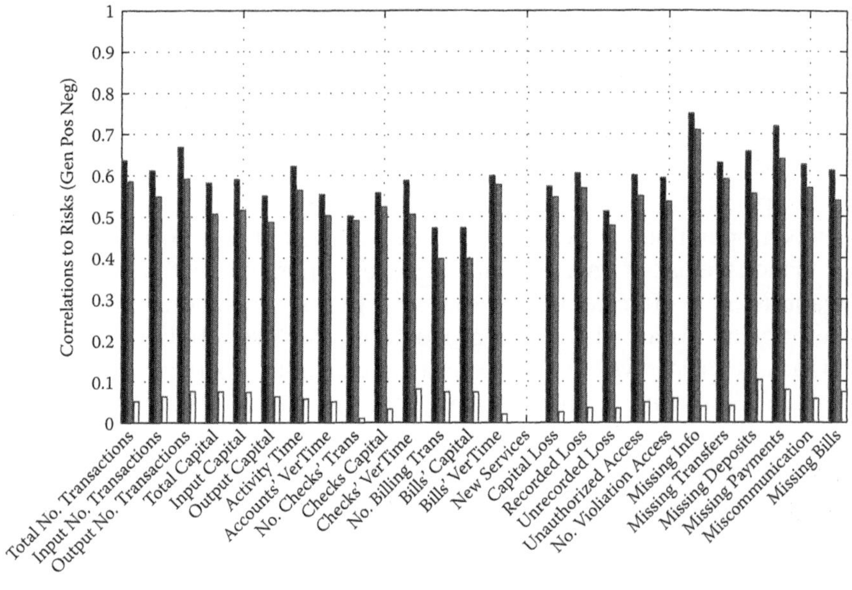

Figure 5.11 Bar chart representing the degree of correlations between the operational risk referring to "failures in new services" with all other operational risks; the first bar indicates the general, the second the positive, and the third the negative correlations.

refers to "unauthorized access" and the rest of the operational risks. In this case study, the highest degree of correlation appears in the risks referring to "transactions," "unrecorded loss," and "violation access." This means that "unauthorized access" is strongly related to "transactions," "unrecorded loss," and "violation access." So if there are many unauthorized accesses, the risk managers should also investigate the amount of transactions, the amount of unrecorded loss, and the number of times there was a violation access and vice versa.

In Figure 5.13, the bar chart represents the degree of correlation between the affected operations referring to "capital transfer process" with all the other affected operations. In this case the highest correlation appears with operations that refer to "Trader B" and the lowest with the "IT systems" related to insurance accounts. In this case, this means that it is human activities that cause operational risks in the "capital transfer process," rather than IT systems.

Moreover, the correlations between the affected "IT systems" referring to insurance accounts are correlated with all the other operations to different degrees, as illustrated in Figure 5.14. It can be seen that IT systems are mostly correlated with "credit cards" and "ATM" operations.

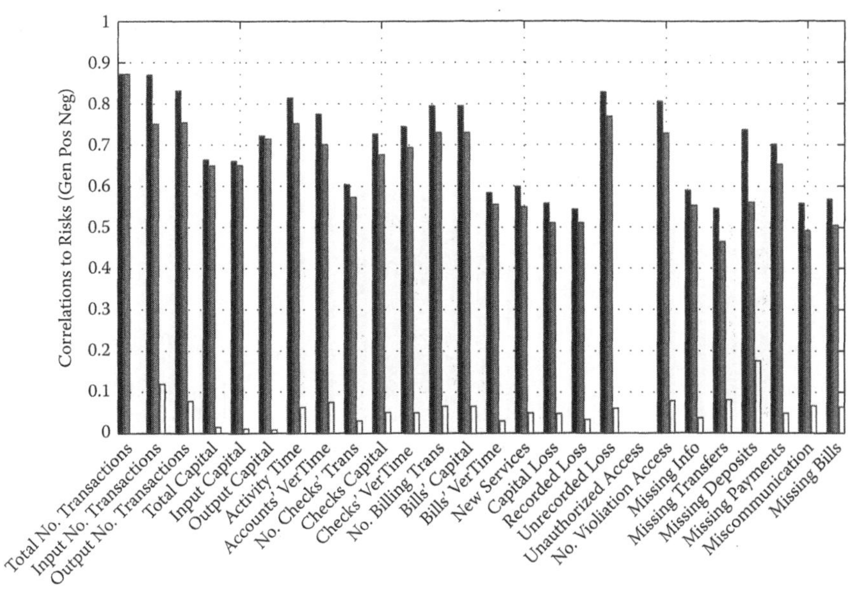

Figure 5.12 Bar chart representing correlations between the operational risk of "unauthorized access" and the other operational risks.

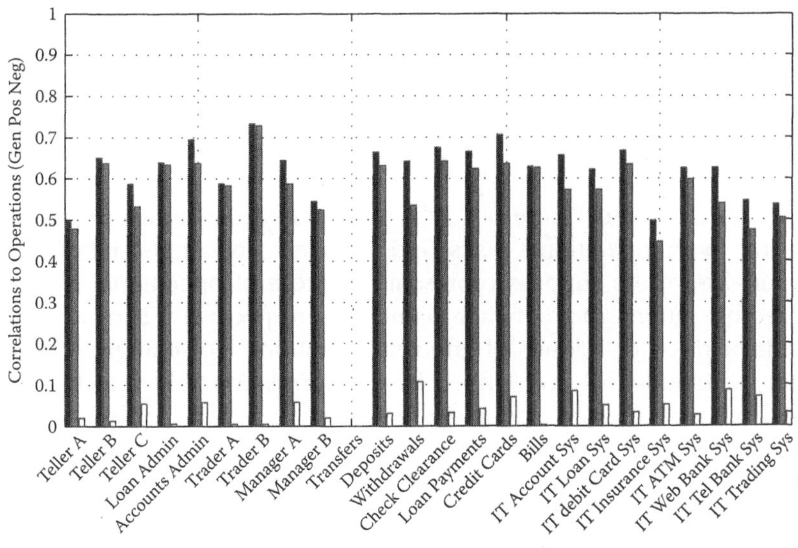

Figure 5.13 Bar chart that defines the correlation between "capital transfers" and all the other affected operations.

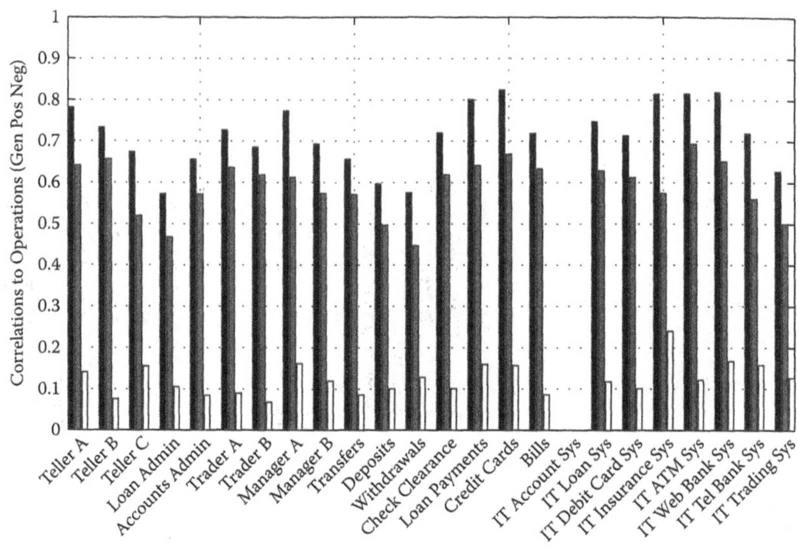

Figure 5.14 Bar chart that defines the correlation between "IT accounting system" and the affected operations.

Moreover, Figure 5.15 and Figure 5.16 illustrate the cartographic topography of the correlations between operational risks using their KRIs, and between the affected operations respectively, using a "topographic" mapping for all types of correlations mentioned earlier. These illustrations indicate the correlation areas and can be useful for monitoring and evaluating the significant values, in terms of interactions, for both operations and risk groups. The different gray scale indicates the different correlation levels (i.e., dark "high" correlation and light "low" correlation).

In Figure 5.7 and Figure 5.8, which illustrated the surface representations for both operational risks and affected operations' models, the contours above the surfaces represent the areas of operational risks and affected operations above their conjunctions, respectively. They are called "clouds of risks" or "clouds of affected operations" accordingly. The dots within the clouds that are defined by the correlation values of the operational risks or affected operations are clusters that are called "storms." This geographical and meteorological representation facilitates in monitoring large amounts of operational risks and affected operations by viewing their risk status in a single figure.

All of the above representations play a vital role in viewing the smaller as well as the larger picture of the operational risks and affected operations. The definition and understanding of correlation is the basis for constructing an efficient operational risk monitoring system. It also plays a vital role

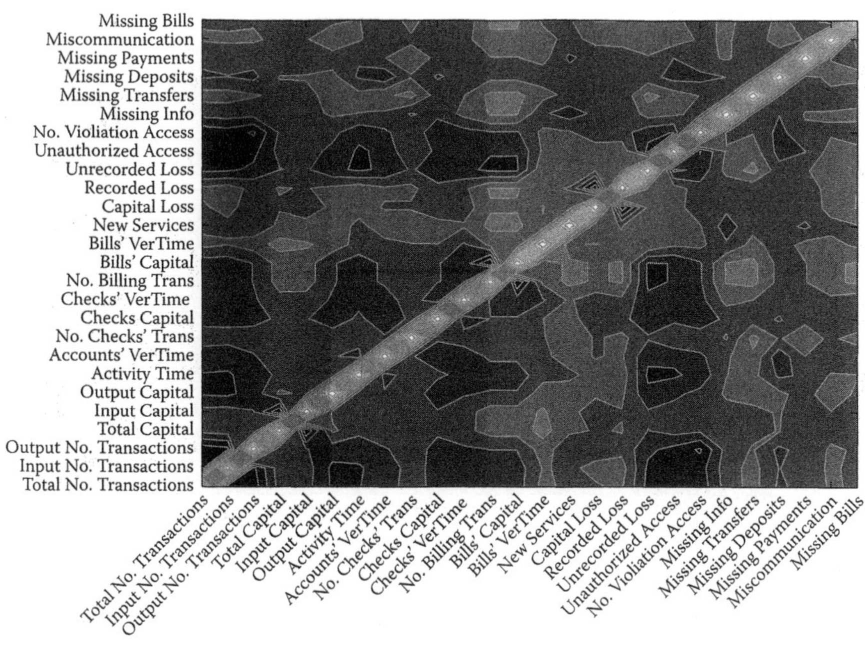

Figure 5.15 "Topographic" mapping representations for monitoring the correlations between the operational risks. Different gray colors indicate different levels of correlation. Dark gray means a high level of correlations and light gray means a low level of correlation.

in constructing the operational risk evaluation system, as discussed in the next chapter.

Essential Guides for Operational Risk Monitoring Management

In operational risks management frameworks, it is essential to have a well-established monitoring management system. In banking organizations, senior management should establish a program to:

- Monitor both the qualitative and quantitative assessments of the exposure to all types of operational risk faced by the organization.
- Assess the quality and appropriateness of mitigating actions, including the extent to which identifiable operational risks can be transferred outside the organization.
- Ensure that adequate controls and systems are in place to identify and address problems before they become major concerns.

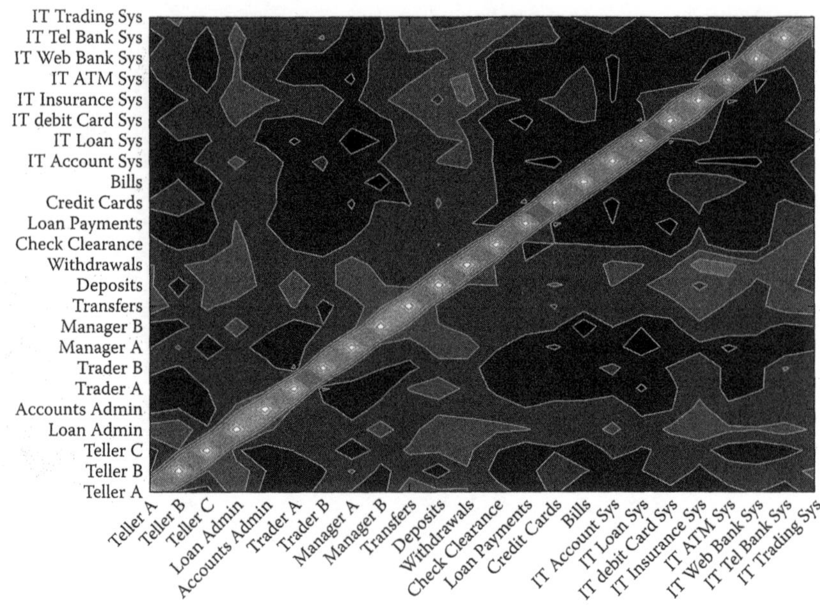

Figure 5.16 "Topographic" mapping representations for monitoring the correlations between the affected operations. Different gray colors indicate different levels of correlation.

Monitoring systems are used to determine the operational risk's severity level and thus monitor the operational risk profile on an ongoing basis.

In the framework of operational risk monitoring systems, it is essential that:

- Responsibility for the monitoring and controlling of operational risk should follow the same type of organizational structure that has been adopted for other risks, including market and credit risk.
- Senior management ensures that an agreed definition of operational risk together with a mechanism for monitoring, alerting, and reporting is designed and implemented.
- This mechanism should be appropriate to the scale of operational risks and activities undertaken by the organization.

The periodic review of operational risks and affected performances should be used as a basis to alert financial organizations and to indicate potential risk concerns. Regular monitoring activities can offer the advantage of quickly detecting and correcting deficiencies in the policies, processes, and procedures for optimizing and managing operational risks. The results of these monitoring activities should be included in regular management and board reports. A strong operational risk measurement and monitoring system gives detailed information to senior management for better understanding and decision making. Senior management should establish a program to monitor both the qualitative and quantitative exposure to all types of operational risk faced by the organization.

Summary

Operational risk identification is the first element of the assessment phase in the process of designing efficient operational risk management systems. During the identification step, operational risk mapping and operations process mapping are used to define the general inputs and outputs and linkage between the operational risks and the operations. The mapping is used for the purpose of identifying key operations and key performance and risks indicators, together with key business objectives. The influences on operational performances and by operational risks are initially defined qualitatively; however, they have also to be defined quantitatively to allow for their measurement. The latter is achieved by using key performance and risk indicators, which were discussed extensively in this chapter, with examples of KRIs given. The definition of these indicators relies on the parameters that are used to measure the operations and risks under study. Operations together with their associated risks construct the operational risk matrix.

Key performance indicators are used to define and extract the information data related to operational risks and undesirable performances. These are then utilized to complete the matrix of risk measurements. Based on the correlation analysis of the above information, the models referring to both operational risks and affected operations are defined. Three types of data that refer to causes, events, and consequences are used to define these models. Modeling and monitoring the operational risks and affected operations give an outlined view that illustrates the banking organization's current state in terms of risk hazards. The models of the operational risks as well as of the affected operations are defined through correlation analysis. Managers of operational risks must be able to have a clear view of how the affected operations are linked to one another in terms of risks. They must also know how the operational risks are related to one another and what their level of exposure within the business lines is. They also need to know the possible degree of correlation with the other operational risks under study, or in other words how the operational risks are linked to one another and to what degree. This gives a good view and understanding of what is happening, or will happen, in a short term to a longer term, when an operational risk occurs. Moreover, the correlations between the affected operations also need to be reviewed. Operational risk managers and all those who are involved in operational risk management must be able to have a good picture of how an affected operation may result or is behaving in similar ways with other affected operations. The above monitoring of both operational risks and affected operations is achieved by analyzing correlations between them, as discussed in this chapter. This facilitates a sophisticated monitoring of both operational risks and affected operations. This can be used as a "warning signal" of what is going on and what the future holds, and where actions can be taken accordingly.

The next chapter discusses the remaining main element of the assessment phase: the evaluation of operational risks.

References

1. Basel Committee on Banking Supervision, Sound Practices for the Management and Supervision of Operational Risk, February 2003.
2. One of the main criteria for using the Advanced Measurement Approach in Basel II.
3. Basel Committee on Banking Supervision, Working Paper on the Regulatory Treatment of Operational Risk, September 2001.
4. Basel Committee on Banking Supervision, International Convergence of Capital Measurement and Capital Standards: A Revised Framework, June 2004.
5. Optimisation for Business Ltd., KRI and KPI DataBases, http://www.optimisation4risk.com, 2005.

Chapter 6

Operational Risk Assessment via Evaluation Analysis

It is likely that the unlikely will happen.

—Aristotle

Introduction

This chapter refers to the evaluation analysis of operational risks and affected operations. The calculation of the degree of significance and actual values, referring to cause, events, and consequences, by applying correlation analysis is discussed comprehensively. The calculation of the significance values for the events, causes, and consequences that refer to the risks and operations under study are defined mathematically in this chapter. Moreover, the calculations of the actual values of the affected operations as well as the corresponding beta points are illustrated. The importance of having common measurement values and scales together with the use of data normalization is also discussed. Clustering analysis as a main tool in the evaluation process is presented and discussed analytically. This chapter begins with the definition of clusters for operational risk and affected operations. Clustering approaches based on fuzzy logic theory are presented to show their implementation in operational risk analysis.

An important aspect in the evaluation process is the identification of the equilibrium points referring to operational risk and affected operations. Two methods, clustering operational risk equilibrium (CORE) and clustering affected operations equilibrium (CAOE), are illustrated in this book to identify these equilibrium points. Based on the equilibrium analysis, the associated trends are also defined. Finally, and most important, the evaluation of the severity of operational risks and affected operations, is defined by applying a method called mountain surface evaluation. This method, which is based on distribution and mountain surface analysis, is discussed extensively in this chapter. Advanced graphical results are illustrated to show results of the evaluation process.

The estimation and evaluation of the economic capital reserves is also described in this chapter. Unexpected losses initiated by people, processes, and systems are characterized, together with the identification of the direct and indirect potential losses. The representation of the unexpected performances based on internal, external, and "received" potential losses is illustrated. The estimation of the economic capital reserve for operational risks, using the operational value-at-risk (VaR) and applying extreme value theory (EVT), is described in this chapter.

Figure 6.1 illustrates the main elements of this chapter.

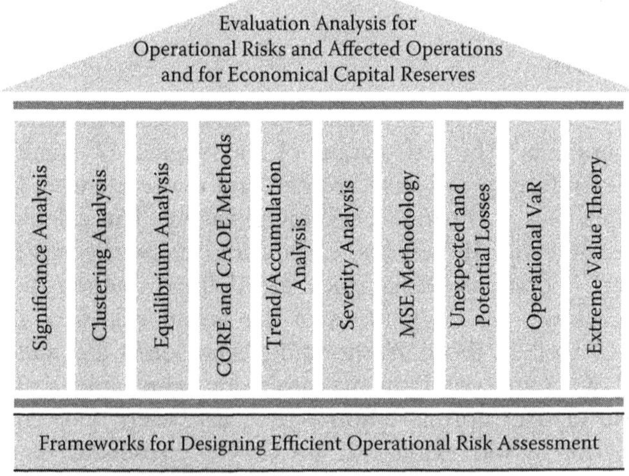

Figure 6.1 Layout of Chapter 6.

Operational Risk Evaluation Analysis

Operational risk managers and all those who are responsible for managing operational risks must be able to evaluate the current status and the trend for all operational risks and affected operations within any business line under study. In banking organizations, there are large numbers of both operational risks and operations. In most cases, however, not enough reliable information data is available to apply statistical approaches for assessing and evaluating performances and risks in operations. Moreover, historical information usually needs extensive and time-consuming analysis that gives rise to large amounts of different results and conclusions. More important, in operational risk analysis historical, information has low significance. That is because with operational risks, what has occurred in the past is not always likely to happen again. Note also that statistical analysis has great reliance on expert input, can be manipulated to show only certain aspects of the analysis, and in most cases is very much subjective to the analyst's views.

Using advanced evaluation analysis of the distributions referring to both operational risks and affected operations, their current status and future trends can be evaluated as discussed in the following sections of this chapter. Therefore, in this book the operational risk evaluation analysis is based on advanced mathematical algorithmic techniques and methodologies that combine:

- The overall significance and actual values for each of the operational risks
- Distribution of the:
  - Operational risks versus the affected operations
  - Affected operations with their associated operational risks
- The operational risk equilibrium points defined by the analysis of distributions/clusters mentioned above
- Trend analysis for:
  - Operational risks
  - Affected operations

The above aspects are approached by methodologies that are based on significance and clustering analysis. Both methodologies are used as the main elements in the evaluation process. Moreover, trend analysis is also an important phase in the evaluation process. The results are illustrated using advanced multidimensional graphical representations.

The estimation of the economical capital reserve needed to cover the potential losses resulting from operational risks is also a main aspect in the evaluation analysis. Operational value-at-risk (VaR) is used for this estimation, by implementing approaches that are based on extreme value theory (EVT), as discussed later in this chapter.

Evaluating the Degree of Significance and Actual Values of Operational Risks

The key aspects in evaluating the value of an event, a cause, or a consequence are its degrees of significance and its actual values. The term "significance" implies the importance of the events, causes, and consequences under study according to the correlation that they may have with the other events, causes, and consequences. The term "actual value" indicates the value that results from integrating the real value and the above degrees of significance for each operational risk events, causes, and consequences. The following sections describe how to evaluate the degrees of significance and actual values.

Significance Value of a Cause

A cause of a risk is a measurement value that may result from different internal or external events and from consequences of other risks. A cause always results in one or more events or consequences. In this book the calculation of the significance value of a cause (SVΔ) is approached by considering and evaluating the particular cause with:

- All other causes of risks
- All possible internal and external event(s) that generate the risk cause under study
- All possible event(s) that the cause may generate
- All possible consequences that generate the cause of operational risk under study

Thus, the mathematical function calculating the SVΔ is as shown in Equation 6.1:

$$SV\Delta = \left[cor(\Delta\Delta) + cor(\Delta\Gamma) + cor(\Delta C)\right]/3 \text{ where } SV\Delta \in \{0,..,1\} \quad (6.1)$$

where

$cor(\Delta\Delta)$ is the correlation between the cause δ under study and the rest of the n causes are as defined in Equation 6.2.

cor(ΔΓ) defined in Equation 6.3 combines the correlations between:

- The cause δ and its resulting events γ.
- The external or internal events γ that may generate the cause δ.

cor(Δ*C*), defined in Equation 6.4, is the correlation between the consequences *c* that may initiate the cause δ.

$$cor(\Delta\Delta) = \sum_{i=1}^{n-1} cor_T(\mathbf{z}^{\delta}\mathbf{z}_i^{\delta}) \Big/ (n-1) \tag{6.2}$$

$$cor(\Delta\Gamma) = \left[\sum_{j=1}^{h} cor_T(\mathbf{z}^{\delta}\mathbf{z}_j^{\gamma}) \Big/ h\right] + \left[\sum_{q=1}^{p} cor_T(\mathbf{z}^{\delta}\mathbf{z}_q^{\gamma}) \Big/ p\right] \tag{6.3}$$

$$cor(\Delta C) = \sum_{k=1}^{w} cor_T(\mathbf{z}^{\delta}\mathbf{z}_k^{c}) \Big/ w \tag{6.4}$$

where

n is the number of the causes.

h is the number of the events that are generated by the cause under study.

p is the number of the events that may generate the cause under study.

w is the number of the consequences that may initiate the cause under study.

T is the type of correlation (i.e., general, positive, negative, or differential between positive and negative).

Actual Value of a Cause

The actual value of operational risk causes is evaluated and defined by considering the real value of the cause together with its significance value. The measured value of a cause has a pragmatic meaning according to its significance value. If the latter has a low value, then the former would also lose its real value, and vice versa. Equation 6.5 describes this relationship and defines how to evaluate the actual value of risk AVΔ:

$$AV\Delta = \mathbf{z}^{\delta} \cdot SV\Delta \tag{6.5}$$

where

$\mathbf{z}^{\delta}$ is the matrix of the measured values referring to risk causes defined by the corresponding KRIs. These KRIs are defined by the parameters that describe the cause of operational risk — for example, in the trading process, the number of mistyping errors per week.

SVΔ is the significance value of the cause $SV\Delta \in \{0, \ldots, 1\}$.

The initial estimation of SVΔ may have an approximate value because the initial actual value of the cause may not be available as well as some of the correlations. The system of estimating the SVΔ should be designed in a manner so as to update its parametric values and thus increase its accuracy.

Levels of Acceptance for Causes

A cause may be characterized as "acceptable," "partly acceptable," or "nonacceptable," depending on its nature, its prevention activities before it appears, and the consequence of the events that it may create. Causes that come from physical or natural phenomena are usually acceptable. A power cut from the main supplier may be partly acceptable if it affects minor operations or has been prevented by the local electrical generators or uninterruptible power supplies (UPS). Computer virus attacks and security breaches are nonacceptable because they could be prevented and may result in catastrophic consequences.

Significance Value of an Event

In operational risk management analysis, two types of events are considered: "internal" and "external." Measuring the significance value of an event (SVΓ) is a complicated process because there are large numbers of mainly qualitative parameters that are describing and defining them. The types of values that should be considered to define the SVΓ include the degree of correlations between the event under study and:

- All other external and internal events
- The possible causes that may be initiated from the event under study
- All resulting consequences

The mathematical function for calculating the SVΓ is defined as per Equation 6.6:

$$SV\Gamma = \left[cor(\Gamma\Gamma) + cor(\Gamma\Delta) + cor(\Gamma C)\right]/3 \tag{6.6}$$

where

$cor(\Gamma\Gamma)$ describes the correlation between the event under study γ with the rest of the internal or external events, defined mathematically in Equation 6.7.

$cor(\Gamma\Delta)$ is defined in Equation 6.8 and describes the correlation between:

- cause δ and its resulting event γ under study
- the event γ under study and the new cause δ that it may initiate

$cor(\Gamma C)$ is defined in Equation 6.9 and describes the correlation between the event γ and its resulting consequences c.

$$cor(\Gamma\Gamma) = \sum_{i=1}^{h-1} cor_T(\mathbf{z}^{\gamma}\mathbf{z}_i^{\gamma}) \Big/ (h-1) \tag{6.7}$$

$$cor(\Gamma\Delta) = \left[\sum_{j=1}^{n} cor_T\left(\mathbf{z}^{\gamma}\mathbf{z}_j^{\delta}\right) \Big/ n\right] + \left[\sum_{q=1}^{p} cor_T\left(\mathbf{z}^{\gamma}\mathbf{z}_q^{\delta}\right) \Big/ p\right] \tag{6.8}$$

$$cor(\Gamma C) = \sum_{k=1}^{l} cor_T(\mathbf{z}^{\gamma}\mathbf{z}_k^{c}) \Big/ w \tag{6.9}$$

where

h is the number of events.

n is the number of the causes that initiates the event under study.

p is the number of causes that may be initiated from the event under study.

w is the number of consequences that may initiate the cause under study.

T is the type of correlation.

Note that the above correlations can be reasonably evaluated for internal events, whereas this is not always viable for the external events. In reality it is very hard to identify and measure the correlations between the external events and their causes. Moreover, it is even harder to do such correlation analysis with their direct consequences. In the correlation analysis for the external events, the easiest and most sensible way is defining the correlation of the causes of new events and consequences.

Actual Value of an Event

The significance value of a risk event gives added value to its real value. The real value of an event loses its initial importance if the event's significance value is minor. The significance value of an event $SV\Gamma$ combined with its real value gives the actual value. Equation 6.10 describes the function for an event's actual value $AV\Gamma$:

$$AV\Gamma = \mathbf{z}^{\gamma} \cdot SV\Gamma \tag{6.10}$$

where

$\mathbf{z}^{\gamma}$ is the matrix of the measured values referring to the risk event under study, defined by the corresponding KRI. These KRIs are defined by the parameters that describe the cause of the event. Although in many cases events are defined qualitatively, it is important to define and measure them quantitatively. Nevertheless, in cases where it is impossible or the definitions include high levels of assumptions, it is advisable to estimate the $SV\Gamma$ based only on the second part of Equation 6.6, i.e., the correlation values.

m is the number of operations related to the event.

$SV\Gamma$ is the significance value of the event $SV\Gamma \in \{0, \ldots, 1\}$.

Levels of Acceptance for Events

Events that result from operational risk causes can be "acceptable," "partly acceptable," or "nonacceptable." The degree of acceptance is related to its nature, its prevention activities before it occurs, and the resulting consequences that it may create. An event such as fraud can be acceptable or partly acceptable when its impact is low even though its probability is high. However, there are frauds that have high financial impact and cannot be accepted even if their probability may be low.

Significance Value of a Consequence

Consequences result from events and are directly linked to the impact of risks. They usually generate causes of new risks. Therefore, to measure the significance value of a consequence C, the following correlations should be considered:

- Its correlation with all the events that result in the cause under study
- Its correlation with all possible causes that it generates
- Its correlation with all other consequences

Thus, the mathematical function calculating the significance value of a consequence (SVC) is described in Equation 6.11:

$$SVC = \left[cor(C\Gamma) + cor(C\Delta) + cor(CC)\right]/3 \tag{6.11}$$

where

$cor(C\Gamma)$ defined mathematically in Equation 6.12, describes the correlation between the internal or external events γ, and their resulting consequences c under study.

$cor(C\Delta)$ describes the correlation between the consequence c and the causes δ it generates as defined in Equation 6.13.

$cor(CC)$ describes the correlation between the consequences c under study and the rest of the consequences as defined in Equation 6.14.

$$cor(C\Gamma) = \sum_{i=1}^{h} cor_T(\mathbf{z}^c\mathbf{z}_i^\gamma) \Big/ h \tag{6.12}$$

$$cor(C\Delta) = \sum_{j=1}^{p} cor_T(\mathbf{z}^c\mathbf{z}_j^\delta) \Big/ p \tag{6.13}$$

$$cor(CC) = \sum_{k=1}^{w-1} cor_T(\mathbf{z}^c\mathbf{z}_k^c) \Big/ (w-1) \tag{6.14}$$

where

h is the number of events.
p is the number of causes.
w is the number of consequences.
T is the type of correlation.

Actual Value of a Consequence

Similar to the estimation of the AVΔ and AVΓ, the actual value of a consequence (AVC) is defined by integrating its real value with its SVC. Equation 6.15 describes the function of AVC:

$$AVC = \mathbf{z}^c \cdot SVC \tag{6.15}$$

where

$\mathbf{z}^{\gamma}$ is the matrix of the measured values referring to the risk consequences in all operations, measured by KRIs that describe its quantitative parameters. All consequences must be well defined to be used as a basis for evaluating the operational risk impacts.

m is the number of operations related to the consequence.

SVC is the significance value of the consequence, $SVC \in \{0, \ldots, 1\}$.

Note that, similar to the comment on the initial estimation of SVΔ, the SVC may initially have an approximate value that will increase its accuracy through the updates of its parameters.

Levels of Acceptance for Consequences

A consequence of an event may be characterized as "acceptable," "partly acceptable," or "catastrophic" according to the level of its direct or indirect impact (mainly financial) and chain reactions in generating new causes of unexpected operational risk events. Consequences that have minor financial impact on or minor implications for the other operations are often characterized as acceptable. Those that have limited financial costs or a small degree of implications to the other operations are usually characterized as partly acceptable. Finally, those that have major financial costs or multiple implications to the other operations are characterized as catastrophic. It is important to note that the scoring system for defining consequential losses (especially monetary) should reflect on the organization's values and policies. For instance, a $10,000 monetary loss that is tolerable for one organization may be unacceptable for another.

Measurements Values and Scales for Causes, Events, and Consequences

In evaluating and defining SVΔ, SVΓ, and SVC, it is useful to convert their actual values of causes, events, and consequences to specific common units such as time or money so they can be compared to the subjective units used elsewhere in the analysis. In this case, a particular cause must not change its measurement value and scale when referring to different events. For example, particular telecommunication failures could be measured with a value for the overall margin of failure time or as a rate of failures within a time period. These failures could be a cause for systems shutting down as well as for events of security breach. It is efficient to stick to one of the above measurement types of cause values (i.e., margin or rate). Measurements that are based on rates of frequency are most preferable. Similarly, a consequence that stems from different events must have a unique normalized type of scale and measurement value, most usually expressed in financial terms.

Data Normalization

The information data used in operational risk identification and evaluation analysis comes from a variety of sources. As a result, there are many different units for measuring this data. Normalizing such data gives a comparative way to make full use of the data, without thinking about the units of measurements, although normalizing such information data may influence its actual and initial meaning.

The simplest type of normalization is the subtraction of the feature average $\bar{z}_j$ as in Equation 6.16. This normalization makes the feature values invariant to rigid displacements of the coordinates. The asterisk denotes the "raw" or normalized (unscaled) values.

$$z_{jk} = z^*_{jk} - \bar{z}_j \tag{6.16}$$

Another type of normalization that is commonly used translates and scales the axes so that all the features have zero mean and unit variance, as described in Equation 6.17.

$$z_{jk} = \frac{z^*_{jk} - \bar{z}_j}{\sigma_j^2} \tag{6.17}$$

The jth feature average, $\bar{z}_j$, defined in Equation 6.18, and the jth feature variance, σ_j^2, defined in Equation 6.19, are the measurement mean value and the sample value variance for the jth feature, respectively.

$$\bar{z}_j = (1/n)\sum_{i=1}^{n} z^*_{jk} \tag{6.18}$$

$$\sigma_j^2 = (1/n)\sum_{i=1}^{n} (z^*_{jk} - \bar{z}_j)^2 \tag{6.19}$$

After the analysis there is a need to de-normalize the initial measurement values. There are many normalization techniques for setting values to a common scale and comparing them based on the "same" degree of measurement characteristics. "Distance norms" are such normalization techniques; they are sensitive to variations in the numerical ranges of the different features. For instance, the Euclidean distance assigns more weighting to features with wide ranges than to those with narrow ranges. Nevertheless, this data is analyzed using clustering approaches, as discussed in the following sections referring to risk evaluation. Clustering approaches are able to adapt such measures in a way that is less sensitive to data scaling.

Estimating the Significance and Actual Value of an Operation

The significance value of an operation, in terms of risks that influence it, is estimated by considering the degree of correlations between particular operations and all the others. The comparative values are all risks that influence the operation under study and are also common risks to the other operations. Equation 6.20 defines the mathematical function that calculates the significance value of an operation (SVΛ).

$$SV\Lambda = \left[\frac{\sum_{i=1}^{m-1} cor_T(\mathbf{z}_a^{\lambda}\mathbf{z}_i^{\lambda})}{(m-1)} \right] \quad \text{where} \quad SV\Lambda \in \{0, \ldots, 1\}, \tag{6.20}$$

note that $\mathbf{z}^{\lambda}$ is defined by the inverse matrices $\mathbf{z}^{\delta}$, $\mathbf{z}^{\gamma}$, $\mathbf{z}^{c}$ defined in Equation 5.3, thus

$$\mathbf{z}^{\lambda} = \left[\mathbf{z}^{\delta}, \mathbf{z}^{\gamma}, \mathbf{z}^{c}\right]^{T}$$

where:

- m is the number of the operations influenced by the operational risks under study,
- $cor_T(\mathbf{z}_a^{\lambda}\mathbf{z}_i^{\lambda})$ defines the correlation between the z risks that affects operation a with their common risks that also affects the rest of the m-1 operations.

Moreover, T is the type of correlation (i.e., general, positive, negative, or differential between positive and negative).

Therefore, the actual value of an operation is estimated by integrating its real value with its significance value, as defined in Equation 6.21.

$$AV\Lambda = \mathbf{z}^{\lambda} \cdot SV\Lambda \tag{6.21}$$

where

$\mathbf{z}^{\lambda}$ is the matrix of the measured risk values referring to the operation under study.

SVΛ is the significance value of the operation, $SV\Lambda \in \{0, \ldots, 1\}$.

The significance and actual values of an operation are very useful in the operational risk assessment analysis, as described later in this book.

Beta Point for an Operational Risk or an Operation

In the evaluation phase of operational risk management, there are some operational risks that are well known and considered very significant at the time of the operational risk evaluation. This will be considered the "beta" operational risks. For example, a reengineering process of the banking systems has causes and events that may be well known to the risk managers. It is therefore very effective in operational risk management evaluation to understand and calculate their influences on the rest of the operational risks.

Estimating the Significance and Actual Value of a Beta

The estimation of a beta's significance value is defined by considering the degree of correlations between the values of beta set point and risks or operations. The two matrices in Equation 6.22 define the elements of the beta sets referring to operational risks r or affected operations λ respectively.

$$\mathbf{b}_r = \begin{bmatrix} b_1^r \\ b_2^r \\ \ldots \\ b_n^r \end{bmatrix} \text{ or } \mathbf{b}_\lambda = \begin{bmatrix} b_1^\lambda \\ b_2^\lambda \\ \ldots \\ b_m^\lambda \end{bmatrix} \tag{6.22}$$

where $\mathbf{b}_r$ may refer to beta values for risk cause $\mathbf{b}_r^\delta$, event $\mathbf{b}_r^\gamma$, or consequence $\mathbf{b}_r^c$, whereas $\mathbf{b}_\lambda$ refers to a beta value for an affected operation. Moreover, Equation 6.23 and Equation 6.24 define the mathematical functions of calculating the significance value of a beta with the different types of risks (i.e., SVB_Δ, SVB_Γ, and SVB_C) as well as with all operations SVB_Λ.

$$SVB_\Delta = \left[\frac{\sum_{i=1}^{d} cor_T(\mathbf{b}_r^\delta \mathbf{z}_i^\delta)}{d}\right],$$

$$SVB_\Gamma = \left[\frac{\sum_{i=1}^{g} cor_T(\mathbf{b}_r^\gamma \mathbf{z}_i^\gamma)}{g}\right], \tag{6.23}$$

$$SVB_C = \left[\frac{\sum_{i=1}^{c} cor_T(\mathbf{b}_r^c \mathbf{z}_i^c)}{c}\right]$$

$$SVB_\Lambda = \left[\frac{\sum_{i=1}^{m} cor_T(\mathbf{b}_\lambda \mathbf{z}_i^\lambda)}{m}\right] \tag{6.24}$$

where

$cor_T(\mathbf{b}_r^\delta \mathbf{z}_i^\delta)$, $cor_T(\mathbf{b}_r^\gamma \mathbf{z}_i^\gamma)$, $cor_T(\mathbf{b}_r^c \mathbf{z}_i^c)$, and $cor_T(\mathbf{b}_\lambda \mathbf{z}_i^\lambda)$ define the correlations between the beta values with the comparing risks' cause γ, risk event δ, consequence or risks c or operations λ. T indicates the type of correlation (i.e., general, positive, negative, or differential between positive and negative).

d, g and q are the number of the corresponding operational risks (measured by the KRIs) that refer to risk causes, events and consequences.

m is the number of the operations influenced by the risk under study.

The actual values of the above betas are estimated by integrating their real beta values with their significant ones, as defined in Equation 6.25 and Equation 6.26.

$$AVB_{(\Delta,H,C)} = \mathbf{b}_{(\Delta,H,C)} \cdot SVB_{(\Delta,H,C)} \tag{6.25}$$

$$AVB_{\Lambda} = \mathbf{b}_{\Lambda} \cdot SVB_{\Lambda} \quad (6.26)$$

where

$AVB_{(\Delta,\mathrm{H},C)}$ and $SVB_{(\Delta,\mathrm{H},C)}$ are the actual and significance values of a beta risk that exist within all m operations. Accordingly, AVB_{Λ} and SVB_{Λ} are the actual and significance values of a beta operation that is influenced by n number of risks.

$\mathbf{b}$ is the coordination array of the beta point.

Illustrating the Significance and Actual Values

In the estimation of the significance values (SV), the important factor is the degree of correlation. When this is high in operational risk or affected operations, its value indicates that other risks or operations are also affected to a corresponding degree. The bar plots in Figure 6.2 and Figure 6.3 illustrate the significance values for both operational risks and affected operations, respectively, defined by the equations mentioned above. Note that in these results the correlation type must be set as general.

In banking organizations, the complexity of the operations is very high and the operational risks influencing them have different degrees. A way to determine the significance of each operation and operational risk is critical for evaluating them.

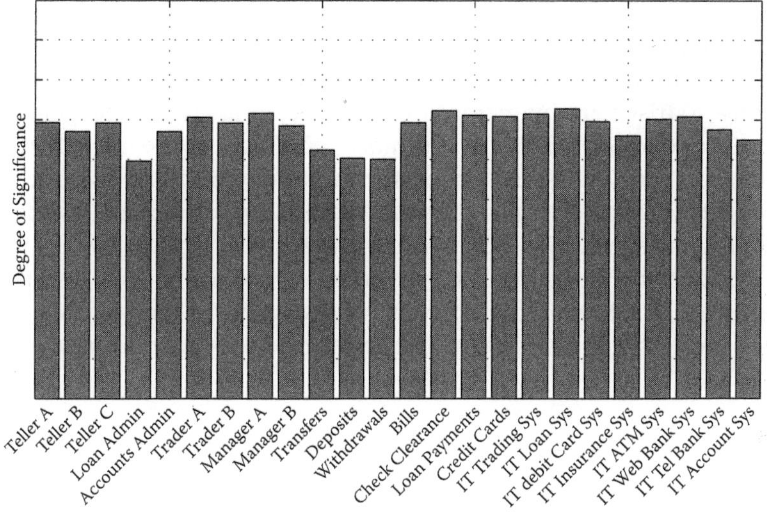

Figure 6.2 Overall significance values for each affected operation.

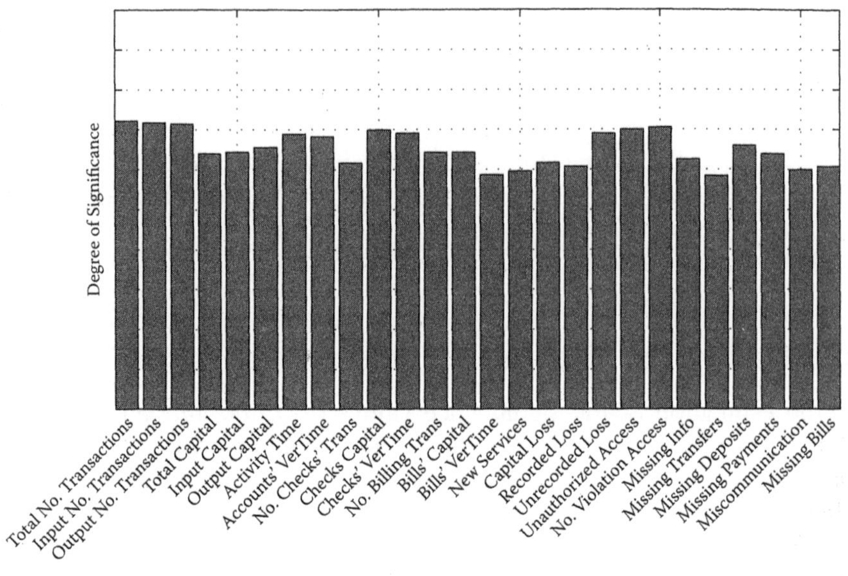

Figure 6.3 Overall significance values for each operational risk.

Cluster Analysis as a Tool in the Evaluation Process

For operational risk management, "cluster" analysis can be used to partition information data referring to operational risks or affected operations into subsets or groups. Cluster analysis is used for operational risk identification, evaluation, and control as a technique to seek out natural clusters referring to risks in operations. Using cluster analysis, the similarities between operational risks or affected operations can be identified. This identification analysis is used extensively for the operational risk evaluation process, as illustrated in this chapter. Additionally, cluster analysis is used to identify the similarities between operational risk probability and impact and evaluate their exposure. Furthermore, clustering is used extensively in operational risk profiling analysis, as discussed in Chapter 7.

The clusters that are used in the above-mentioned evaluation analyses are defined by:

- The affected operations that are distributed in axes defined by the operational risks
- The operational risks that are distributed in axes defined by the affected operations
- The distribution of the operational risks' probability and impact values

As already discussed, the operations are defined by the risks that affect them, whereas the risks are defined by the operations that they affect. Based on these definitions, in clustering analysis, the affected operations are distributed in a multidimensional space where each dimension is defined by the risks that effect these operations. On the other hand, the operational risks are distributed in a multidimensional space where each dimension is defined by the operations that they affect. Finally, the degree of probability and impact for the losses that refer to operational risks or affected operations are used to define their corresponding distribution in probability and impact axes.

Clusters divide all objects (samples) related to the above values into smaller subgroups, and classify them according to the similarities between them. They also extract the information encapsulated in the data by extrapolating class membership to unlabeled information or simply to better understand the operational risk identification characteristics. Clustering techniques belong to the classes of *unsupervised* (learning) methods because they do not use prior class identifiers or knowledge. Furthermore, most clustering algorithms do not rely on assumptions common to conventional statistical methods, such as the underlying statistical distribution of data, and therefore they are useful in situations where little prior knowledge exists or when this knowledge is not structured very well.

Definition of Clusters for Operational Risk and Affected Operations

Various definitions of clusters have been formulated in the literature, depending on the objective of clustering. In operational risk evaluation analysis, a cluster is defined by the group of homogeneous operational risks or affected operations that displays similar characteristics to each other rather than to members of other clusters. The term "similarity" has an important effect on the clustering results because it indicates which mathematical properties of the data set (i.e., distance, connectivity, and intensity), should be used and in what way the clusters should be identified. Distance can be measured among the data vectors themselves, or as a distance from a data vector to some prototypical object of the cluster. The prototypes (which are usually the centers of the clusters) or centroids are usually unknown beforehand, and are sought by the clustering algorithms simultaneously with the partitioning of the data. The prototypes may be vectors of the same dimension as the data clusters, but they can also be defined as "high-level" geometrical objects, such as linear or nonlinear subspaces or functions.

Operational risk cluster analysis is an analysis that visualizes the group distribution of operations and their associated risks by projecting their actual values onto operational performances and risks' probability and impact axes. The resulting clusters are defined by considering the distribution in n-dimensional axes together with the degree of membership for each operational risk or affected operations within the groups. Cluster analysis for operational risk or affected operations is introduced and discussed extensively in this book as it is effective during the operational risk evaluation phase and for constructing effective decision-making processes in operational risk management systems.

Data Used for Clustering Analysis

One of the important advantages of clustering techniques that can be used in operational risk evaluation is that they can be applied to information data that is *quantitative* (numerical), *qualitative* (categoric), or a *mixture* of both. In the operational risk management analysis presented in this book, the clustering of quantitative operational risk data is considered. The data is typically measurement records of operational performance variances, operational risk values, and losses. Each measurement consists of n measured variables, grouped into an n-dimensional Euclidean space $\Re^n$ column vector $\mathrm{z}_k = [z_{1k}, z_{2k}, \ldots, z_{nk},]^T$, $z_k \in \Re^n$. A set of N records is denoted by $Z = \{\mathrm{z}_k \mid k = 1, 2, \ldots, N\}$, and is represented as an $n \times N$ matrix as in Equation 6.27:

$$\mathrm{Z} = \begin{bmatrix} z_{11} & z_{12} & \cdots & z_{1N} \\ z_{21} & z_{22} & \cdots & z_{2N} \\ \cdot & \cdot & \cdot & \cdot \\ \cdot & \cdot & \cdot & \cdot \\ \cdot & \cdot & \cdot & \cdot \\ z_{n1} & z_{n2} & \cdots & z_{nN} \end{bmatrix} \tag{6.27}$$

Z is called the *pattern* or *risk data matrix*. The meaning of the *columns* and *rows* of Z depends on the context of the classification problem. In the risk distribution analysis of the operational risks or affected operations, the rows and columns of the matrix are operational risk values. Moreover, in the risk profiling analysis (discussed in Chapter 7), the rows of the matrix represents the risk impact, whereas the columns defines the probability of the operational risks.

Clustering Approaches in Operational Risk

There are several clustering approaches that can be used in identifying the clusters constructed by the operational risk probability and impact values or from the operational risks and affected operational values. The objective of clustering methods in this case is to perform a partition of the collection of elements in Equation 6.27 into c data sets with respect to a given criterion, where c is defined as the number of clusters. The criterion is usually to optimize an *objective function* that acts as a performance index of clustering.

In classical "hard" clustering analysis, the data is distributed into partitions so that the degree of their association is strong within blocks of the same partition and weak in different blocks. In other words, each information data is assigned to only one cluster, and all clusters are regarded as a disjoint gathering of the data set. In practice, however, there are many cases in which the clusters are not completely disjointed and data could be classified as belonging to one cluster almost as well as to another. A crisp classification process is thus unable to cater to such situations. Therefore, the separation of the clusters becomes a fuzzy notion, and the representations of real data structures can then be more accurately handled by fuzzy clustering methods. In these cases, it is necessary to describe the data structure in terms of fuzzy clusters. Thus, the end result of the fuzzy clustering is the *partition matrix* $U = [\mu_{ik}]_{i=1\ldots c,\ k=1\ldots N}$, where μ_{ik} is a numerical value in [0,1] (i.e., $\mu_{ik} \in \{0,1\}$) and expresses the degree to which the element z_k belongs to the i cluster.

However, there are two additional constraints on the value of μ_{ik}:

1. A total membership of the element $z_k \in RP_{matrix}$ in all classes is equal to 1.0; that is,

$$\sum_{i=1}^{c} \mu_{ik} = 1 \qquad \text{for all } k = 1, 2, \ldots, N$$

2. Every constructed cluster is nonempty and different from the entire set; that is,

$$0 < \sum_{k=1}^{N} \mu_{ik} < N \qquad \text{for all } i = 1, 2, \ldots, c$$

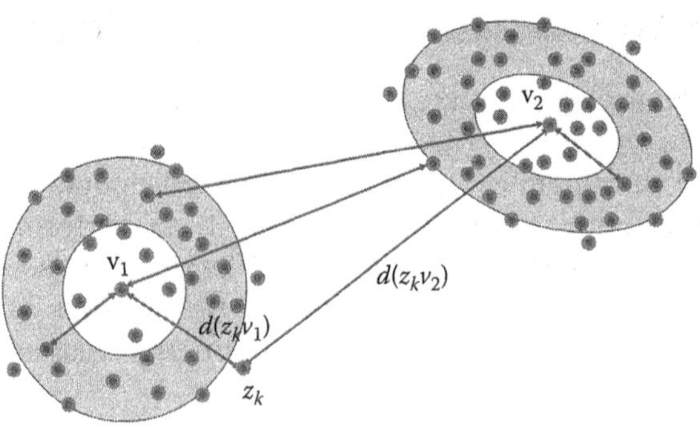

Figure 6.4 Fuzzy clustering representation.

A general form of the objective function is as defined in Equation 6.28:

$$J(\mu_{ik}, v_i) = \sum_{i=1}^{c}\sum_{k=1}^{N}\sum_{i=1}^{c} g[w(z_i),\mu_{ik}] \cdot d(z_k, v_i) \tag{6.28}$$

where $w(z_i)$ is the *a priori* weight for each z_k and $d(z_k,v_i)$ is the degree of dissimilarity between the data z_k and the supplemental element v_i, which can be considered the central vector of the *i*th cluster. The degree of dissimilarities is defined as a measure that satisfies two axioms:

1. $d(z_k, v_i) \geq 0$
2. $d(z_k, v_i) = d(v_i, z_k)$

With the above settings, fuzzy clustering can be precisely formulated as an optimization problem:

$$\text{Minimize: } J(\mu_{ik}, v_i),\ i = 1, 2, \ldots, c;\ k = 1, 2, \ldots, N \tag{6.29}$$

Figure 6.4 illustrates these types of clusters, with cluster centers $V = [v_1, v_2]$ and *partition matrix U*; that is,

$$U = \begin{bmatrix} \mu_{11} & \mu_{12} & \cdots & \mu_{1N} \\ \mu_{21} & \mu_{22} & \cdots & \mu_{2N} \end{bmatrix}$$

In the literature, numerous clustering approaches have been developed on iterative minimization of the criterion function in Equation 6.29. In this book some of these approaches are introduced in terms of their relevance and importance in the identification, monitoring, evaluation, and control strategies for operational risk management systems. Most widely used fuzzy clustering methods are based on the fuzzy *c*-means (FCM) algorithm.[1]

Fuzzy C-Means Clustering Approach

The objective (or cost) function of the FCM algorithm takes the form of:

$$J(\mu_{ik}, \mathbf{v}_i) = \sum_{i=1}^{c}\sum_{k=1}^{N} \mu_{ik}^{m} \cdot \left\|\mathbf{z}_k, \mathbf{v}_i\right\|^2 \qquad m > 1 \tag{6.30}$$

where m is called the *exponential weight*, which determines the fuzziness of the resulting cluster. To solve this minimization problem, the objective function in Equation 6.29 is differentiated with respect to $\mathbf{v}_i$ (for fixed μ_{ik}, $i = 1, 2, \ldots, c$; $k = 1, 2, \ldots, N$) and to μ_{ik} (for fixed $\mathbf{v}_i$, $i = 1, 2, \ldots, c$) and the condition of Equation 6.27 is applied.

$$\mathbf{v}_i^{(l)} = \frac{\sum_{k=1}^{N} (\mu_{ik}^{l-1})^m \cdot \mathbf{z}_k}{\sum_{k=1}^{N} (\mu_{ik}^{l-1})^m}, \qquad i = 1, 2, \ldots, c \tag{6.31}$$

$$\mu_{ik}^{l} = \frac{1}{\sum_{j=1}^{c} (D_{ikA}/D_{jkA})^{2/(m-1)}}, \qquad i = 1, 2, \ldots, c;\ k = 1, 2, \ldots, N \tag{6.32}$$

where l is the number of repeats and

$$D_{ikA}^2 = \left\|\mathbf{z}_k - \mathbf{v}_i\right\|_A^2 = (\mathbf{z}_k - \mathbf{v}_i)^T \mathbf{A}(\mathbf{z}_k - \mathbf{v}_i) \tag{6.33}$$

is a square inner product distance norm.

The algorithm of the FCM approach is simply an iteration through the preceding three steps, which are summarized next.

Algorithm FCM

Select the data set Z, allocate a number of clusters c $(2 \le c \le N)$, the exponential weight $(1 < m < \infty)$, the termination tolerance $\varepsilon > 0$ and the norm-inducting matrix $\mathbf{A}$. Choose an initial partition matrix $\mathbf{U}^{(0)}$.

Repeat for $l = 1, 2, \ldots$

1. Compute the fuzzy cluster prototypes — centers of clusters — $\{v_i^{(l)} | i = 1, 2, \ldots, c\}$ using $\mathbf{U}^l$ and Equation 6.31.
2. Compute the distance using Equation 6.33.
3. Update the partition matrix $\mathbf{U}^{l+1}$ using $\{\mathbf{v}_i^{(l)} | i = 1, 2, \ldots, c\}$ and Equation 6.30

   until $\left\| \mathbf{U}^l \text{-} \mathbf{U}^{l+1} \right\| < \varepsilon$

The hard c-means (HCM) clustering algorithms can be considered a special case of the fuzzy c-means clustering algorithm. In Equation 6.29, if μ_{ik} is one for only one class and zero for all other classes, then the criterion function $J(\mu_{ik}, \mathbf{v}_i)$ used in the FCM is the same as in the hard c-means clustering algorithm. The use of membership values in the FCM method provides more flexibility and formulates the clustering results in a more useful form for practical applications. However, both algorithms are iterative, and therefore there are no guarantees that they will converge to an optimum solution. The performance depends on the selection of the *initial positions of the cluster centers,* whereby another fast algorithm can be used to determine the initial clusters or to run HCM/FCM algorithms several times, each starting with a different set of initial cluster center(s). Moreover, an important parameter that also must be selected in applying these algorithms is *the number of clusters*. The number of clusters should ideally correspond to the number of substructures naturally present in the data.

Inner-Product Norms

The shape of the clusters is determined by the choice of the matrix A in the distance measured (Equation 6.31). One choice of $\mathbf{A}$ is $\mathbf{A} = \mathbf{I}$. This induces the standard Euclidean norm as in Equation 6.34:

$$D_{ik}^2 = (\mathbf{z}_k - \mathbf{v}_i)^T (\mathbf{z}_k - \mathbf{v}_i) \tag{6.34}$$

which actually stimulates hyper-spherical clusters, that is, clusters whose surfaces of constant membership are hyper-spheres.

An $n \times n$ diagonal matrix that accounts for different variances in the directions of the coordinate axes of RP_{matrix} can be another choice of **A**, as in Equation 6.35:

$$A = \begin{bmatrix} (1/\sigma_1)^2 & 0 & \cdots & 0 \\ 0 & (1/\sigma_2)^2 & \cdots & 0 \\ \cdot & \cdot & \cdot & \cdot \\ \cdot & \cdot & \cdot & \cdot \\ \cdot & \cdot & \cdot & \cdot \\ 0 & 0 & \cdots & (1/\sigma_n)^2 \end{bmatrix} \tag{6.35}$$

This matrix induces a diagonal norm on $\Re^n$.

Finally, **A** can be defined as the inverse of the $n \times n$ sample covariance matrix of RP_{matrix}: $\mathbf{A} = \mathbf{R}^{-1}$, where

$$\mathbf{R} = \frac{1}{N}\sum_{k=1}^{N}(\mathbf{z}_k - \bar{\mathbf{z}})(\mathbf{z}_k - \bar{\mathbf{z}})^T \tag{6.36}$$

Here $\bar{\mathbf{z}}$ denotes the sample mean of the data. In this case, **A** induces the Mahalanobis[1] norm on $\Re^n$. Both the diagonal and Mahalanobis norms generate hyper-ellipsoidal clusters. The only difference is that with the diagonal norm, the axes of the hyper-ellipsoids are parallel to the coordinate axes while with the Mahalanobis norm, the orientation of the hyper-ellipsoid is arbitrary.

The choice of which norm to use depends on the data itself. Euclidean distance is the overwhelming favorite because it is considered closer to what human observations are like. Mahalanobis distance is useful when there are large disparities in the ranges of the measured features because it rotates the basis $\Re^n$ so that the data is scaled equally and is pair-wise uncorrelated.

A common limitation of cluster algorithms based on a fixed distance norm is that such a norm induces a fixed topological structure on $\Re^n$ and forces the objective function to prefer clusters of that shape even if they are not present. However, a method using the norm-inducing matrix A can be adapted to the local topological structure of the data. This method can be used to estimate the dependence of the data in each cluster, as described in the next sections.

Extensions of the Fuzzy C-Means Algorithm Using Fuzzy Covariance Matrix

Several algorithms can be derived from the basic FCM scheme by adapting the inner-product norm (Equation 6.31). The most used and successful clustering algorithms are the Gustafson and Kessel (G-K) proposed by Gustafson and Kessel[2] and fuzzy maximum likelihood estimates (FMLE) proposed by Bezdek and Dunn.[3] Both algorithms recognize the fact that different clusters in the same data set may have different geometrical shapes and to detect them, the standard fuzzy c-mean algorithm is extended, by employing an adaptive distance norm. The analytical description of these algorithms is outside the scope of this book; however, some important aspects should be noted:

The fuzzy covariance matrix defined for the ith cluster using the GK method as in Equation 6.37 is denoted as F_i, whereas for the FMLE method uses Equation 6.38 and is denoted as Σ_i.

$$\mathbf{F}_i = \frac{\sum_{k=1}^{N} (\mu_{ik})^m (\mathbf{z}_k - \mathbf{v}_i)(\mathbf{z}_k - \mathbf{v}_i)^T}{\sum_{k=1}^{N} (\mu_{ik})^m} \tag{6.37}$$

$$\mathbf{\Sigma}_i = \frac{\sum_{k=1}^{N} \mu_{ik} (\mathbf{z}_k - \mathbf{v}_i)(\mathbf{z}_k - \mathbf{v}_i)^T}{\sum_{k=1}^{N} \mu_{ik}} \tag{6.38}$$

The difference between the fuzzy covariance matrices $\mathbf{F}_i$ and $\mathbf{\Sigma}_i$ is that the latter does not include the weighting exponent m. This is simply because the two weighted covariance matrices arise as generalizations of the classical covariance from two different concepts. Note that the choice of *weighting exponent m* is as in the case of FCM algorithm (i.e., $1 < m < \infty$).

Each cluster has its own inner product distance norm. The first method is as in Equation 6.39 and the second as in Equation 6.40.

$$D^2_{ikA_i} = (z_k - v_i)^T \left[\rho_i \mathbf{det}(\mathbf{F}_i)^{1/n} \mathbf{F}_i^{-1} \right] (\mathbf{z}_k - \mathbf{v}_i) \tag{6.39}$$

$$D^2_{ikA_i} = \frac{\left[\det \Sigma_i\right]^{1/2}}{P_i} \exp\left[\frac{1}{2}(\mathbf{z}_k - \mathbf{v}_i)^T \Sigma_i^{-1}(\mathbf{z}_k - \mathbf{v}_i)\right] \tag{6.40}$$

In Equation 6.39, the *cluster volumes* ρ_i are simply fixed at one for each cluster if no *prior knowledge* is available. In Equation 6.40, P_i is the prior probability of selecting cluster i and is defined as in Equation 6.41.

$$P_i = \frac{1}{N}\sum_{k=1}^{N} \mu_{ik} \tag{6.41}$$

Note that Equation 6.40 involves an exponential term and thus $D^2_{ikA_i}$ decreases faster for a given change in distance measure than the inner product norm in Equation 6.39. Therefore, the clusters are not constrained in volume as may happen when using the G-K algorithm. Thus, the algorithm is able to detect clusters of varying shapes, sizes, and distances. However, FMLE needs good initializations (i.e., close to the optimal), because, due to the exponential distance norm, it tends to converge to a nearby local optimum.

Determination of the Number of Clusters

One issue in operational risk cluster analysis is the definition of the number of c clusters. In the distribution analysis of operational risks and affected operations where the coordinates of the elements that construct the clusters are values of an n-dimensional space, the clusters cannot be visually recognized. Thus, it is very difficult to estimate their actual number. Each of the n-dimensional clusters has a centroid that defines its unique equilibrium point, as explained in the risk equilibrium section. There is no warranty for predefining the number of these operational risk centroids. However, by using clustering methodological techniques, this number can be defined. The idea behind such approaches is that "overnumbering" will end up defining the same centroid when it will exceed its real number of clusters. In that case, a large number of centroids should initially be defined. For instance, if the actual number of clusters is five and the algorithm has been set to look for seven centroids, then two of its resulting coordinates will have the same or very similar values. This will also indicate that the maximum number of the clusters is five. This technique results in a very good approximation of the real number of the clusters and its centroids; however, it may be very time consuming during the algorithmic calculations. Finally, in many cases the number of centroids is defined by the analyst, due to the analyst's desire to perform a specific analysis, that is, looking for the equilibrium of all operational risks, the number of the centroids must be set to one.

Normalization in Clustering Analysis

In the literature on clustering analysis, it is often suggested that the data should be appropriately normalized. Thus, considering Equation 6.27, the elements of the **Z** matrix should be normalized in the values [–1 1]. Normalization, however, is not always desirable; it may influence the result of clustering when the separation between clusters is altered. The result of clustering can thus be negatively influenced by, for instance, choosing different measurement units. Nevertheless, clustering algorithms that are based on adaptive distance measure are less sensitive to data scaling because the adaptation of the distance measure automatically compensates for the distance in scale.

Equilibrium Identification Analysis for Operational Risk Management

In banking organizations where the number of operational risks or undesirable performances may be extensive, there is a specific point or points that defines their risk equilibrium point(s). Moreover, there is a large number of affected systems, people, and processes that also have one or more equilibrium point(s). The identification of the operational risk equilibrium points $\mathbf{e}_r$ as well as between all affected operations $\mathbf{e}_o$ is defined using multidimensional space clustering analysis. The methods for this identification analysis are called clustering operational risk equilibrium (CORE) and clustering affected operations equilibrium (CAOE) for the above two cases accordingly in this book.

In the CORE method, the equilibrium identification analysis is based on the values of operational risks that are distributed in multidimensional space of all affected operations. The clusters of the operational risks that emerge within the multidimensional space are analyzed to define their equilibrium points. The aim therefore in this case is to minimize the cost function defined in Equation 6.42:

$$J(\mu_i, \mathbf{e}_{r_i}) = \sum_{i=1}^{c} \sum_{k=1}^{n} \mu_i \cdot \left\| \mathbf{z}_k, e_{r_i} \right\|^2 \tag{6.42}$$

In the CAOE method, the affected operations are distributed in a multidimensional space of the operational risks. The clusters defined by the affected operational risks in the multidimensional space are also analyzed. The target in this case is to minimize the cost function defined in Equation 6.43:

$$J(\mu_i, \mathbf{e}_{\lambda_i}) = \sum_{i=1}^{c}\sum_{k=1}^{m} \mu_i \cdot \left\| \mathbf{z}_k, e_{\lambda_i} \right\|^2 \tag{6.43}$$

where

μ is the membership functions and

$$\sum_{i=1}^{n} \mu_i = 1 \quad \text{and} \quad \sum_{i=1}^{k} \mu_i = 1 \tag{6.44}$$

z are the elements of multidimensional matrix where each dimension represents the different operational risks or affected operations.

e_r and e_λ are the equilibrium points.

n is the number of operational risks.

m is the number of the affected operations.

c is the number of the "suggested" equilibrium points.

The resulting vectors of the equilibriums points of operational risks $\mathbf{e}_r$ as well as for the affected operations $\mathbf{e}_\lambda$ are defined in Equation 6.45 and Equation 6.46, respectively.

$$\mathbf{e}_r = \begin{bmatrix} e_1^r \\ e_2^r \\ \dots \\ e_n^r \end{bmatrix} \tag{6.45}$$

$$\mathbf{e}_\lambda = \begin{bmatrix} e_1^\lambda \\ e_2^\lambda \\ \dots \\ e_m^\lambda \end{bmatrix} \tag{6.46}$$

The centroids of these multidimensional clusters identify both the operational risks and the affected operations' equilibrium points.

The implementation of both CORE and CAOE methods proposed in this book identify the equilibriums points for the operational risks and affected operations. The number of these equilibrium points is dependent on the actual number of clusters of the operational risks or operations' subspaces. In the case of searching for one equilibrium point, the resulting point defines the overall equilibrium for the operational risk or affected operations. However, if several equilibrium points have been identified, the resulting points will represent the equilibrium of the different clusters. The number of clusters is not always clearly defined, especially when these clusters construct the multidimensional subspaces. When this is the case, the clustering algorithms are set to search for a large number of centroids. Clustering algorithms can find the actual number of centroids. Equilibrium points are used in analyzing the trends of the operational risks and undesirable performances in operations, as explained in the following section.

Trend Analysis for Operational Risk

In the operational risk evaluation analysis, the operational risk equilibrium points indicate the tendency of the operational risks. This is because all operational performances and operational risks have the tendency to "shift" or, in other words, "slide" into their equilibrium. This is a natural "force" like gravity, where in the case of performance analysis, it defines the business tendency to move toward its stability point. However, in the case of operational risks, the equilibrium point defines the business overall operational risk point. In this case when the operational risk values are close to their equilibrium points or when they are "forced" to that point, the business operations are close to reaching their critical stability points, which may result in ruining the business. Note that the magnitude of the force is measured by its correlation or, in other words, gravitation toward the operational risk equilibrium points. Thus, these gravitational forces of the equilibrium points are called "trends" T. For each of them, the magnitude of their trends is estimated by the degree of correlations between:

- The real value of each operational risk with the risk equilibrium point of all operational risks in operations, as defined in Equation 6.47
- The real values of the affected operations with the operational risks equilibrium point for all operations, as defined in Equation 6.48

$$T_r^{\delta} = cor(\mathbf{z}^{\delta}\mathbf{e}_r),\ T_r^{\gamma} = cor(\mathbf{z}^{\gamma}\mathbf{e}_r),\ T_r^{c} = cor(\mathbf{z}^{c}\mathbf{e}_r) \tag{6.47}$$

$$T_{\lambda} = cor(\mathbf{z}^{\lambda}\mathbf{e}_{\lambda}) \tag{6.48}$$

where T_r^{δ}, T_r^{γ}, T_r^{c} and T_{λ} are the Force of Risk Gravity (FRG) of the operational risks, (referring to cause, events, or consequences) and the affected operations λ, respectively.

The overall degree of the above trends is estimated, for the risks and for the operations, by Equation 6.49 and Equation 6.50, respectively:

$$T_R = \sum_{i=1}^{d} cor(\mathbf{z}_i^{\delta}\mathbf{e}_r) + \sum_{j=1}^{g} cor(\mathbf{z}_j^{\gamma}\mathbf{e}_r) + \sum_{k=1}^{q} cor(\mathbf{z}_k^{c}\mathbf{e}_r) \tag{6.49}$$

$$T_{\Lambda} = \sum_{i=1}^{m} cor(\mathbf{z}_i^{\lambda}\mathbf{e}_{\lambda}) \tag{6.50}$$

where

- d, g, and q are the number of the operational risks (measured by their corresponding KRIs) that refer to risk causes, events, and consequences accordingly
- m is the number of the affected operations

Note that the general values that the above correlations have in certain value is positive and in another value negative. Note also that this equilibrium and trend analysis is based on current or short-time (according to the data that is used) measurements that indicate the current operational risk stability point and future operational risk trends accordingly.

Trend Accumulation for the Operational Risks and Affected Operations

The equilibrium and trend analyses are used to define the trend accumulation for the operational risk and affected operations. The differences between the values of the equilibrium points and the actual values of the operational risks or affected operations define their accumulation RA degrees accordingly. Moreover, by integrating the magnitude and direction of their trends, the degree of trend accumulation RA_T can also be defined.

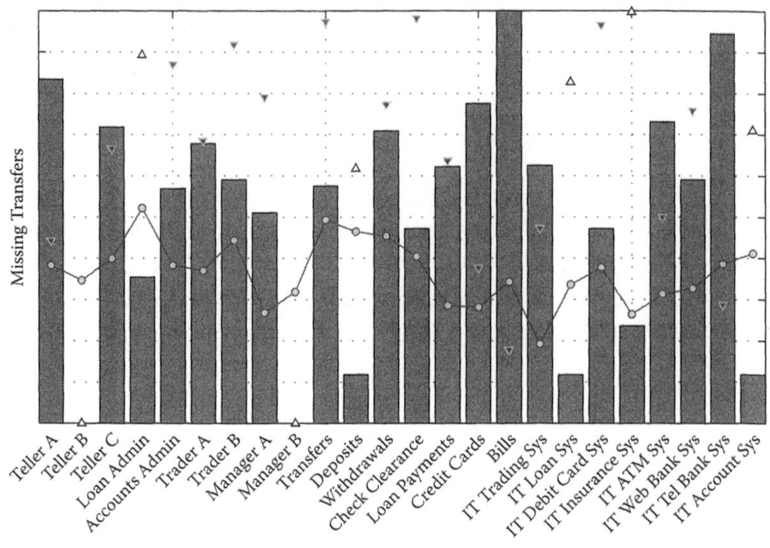

Figure 6.5 Trend analysis for the operational risk that refers to missing capital transfers. The bar plots illustrates the real normalized values of the operational risk in each of the affected operations. The dots illustrate the corresponding operational risk equilibrium points. The arrows define the trends of the operational risk and their magnitude, which defines their force in different affected operations.

If the accumulation degree and its trend are very high, the exposure of the affected operations is becoming high and the business may fail. The aim in the operational risk and affected operations' equilibrium identification analysis is to minimize the above-mentioned degree of accumulation. This can be done by moving their trend values away from their equilibrium points. This process is very desirable, especially for those values that indicate a high degree of tendency to their operational risk equilibrium points. The accumulation of the operational risk and affected operations plays a vital role in operational risk profiling and optimization analysis, as discussed extensively in Part IV of this book.

By implementing the CORE and CAOE methods, Figure 6.5 and Figure 6.6 illustrate the equilibrium points and trends, together with the significance values for operational risks and affected operations, respectively. Analytically, Figure 6.5 illustrates the trends for an operational risk that is referring to "missing capital transfers." The bars in this figure define the magnitude of significance for the operational risk in each of the affected operations. These values indicate where the operational risk under study has its maximum value (i.e., the operation referring to "bills"), its minimum (i.e., in operations referring to "Teller B" and "Manager B"), etc. The dots

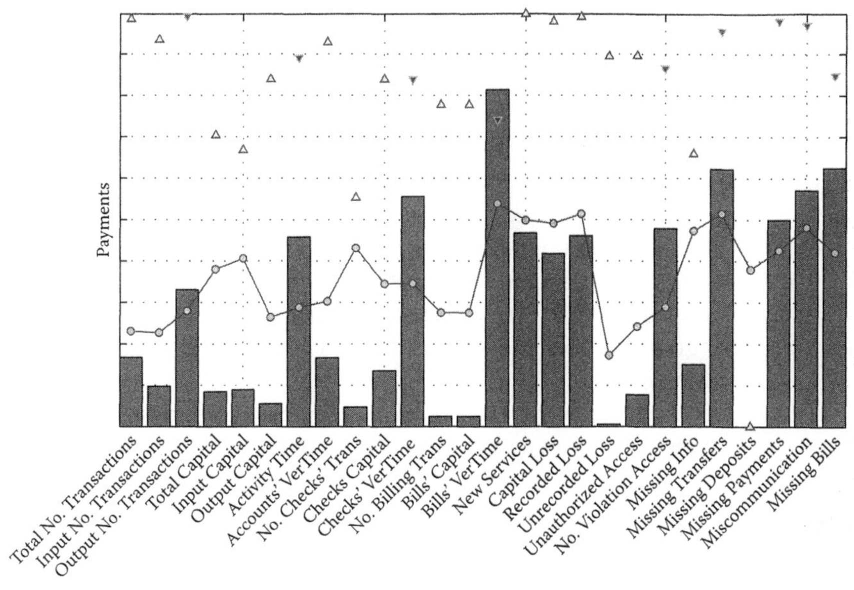

Figure 6.6 Trend analysis for each operational risk in the affected operation that refers to "payments". The bars illustrate the normalized values for all operational risks in the affected operation. The dots illustrate their corresponding equilibrium points for each of the operational risks.

indicate the corresponding equilibrium points of the operational risk. As can be observed from the figure, these values vary from one affected operation to the other. Finally, the arrows define the trends of the operational risk within the different affected operations. The downward-facing arrow indicates the trend of operational risk to reduce its value and vice versa. Note that the trend of the operational risk is to reach the value that is close to equilibrium. The forces of these trends are defined from the magnitudes of these trend arrows, that is, high trend magnitudes indicate a big force, whereas low magnitudes indicate a small force. Thus, the trend force of the operational risk to increase its value in the operations referring to "IT systems," related to insurance services, is very high. Thus for the operation "IT insurance system", the trend in the operational risk is on the increase. This means attention should be given to this operation. On the contrary, for the operation associated with "bills", the tendency is to decrease operational risks. This means that this operation tends to perform well and decrease operational risks.

Figure 6.6 illustrates the trends of all operational risks that affect a particular operation, that is, the one that is referring to "payments." Similar to the above description (Figure 6.5), the bars illustrate the normalized values for all operational risks that affect the operation under study. Thus, the operational risk referring to "bills' verification time" has the highest magnitude on the affected operation, whereas the operational risk referring to "missing deposit" has the lowest value. The dots illustrate the corresponding equilibrium points for each of the operational risks in their affected operations. The downward-facing and upward-facing arrows indicate the direction of the trend force in the affected operations and their movement to reach their equilibrium points. Their magnitude indicates their volume of force. As can be observed from Figure 6.6, most of the operational risks that affect the operation referring to "payments" have a high trend magnitude. This means that they have a high tendency to reach their equilibrium points.

The above analysis is vital in the evaluation phase and, more important, in the risk control and management phase. Determining the trend of operational risks and undesirable operational performances is very valuable in operational risk management systems. It is used as a base for designing prevention systems that are implemented to avoid or plan how to minimize or mitigate the operational risks before they actually occur. In dynamic environments such as in banking organizations, the operational risk equilibrium point is dynamic. Operational risk equilibrium points are dynamically varying because they are directly dependent on the operational risks and affected operations.

Evaluating the Severity of Operational Risks and Affected Operations

In this book, a methodology called mountain surface evaluation (MSE) is used to evaluate the severity of the operational risks and the affected operations. The method is based on distribution, significance, and trend analysis of the operational risks and the affected operations under study.

Distribution Analysis

Distribution analysis is a key element for evaluating the severity of the operational risks and the affected operations. The analysis is based on their positions in the space constructed by the operational risks or the affected operations and their significance and trend values. Thus, in this analysis, two types of distributions are considered:

1. In the first case, the distribution of the operational risks is defined by the risks' coordinating positions in a space that are constructed

by their affected operations. In this analysis, a combination of two affected operations defines a two-axis operational space where the values of their common operational risks define the coordinates of the operational risks' distribution. An additional third axis defines the significance value or trend or accumulation degree of the operational risks under study. The evaluation analysis examines the severity and similarity of the distributed operational risks. This is based on their significance value or their trend or accumulation degrees, together with the value and density of the operational risks that are distributed within the same operational space.

2. The second case analyzes the distribution of the affected operations within the axes that are defined by their common operational risks. Thus, in this case, a pair of operational risks defines the operational risk space. The coordinates of the distributed values within this space are defined by the different degrees of their effect to the operations. The significance value or the degrees of trends or accumulation that refer to the distributed operations define the coordinates of the third axis of the distributional space under study. The evaluation of the severity of the operational effects is based on the above distribution analysis.

When the significance values are used, the analysis refers to the evaluation of the current status. However, the evaluation analysis referring to trends is defined by the use of the degree of trend or accumulation values. Techniques and methodologies that are based on clustering analysis are used in distribution analysis where their results are illustrated using mountain surface representations. The following sections present and analyze these representations.

Mountain Surface Evaluation (MSE) Methodology

In the MSE methodology, the volume at the surface of the mountains represents the degree of severity of the cluster areas defined by the operational risks or affected operations. As discussed above, when the operational risks are under study, they are distributed in the space of the affected operations. On the other hand, when the affected operations are under study, their distribution is defined in the operational risks' space. Moreover, in the distribution analysis, the significance value or the trend or its accumulation values are also considered. The mountain surfaces in both of the above spaces are constructed by integrating the density of the distributed operational risks or distributed affected operations together with their significance and trend values.

Thus, the mountain is a function that is defined by the density *den* in each point of the clusters together with the significance *SV* or trend *T* values. The estimation of the mountain surfaces for the distribution of the operational risks and for the distribution of the affected operations is defined in Equation 6.51 and Equation 6.52, respectively.

$$M_{OpR} = f\left(den\left(\mathbf{z}^{\delta},\mathbf{z}^{\gamma},\mathbf{z}^{c}\right),\left[SV_{\delta},T_{\delta}\right],\left[SV_{\gamma},T_{\gamma}\right],\left[SV_{c},T_{c}\right]\right) \quad (6.51)$$

$$M_{\Lambda} = f\left(den\left(\mathbf{z}^{\lambda}\right),\left[SV_{\lambda},T_{\lambda}\right]\right) \quad (6.52)$$

where

$den\left(\mathbf{z}^{\delta},\mathbf{z}^{\gamma},\mathbf{z}^{c}\right)$ and $den\left(\mathbf{z}^{\lambda}\right)$ define the density of the operational risk and the affected operations respectively,

$\left[SV_{\delta},T_{\delta}\right],\left[SV_{\gamma},T_{\gamma}\right],\left[SV_{c},T_{c}\right]$ and $\left[SV_{\lambda},T_{\lambda}\right]$ define the significance and trend values for the operational risks and the affected operations, respectively.

Note that the two dimensions of the distribution space refer to a pair of operational risks or the affected operations. However, it is important to note that both significance *SV* and trend *T* or accumulation values include all the associated values of the affected operations and operational risks, respectively. This means that the mountain function uses the significance *SV* and trend *T* values and considers all information of the multidimensional correlation space.

The volume of the resulting mountains, defined by their size and height, is used to evaluate the current or trend severity of the areas referring to operational risks or affected operations. The contour areas resulting from the cross section of the above mountains indicate the boundaries of severity referring to clusters. These are defined from the operational risks or affected operations to different significant level. Thus, each contour for each cluster has different space area according to the level of the mountains that the cross sections represent. The smaller and the more centralized the cluster, the higher the mountain and so the higher the severity. These contour areas indicate the area where a synergy may exist between different operational risks or affected operations that belong to the same risk levels. The very small/centroid contour represents the top of the mountains. This also is used as one way to indicate the center of the cluster under study. A comparison with the operational risk equilibrium point(s) shows how close or how far the clusters are from the equilibrium point(s).

Resulting Views from Distribution Analysis

There are many different ways of viewing and extracting considerable information about operational risks using the two types of distribution mentioned in the above sections. For instance, Figure 6.7 and Figure 6.8 show the distribution of several operational risks in the space that is defined by two different operations referring to "Teller B" and "IT Account Systems."

The dots in both figures are defined by the values of the common operational risk that appears in the two operations. The different gray color spectrum indicates their values of significance (Figure 6.7) or degree of their trends (Figure 6.8). The dark gray indicates high significance and high trend, whereas the light gray indicates low significance and low trend. The contours define the area of the current and trends' operational risk severity. Figure 6.9 and Figure 6.10 illustrate the mountain surfaces that define the current and trend severity of the two affected operations. The volume of these mountains in the plot of the affected operations evaluates the participation of operations referring to "IT Account Systems"

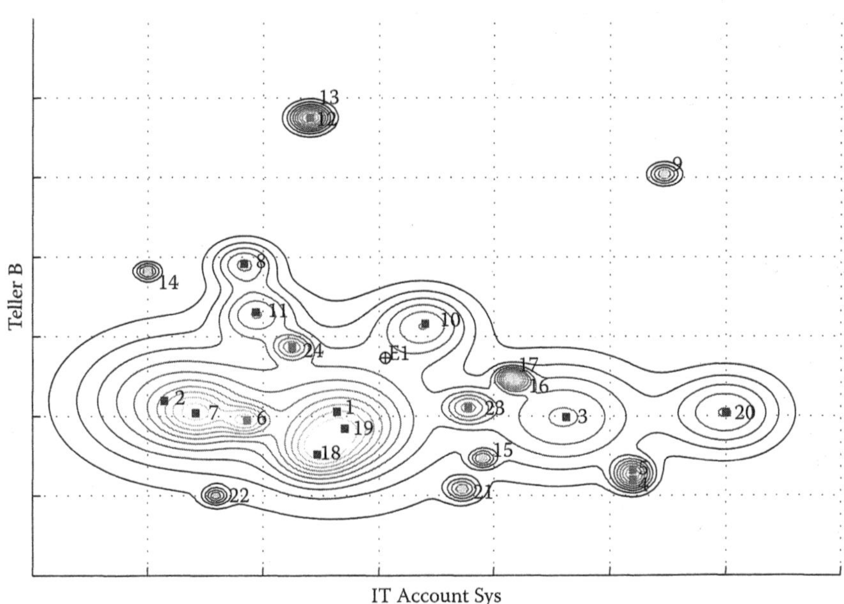

Figure 6.7 Distribution of several operational risks in the space that is defined by two different affected operations referring to "IT Account Sys" and "Teller B." The gray scales of the dots define the significance values of the operational risks under study.

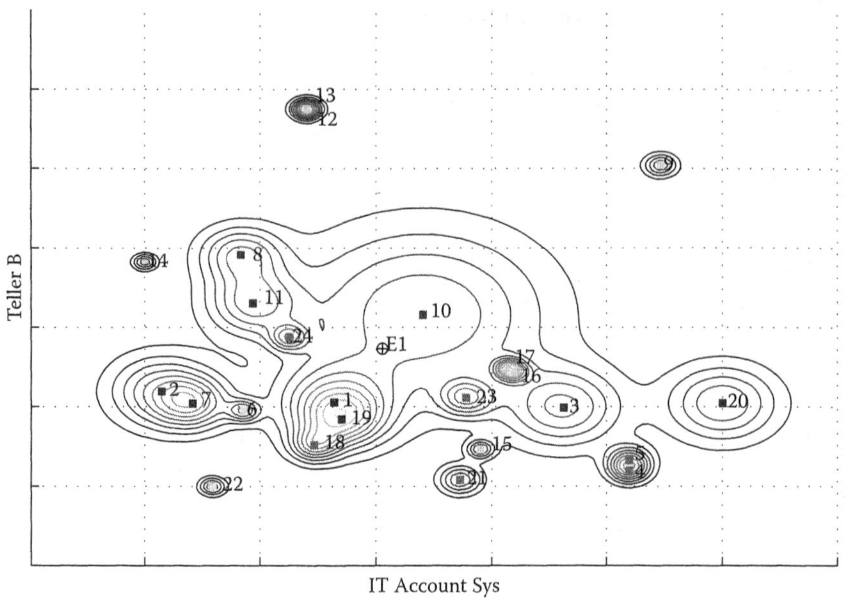

Figure 6.8 Distribution of operational risks referring to Figure 6.7 where the variations of the gray scales of the dots define the trend values of the operational risks under study.

and "Teller B" refers to the quantification of operational risks. Moreover, the evaluation on how these operational risks are affecting or will tend to affect the two operations that define the two axes of the operational risk distribution is also defined and illustrated graphically. The z axis defines their corresponding degree of severity.

The distribution of the groups defines a number of different affected operations, as illustrated in Figure 6.11 and Figure 6.12. The coordinates of the elements, represented by the dots and construct the clusters, are defined by the values of the operational risks that affect the associated operations. Thus, the x and y axes define the operational risks' space. The gray dots define the different significance values in Figure 6.11 and degree of trends in Figure 6.12, which refer to our exampled case twenty-four (24) different affected operations from their associated operational risks. The area of severity for the current and trend effect to the operations is illustrated by the contour plotted in both Figure 6.11 and Figure 6.12. The surface of mountains in Figure 6.13 and Figure 6.14 illustrates the current and trend degree of the severity of the impact of a preselected combination of operational risks (referring to "Missing Transfers" and "Account Verification Time") on the set of the affected operations. Note

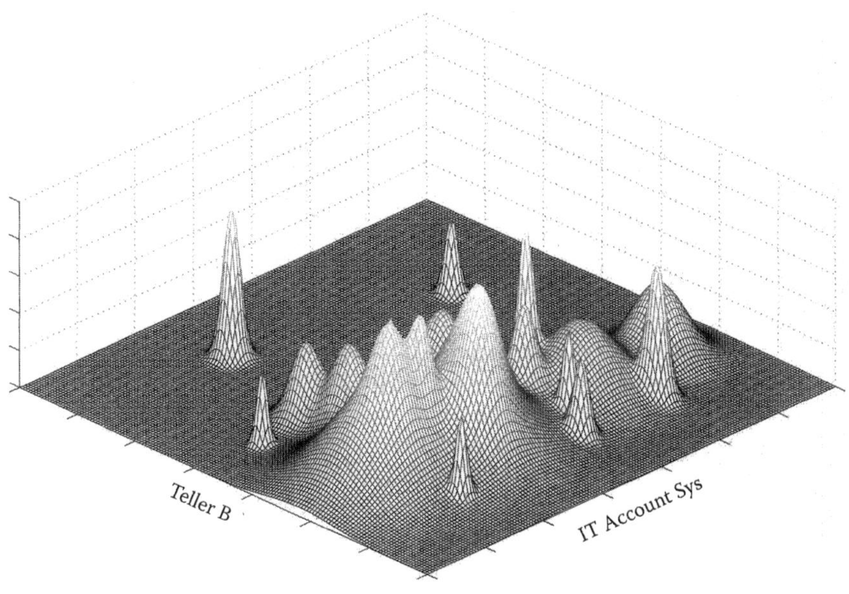

Figure 6.9 Mountain surfaces that evaluate the current severity of the affected operations referring to the quantification of risks.

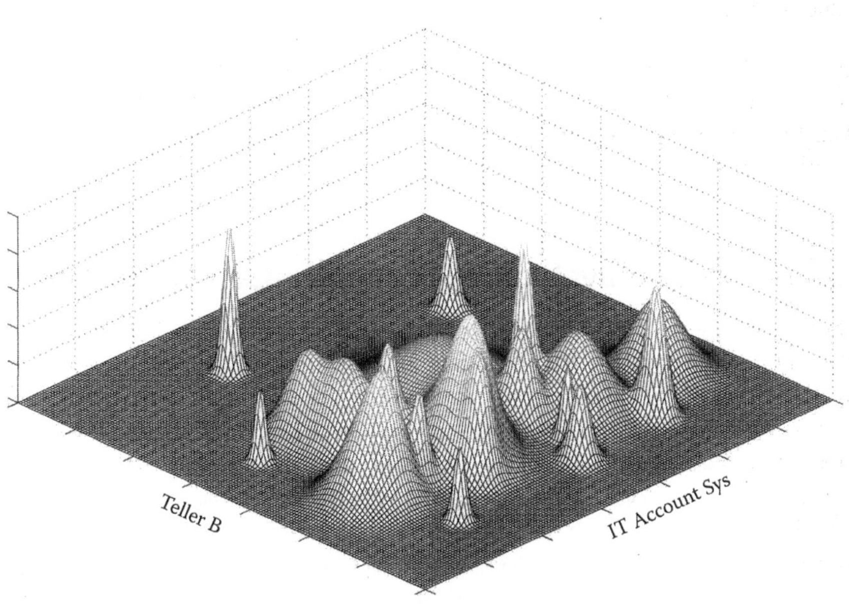

Figure 6.10 Mountain surfaces that evaluate the severity of the future trend for the affected operations.

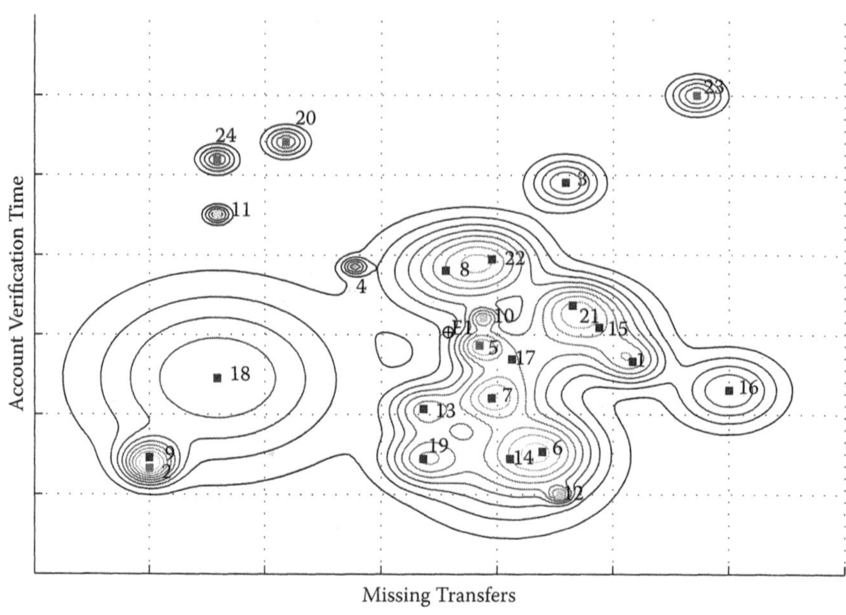

Figure 6.11 Distribution of affected operations in the space that is defined by two common associated operational risks. The contours define the area of current value of severity.

that the degree of operational risk severity is defined by the volume of the mountains, that is, size and height. This is defined by considering the distribution of the affected operations, together with their significance or trend values.

Estimating and Evaluating Economic Capital Reserves

The second part of this chapter is about the estimation and evaluation of the economic capital that banking organizations need to reserve for covering potential losses that are initiated from operational risks. In banking organizations, losses that are initiated from operational risks are measured and evaluated by quantifying unexpected (or unaffordable) performance of people, processes, and systems that cause potential losses. Consider that a given actual value of an operation's performance results in expected profit. A variation of the actual operation's value due to operational inefficiencies can result in a decrease in this expected profit (opportunity loss) or an increase of the realized loss (a realization of an absolute loss). If this is the case, the organization faces a potential loss.

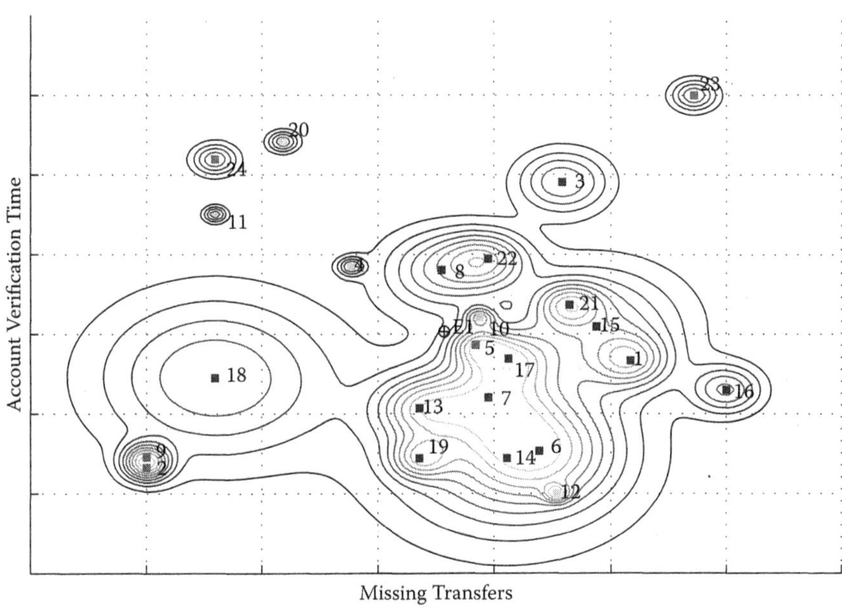

Figure 6.12 Trend distribution of the affected operations defined in Figure 6.11. The contours define the severity areas of the above trends.

The potential loss is the difference between the actual profits/losses and the expected profits/losses. Potential losses should be efficiently defined, measured, and represented in matrices, and categorized according to where they may initiate from, that is, people, systems, and processes. Operational value-at-risk (VaR) is used for estimating the capital needed to cover the potential losses resulting from operational risks. In this book, approaches from the well-known and widely used extreme value theory (EVT) are introduced as techniques for estimating the operational VaR.

Unexpected Losses Relating to People

It is suspected, but not always provable, that losses initiated from employees' performances are the most critical in the organization's overall performance. The term "critical" usually refers to the degree of financial disaster that may affect the business. A few such disasters were listed in Table 1.2 in Chapter 1. As discussed in that chapter, fraud is one of the major and most common sources of losses in banking organizations. In operational risk management, the estimation of the overall potential loss that the organization could possibly sustain from employees' unauthorized activities

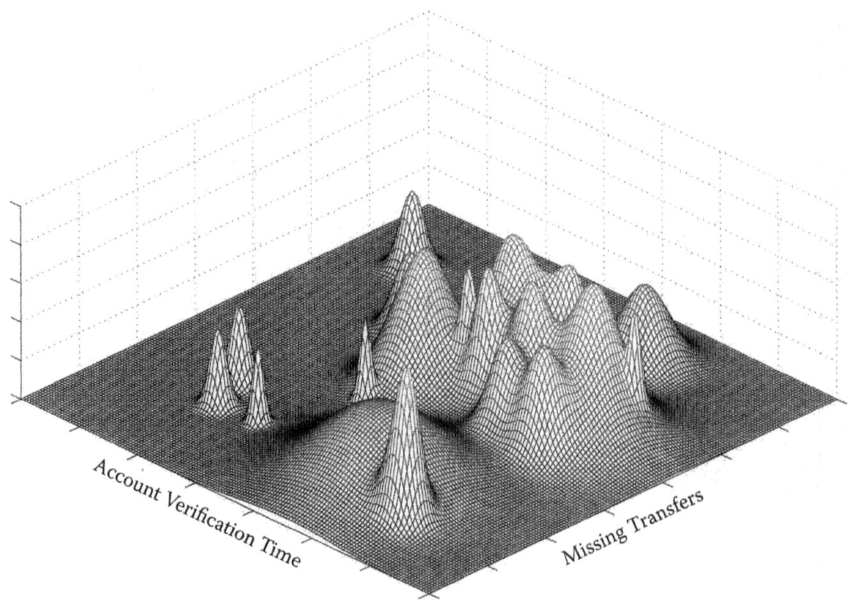

Figure 6.13 Evaluation of the current volume of impact severity concerning a preselected combination of operational risks on the set of affected operations illustrated by a mountain representation.

is defined from the degree of correlation between these business activities with:

- Other employees' business activities
- Supported system activities
- Involved process activities

When trading, the banking organization is exposed to three types of risks: market risk, credit risk, and operational risk. If the banking organization is on the selling side of the transaction, it carries a credit risk resulting from the inability or the unwillingness of the counterparty to fulfill its obligations during the settlement procedure (otherwise known as "settlement risk"). Moreover, the banking organization has a postsettlement risk from the adverse movement of market prices. Finally, the most important risk for our analysis is the operational risk. For instance, assume a case where a bank trader has a trading authorization limit of $100,000 per day. The bank pays a fee to third parties that carry out transactions on behalf of the banking organization. Consequently, suppose that the transaction fees are equal to 0.5 percent for every transaction. This means that the bank is willing to pay a maximum fee of $500 per transaction

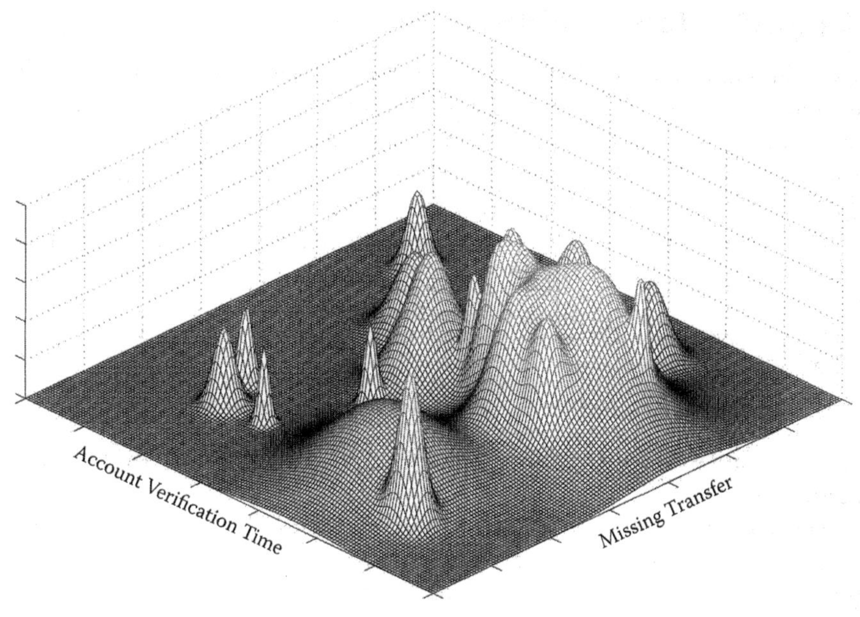

Figure 6.14 Mountain surface that represents the evaluation of the severity trend impact of a preselected combination of operational risks on the set of affected operations.

corresponding to the aforementioned trader. However, if the trader breaches the limit and trades \$1,000,000, the fees will be \$5,000. Thus, in this case the realized loss would be \$4,500 per day.

Exactly the opposite would have happened if the banking organization was going to receive the aforementioned fees. Imagine the case in which the banking organization receives a selling order from its client. The order equals \$100,000, but the trader, accidentally or intentionally, puts an order of \$1,000. The banking organization will actually receive \$5 instead of the expected amount of \$500. Thus, there is an opportunity loss of \$495.

The maximum potential loss that the organization could have from an unintentional (but even so unprofitable) trading in, for example, a 21-day period, is \$100,000 × 21 = \$2,100,000 (adjustment). Stated otherwise, the potential loss is a function of either the reduction in profit or the realized loss.

The above loss is accurate if and only if the trading process would be independent in terms of other people's business activities, monitoring systems, and processes involved in these particular trading activities. Note that the banking organization's policies must always be integrated with the people's operational activities, systems, and processes of the business.

Unexpected Losses Related to Systems

Potential financial losses initiated from systems usually refer to their failures or their weaknesses for preventing other potential losses that are initiated by people and processes and that are undesirable for business activities. System failures could appear independently, or in parallel, and within several business lines and with different degrees of financial significance.

The resulting potential loss to systems is estimated by considering their correlation to:

- Employees' activities
- Process workflows
- Other system activities within the organization

that are related to business performance and usually transferred to their financial profits.

The volume of potential losses related to systems is therefore estimated by considering and analyzing the above correlations in comparison to their individual expected financial performances.

Unexpected Losses Related to Processes

Operational business processes in banking consist of a set of business activities and procedures, undertaken by the organization, in the pursuit to reach the overall business targets and objectives. Typical business processes in banking organizations include managing trading orders, delivering financial services, managing money, managing credits and loans, etc. The operational business processes depend on several business functions for support, e.g., IT systems, personnel, and activities from other processes. Thus, the business process rarely operates in isolation; in fact, other business processes, systems, and people will depend on it to a certain degree.

The process activities and procedures may have failed in its application and, thus, may initiate potential internal or external losses, that is, from the actual process failure or from the correlated processes, people, and systems, respectively. The loss from these risks of failure needs to be evaluated. This evaluation is achieved by considering the correlation between the processes with the affected:

- Employees' activities
- System activities
- Other process workflows within the organization

that are related to their performances. These performances are translated, if possible, to financial impact. Thus, the potential unexpected losses of processes refer to people and system operational activities and their relation to the expected performances.

Considering the above issues, the estimation of the potential loss, initiated from processes and their amount of correlation with people or systems, is defined by the performance analysis among their operational activities. The operational risks are initiated from insufficient management within the operational activities. The use of the correlation analysis quantifies the loss impact across the operations and is used as a basis for evaluating the operational potential losses, as described in the following sections.

Identifying Potential Losses

One of the main tasks of designing an optimal operational risk management system is to define the maximum probabilistic financial impact (or in other words financial loss) that could be caused from each of the operational risks that may occur. The financial impact is defined as a downstream effect of the consequences of risks. The consequences of risks result from the events that are caused by the undesirable or unexpected performances of people, processes, or systems. Thus, the identification of the financial impact should be categorized according to these three types of risk initiatives: people, processes, and systems.

Banking organizations subjected to operational risk must keep an effective database of financial losses that have occurred. This type of database usually refers to a sequence of realized losses or opportunity losses that have initiated from operational risks and have already appeared. These operational risks define the insufficient manipulation of the operational activities within the business lines and thus the losses appear to be related to undesirable operational performances.

Defining Potential Losses

The first step is to define the losses for each operational activity within all business lines that result from both internal and external risks. There are two main types of potential losses according to the effect of operational risks:

1. Direct: those that are initiated directly from the risks in operations
2. Indirect: those that are initiated from the risk affecting other operations that are linked to the operations under study

Both types of losses are presented in the next two subsections.

Potential Losses from Influences of Direct Operational Risks

In this book, the estimation of the above losses is approached using the performance and correlation analysis among the operations affected from risks. The analysis must include all affected operations within all business lines. It also includes expected and unexpected performance analysis, together with the operational profit, corresponding to expected and unexpected values.

First, in the definition of losses, it is important to define the actual "value" V for each of the operational activity in relation to overall business performance and objectives. In general, the term "value" indicates the degree of financial significance of each operational activity. This significance mainly results from its level of financial correlation to:

- The operations related to performance of processes, people, and systems
- Its impact on business objectives

Thus, $V = f(cor(op,r), cor(op,obj))$, where *op* defines the operational activity; *r* the performance of processes, people, and systems; and *obj* the merit of the business objective. In both cases, performances and objectives are related to the financial profits.

The second analysis refers to the actual degree of the desirable or "expected performance" (*ExP*) before any disturbance(s), from risk(s), occur in each operational activity. The term "expected" includes the value of financial performances (mainly expressed in terms of profit) of the operational activities. This expectation is usually defined through the organization's quality management system. This system defines the interrelation workflow activities of processes, people, and the systems and the return (i.e., profit, better performance, etc.) in relation to their contribution toward reaching the overall business targets and objectives.

The combination of the actual operational value, together with its expected performance, defines the desirable or "expected profit" that the operational activity exhibit, that is, $ExT = (ExP, V)$. Note that, in this definition, the operations are not under operational risk influences.

When an operational risk is initiated, a variation of its affected operations' performances occurs to different degrees. Thus, this variation is used for indicating the operational risks appearances as well as participation in the measurement analysis of its value. The actual performance *AcP* of the operations, under operational risk influences, is different from the expected one (*ExP*) by some value, that is, $AcP \neq ExP$. Thus, the resultant unexpected performance ($UExP_{Risk}$) that is initiated from the operational risk(s) is estimated from the absolute value of the difference between the expected and actual performance, that is, $UExP = abs(ExP - AcP)$.

The actual undesirable or "unexpected profit" of the operations that are affected by operational risks is defined similarly to the expected one. In this case, the unexpected performance $UExP_{Risk}$ is multiplied by the actual operational value of the operations under study, that is, $UExT = UExP_{Risk} \times V$.

The overall direct loss of an operation that is under operational risk influence is estimated by considering the expected and unexpected profits. Thus, the absolute value of the difference between these expected and unexpected values defines the operational unexpected loss that is caused by the operational risk(s), as illustrated in Equation 6.53.

$$UnExOpLoss_D = abs\left(ExT - UExT\right) \tag{6.53}$$

This estimation of unexpected losses refers to all those operational activities that are directly affected by one or more operational risks.

Potential Losses from Indirect Operational Risk Influences

When an operational risk occurs, the affected operational activities change their performances to unexpected values. This is a direct risk influence on the affected operations under study. However, in large organizations such as banking where people, processes, and systems are linked and interacting with one another, performance variation in one operation generates a chain reaction of performance variation in other linked/related operations. Therefore, this resultant unexpected performance $UExP_{Op}$ of the related/linked operations is in this case initiated from the unexpected and undesirable performances of the affected operations due to operational risks. This is an "indirect" operational risk influencing the related operations.

The "expected performance" ExP, as well as their actual values, V, of the related operations are defined as explained in the previous section. Moreover, similar to the definition described in the above subsections, the "expected profit" of this indirectly influenced operation is defined by integrating the actual operational value together with its expected performance, that is, $ExT = (ExP, V)$. Note that in this case, the linked operations under study do not have any direct or indirect influence on operational risks.

Furthermore, in this analysis the unexpected performance $UExP_{Op}$ that occurs due to a linked operation is also calculated. This performance $UExP_{Op}$ is initiated from another operation(s) that is directly influenced by operational risk(s). In this case, the actual performances AcP of the linked operation(s) that are under operational risk influence(s) are compared to their expected ExP ones, that is, $AcP \neq ExP$. Thus, in this analysis, the resultant unexpected performance $UExP_{Op}$ is defined by the absolute value of the difference between its expected and actual performance referring to linked operations, that is, $UExP_{Op} = abs(ExP - AcP)$. Finally, the actual undesirable or unexpected "profit" of these operations is calculated by integrating the unexpected performance $UExP_{Op}$ with their actual operational value, that is, $UExT = UExP_{Op} \times V$.

For the indirectly influenced operations, the overall indirect unexpected, potential losses are defined similarly to that of the directly influenced operations. Therefore, in this case such calculation is also done by considering the expected and unexpected profits, as defined in Equation 6.54:

$$UnExOpLoss_I = abs\left(ExT - UExT\right) \tag{6.54}$$

This calculation of indirect losses refers to linked operational activities that are in this case indirectly affected by one or more operational risks.

It is important to note that in both of the above cases, direct and indirect, the operational performances related to people, systems, and processes are ongoing processes that all banking organizations must monitor and measure. As mentioned in previous chapters of this book, performance is usually measured through key performance indicators, KPIs, and operational risks are measured through KRIs. In this part of the risk management evaluation analysis, therefore, the two different types of key indicators (i.e., performance and risk) are combined to measure the losses. They have therefore equal importance in this part of the operational risk evaluation analysis. Moreover, the measurement of the profit should be defined in financial terms. The actual operational value therefore should also be defined in financial terms.

Representing Unexpected Performances

The representation of the potential losses within the operational activities can be illustrated in a matrix that includes all activities, together with their direct and indirect losses. Moreover, three types of unexpected losses that are initiated directly or indirectly from the operational risks are illustrated in this representation:

1. Internal potential losses: all the actual losses that result from the affected operations and that refer (internally) to the same operation
2. External potential losses: all the losses that are initiated from the affected operations and that refer (targeting) to the other operations
3. Receiver potential losses: all losses that an operation exhibits but that are initiated (received) from other affected operations

There are two alternative ways of looking at potential losses initiated from operational risks and assigned to each operational activity within each business line:

1. The first way is to assign all these potential losses that are initiated from a particular operation and that affect the other operational activities to each operational activity. In this case the quantification of losses results in the measurement of the losses of the affected operations. This representation of "loss dispersion" illustrates the quantitative value of losses for each affected operation.
2. The second way is to identify and measure all these potential losses resulting from the contagion effect of operations that are initiated from the performance variation of the related/linked operations. These linked operational activities are directly affected by operational risks. This "loss reception" representation shows the losses of each operational activity that are initiated indirectly from internal or external linked operations within all business lines.

In both of the above cases, these potential losses resulting from the operational risks can be assigned to each operational activity.

For instance, suppose that in a banking organization there are three different operational activities under consideration, such as "Cash Transactions" (Act 1), "Billing Payments" (Act 2) and "Check Transactions" (Act 3), as defined in Table 6.1. Let's assume that operational risks initiated from insufficient operation of "Cash Transactions" result in an internal potential loss of $9000 toward itself. This underperformed "Cash Transactions" operation initiates losses in "Billing Payments" and "Check Transactions" that amount to $900 and $1800, respectively. Similarly, the internal loss of "Billing Payments" is $10,000 and the resultant indirect potential losses

Table 6.1 Loss Representation of Three Operational Activities: Cash Transactions, Billing Payments, and Check Transactions

	Response			
Impulse	*Act 1*	*Act 2*	*Act 3*	*Loss Dispersion*
Act 1	$9,000	$900	$1,800	$11,700
Act 2	$100	$10,000	$200	$10,300
Act 3	$0	$300	$0	$300
Loss Reception	$9,100	$11,200	$2,000	$22,300

to the other operational activities are $100 and $200, respectively (see Table 6.1). Finally, the "Check Transactions" activity causes operational loss only to itself. The "Loss Dispersion" representation gives a summation of the overall losses of $11,700, $10,300, and $300 for each of the operations. This results from adding the row elements of Table 6.1, that is, *sum* ($9,000 + $900 + $1,800) = $11,700 for the first case. The overall "Loss Dispersion," which is the potential loss from all operations, is thus $22,300. Considering the columns of the same table, a representation of the "loss reception" is illustrated. Thus, in the first column, the operational activity of "Cash Transactions" has internal direct losses of $9000 and indirect losses from the "Billing Payments" of $100. The resultant "Loss Reception" representation is $9,100, $11,200, and $2,000 for each of the operational activities under study. Their estimation is defined by the summation of the column elements. Moreover, overall "Loss Dispersion" from all operations is $22,300. Note that both "Loss Dispersion" and "Loss Reception" values for analyzing the potential losses are equal.

Estimation of the Economic Capital of Operational Risks Using the Operational VaR

The Basel II Accord for Banking Supervision has already defined the capital requirements, related to operational losses, for the basic indicator and standardized approaches. According to the paper of the Basel Committee on banking supervision, "Supervisors will require the bank to calculate its regulatory capital requirement as the sum of Expected Loss (EL) and Unexpected Loss (UL)."[4] For the advanced measurement approach (AMA), banking organizations are free to implement their own, tailor-made approaches that better describe the operational risk profile of their operations.

The Basel II Committee does not explicitly define the relationship between economic and regulatory capital. Thus, it allows banking organizations to develop their individual interpretations for the determination of regulatory capital, given that internal models are fully incorporated in the business culture. In banking organizations, the economic capital corresponding to market and credit risks is approximated by VaR measurements.[5] In turn, the economic capital, corresponding to market risk and credit risk, is used as the starting point for regulatory capital calculation by regulatory authorities. The operational risk can use an equivalent measurement, called the "operational VaR." Because the operational VaR is the cornerstone element for the determination of regulatory capital, it is important to explain the main approaches to measure it. The estimation of the operational VaR is based on EVT, as described in the following sections.

Extreme Value Theory to Operational Risk

The extreme value theory, or Fisher–Tippett theorem,[6] was originally applied to model rare phenomena that came from hydrology and climatology. It has only recently been systematically employed to explain extreme behaviors in the fields of insurance and finance.[7,8] This section uses an adjustment of the Fisher–Tippett theorem for modeling operational losses. It is important to note that the need for EVT follows the operational modeling suggested by the Basel II regulatory framework. EVT is used as a basis for estimating the operational VaR.

The basic indicator and standardized approaches are the main measuring strategies for estimating operational losses for "nonsophisticated" banking organizations. However, a natural candidate for advanced measuring approaches is the EVT. In contrast to traditional approaches that presume a prespecified distribution, the EVT approach identifies extreme losses of low density and high magnitude based on the actual distribution of losses and covers a large set of distributions[9] (normal, log-normal, χ^2, Student–t, F, gamma, exponential beta, uniform, etc.).

In contrast to market and credit risk quantification, operational risk factors do not follow ordinary density distributions. Alternatively, they exhibit fat tails and in many cases the tails themselves follow independent distributions from the distribution of the dataset. As illustrated in Table 6.2,[10] the ratio of losses to insurance fees resulted from the earthquakes in California for the period between 1971 and 1994, the tail events are more catastrophic than expected from the normal density distribution. For instance, the earthquake in 1994 caused losses that were approximately 17 times more than the maximum amount of losses that appeared within this period.

EVT is explicitly or implicitly based on the distribution of business losses, defined in Equation 6.53 and Equation 6.54, within the probability and impact axes. Moreover, it may also use the distribution of residuals (errors). The probability is defined in terms of frequency whereas the impact is described in terms of financial losses.

Extreme Value Theory Approaches

The EVT is divided in two main categories: the block maxima and the peaks over threshold. The peaks over threshold approach is divided into two subcategories: the semi-parametric and parametric approaches. Finally, the parametric approach is based on either conditional or unconditional approaches. Figure 6.15 illustrates this categorization.

Table 6.2 Ratio of Losses to Insurance Fees Resulting from the Earthquakes in California for the Period between 1971 and 1994

Year	*Rate of Losses*	*Frequency*
1971	17.4	5
1972	0.0	21
1973	0.6	20
1974	3.4	12
1975	0.0	21
1976	0.0	21
1977	0.7	19
1978	1.5	16
1979	2.2	15
1980	9.2	10
1981	0.9	18
1982	0.0	21
1983	2.9	14
1984	5.0	11
1985	1.3	17
1986	9.3	9
1987	22.8	4
1988	11.5	8
1989	129.8	2
1990	47.0	3
1991	17.2	6
1992	12.8	7
1993	3.2	13
1994	2272.7	1

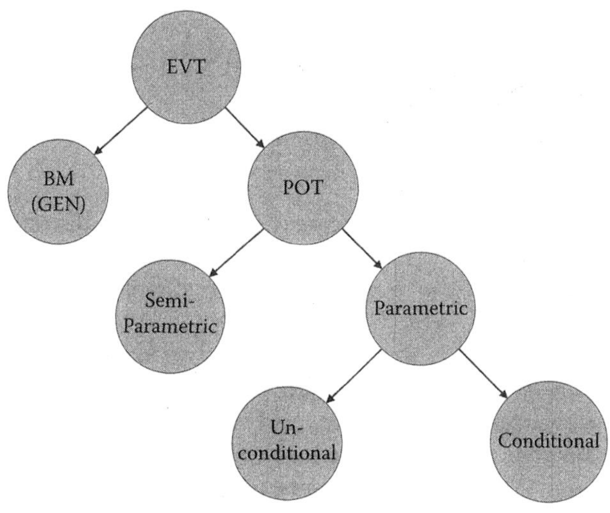

Figure 6.15 Categorizing the approaches in extreme value theory (EVT): block maxima (BM) and peaks over threshold (POT). The POT approach is divided into the subcategories "semi-parametric" and "parametric." The parametric approach is based on conditional or unconditional approaches.

Block Maxima Approach

This method is used when all the loss events that are related to operational performances and risk variations are independently and identically distributed (IID). Thus, the observations denoted as X_n ($n \in \mathbf{Z}$) are drawn from an unknown distribution F. Using the block maxima approach, the distribution of losses is separated into nonoverlapping (periodical) consecutive blocks of n length. The size of the length is based on an ad hoc decision chosen by the analyst. The maximum values of each block are selected to define the vector **M**. This vector of maximal distributed values is normalized into y normalized values as defined in Equation 6.55:

$$y_{ni} = \frac{M_{ni} - \mu_n}{\sigma_n} \tag{6.55}$$

where the parameters μ_n and σ_n define the location (mean) and scale (standard deviation) of the **M**'s vector distribution of its i element.

Fisher and Tippett as well as Gnedenko[11] proved that, when $n \to \infty$, the variable y follows the nondegenerate distribution function H defined in Equation 6.56:

$$H_{\xi}(y) = \begin{cases} \exp\left(-(1+\xi y)^{-\frac{1}{\xi}}\right) & \xi \neq 0 \\ \exp\left(-e^{-y}\right) & \xi = 0 \end{cases} \tag{6.56}$$

where ξ is the generalized parameter of the unknown distribution F. This parameter is defined by applying the maximum likelihood method on the observed values. Equation 6.56 defines the distribution of maxima in probability and impact axes.

The return level VaR is the level expected to be exceeded in one out of k block-length periods. For instance, taking 20 blocks (i.e., $k = 20$) that each one equals one year in length, and obtaining for the data VaR = 7.2 percent, means that the maximum loss observed during a period of one year will exceed 7.2 percent in one out of 20 years, on average. Equation 6.57 defines the aforementioned VaR value:

$$VaR = H^{-1}\left(1 - \frac{1}{k}\right) \tag{6.57}$$

This method is suitable when there are adequate available extreme operational losses for each "block" in order to model the operational losses from the available set of information data.

Peaks over Threshold (POT) Approach

The peaks over threshold (POT) approach is divided into the *semi-parametric version*, constructed around the Hill estimator, and the *parametric version*, based on the generalized Pareto distribution (GPD).

Semi-parametric POT

The *semi-parametric POT* approach is based on the assumption that all extreme values are laid above a threshold that is, more or less, subjectively determined. Thus, the determination of the threshold **u** is mainly based on the quantile–quantile regression method.

Operational risk management, in general, is focused on heavy-tailed distributions in the maximum domain of attraction of generalized extreme value (GEV) distribution. In such cases the estimation of ξ is defined using Hill's[12] estimator. Based on this method, the original X_i opportunity loss data, which is assumed to be independently identically distributed, is arranged in descending order, that is, $X_1 \geq X_2 \geq \ldots \geq X_n$. The tail index ξ is defined by Equation 6.58:

$$\xi = \frac{1}{m-1} \sum_{i=1}^{m-1} \ln X_i - \ln X_m \tag{6.58}$$

Position index m denotes the mth threshold element or, otherwise stated, the cut-off point of the descending ordered sample, over which extreme values are realized. The difficulty in threshold determination is that a high threshold provides very little information about the behavior of extremes, while a low threshold introduces some of the average observations from the dataset distribution, increasing the bias incorporated in the estimation. Dacorogna et al.[13] and Blum and Dacorogna[14] defined m as the square root of the number of observations of business losses. In practice, this is a fairly good approximation of the true value, retaining the trade-off between bias and availability of data.

To estimate the extreme quantile that corresponds to VaR, without bias, the following formula, proposed by Dacorogna,[13] is applied to large samples. Thus, for a given probability level q, the extreme value quantile that corresponds to VaR is given by

$$VaR = X_{(m)} \left(\frac{m}{nq} \right)^{\xi} \tag{6.59}$$

This method is suitable when there are large samples of observed data referring to the extreme business operational losses. In this case, maximum use of available information is needed to identify a semi-parametric model of the operational losses. Moreover, the method is easy to implement because it is relatively simple for a naïve determination of the tail characteristics.

Unconditional Parametric POT

The unconditional parametric, POT approach is based on the determination of the threshold but beyond the estimation of the full business loss distribution characteristics of the tail. The method estimates both the position and scale parameters of the distribution. Based on this method, for the X_i opportunity loss data that follow an F distribution, it is assumed that for a certain u, the excess distribution may be taken to be exactly generalized Pareto distribution for some ξ and β (i.e., $F_u(y) = G_{\xi,\beta}(y)$), where

$$G_{\xi,\beta}(y) = \begin{cases} 1-\left(1+\xi\dfrac{y}{\beta}\right)^{-\frac{1}{\xi}} & \xi \neq 0 \\ 1-e^{-\frac{y}{\beta}} & \xi = 0 \end{cases}, \tag{6.60}$$

$$\beta > 0 \text{ and } y \geq 0 \,\forall\, \xi \geq 0 \text{ and } -\beta/\varepsilon \geq y \geq 0 \,\forall\, \xi < 0$$

The VaR for the unconditional parametric approach is defined as in Equation 6.61:

$$VaR = u + \frac{\hat{\beta}}{\hat{\xi}}\left\{\left[(1-q)\frac{n}{N_u}\right]^{-\xi} - 1\right\} \tag{6.61}$$

The parametric method is suitable when the available observed information data referring to business opportunity losses are described by complex probability distribution. Thus, the unconditional parametric method is used when reliable information data is available that describes the operational business losses for banking organizations.

Conditional Parametric Approach

The unconditional EVT is not based on any behavioral assumptions related to opportunity losses. The operational environment of a business may follow a specific trend described by an econometric model specification. This specification describes the behavior of opportunity operational losses in a dynamic manner, in contrast to the conditional approach that takes a picture of all past observations. On the other hand, the model is not likely to hold for every point in time, because the environment changes dynamically.

Moving further, the residuals of the econometric estimation are taken as the starting point to correct any error in estimation. In other words, past residuals are used from a corrective mechanism to eliminate any error resulting from misspecification. Thus, if the model underestimates the true potential losses, similarly, past residuals are used to eliminate this bias. To construct the above-mentioned mechanism, the model of the residuals must be defined according to the same approach used in the above paragraph for the pure data.

The operational VaR for the conditional parametric approach is given by Equation 6.62:

$$VaR = f\left(VaR\left(e_i\right)\right) \tag{6.62}$$

Equation 6.62 models the historical potential losses to estimate the current level of potential loss for a specific activity in a business line. The element e_i represents the residuals series taken from a specification that model past potential losses. In turn, the overall operational VaR is calculated using the VaR of these residuals. The specification of f is subject to a model based on a moving time frame of potential losses. Table 6.3 summarizes the main functions used in estimating operational VaR for Block Maxima (BM) and Peaks Over Threshold (POT) approaches together with their advantages and disadvantages.

Summary

In the analysis of a great number of operational risks and affected operations, it is easy to try to apply complex solutions. Increasing the complexity of the analysis used in operational risk management may increase its actual operational risks. In banking organizations, it is essential to use evaluation methods for the current status and the trend for all operational risks and affected operations that are transparent and well defined. One of the initial and fundamental steps in the evaluation process is to define the significance value of each of the operational risks that refer to causes, events, or consequences. As discussed in this chapter, the main elements in significance analysis are the correlation analysis that refers to any dimension of operational risks, their effects, and their equilibrium points. The corresponding actual values are defined by integrating the degree of significance together with the real values of operational risks. Similarly, the significance and actual values of the affected operations are also defined using correlation analysis. Finally, the correlation analysis is also utilized in the evaluation of the degree of significance for the "beta points" of operational risks and affected operations. Because data originates from various inhomogeneous sources, it needs to be normalized, and this chapter discussed this. Some illustrations referring to the significance and actual values were also presented. The identified significance values defined in this chapter are used extensively in all steps in the design of operational risk assessment and control/management framework. Significance analysis is used as the basis in the clustering and optimization analysis.

Cluster analysis is a novel approach in finance, even though it is highly suitable in the design phase of operational risk management systems. Clusters, in operational risk management, are the groups of homogeneous operational risks or affected operations that have more similarities to one

Table 6.3 Main Functions Used in Estimation of Operational VaR for Block Maxima (BM) and Peaks Over Threshold (POT) Approaches, Together with Their Advantages and Disadvantages

Approach		*Function*	*Advantages*	*Disadvantages*
Block Maxima (BM)		$VaR = H^{-1}\left(1-\frac{1}{k}\right)$	Used when there are adequate available extreme operational losses for each block	The maximum value in a block could be nonsignificant in the entire data set
Peaks Over Threshold (POT)	Semi-parametric	$VaR_q = X_{(m)}\left(\frac{m}{nq}\right)^{\xi}$	Used when there are large samples of observed data referring to the extreme business operational losses Method is easy to implement because it is relatively simple to achieve a naïve determination of the tail characteristics	Do not use information concerning extreme value distribution

	Parametric	Conditional	$VaR_q = f\left(VaR\left(e\right)_q\right)$	Describes the behavior of opportunity operational losses in a dynamic manner Is not based on any behavioral assumptions related to opportunity losses	Significantly, in a better position than the aforementioned approaches However, assumes that distribution remains stable over time.
		Unconditional	$VaR_q = u + \frac{\hat{\beta}}{\hat{\xi}}\left\{\left[\left(1-q\right)\frac{n}{N_u}\right]^{-\xi} - 1\right\}$	Used when reliable information data is available that describes the operational business losses for banking organizations	Subject to model error risk

another than to members of other clusters. Applying clustering techniques in operational risk analysis, information data that is quantitative, qualitative, or a mixture of both can be more easily analyzed. The main clustering approaches together with their extensions that can be used in operational risk analysis are the ones that are based on fuzzy set theory, as discussed in this chapter. Clustering analysis is also used extensively in the process of risk profiling, as discussed in the next chapter.

Another important aspect in the evaluation process is the definition of the equilibrium point(s) for both operational risk and affected operations. Two methodologies for this identification analysis, called CORE and CAOE, were introduced in this chapter. The operational risk equilibrium point(s) and the equilibrium point(s) of the affected operations were defined using the above methods. Based on these methodologies, the corresponding trends and their accumulations were also defined. Note that trend analysis is essential in evaluation analysis because it shows the tendencies (trend) of the operational risk "behaviors" and their associated affected operations "behavior."

Furthermore, a method called the mountain surface evaluation (MSE) is used to evaluate the severity of the operational risks and the affected operations. The level of severity is defined based on mathematical algorithmic techniques and methodologies. Distribution, significance, and trend analysis of the operational risks and the affected operations under study are the main elements used in this MSE method.

The above types of evaluation analysis are straightforward and transparent where their results are illustrated using advanced graphical representations. These are important aspects in operational risk management analysis. Note finally that, for confidentiality reasons, some data referring to operational risk and affected operations has been modified.

The estimation and evaluation of the economic capital that banking organizations using the AMA need to reserve for covering potential losses initiated from operational risks were defined in the second part of this chapter. In this chapter, the unexpected losses initiated from people were defined from the degree of correlation between their business activities and the business activities of other people, systems, and processes. Moreover, the unexpected losses initiated from systems and processes were estimated considering their correlation to people's activities, process workflows, and other system activities within the financial organization. The potential losses were categorized according to the effect of operational risks as direct and indirect ones, and their estimation was related to the expected and unexpected operational performances combined with their actual values. The unexpected performances matrix was constructed by presenting it in the same matrix as the internal, external, and receiver potential losses.

The estimation of the capital needed to cover the potential losses coming from operational risks is based on operational VaR, as discussed in this chapter. Moreover, this chapter introduced two categories, the block maxima and the peaks over threshold approaches from extreme value theory, that can be used to estimate the operational VaR. The mathematical equations together with their advantages and disadvantages for these approaches were also discussed (see Table 6.3).

References

1. Bezdek, J.C., *Pattern Recognition with Fuzzy Objective Function Algorithms*, Plenum Press, New York, 0-306-40671-3, 1981.
2. Gustafson, D. and Kessel, W., *Fuzzy Clustering with a Fuzzy Covariance Matrix,* IEEE CDC, San Diego, 1979.
3. Bezdek, J. and Dunn, J., Optimal Fuzzy Partition: A Heuristic for Estimating the Parameters in a Mixture of Normal Distributions, *IEEE Trans. Computers*, C-24, pp. 835–838, 1975.
4. Basel Committee on Banking Supervision, International Convergence of Capital Measurement and Capital Standards: A Revised Framework, June 2004.
5. Kalyvas, L., Sfetsos, A., Georgopoulos, A., and Siriopoulos, C., An Investigation of Riskiness in South and Eastern European Markets, *International Journal of Financial Services Management*, forthcoming, 2005.
6. Fisher, R.A. and Tippett, L.H.C., Limiting Forms of the Frequency Distribution of the Largest and Smallest Member of a Sample, *Proc. Cambridge Phil. Soc.*, 24, 180–190, 1928.
7. McNeil, A.., Internal Modeling and CAD II, RISK Books, pp. 93–113, 1999.
8. Kellezi, E. and Gilli, M., Extreme Value Theory for Tail-Related Risk Measures, preprint, Department of Econometrics and FAME, University of Geneva, 2000.
9. De Fontnouvelle, P., Rosengren, E., and Jordan, J., Implications of Alternative Operational Risk Modeling Techniques, June 2004.
10. Jaffe, D.M. and Russell, T., *Catastrophe Insurance, Capital Markets and Uninsurable Risk,* Financial Institutions Center, The Wharton School, Philadelphia, pp. 96–112, 1996.
11. Gnedenko, B., Sur la Distribution Limite du Terme Maximum d'une Serie Aleatoire, *The Annals of Mathematics*, 2nd Ser., Vol. 44, No. 3., pp. 423–453, July 1943.
12. Hill, B., A Simple General Approach to Inference about the Tail of a Distribution, *Annals of Statistics*, 3, pp. 1163–1174, 1975.
13. Dacorogna, M., Gencay, R., Muller, U., Olsen, R., and Pictet, O., *An Introduction to High Frequency Finance*, Academic Press, 2001.
14. Blum P. and Dacorogna, M., *Extreme Forex Moves,* RISK, pp. 63–66, February 2003.

IV

FRAMEWORKS FOR DESIGNING AND IMPLEMENTING EFFICIENT OPERATIONAL RISK CONTROL AND MANAGEMENT SYSTEMS

Controlling and Managing Operational Risks

Controlling and managing operational risks is the second major part of the operational risk pyramid for designing and implementing efficient operational risk management systems. The principles of operational risk control and management can be directed both to minimizing operational risk significances and adverse operational performances, as well as achieving desirable results and reaching the overall business targets and objectives.

Operational risk profiling analysis is a key part of designing efficient operational risk control and management systems. The degree of operational risk probability and impact is estimated based on correlation, significance, actual, and loss analysis. Moreover, the distribution value is used to define the operational risk exposure. The values of probability, impact, and exposure are combined using clustering and fuzzy set techniques to define and support the decision making needed in designing efficient operational risk management systems. Operational risk profiling is discussed in Chapter 7.

When operational risks occur, the performance of the affected operations is likely to fail to a certain degree. The operational risks may be controllable, partly controllable, or uncontrollable in nature. The result from operational risks may be catastrophic, mostly if they cause a chain reaction to those performances that negatively affect the business objectives and economical target values. Natural disasters, such as tornadoes in a local business area, may be uncontrollable but may not necessarily be catastrophic — that is, if the local businesses and operations can perform independently and their resulting isolation does not affect the global business activities. However, if isolation is not adequate due to constraints (such as being the main support site), the resulting consequences could be catastrophic. It is important to evaluate the degree of operational controllability in relation to business consequences, constraints, and objectives. Moreover, how levels of operational risk controllability should be managed through avoidance, transfer, or mitigation must be clearly defined, and it must also be determined whether these risks should be accepted in case of uncontrollability. However, even though an operational risk can be controlled and managed through prevention and mitigation, prevention does not always mean additional financing; moreover, mitigation does not always mean transfer to external insurance vendors.

The main objective in operational risk control and management is to minimize the overall degree of the operational risks so as to minimize the implications to operations as well as to the overall business objectives. To minimize the overall operational risk level, optimizing each operational risk level within the business lines is desirable. This is because it is almost impossible, as well as very expensive, to try to minimize all operational risks to zero. This means that, to understand the operational risks involved, organizations need to measure their actual significances and then adjust them to the levels that minimize them to the optimal degree. The problem becomes more complex because operational business processes and risks are dynamically changing, are correlated to each other, and are being influenced by many internal and external parameters. Moreover, in the global market where businesses are so related to each other, controlling and managing operational risks through the use of optimization are key elements for business financial stability and efficient growth. Obtaining optimal levels of operational risks involves determining the appropriate minimal possible level of these risks so that they will affect the operations minimally. The term "appropriate" means just enough. "Possible" indicates their constrained values that result from either the fact that other risks may be correlated negatively with them or the case where they need to have predefined values due to some external factors. In most cases of applying optimization techniques, there are constraints that should be taken into account when defining the value of the optimal points. Thus, both constrained and unconstrained optimization analyses are the two main approaches in optimization theory and should be considered in operational risk optimization analysis.

Optimizing the level of risks in operations, taking into account possible constraints, balances their values to optimal levels so that it reduces the overall operational risk implications to the minimum level. In this optimization analysis, discussed in Chapter 8, analyzing the interactions and correlations between the operational risks and between operational processes (taking into account any constraints) helps to define the optimal operational risk level. This analysis also shows the present and future trends in operational risks. The optimal allocation of resources needed for the management of the existing or optimal operational risks within each site, department, business lines, etc. is also calculated to ensure cost-effective operational risk management systems.

In addition to optimizing the levels of operational risks, the control and management strategy involve having systems in place to gain access to reliable, up-to-date information about operational risks, having an appropriate level of internal control in place to deal with these risks, and having adequate decision-making processes. It also involves planning and scheduling operational risk actions and policies. The results of these steps are used to form the inputs to the continuity planning and operational risk reviews and reports, which are discussed in Chapter 9, to enable better decision making and the establishment of appropriate risk policies. Business continuity or contingency planning through optimization is also part of operational risk control and management. This involves identifying the "what to do" actions in case a major risk occurs, and also ways to minimize its impact. Scenarios also must be planned and written, so that any reaction to a major loss will initiate the business continuity plan and be handled by predefined actions and appropriate personnel. The contents, presentation, and the frequency of the operational risk reports must also be designed and defined.

The top of the pyramid results in a dynamic operational risk control and management system that is robust and transparent and controls efficiently and optimally all risks in operations, while minimizing overall operational risks and cost and maximizing efficiency.

Chapter 7

Operational Risk Profiling

Risk without knowledge is dangerous. Knowledge without risk is rather useless.

—Peter Jennings

Introduction

Operational risk profiling in banking organizations describes actual exposure to all types of operational risks that they face. The analysis of the operational risk profile is essential in designing and implementing effective operational risk management systems. In this analysis, the values of operational risks and their associated losses are distributed into two- or three-dimensional spaces. These spaces are defined by the values of the operational risk probabilities, their impacts, and their exposures. Exposure to operational risks means the actual degree of severity of the operational risk that a bank faces. This chapter defines how to estimate the values referring to probability and impact based on the analysis of the operational risk causes, events, and consequences. This analysis mainly focused on the correlations, significance, actual, and loss values. Based on the distribution analysis of the operational risk values within the probability and impact axes, the degree of exposure is defined. Moreover, the monitoring of the operational risk profile is presented. Some main aspects, such as the deviation and curves used for evaluating the operational risk profile

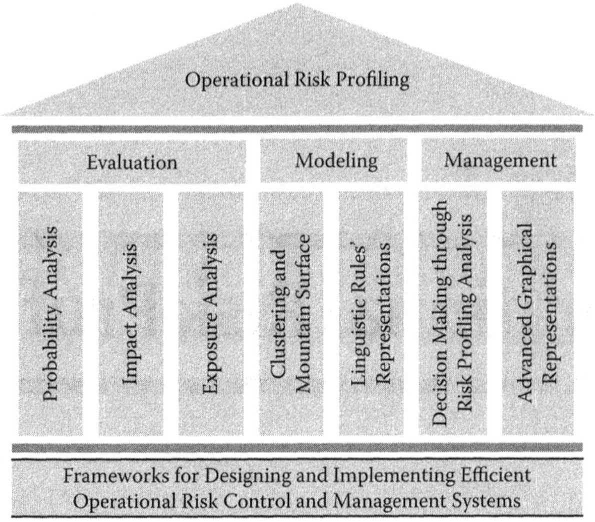

Operational Risk Profiling

Evaluation | Modeling | Management

Probability Analysis
Impact Analysis
Exposure Analysis
Clustering and Mountain Surface
Linguistic Rules' Representations
Decision Making through Risk Profiling Analysis
Advanced Graphical Representations

Frameworks for Designing and Implementing Efficient Operational Risk Control and Management Systems

Figure 7.1 Main elements of Chapter 7.

as well as the controllability zones and distribution tails, are examined. A methodology called clustering operational risk profile is used to identify, model, and evaluate the operational risks and construct the decision rules for their management. The monitoring of the operational risk profile, based on fuzzy clustering and fuzzy logic techniques and methodologies, is also discussed. The use of these models in the construction of the decision-making rules is further described. Fuzzy set theory is also used to define the linguistic membership functions. These advanced approaches for decision making are implemented in two different cases of operational risks in banking organizations. Advanced graphical representations of the results are presented and discussed extensively. The goal is to show the steps of the operational risk profiling analysis and their applicability in the construction of decision-making processes used in operational risk management systems. Figure 7.1 illustrates the main elements that make up Chapter 7.

Operational Risk Profiling

Once identified and modeled, operational risks should be evaluated by considering their causes (risk drivers), events, and consequences to determine their nature in terms of:

- The likelihood or probability of operational risks occurring and leading to an undesirable event
- The resulting impact of operational risks before and after undertaking risk control actions
- The overall exposure areas of the operations in all types of operational risks

Thus, from a high-level view, the operational risk profiling evaluation process is a three-dimensional problem constructed from multiple analysis of their probability, impact, and resulting exposure. Ways for determining their values from managers' assumptions are bound to be biased and most probably unrealistic. This is because staff members will have different experiences or viewpoints and will rate probability and impact differently.

In this book, the process of defining probability of operational risk appearances is based on multiparameter analysis that considers and combines possible and actual operational risk parameters of internal or external causes of operational risks. Moreover, causes that resulted from consequences of other operational risks are also considered. On the other hand, the estimation of operational risk impact is measured in terms of losses. Its computation is a complex process that considers all direct and indirect consequences and downstream effects resulting from the operational risks. These include the realized and opportunity losses. Moreover, the potential impacts are assessed broadly with reference to the potential effects on the realization of corporate objectives. Finally, the operational risk exposure measures the value of the risk threat by combining the likelihood of actual losses (probability), together with the magnitude of the potential losses (impact). The analysis is based on the operational risk value distribution in probability and impact axes as well as their degree of significance. The application of cluster analysis in two- or three-dimensional space, introduced in Chapter 6, is used as the backbone for analyzing and evaluating the operational risk profile.

Defining the Value of Operational Risk Probability

It is very difficult to calculate the value of operational risk probability by applying only statistical approaches that mainly rely on historical information data. This is simply because in the operational risk evaluation process, many different operational risk indicators must be considered and analyzed. As a result, many statistical approaches that could be used with such a high degree of information will be very complicated and time consuming. This may also increase the actual operational risks of the operational risk profiling analysis solution(s). Additionally, and more important in operational risk management, it is a fact that what will happen is not necessarily "similar" to what happened in the past. This concept must always be considered during the analysis and evaluation of the operational risk profile. Therefore, in the probability analysis, the information referring to the operational risk values and their resulting losses should be considered for a short length of time.

What should be considered in the probability analysis is all those operational risks that refer to people, processes, and systems that may cause financial impacts or losses. In banking organizations, the number of these operational risks is very high and their "multisource" analysis to define the operational risks' likelihood is based on correlation analysis between the risk causes, events, and consequences, as discussed later in this chapter. Finally, note that the frequency of the operational risks appearance is highly nonlinear.

Operational Risk Probability

Operational risk probability is expressed as a numerical value of the likelihood of operational risk existence within the operations of banking organizations. An operational risk usually appears in more than one operation and may be characterized as an unexpected or adverse cause, event, or consequence. The frequency of this operational risk appearance together with its correlation and significance value, indicates their probability. Moreover, the actual values of the correlated operational risks should also be considered. Note that, as discussed in the section "Defining Key Operational Risk Indicators" in Chapter 5, all operational risks should be defined quantitatively through KRIs that can be measured at any time.

The probability of the risk *cause* depends on the events and consequences that together initiate it. In other words, the probability of a cause of an operational risk is determined by the degree of correlation that the cause has with the events and consequences that initiate it. Moreover, the actual values of the events and consequences are also considered. The representation of what is considered as a probability of an operational risk cause is defined as follows:

Correlation and actual values of events ⇒ Probability of a cause ⇐
Correlation and actual values of consequences

For instance, an event of a power cut can generate a new operational risk causing an IT system failure. It is important to investigate how and by how much the parameters of the operational risk concerning a power cut correlates with the parameters of the IT system failure. High correlation indicates high probability, and vice versa.

Equation 7.1 describes the mathematical function for defining the probability of a cause of risk PR_Δ:

$$PR_\Delta = \left[\overbrace{\frac{\sum_{i=1}^{m}\left(cor(\mathbf{z}^\delta \mathbf{z}_i^\gamma)\cdot AV\Gamma_i\right)}{m}\times 100\%}^{events\rightarrow probability\_of\_cause} \right] + \left[\overbrace{\frac{\sum_{j=1}^{l}\left(cor(\mathbf{z}^\delta \mathbf{z}_i^c)\cdot AVC_j\right)}{l}\times 100\%}^{consequences\rightarrow probability\_of\_cause} \right] \tag{7.1}$$

where

$cor(\mathbf{z}^\delta \mathbf{z}^\gamma)$ and $cor(\mathbf{z}^\delta \mathbf{z}^c)$ define the correlation between:

- The external or internal events γ that may initiate the cause δ.
- The consequences c that may initiate the cause δ.

AVΓ and AVC are the actual values of the events and consequences, respectively, as defined in the operational risk identification process.

m and l are the number of the related events and consequences.

In the operational risk *event* analysis, its probability mainly depends on and is related to the causes that initiate it. Thus, the correlation degree between the causes and events, together with the actual value of the causes, defines the probability of an event; that is,

Correlation and actual values of cause ⇒ Probability of events

The mathematical function for defining the probability of an operational risk event PR_Γ is defined in Equation 7.2:

$$PR_\Gamma = \left[\overbrace{\frac{\sum_{i=1}^{n}\left(cor(\mathbf{z}^\gamma \mathbf{z}_i^\delta)\cdot AV\Delta_i\right)}{n}\times 100\%}^{causes\rightarrow event} \right] \tag{7.2}$$

where

$cor(\mathbf{z}^{\gamma}\mathbf{z}^{\delta})$ defines the correlation between the event γ under study and the causes δ.

$AV\Delta$ is the actual value of the causes as defined in the operational risk identification process.

n is the number of related causes.

The operational risk *consequences* are initiated from risk events. Thus, the probability of a consequence mainly depends on its correlation with the events that initiate it as well as with its actual value; that is:

Correlation and actual values of events ⇒ Probability of consequences

Thus, the mathematical function of defining the probability of risk consequences PR_C is defined as in Equation 7.3:

$$PR_C = \left[\overbrace{\frac{\sum_{i=1}^{n} \left(cor(\mathbf{z}^{c}\mathbf{z}_i^{\gamma}) \cdot AV\Gamma_i \right)}{n}}^{events \rightarrow consequence} \times 100\% \right] \quad (7.3)$$

where

$cor(\mathbf{z}^{c}\mathbf{z}^{\gamma})$ defines the correlation between the consequence c and events γ.

$AV\Gamma$ is the actual value of the events as defined in the operational risk identification process.

n is the number of the related events.

The above probability values are used during operational risk profiling analysis. These values define the coordinates of the probability axis in the operational risk space used in operational risk profiling analysis.

Defining the Value of Operational Risk Impact

Operational risks always have a direct or indirect impact on business outcomes. This is because operational risks "disturb" the stability of operations, where their performances are linked to business targets and objectives. In other words, operational risks affect the courses of action employed to reach the business targets and objectives. Defining and understanding the business effects, mainly defined as loss, help to actually evaluate the real "impacts" that the operational risks instigate in the organization. There are four types of impacts that operational risk may initiate:

1. Cost:
   Operational risks may result in:
   - Reduction of business income (i.e., reduction of activities on customers' accounts resulting from operational risks)
   - Increased expenses (i.e., additional effort and investments for supporting operations under operational risk influences)
   - Direct or indirect cost from loss opportunities
2. Performance:
   The overall combined performances of people, processes, and systems fail to meet the business' expectations, either because the business' targets and objectives were unrealistic or because they perform inefficiently. Note that the reliability or unreliability of one of the systems, people, or processes affects others' performances.
3. Capability:
   The overall combined capability of people, processes, and systems fails to provide the components needed for the end-to-end services to function/work properly or even function/work at all. For example, consider an organization's e-mail system that relies on mail servers, IT administrators, spam processes related to physical network components, and business policies. Their failures would impact the e-mail service and hence would directly impact the business' capability to communicate effectively.
4. Security:
   Incomplete information data, inefficient system monitoring, uncontrollable trading, etc. harm the business by having limited security knowledge and thus expose the organization's systems to security breaches and jeopardize the trading process.

Note that over-performance or over-capability may increase the business complexities, whereas over-security may reduce employees' or customers' confidence concerning business loyalty. Therefore, a balance must be sought between all these parameters.

In the operational risk profiling analysis process, it is vital to define the resulting characteristics of their impacts. Therefore, when the values of the impact for each operational risk are evaluated, the ones with the highest impacts must be investigated further.

Operational Risk Impact

The impact from an operational risk event and consequence is an estimation of its severity effects on the overall business cost, performance, capability, and security. This results in a magnitude of direct and indirect losses that have different degrees of significance. Thus, risk impact should be directly or indirectly measured with techniques and methodological approaches so that it can have comprehensive meanings. In most cases, losses are measured in financial terms, referring most of the time to costs or losses. Thus, financial impact might be long-term costs or losses in operations, short-term costs or losses such as losses of short-term market share, etc. The use of financial indicators to quantify the magnitude of loss has great advantages; it is familiar to business managers and boards of directors, and whenever there are discussions concerning financial cost or losses, attention is aroused. Moreover, the financial terms help in the planning step to ensure that the cost of preventing a risk is lower than the loss or losses that it initiates. In addition, there is a possible cost of opportunity loss that could be considered in the estimation of the overall impact. For instance, losses may result from a major contract failure because of operational risk consequences such as the organization being exposed to a security breakdown just before the contract.

It might seem that the estimation of the financial values is preferable and should be used in place of other performance indicators. In practice, however, any other objective measurement such as transaction rate, systems response time, and so forth should be used if it is justified as more appropriate and gives a clearer view of the situation. It is very important to note that *the same measurement scale must be used for all risks impacts*. This is because in situations where they are mixed, it is almost impossible to compare their direct or indirect relations, or to analyze their correlations. To overcome the problem of multimeasurements and multiscaling, it is proposed to normalize all measurements on a common unit scale, as discussed in Chapter 6.

Impact Initiated from Operational Risk Cause

The operational risk cause initiates, directly or indirectly, impact(s) on the organization's business performances. Thus, a cause has impact on one or more events, for example, the high volatility of an operational process. It may also affect opportunity losses that arises from the cause under study.

The value of the impact creates operational risk causes. Such impacts are defined by considering their actual values together with the degree of correlation(s) between the cause(s) under study and their resulting events. Moreover, the actual values of these events as well as the value of the opportunity losses, where available, are also considered in calculating the impact that results from the operational risk causes. Note that in the function for estimating the impact of operational risks, the element referring to losses should be considered with a higher degree than the other elements.

As a result, the estimation of the impact that is initiated from the operational risk causes refers to:

Cause ⇒ Impact from the actual value of the cause

⇒ Impact resulting from the causes to events

⇒ Impact from the opportunity or realized loss initiated from the cause

Equation 7.4 describes the mathematical function for estimating the impact of a cause IR_{Δ}:

$$IR_{\Delta} = \left[\left(AV\Delta + \frac{\overbrace{\sum_{i=1}^{n}\left(cor(\mathbf{z}^{\delta}\mathbf{z}_{i}^{\gamma}) \cdot AV\Gamma_{i}\right)}^{\substack{cause\rightarrow \\ impact\_to\_events}}}{n} + \overbrace{\left(Norm(\Delta Loss) \cdot AV\Delta\right) \cdot f(w_{\delta})}^{\substack{cause\rightarrow \\ impact\_to\_OpLoss}}\right) \cdot \left(\varepsilon_{\delta}^{-1}\right)\right] \tag{7.4}$$

where

$cor(\mathbf{z}^{\delta}\mathbf{z}^{\gamma})$ defines the correlations between the cause δ and the events γ that may be initiated.

AVΔ and AVΓ are defined in the operational risk identification process in Chapter 6, and represent the actual values of the cause and events, respectively.

ε_{δ} is equal to 3 and represents the number of impact types under consideration in the impact analysis from risk causes.

n is the number of related events.

$\Delta Loss$ is the opportunity loss from the appearance of the risk cause. "Norm" is its normalized value in the scale of zero to one [0,1]. The opportunity loss is related exponentially to the degree of the actual value of the cause.

$f(w_{\delta})$ is the weight function that gives an added value to losses that are initiated from the operational risk causes.

Impact Initiated from Operational Risk Events

The actual value of an event is also considered an impact to the business. Moreover, in the estimation of the event, impacts are also considered in the resulting consequences and new causes that arise from the event's appearance. The opportunity losses incurred from the event are also accounted for in the impact analysis. To define the impact value of an event, therefore, it is desirable to consider its actual value and the correlations with its resulting consequences and causes of risks. Moreover, the actual value of these consequences and causes should also be considered. Finally, in the estimation of the impact of an event, the opportunity loss resulting from the event should also be considered if its value is available. Thus, an event may result in the following impacts:

Event ⇒ Impact from the actual value of the event

⇒ Impact from the resulting consequences

⇒ Impact from the resulting (from the event) causes

⇒ Impact from the opportunity loss (initiated from the events)

Thus, the above impacts are considered in the estimation of the event's impact analysis. The mathematical function for estimating the Impact of an Event IR_Γ is as defined in Equation 7.5:

$$IR_\Gamma = \tag{7.5}$$

$$\left[\left(\begin{array}{l} AV\Gamma + \dfrac{\overbrace{\sum_{i=1}^{n}\left(cor(\mathbf{z}^{\gamma}\mathbf{z}_i^{c})\cdot AVC_i\right)}^{\substack{event\rightarrow\\ impact\_to\_consequences}}}{n} + \dfrac{\overbrace{\sum_{j=1}^{m}\left(cor(\mathbf{z}^{\gamma}\mathbf{z}_j^{\delta})\cdot AV\Delta_j\right)}^{\substack{event\rightarrow\\ impact\_to\_causes}}}{m} + \\ \overbrace{\left(Norm(\Gamma Loss)\cdot AV\Gamma\right)\cdot f(w_\gamma)}^{\substack{event\rightarrow\\ impact\_to\_OpLosses}} \end{array}\right)\cdot\left(\varepsilon_\gamma^{-1}\right)\right]$$

where

$cor(\mathbf{z}^{\gamma}\mathbf{z}^{c})$ and $cor(\mathbf{z}^{\gamma}\mathbf{z}^{\delta})$ define the correlations between the event γ with its resulting consequences c and causes δ, respectively.

AVΓ, AVC, and AVΔ are defined in the operational risk identification process (Chapter 6) and represent the actual values of the event, consequences, and causes, respectively.

ε_γ is equal to 4 and represents the number of impact types under consideration in the impact analysis from operational risk events.

n and m are the number of related consequences and causes, respectively.

$\Gamma Loss$ is the opportunity loss from the risk event appearance.

$f(w_\gamma)$ is the weight function that gives an increased emphasis on the significance of the losses that are initiated from the operational risk events.

Impact Initiated from Operational Risk Consequences

The actual value of a consequence measures the business impact, mainly in terms of losses. It also refers to downstream effects such as the reduced customer satisfaction. Even though many of the downstream effects are rarely measured quantitatively, their implications usually generate new causes as an additional impact to the business. Thus, the degree of correlations between the consequences and the new operational risk causes is also considered in the impact analysis. Finally, in the analysis of the impacts related to operational risk consequences, the opportunity losses are also considered. In summary, the consequences may result in the following impacts:

Event ⇒ Impact from the actual value of the consequence

⇒ Impact from the resulting downstream effects and causes

⇒ Impact from the opportunity losses resulting from the consequence

Thus, the above impacts are considered in the calculation of the event's impact analysis. Equation 7.6 describes the mathematical function for calculating the impact of a cause IR_C.

$$IR_C = \tag{7.6}$$

$$\left[\left(AVC + \frac{\overbrace{\sum_{i=1}^{n}\left(cor(\mathbf{z}^c\mathbf{z}_i^\delta)\cdot AV\Delta_i\right)}^{\substack{consequence\rightarrow\\ impact\_to\_causes}}}{n} + \overbrace{\left(Norm(CLoss)\cdot AVC\right)\cdot f(w_c)}^{\substack{consequence\rightarrow\\ impact\_to\_OpLoss}} \right)\cdot\left(\varepsilon_c^{-1}\right)\right]$$

where

$cor(\mathbf{z}^c\mathbf{z}^\delta)$ defines the correlations between the consequence c and the cause δ.

AVC is defined in the identification of the operational risks analysis (Chapter 6) and represents the actual values of the consequence.

ε_c is equal to 3 and represents the number of impact types under consideration in the impact analysis from risk consequences.

n is the number of related causes.

Closs is the opportunity loss from the appearance of a risk consequences.

$f(w_c)$ is the weight function that gives an increased emphasis on the significance of the losses that are initiated from the operational risk consequences.

The values resulting from the impact analysis are used to set the impact axes of the operational risk profiling analysis, as discussed in the following sections.

The Exposure of Operations to Operational Risks

The probability and impact of operational risks are the two main parameters used in the analysis and design of the operational risk profile. In the representation of the risk profile space, probability and impact define the two space axes. In addition to these axes, a third one is used to define the exposure of the operations to operational risks as well as the resulting losses from these operational risks. The analysis of the operational risk exposure is an important element used in the process of designing efficient operational risk management systems.

Banking organizations need to identify, combine, and analyze the degree of operational risks' probability and impact that could result in hazardous exposures. In this book, operational risks exposure is defined based on:

- The extent of operational risk values distributed in the probability and impact axes
- The values of risks' probability and impact as defined in the preceding sections.

Thus, the operational risk exposure is a function of the coordinating values of both probability (i.e., PR_Δ, PR_Γ, and PR_C) and impact (i.e., IR_Δ, IR_Γ, and IR_C) that are combined considering their density (*den*), as defined in Equation 7.7. The calculation of the operational risk exposure is based on the analysis of the clusters that are defined for the above coordinates.

$$REx = f(den(PR, IR), PR_{(\Delta,\Gamma,C)}, IR_{(\Delta,\Gamma,C)}) \tag{7.7}$$

In addition to the above probability and impact parameters, the degree of accumulation RA and its trend RA_T of the operational risk and affected operations under study, discussed in Chapter 6, can also be considered in the calculation of the operational risk exposure, as defined in Equation 7.8.

$$REx = f(den(PR, IR), PR_{(\Delta,\Gamma,C)}, IR_{(\Delta,\Gamma,C)}, RA, RA_T) \tag{7.8}$$

Banking organizations are exposed to several operational risks in the ordinary course of operations. Some of the main tasks in operational risk management in reference to the exposures are as follows:

- Identify their "area" and degree of significance.
- Limit them to a minimum level.
- Shift or distribute them to acceptable "areas."

The term "area" indicates the space within the probability and impact axes.

Advanced algorithmic approaches based on multidimensional cluster analysis are used for identifying and calculating the exposure to operational risks. Using such approaches, the exposed areas together with their degree of significance are illustrated using mountain surface representations as explained in the following sections. The surface of the mountains is constructed within the probability, impact, and exposure space.

It is important to note that during the optimization process, described in Chapter 8, most of the parameters that define the values of probability, impact, and exposure are minimized to an optimal level. Thus, the optimal values of the operational risks are used to drive or shift the distributed operational risk exposures to acceptable and controllable areas.

The Operational Risk Profiling Matrix

In the operational risk profiling analysis, a set of observations (or records) of the operational risks is denoted by $RP = \{z_k \mid k = 1,2,\ldots,N\}$, and is represented as an $n \times N$ matrix defined as in Equation 7.9.

$$RP_{matrix} = \begin{bmatrix} z_{11} & z_{12} & \cdots & z_{1N} \\ z_{21} & z_{22} & \cdots & z_{2N} \\ . & . & . & . \\ . & . & . & . \\ . & . & . & . \\ z_{n1} & z_{n2} & \cdots & z_{nN} \end{bmatrix}, \; z_k = \begin{bmatrix} PR \\ IR \\ ExR \end{bmatrix}, \; z_k \in \Re^n \quad (7.9)$$

where n and N are the numbers of the affected operations and operational risks, respectively.

Each element is a Euclidean space $\Re^n$ column vector that contains the values of operational risk probability, impact, and exposure as defined in Equation 7.1 through Equation 7.6.

The matrix **P** used in risk profiling analysis has three dimensions, where each of them represents the coordinates of the space defined from the values of operational risk probability, impact, and exposures. Thus, the matrix **P** is defined as in Equation 7.10.

$$\mathbf{P} = \begin{bmatrix} \overbrace{\mathbf{p}_{11}}^{pro} & \overbrace{\mathbf{p}_{12}}^{imp} & \overbrace{\mathbf{p}_{13}}^{exs} \\ \mathbf{p}_{21} & \mathbf{p}_{22} & \mathbf{p}_{23} \\ \cdots & \cdots & \cdots \\ \mathbf{p}_{N1} & \mathbf{p}_{N2} & \mathbf{p}_{N3} \end{bmatrix}, \quad \mathbf{p} = \{IR_\Delta, IR_\Gamma, IR_C, ExR\} \quad (7.10)$$

The data in the **P** matrix is used in the design of the operational risk patterns illustrated within probability and impact axes and analyzed by clustering techniques and methodologies as described in the following sections.

Operational Risk Probability, Impact, and Exposure Analysis

The operational risk profiling analysis is based on their position within the space of the axes that defines the risk probability, impact, and exposure values. Thus, the analysis is based on the distribution of the operational risk values that are defined from the coordinates of the three axes mentioned above. Therefore, if a financial organization decides to better control certain internal operational risks, such as personnel mistakes, fraud,

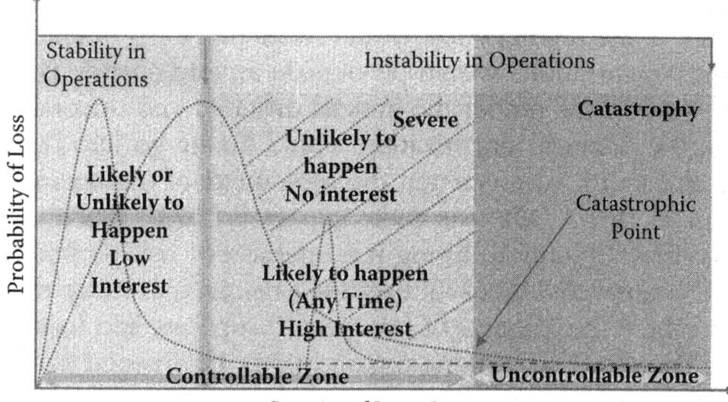

Figure 7.2 Risk profiling illustrated in the probability and impact axes. Severity of risks and their interest for the operational risk management systems.

system failures, etc., the operational risk profiling model is capable of directly identifying how much is the actual risk exposure to all operations within the organization's business lines. Moreover, it can define how much this exposure affects the organization without waiting months or years to see the results of operational risk implications. Operational risk profiling analysis is also used as one of the main elements in the construction of the operational risk control and management systems, as discussed earlier in this chapter.

First, the space that is defined by the probability and impact axes is analyzed by dividing it in four subspaces, as illustrated in Figure 7.2. These four areas indicate the severity of the operational risks based on their probability and impact as follows:

1. Low impact and low probability
2. Low impact and high probability
3. High impact and high probability
4. High impact and low probability

In the first and second cases, the severity of impact is "low" for any probability of risks appearances, which indicates trivial operational risks in businesses and low business implications. Therefore, their management and control are not of utmost importance to banking organizations. Note that business implications are mainly measured by the magnitude of financial losses.

The third case is out of the operational risk pragmatic state of existence for any banking organization. This is because it is impossible for any banking organization to stand alone in the market if both its operational risks probability and impact appear with a "high" degree. In such cases, the existence of the high impacts would mean that most operations within the banking organizations would be outside any acceptable performance range and would thus render the system unstable and uncontrollable. In such cases, the financial organization would finally go into bankruptcy.

Finally, the fourth case is when the probability of the operational risks appearances is "low," whereas their impact is "high." Such cases must receive significant attention during the operational risk profiling analysis. Note that at unexpected times all banking organizations have experienced such cases where the impacts of business disruptions and losses are very significant. Therefore, in banking organizations, heightened attention must be given to potential operational implications that arise from "low-frequency, high-impact" events such as major frauds, external attacks, and natural disasters. Note that for these cases, ongoing controls and management must be in place within all main business lines of banking organizations to capture these operational risks.

The probability and impact of an operational risk can be generally grouped under low and high values. However, for more accurate risk profiling models, a *medium* zone can be used, as illustrated in Figure 7.3. The definition of where and how to separate these areas is based on fuzzy modeling analysis in this book, as explained in the following sections.

In banking organizations, the exposure of the operations to operational risks, which arises within different business lines, is defined through risk profiling analysis. Operational risk exposure uses the information from the probability and impact axes to define the coordinate values of the

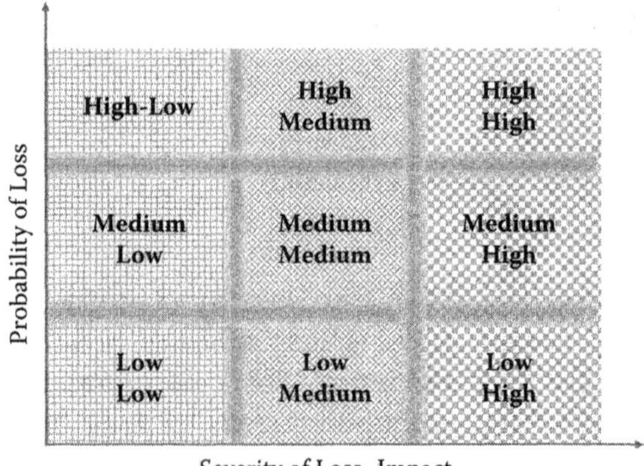

Figure 7.3 Operational risk profiling grouped under low, medium, and high values.

third dimension of the risk profiling axes. Thus, operational risk exposure analysis considers the density of the operational risks within the probability and impact axes, together with their significance values. This analysis is explained analytically in the following sections, where the risk exposure is represented using advanced graphical illustrations.

Values for Monitoring the Operational Risk Profile

In the ongoing monitoring process of the operational risk profile, three primary values should be considered:

1. The ongoing impact to the business
2. The ongoing probability or likelihood of an event occurring
3. The ongoing exposure of the operations to operational risks and losses

Furthermore, data that is used as part of the monitoring process also includes the cost or loss of an incident to the business line (actual, projected, labor hours, etc.).

Aspects for Consideration in Operational Risk Profiling

This section examines some important aspects to consider in the risk profiling design and implementation process.

Dividing the Risk Profile

Values referring to operational risk probability and impact rank from *high-frequency, low-impact*, such as transaction processing errors at one end, to *low-frequency, high-impact* catastrophic events at the other. Business losses arising from high-frequency, low-impact, such as small accounting errors or tellers' mistakes, are generally available from a financial organization's internal systems. However, information referring to low-frequency, high-impact operational risk events must be collected over some years. Modeling and budgeting for operational risks with high-frequency, low-impact can be designed quite accurately. On the other hand, those with low-frequency, high-impact are uncommon, and a single financial organization is thus unable to have sufficient data for such modeling purposes. The low frequency aspect of the operational risks makes it difficult to gather data for quantification. Note that losses that occur at a low frequency are insensitive to quantification for yielding meaningful loss event data. For such events, a financial organization may have to supplement its data with data from external organizations. However, nowadays many banking organizations are collecting such information from other external financial resources, as discussed in Chapter 2.

Defining the Elements of Risk Profiling Analysis

The elements included within the risk profiling axes are the operational risks that refer to either the individual or the groups of operations. In the first case, the risk profiling analysis refers to several operational risks that affect a single operation. In the second case, operational risks are affecting a group of operations (usually they are members of a common business line). In the latter case, the number of dimensions *d* that each operational risk value is projected on the probability and impact axes is defined in Equation 7.11:

$$d = \sum_{i=1}^{\lambda} (\delta_i + \varepsilon_i) \tag{7.11}$$

where

δ and ε are the probability and impact axes, accordingly, for each operation under study.

λ is the number of operations.

Controllable Zones and Distribution Tails

Figure 7.2 also illustrates the pattern of operational risk values' controllability zones in relation to their distribution in the probability and impact axes. Moreover, the severe and catastrophic zones are also defined. Note that the tail of the distribution curve defines the uncontrollable catastrophic zone. It is important to note that in the tail, the operational risk does not follow the normal distribution. Unexpected impacts with high degrees result in random peaks on the tail. The aim in the design process of the operational risk management system is to move any highly probable impact of operational risk toward the area of its low impact and controllable zones.

Modeling and Monitoring the Operational Risk Profile

The risk profile should be identified in terms of the different degrees of probability and impact values. The zones between the low, medium, and high areas are also defined. In this book, the justification for what the actual boundaries of these areas are and how to analyze them is also discussed. The modeling analysis for the operational risk profile is based mainly on clustering analysis and fuzzy set theory. Moreover, the boundary between the zones that define the pattern between low, medium, high, etc., operational risks probability, and impact is *gray*, or, in other words, not crisp. In this book, sophisticated approaches that are based on advanced mathematics, together with the application of clustering analysis and fuzzy logic techniques and methodologies, are used to measure and monitor the probability and impact of risks in the operations.

Clustering Analysis in Risk Profiling Analysis

In this book, a methodology called clustering operational risk profile (ClORiP) is used to identify, model, and evaluate the operational risks and to construct the decision rules for their management systems. In the space axes of the operational risk profiling, the coordinates defined by the probability, impact, and significance degrees construct groups using position dots. These dots, which are distributed in the subspace areas, are called *clusters*. These clusters define whether different operational risks are grouped in terms of having similar probability, impact, and significance values. Analysis of these clusters includes identification of their centers, boundaries, and exposure degrees. The centroids of the clusters are defined through fuzzy clustering analysis. Moreover, the boundaries of operational risks clusters as well as their value of exposure are defined using the mountain surfaces. The main elements of the methodology are presented in the following sections.

Mountain Surfaces in Operational Risk Profiling

The mountain surfaces in operational risk profiling illustrate the value of operational risk exposure in the probability and impact axes. To build this surface, a combination of two types of estimation is needed for each point in the probability and impact axes:

1. The density of the constructed clusters
2. The significance value of the operational risks

Therefore, the function that defines the mountain surface is constructed by combining the density of clusters and the significance value of its elements.

The characteristics of the resulting mountain surface (i.e., height and size) indicate the value of the degree of effect that each risk initiates within the operations. In other words, it defines the exposure of the operations to operational risks. This indication refers to each point within the probability and impact space. Thus, the size of the mountain surfaces refers to the exposure area, whereas the height indicates the degree of this exposure. Finally, the cross section of the mountains in different zones of height defines the contour map of the clusters. Thus, the lower the height, the larger the coverage area of the contour. These contours can be used to indicate the different zones of cluster boundaries.

Centroids of Operational Risk Profiling Clusters

In the analysis of the mountain surface, the top of the mountains can also be used to indicate the centers of the clusters. Thus, each subgroup that constructs a mountain has a center at its top point. This is also an efficient way of identifying the number of the cluster centroids. However, when this number is set, the centroids of the risk profiling clusters are identified using the approaches defined in the section on "Clustering Approaches in Operational Risk" in Chapter 6. The centers of the clusters that are constructed by the elements of the matrix **P** (Equation 7.10) are defined by implementing fuzzy clustering algorithmic approaches. Using such approaches, the cost function of a fuzzy *c*-means is applied. Extensions of the fuzzy c-means approaches could also be implemented. In this case the objective (or cost) functions such as that defined in Equation 7.12 is used for identifying the centroids of risk profiling clusters.

$$J(\mu_{ik}, \mathbf{v}_i) = \sum_{i=1}^{c}\sum_{k=1}^{N} \mu_{ik}^{m} \cdot \left\| \mathbf{p}_k, \mathbf{v}_i \right\|^2 \qquad m > 1 \tag{7.12}$$

The fuzziness of the resulting cluster is determined by the exponential weight m. $\mathbf{v}_i$ is a vector where its elements are the identified centroids. Note that the number of the centroids is set during the operational risk analysis (i.e., $\mathbf{v}_i$, $i = 1, 2, \ldots, c$). Finally, μ_{ik} refers to the membership function that measures how much each of the elements in Equation 7.10 belongs to a particular cluster.

Projection of Cluster Centers and Variances

The clusters or the operational risk profile can also be used for incorporating the zones of values in their probability and impact axes. These zones have linguistic meanings used in the operational risk profiling analysis. Therefore, each cluster and zone is described by the associated membership functions (MFs) that are assigned by linguistic labels. Thus, linguistic labels such as *low*, *medium*, and *high* are referring to zones of operational risk probability or impact.

In two- and three-dimensional operational risk profiling space, the actual meaning and size of the labeled zones are defined by using the centroids and the boundaries of their clusters. The method is based on projecting the centers and the end limits of the cluster boundaries into the probability and impact axes. This method defines the MFs with the corresponding linguistic terms. For instance, if the number of the clusters and thus their number of centroids are 3, the linguistic terms *low*, *medium*, and *high* can be used accordingly. Moreover, if this number is 4, an additional label to the above ones such as *very high* could be defined (depending on which zone area the associated cluster is in). Therefore, the definition of the labels is driven according to the place where the centroids are distributed in the subspaces within the probability and impact axes. Note that in cases where the number of the cluster center is a set number, the amount of linguistic terms is also set to this number.

There are different types of projections that can be used, mainly depending on which clustering method is being used to identify the cluster centers and variances. In general, if the c cluster centers are under consideration and the fuzzy c-means (FCM) method (or its extensions) is used, their projections on each dimension n define the peak values p_i^j $\{i = 1, \ldots, c, j = 1, \ldots, n\}$ of the projected MFs.

Sorting these values on each dimension as in Equation 7.13, triangular MFs are constructed with 1/2 overlap using Equation 7.14:

$$p_i^j \leq p_{i+1}^j \qquad \forall j \tag{7.13}$$

$$\mu_i^j(v^j) = \max\left[0, \min\left(\frac{v^j - p_{i-1}^j}{p_i^j - p_{i-1}^j}, \frac{v^j - p_{i+1}^j}{p_i^j - p_{i+1}^j}\right)\right] \tag{7.14}$$

where v is the distance between the peak (center) and the end of the membership function.

More efficient ways to define the two ends of the MFs include projecting the cluster boundaries defined by the mountains surfaces in the operational risk profile axes, as explained in the corresponding section. Considering the above analysis, the zones between the low, medium, and high probability and impact are defined.

Fuzzy Set Theory and Membership Functions

Fuzzy set theory[1–3] was proposed by Zadeh[3] in 1965 with many applications in different scientific sectors from engineering to finance. In the definition of the fuzzy sets, if the elements of the probability P or impact axes I are denoted by z, then a fuzzy set FS in P or I is defined as a set of ordered pairs. $FS = \{z, FS(z)\} \mid z \in (P, I)$ is called the membership function (or MF) of z in P or I. The MFs map each element of P or I to a membership value between 0 and 1. Thus, in implementing this theory, a value of operational risk is defined in a way that it belongs at the same time to two zone values of probability and impact to different degrees.

As illustrated in the previous subsection, the MFs are defined by projecting the centroids and boundaries of the operational risk profiling clusters. However, many different shapes of the MFs could be chosen in the risk profiling analysis. Triangular, S shape, Z shape, and Gaussian MFs are the most suitable for identifying linguistically the different zone values of probability and impact as well as the interrelated boundaries. When triangular membership functions are selected, their overlap is mainly set to 50 percent. This means that the height of the intersection of the two fuzzy sets is $hgt(\mu_i \cap \mu_{i+1}) = 1/2$. Thus every point in the probability or impact axes belongs to at least two fuzzy sets.

Advanced Approaches for Decision Making Using Risk Profiling Analysis

The decision-making phase is initiated by an effective risk reporting system, as discussed in Chapter 9. An action-making plan should be defined by the operational risk analysts and senior managers responsible for the operational risk management. Figure 7.2 illustrates the pattern of operational risk severity in relation to their distribution in probability and impact axes. Typical decisions on whether to accept, avoid, or mitigate the operational risks and how to deal with them are also suggested in the table, where L is Low, M is Medium, H is High. However, the real degree of exposure is not as clear as it seems by only looking at their distribution in the probability and impact axes. This is because the severity of the operational risks is increasing dramatically when their degree of significance and impact values are high. Thus, there may be the case of a group of operational risks that includes a major number of operations with high probability and low impact where their significance values are low. The resulting overall exposure may not be as significant as it looks. In this book, advanced mathematical approaches based on clustering analysis are used to construct the actual surface of operational risk exposure. Moreover, fuzzy logic theory is implemented to determine the rules used for decision making according to the degree of risk probability, impact, and exposure.

Table 7.1 illustrates the main types of decisions that could be made based on the probability and impact analysis, whereas Table 7.2 gives particular examples of operational risks together with their probability and potential impact and the kinds of decision and methods for dealing with

Table 7.1 Probability and Impact Decision

Probability	*Impact*	*Decision*
Low	Low	Accept
Low	Medium	Accept/avoid
Low	High	Avoid/mitigate
Medium	Low	Accept
Medium	Medium	Accept/avoid
Medium	High	Avoid/mitigate
High	Low	Avoid
High	Medium	Avoid/mitigate
High	High	Mitigate

these operational risks. Considering these tables, the decisions rules are based on the combinations between the values resulting from the degree of the membership defined in the probability and impact axes (i.e., low, medium, and high). However, the boundaries on where the low, medium, and high values start and end is not very crisp. Finally, the degree of "accepting," "avoiding," or "mitigating" the operational risks depends on the actual value of operational risk probability, impact, and exposure.

Approaches based on fuzzy set and fuzzy logic theory are utilized in this book to efficiently set the combination of the different risk zone values and their boundaries. This helps organizations make more effective decisions on whether and to what degree should the operational risks be accepted, avoided, or mitigated. The actual quantitative values of the linguistic representations low, medium, and high are defined by the degree of the MFs. This degree is defined from the projections of the probability and impact values to the MFs. Based on the above techniques, the antecedent of the decision rules (such as that in Table 7.1) are defined by the "fuzzy set" combinations of the MFs of probability and impact and the operational risk exposure. Thus, the values of the decision degree of the consequences for such rules are defined as in Equation 7.15:

$$d = \frac{\sum_{i=1}^{R} \xi_i \mu_i}{\sum_{i=1}^{R} \mu_i} REx \tag{7.15}$$

Table 7.2 Some Examples of Operational Risks Descriptions and Their Probability and Impact

OR Descirption	*OR Code*	*Probability*	*Impact*	*Decision*	*How?*
1. Fraud	OR 1	M	L	Accept	Monitor
2. Employee errors	OR 2	H	L	Avoid	Training
3. IT failures	OR 3	M	M	Avoid	SW/HW updates
4. Process errors	OR 4	L	L	Accept	Monitor
5. Documentation errors	OR 5	M	L	Accept	Monitor (audits)
6. Power cut	OR 6	M	L	Accept	UPS
7. Software virus attack	OR 7	L	M	Avoid	Anti-virus, firewalls
8. Loss of data	OR 8	L	M	Avoid	Backup systems
9. Security breach	OR 9	L	H	Mitigate	Security vendors
10. Earthquakes	OR 10	M	H	Mitigate	Insurance

where

R is the number of rules.

μ_i is the degree of MFs (e.g., defined in Table 7.1).

ξ_i represents the values referring to the cost of risk acceptance, avoidance, or mitigation.

Note that the cost ξ_i of operational risk acceptance or avoidance is defined by the organization's internal evaluation process, considering the variation of the affected operational performances, direct and indirect losses, etc. On the other hand, the cost of operational risk mitigation is mainly defined by external vendors/contractors such as insurance companies. It is important to note that by knowing the actual degree of the operational risk probability, impact, and exposure, the mitigation policy and cost can be based on factual and not approximated status of operational risks. This is beneficial both for the banking organizations and insurance companies.

Representations of Operational Risk Profile

The values of operational risk probability and impact, calculated using Equation 7.1 through Equation 7.6, define the coordinates of operational risk distribution in risk profiling analysis. As explained earlier in this chapter, the operational risk profiling analysis is based on this distribution together with their significance degree. In this section, a graphical representation of the operational risk profiling analysis for decision making is illustrated. Two cases are presented to show the graphical representations of operational risk profiling. Figures 7.4 to 7.9 represent the first case, whereas Figures 7.10 to 7.15 represent the second case.

Figure 7.4 and Figure 7.10 illustrate two different cases of distribution for several operational risks of a banking organization that is defined by

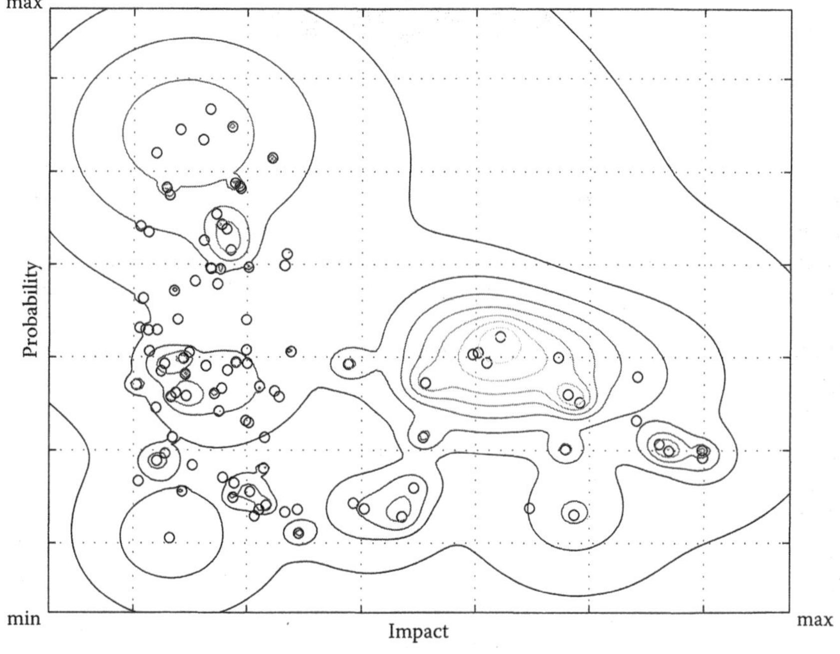

Figure 7.4 Distribution of the values defined by the coordinates set from the degrees of risk probability and impact. The contours show where the peak values are and the different levels of the mountains that are defined in Figure 7.6. The peak of the mountains defines the centroids of the clusters and the contours of the cluster areas. The projection of these values is used to indicate the parameters of the membership functions as defined in Figure 7.7.

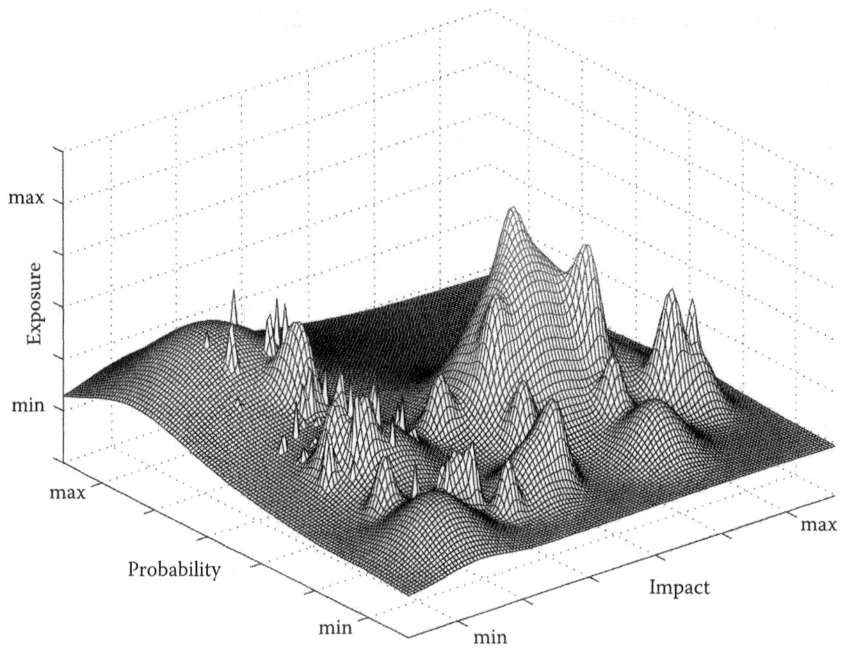

Figure 7.5 Mountain surface representation that illustrates the degree of operational risk exposures for each point within the probability and impact axes. The areas of high degree of impact have the highest exposure of risk and losses.

small circled dots within the probability and impact axes. As can be seen in both figures, most of these values are distributed within the zone of low impact and low to high probability, whereas only a few of them are distributed within the zone of high impact and low probability. Figure 7.5 and Figure 7.11 illustrate surfaces of mountains that represent the exposure of the operational risks distributed as in Figure 7.4 and Figure 7.10. These advanced graphical representations illustrate the areas of exposure within the probability and impact axes. Moreover, they define for each coordinating point, within these axes, the degree of exposure for the operational risk that satisfies this value. In other words, this is the model representation of the operational risk exposure in relation to their probability and impact values. This approach, called mountain operational risk profile, is discussed and highlighted in this book and is capable of modeling any number of operational risks under study.

Although there are few operational risks with low probability and high impact, the surfaces in both Figure 7.5 and Figure 7.11 that illustrate their exposure have the highest and largest mountains within this area. This is because the significance value of the operational risks with high impact

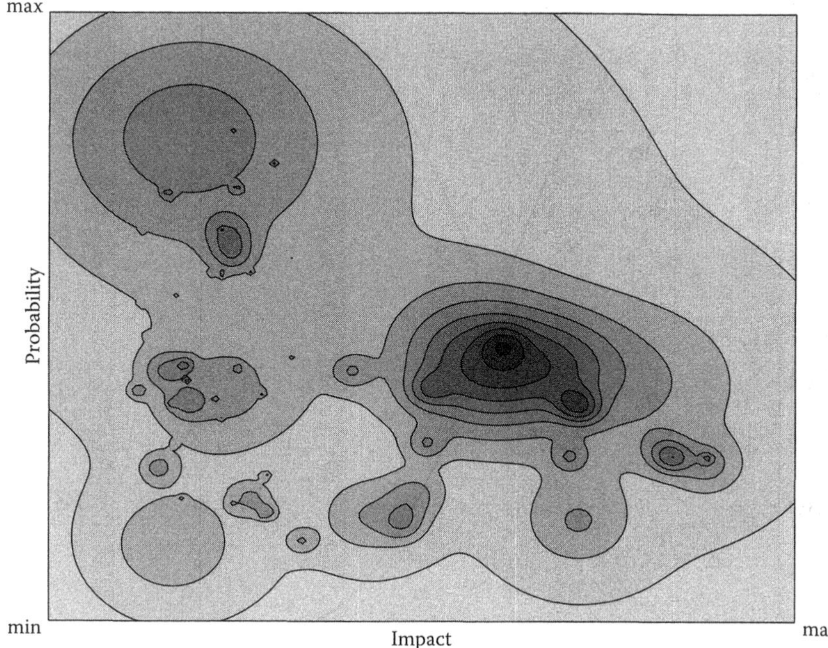

Figure 7.6 Map that illustrates the contour zones for different degrees of risks exposure within the area that is defined by the probability and impact axes.

has a very high degree in terms of initiating implications to business, that is, effect on many operations, losses, etc.

Figure 7.6 and Figure 7.12 illustrate contour maps that define the different zone levels of the mountain surface representations as shown in Figure 7.5 and Figure 7.11, respectively, of the operational risk profile. Note that these zones are defined from the cross section of the mountains. The cross-section number, or in other words, the number of levels, are defined based on the height and size of the mountains, that is, more levels are needed in high and big mountains and vice versa. The gray pallet indicates the different levels, that is dark grays represent higher zones. Note that these contours are also illustrated in Figure 7.4 and Figure 7.10.

The centers or top of the mountains, and the boundaries that are defined by the contour representation analysis, are projected onto the impact axis as illustrated in Figure 7.7 and Figure 7.13 to define their associated MFs. Also, the areas projected in the probability axis to define their associated MFs are shown in Figure 7.9 and Figure 7.15. To visually represent how the projections are defined in the probability axis, the inverse of the distributions defined in Figure 7.4 and Figure 7.10 is used. Thus, Figure 7.8 and Figure 7.14 illustrate these inverse distributions by

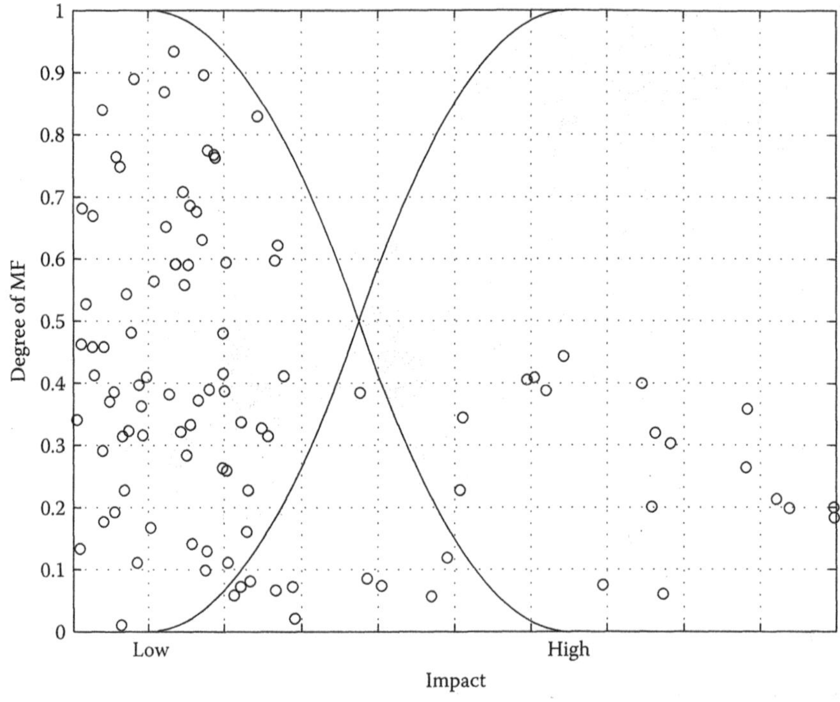

Figure 7.7 Membership functions in Z and S shapes that indicate the linguistic meanings of *low* and *high* impact used in the decision-making process. The parameters of the MFs are defined from the projection of the centroids and contour areas in the impact axis as illustrated in Figure 7.4.

90 degrees. The resulting linguistic membership functions are low and high for the "impact" of the first case and low, medium, and high for their "probability." For the second case, however, where there are three main groups of clusters, the resulting MFs in both probability and impact axes are low, medium, and high. Gaussian, S, and Z are the shapes used to represent these MFs, as shown in Figure 7.7, Figure 7.9, Figure 7.13, and Figure 7.15. The vertical axis of the above figures defines the degree of membership functions (DoMF) with a range between zero and one [0,1]. For instance, an operational risk OR_1 has, for the second case (Figure 7.13 and Figure 7.15), a probability and impact to a certain value (e.g., a and b, respectively). By projecting the value a onto the MFs, it is clearly shown that the operational risk under study has low as well as medium probability to a degree of 0.33 and 0.84, respectively (see Figure 7.15). Similarly, by projecting the value b onto the impact MFs defined in Figure 7.13, the operational risk has medium as well as high impact. Their corresponding degrees are 0.24 and 0.52.

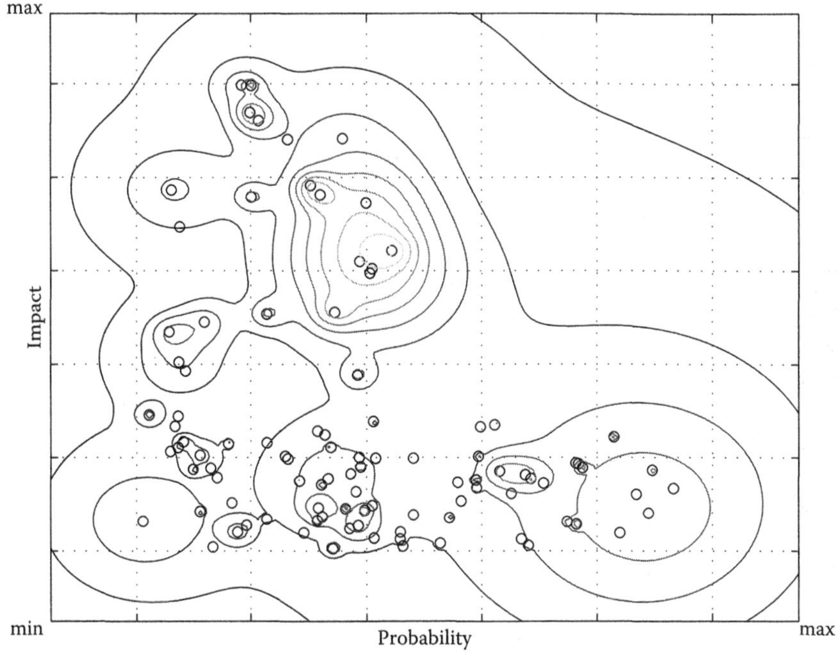

Figure 7.8 Inverse distribution analysis based on the coordinates defined from the risk probability and impact values. The contour of different levels and the tops of the mountains are also illustrated. The resulting centroids of the clusters, together with the limits of the contour areas, are projected to define the parameters of the membership functions.

The combinations of low and medium probability together with medium and high impact define the operational risk decision rules, as illustrated in Table 7.1 and Figure 7.2; that is,

- IF the probability *a* is low AND the impact *b* is medium THEN the operational risk is accepted/avoided.
- IF the probability *a* is low AND the impact *b* is high THEN the operational risk is avoided/mitigated.
- IF the probability *a* is medium AND the impact *b* is medium THEN the operational risk is accepted/avoided.
- IF the probability *a* is medium AND the impact *b* is high THEN the operational risk is avoided/mitigated.

The actual value of the consequence of each of the decision rules is defined by Equation 7.16:

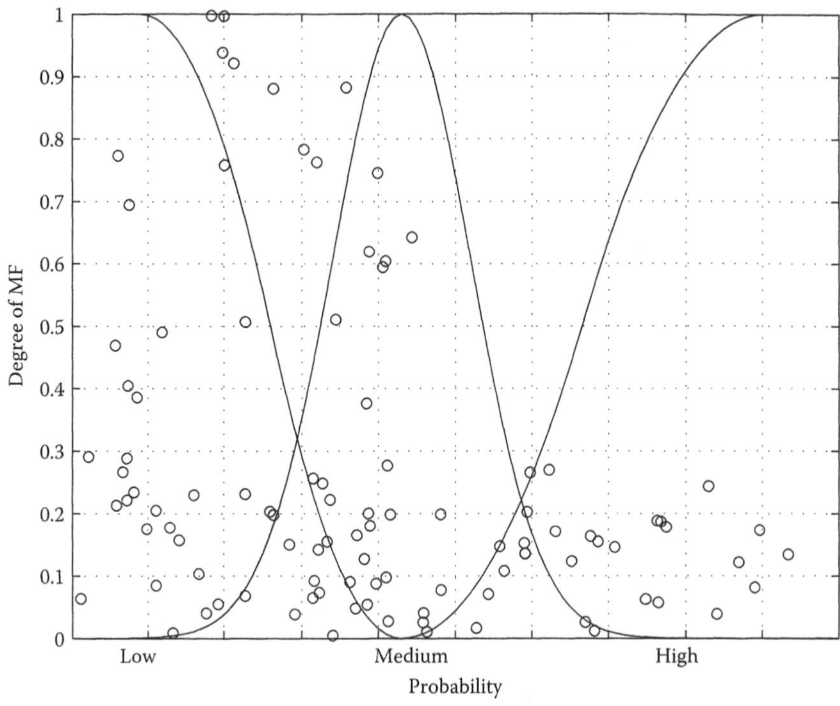

Figure 7.9 Three types of membership functions, indicated by the linguistic terms of low, medium, and high, define the different types of probabilities used in the decision-making process. The parameters of the MFs are defined from the projection of centroids and contour areas in the probability axis where their shapes are the Z, Gaussian, and S, respectively.

$$d = \frac{\begin{bmatrix} (\xi_1 \cdot 0.33 + \xi_1 \cdot 0.24) \cdot REx_1 + (\xi_2 \cdot 0.33 + \xi_2 \cdot 0.52) \cdot REx_2 + \\ (\xi_3 \cdot 0.84 + \xi_3 \cdot 0.24) \cdot REx_3 + (\xi_2 \cdot 0.84 + \xi_2 \cdot 0.52) \cdot REx_4 \end{bmatrix}}{(0.33 + 0.24 + 0.33 + 0.52 + 0.84 + 0.24 + 0.84 + 0.52)} \quad (7.16)$$

where ξ_1, ξ_2, and ξ_3 are the degree of operational risk acceptance, avoidance, and mitigation referring to the above rules. This degree is usually defined in financial terms (i.e., cost).

REx_1, REx_2, REx_3, and REx_4 are the exposure degree of the operations for each of the cases of the above rules.

The above analysis can be implemented for any single operational risk that exists or may appear in the future within any of the business operational activities of banking organizations.

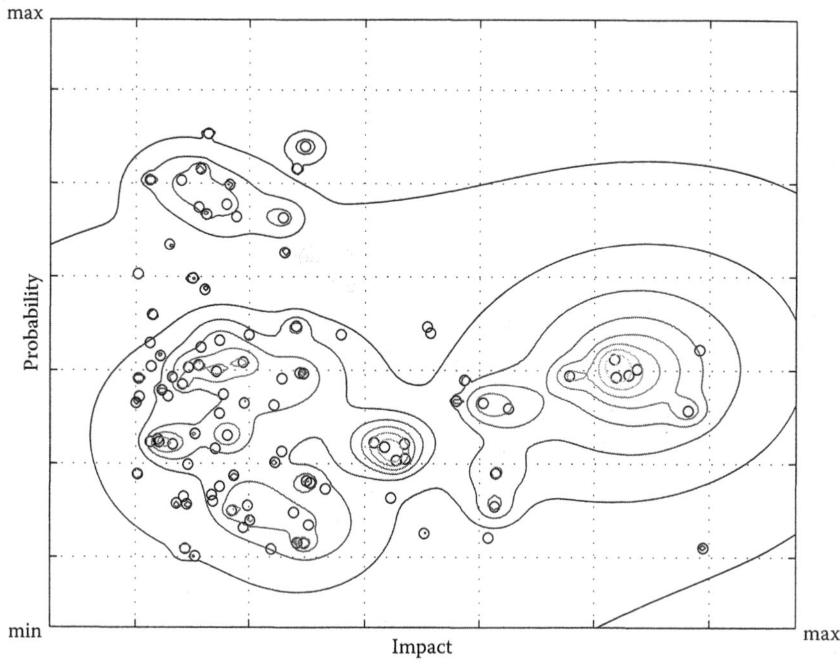

Figure 7.10 Representation of the value distribution defined from the set of coordinates from the degrees of risk probability and impact. The peaks and the contours are defined from the analysis of the mountains' surfaces and are illustrated and projected on the impact axis.

Summary

This chapter showed how to estimate, identify, model, evaluate, and construct decision rules for the operational risks management systems based on ClORiP methodology. The identification of the operational risk profile is based on the probability, impact, and exposure analysis. The value of probability referring to the operational risk cause, events, and consequences is defined by considering the degree of correlations between the risks together with their actual values. The probability of one operational risk occurring might initiate other operational risks and thus increase the probability of new risk appearances. In this case, a chain of operational risks appears, and the actual resulting impact of the initial operational risk result becomes higher. Therefore, understanding the correlations between the operational risks is a vital process to define the actual probability and impact for each operational risk. The estimation of impact referring to the operational risk causes, events, and consequences is also based on cor-

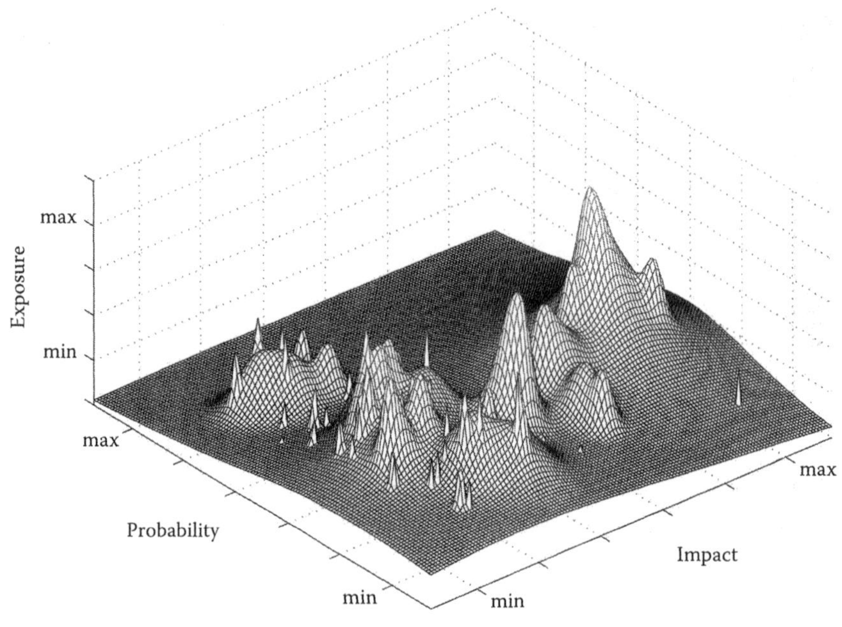

Figure 7.11 Exposure representation in terms of operational risks and losses illustrated by mountain surface within the probability and impact axes. The peaks of the mountains indicate where the operational risks and losses are in the surface area under study. The highest peaks have the highest exposures.

relation analysis. Additionally, any losses that are initiated from the impacts as well as the actual values of operational risk under study are also considered. By identifying the actual probability and by defining the impact through correlation analysis, financial organizations are also able to define the impact on the group of related operational risks. This type of risk modeling analysis can provide financial organizations with an overview of the actual operational risks' probability and impact, instead of being based only on assumptions. The resulting values from the calculations of the probability and impact are used to define the coordinates of their corresponding axes. These axes are used to construct the two-dimensional space of the operational risk profile. For the analysis of the operational risk profile, this space is divided mainly into four subspaces, to define the severity of the operational risks accordingly, as discussed in this chapter. Moreover, their distribution curves together with the tail analysis are also important parts of this operational risk profiling analysis. The exposure of operations to operational risks is defined by analyzing the cluster values that emerge in the probability and impact axes. This analysis

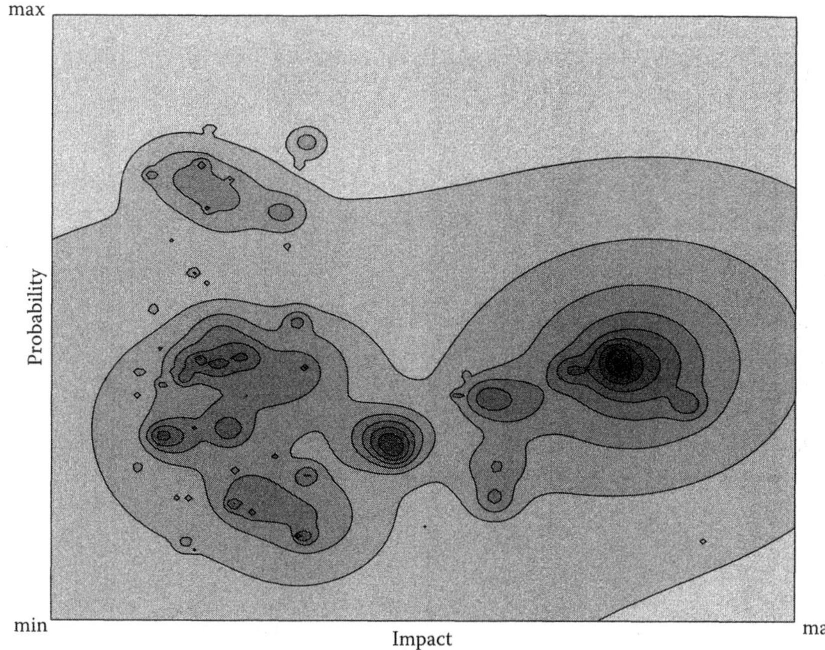

Figure 7.12 Contour zones that define a grayscaled map to illustrate the exposure of operational risks within the probability and impact axes.

is based on algorithmic approaches, and the exposure is presented using an additional axis in the operational risk profiling space. Advanced graphical illustrations of mountain surfaces represent the operational risk exposure for each value of their probability and impact. Representing the distribution of the values of probability, impact, and exposure, the model of the operational risk profiling is defined. This model is used as a basis to construct the decision rules of the operational risk management according to their degree of probability, impact, and exposure. Clustering analysis is applied to define the linguistic terms of the rules expressed as membership functions. Moreover, fuzzy set theory is applied to construct the rules and define how to estimate the values of their consequences. This chapter presented examples to show how operational risk profiling can be used as a powerful operational risk management tool. The analysis of the operational risk profile is a vital process in designing operational risk management systems because it provides the decision-making rules useful to management to gain insight into the organization's exposure to operational risks.

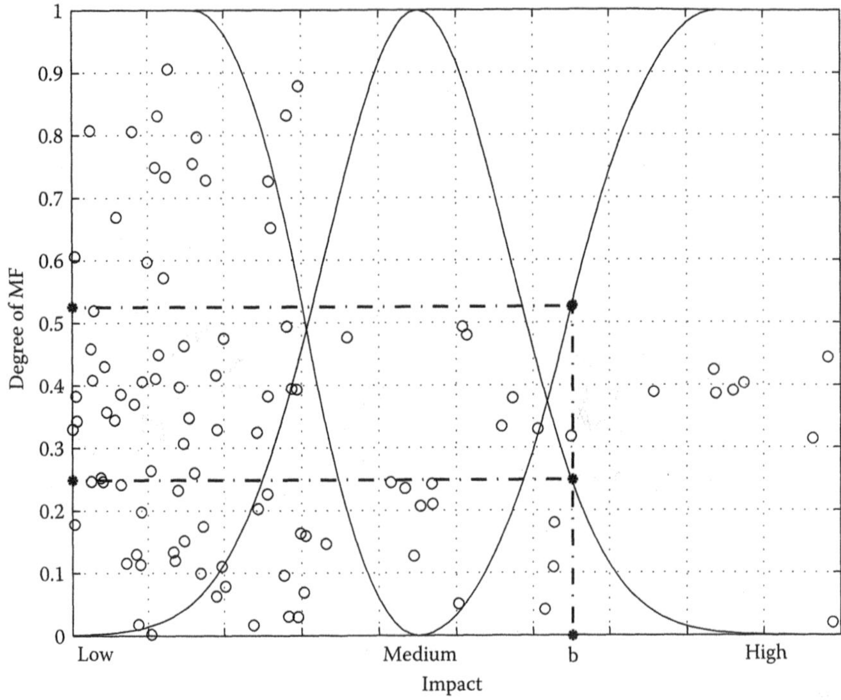

Figure 7.13 The linguistic terms *low, medium,* and *high* are defined by the membership functions that are used in the decision-making process for identifying the degree of impact under consideration. Z, Gaussian, and S are the shapes of these MFs, respectively. An operational risk with value b has medium as well as high impact to a degree of 0.24 and 0.52, respectively.

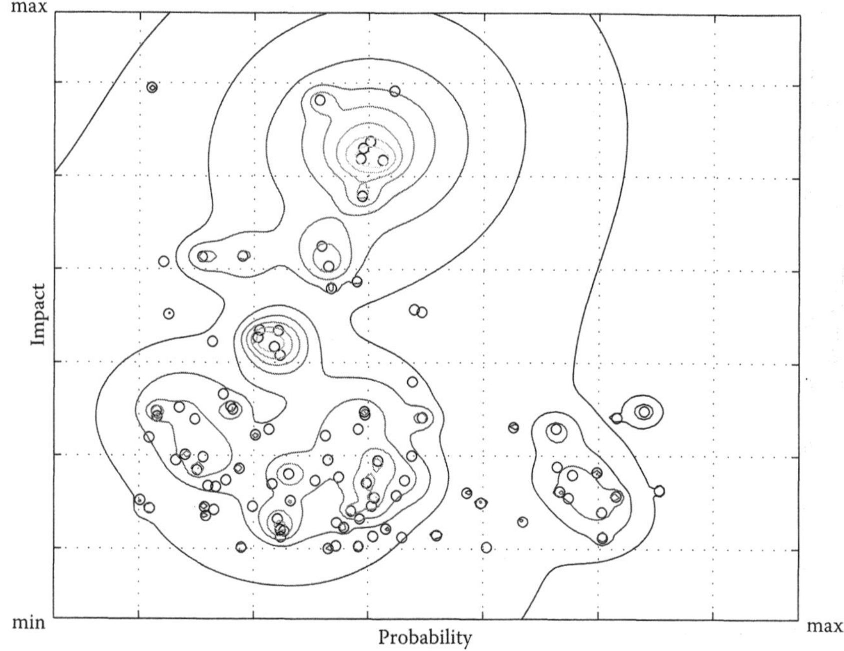

Figure 7.14 Distribution values of risk probability and impact. The contours define the areas of three main clusters of the distributed values, whereas together with their centers they define the parameters of the linguistic MFs illustrated in Figure 7.15.

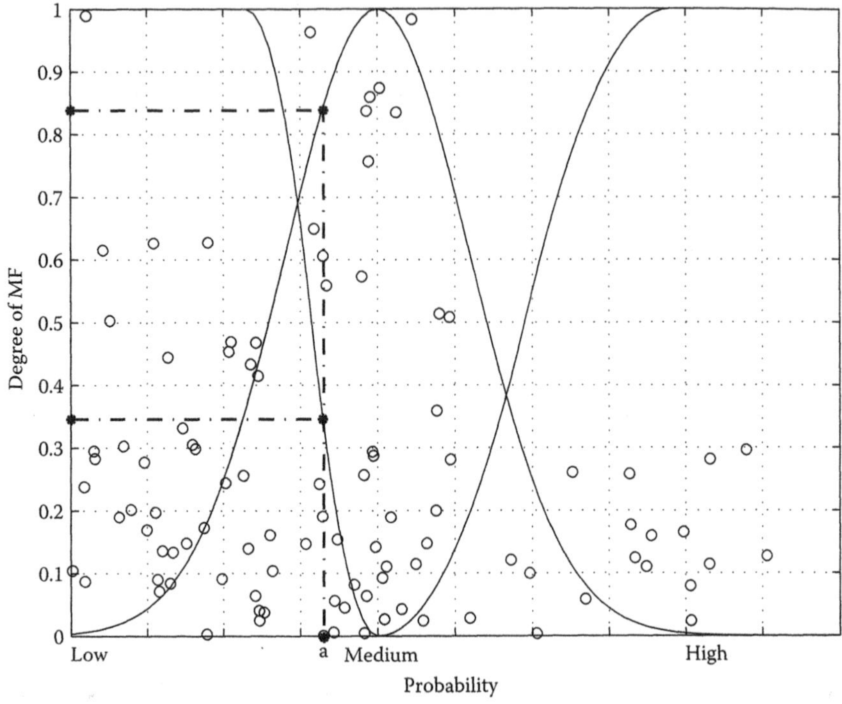

Figure 7.15 ***Low, medium,* and *high* are the linguistic terms of the MFs defined in the probability axes. The shapes used to represent these MFs are the Z, Gaussian, and S. Based on these MFs, an operational risk that has value "a" actually has low and medium probability and "a" has a degree of 0.33 and 0.84, respectively.**

References

1. Sugeno, M. and Kang, G.T., Structure Identification of Fuzzy Model, *Fuzzy Sets and Systems,* 28, pp. 15–33, 1988.
2. Mamdani, E., Application of Fuzzy Logic to Approximate Reasoning Using Linguistic Systems, *Fuzzy Sets and Systems*, 26, pp. 1182–1191, 1977.
3. Zadeh, L.A., Fuzzy Sets, *Journal of Information and Control*, 8, pp. 338–353, 1965.

Chapter 8

Operational Risk Optimization

Efficiency is based on optimizing performances and risks.

—Ioannis S. Akkizidis

Introduction

The design of operational risk optimization systems in terms of optimizing the levels of risks in operations and the resources that should be allocated to manage these risks is presented in this chapter. Different optimization techniques and methodologies that can be implemented for designing an effective and optimal operational risk management system are introduced. These are categorized as derivative-based and derivative-free optimization methods. In this chapter, both methodological approaches are discussed to show their applicability in optimizing the levels of operational risks. Their advantages and disadvantages are highlighted, combined with the main aspects that should be considered during their implementation process. The construction and use of the resulting optimum matrix that includes optimal values of operational risks is also presented. The definition of how to optimize the allocation of resources needed to manage optimally the operational risks is also highlighted. Finally, the importance and use of unconstrained and constrained optimization analysis as well as

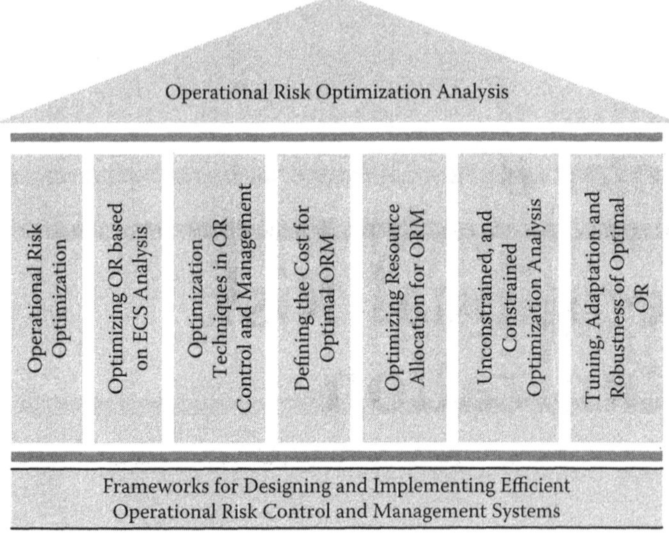

Figure 8.1 Main elements of Chapter 8.

the role of significance and exposure values are also discussed. Figure 8.1 illustrates the main elements of Chapter 8.

Operational Risk Optimization

It is ineffective, expensive, and almost impossible to minimize the impact of risks in operations to zero. This is mainly because the different risks in operations may have variable, opposite, and inhomogeneous relations and correlations. Minimizing one impact of risk alone may cause additional impacts on the other risks or operations that may result in a business imbalance. One of the main challenges in designing operational risk management systems is therefore to optimize all the parameters referring to operational risks and affected operations so that the overall value of operational risks is minimized to a minimal or desirable level. Moreover, it is important to be able to efficiently allocate the resources needed to set these operational risk parameters to their optimal levels. Optimization analysis is a hot topic that should play a big role in today's design of efficient operational risk management systems in banking organizations.

Operational risk optimization is an approach for defining the "balanced" optimal values for each risk in operations, by analyzing its parameters, to minimize the overall risk influences on the operations. By understanding the relationships and trade-offs between operational risks and their associated business performances, organizations can seek the optimal levels of operational risks. The resulting optimal levels of operational risks that exist in the business and system operations set the overall business risks to the minimal possible level with the minimal cost, whereas it helps to maximize overall business performances.

The problem of optimizing operational risks is a nonlinear one because large numbers of operational risk parameters are dynamically changing their values as their degree of correlation varies. The optimization analysis in designing operational risk management systems is approached through algorithmic techniques and methodologies. Such optimization algorithms are able to deal with large, inhomogeneous, and variable operational risk parameters. Thus, the output of such algorithmic parameter analysis gives the optimal values of the operational risks.

Operational risk management analysis is about adopting reasonable and optimal values of operational risks to control and manage potentially undesirable performances or disasters in operations within the business lines in banking organizations. It is also about capturing the optimal global view of the organization and its environment, and the optimal levels of the operational risks, to formulate intelligent decisions while facing such risks. The term "decisions" indicates a set of operational actions linked together by the same rationale, motivations, or preferences, either economic or psychological.

Optimizing Operational Risks Based on Exposure-Correlation-Significant Analysis

In optimizing operational risks, the calculation of the optimal values is based on the combination of types and signs of correlations referring to different types of operational risks within different operations. Moreover, correlation analysis between the affected operations is also considered in the optimization analysis. In addition to the above, the degree of both significance and risk exposure referring to operational risks and affected operations is also considered. It is important to note that risk exposure *RE* plays an important role in operational risk optimization analysis, mainly when the risks under study result in a high impact to banking organizations.

The operational risk matrix defined in Equation 8.1 is constructed by elements that define the values of the risks causes $\mathbf{z}^{\gamma}$, risk events $\mathbf{z}^{\delta}$, consequence of risks $\mathbf{z}^{c}$ (defined in Equation 5.3), set or beta values $\mathbf{b}_{r}$, $\mathbf{b}_{\lambda}$ (defined in Equation 6.22), and equilibriums or critical points $\mathbf{e}_{r}$, $\mathbf{e}_{\lambda}$ (defined in Equations 6.45 and 6.46).

$$\mathbf{Z} = \left[\mathbf{z}^{\delta}, \mathbf{z}^{\gamma}, \mathbf{z}^{c}, \mathbf{b}, \mathbf{e}\right] \tag{8.1}$$

The aim of the optimization process is to minimize the overall degree of operational risks by optimizing the values of the risks in operations. Thus, the optimization process is trying to minimize the cost functions $J(\delta)$, $J(\gamma)$, and $J(c)$ of the correlations between operational risks as defined in Equation 8.2 through Equation 8.4. Moreover, in this analysis, their degree of significance (defined in Chapter 6) and their exposure levels (defined in Chapter 7) are considered:

$$J(\delta) = \sum_{i=1}^{d} \left[\frac{\sum_{j=1}^{d} cor(\mathbf{z}_i^{\delta} \mathbf{z}_j^{\delta})}{(d-1)} \right] [SV\Delta][RE\Delta] \Big/ d \tag{8.2}$$

$$J(\gamma) = \sum_{i=1}^{g} \left[\frac{\sum_{j=1}^{g} cor(\mathbf{z}_i^{\gamma} \mathbf{z}_j^{\gamma})}{(g-1)} \right] [SV\Gamma][RE\Gamma] \Big/ g \tag{8.3}$$

$$J(c) = \sum_{i=1}^{q} \left[\frac{\sum_{j=1}^{q} cor(\mathbf{z}_i^{c} \mathbf{z}_j^{c})}{(q-1)} \right] [SVC][REC] \Big/ q \tag{8.4}$$

where d, g and q are the numbers of KRIs that measure the risk causes δ, events γ and consequences c respectively. Note that these definitions are also applied in the next equations for defining the cost functions.

Moreover, in the optimization analysis, a minimization of the cost functions $J(\delta, \gamma, c)$ for the correlations between other operational risks as well as between all affected operations is also considered. The degree of significance and risk exposure for each risk's causes $\mathbf{z}^{\delta}$, risk events $\mathbf{z}^{\gamma}$, and consequences of risks $\mathbf{z}^{c}$ is also included in the estimation of the cost function for the optimization analysis. The mathematical formula is as defined in Equation 8.5:

$$J((\delta,\gamma,c),(\delta,\gamma,c)) = \tag{8.5}$$

$$\sum_{i=1}^{(d+g+q)} \left[\frac{\sum_{j=1}^{(d+g+q)} cor((z_i^{\delta}, z_i^{\gamma}, z_i^{c}),(z_i^{\delta}, z_j^{\gamma}, z_j^{c}))}{(d+g+q)} \right] \begin{bmatrix} SV\Delta \\ SV\Gamma \\ SVC \end{bmatrix} \begin{bmatrix} RE\Delta \\ RE\Gamma \\ REC \end{bmatrix} \Bigg/ (d+g+q)$$

where $RE\Delta$, $RE\Gamma$, REC indicate the degrees of associated operational risks exposure in relation to causes, events, and consequences, respectively.

Note that the correlations in the above equations indicate how one particular risk affects different operations and to what degree. Moreover, it is important to analyze the relationships of the risks under study within the affected operations and investigate how the same risk affects other operations.

In optimization analysis, it is also important to minimize the actual operational risks' value with their equilibrium point(s). Thus, the aim in this case is to minimize the cost functions $J((\delta,\gamma,c),\mathbf{e})$ for each operational risk, within all influential operations, with its risk equilibrium point(s). Similar to the above consideration, the degree of significance and risk exposure for each risk cause $\mathbf{z}^{\delta}$, risk event $\mathbf{z}^{\gamma}$, and consequence of risk $\mathbf{z}^{c}$ is also included in the estimation of this cost function as defined in Equation 8.6:

$$J((\delta,\gamma,c),\mathbf{e}_r) = \sum_{i=1}^{w} \left[\frac{\sum_{j=1}^{(d+g+q)} cor((\mathbf{z}_j^{\delta}, \mathbf{z}_j^{\gamma}, \mathbf{z}_j^{c}), \mathbf{e}_{r_i})}{(d+g+q)} \right] \begin{bmatrix} SV\Delta \\ SV\Gamma \\ SVC \end{bmatrix} \begin{bmatrix} RE\Delta \\ RE\Gamma \\ REC \end{bmatrix} \Bigg/ w \tag{8.6}$$

where w is the number of the equilibrium point(s) referring to operational risks.

Furthermore, the cost function $J(\lambda)$ of the affected operations λ is as defined in Equation 8.7. The significance level and risk exposure of the affected operations are also considered.

$$J(\lambda) = \sum_{i=1}^{m} \left[\frac{\sum_{j=1}^{m} cor(\mathbf{z}_i^{\lambda} \mathbf{z}_j^{\lambda})}{(m-1)} \right] [SV\Lambda][RE\Lambda] \Big/ m, \tag{8.7}$$

where m is the number of affected operations.

Based on the above same contents, a minimization of the cost function $J(\lambda, \mathbf{e})$ that defines the correlations between the affected operations with their risk equilibrium point(s) as well as with their significance levels is also considered in optimization analysis (Equation 8.8).

$$J(\lambda, \mathbf{e}_\lambda) = \sum_{i=1}^{u} \left[\frac{\sum_{j=1}^{m} cor(\mathbf{z}_j^\lambda, \mathbf{e}_{\lambda_i})}{m} \right] \left[SV\Lambda \right] \Big/ u \tag{8.8}$$

where u is the number of the equilibrium point(s) referring to affected oprations.

Finally, in cases where beta points referring to operational risk(s) or affected operation(s) have been defined, they may also be considered for minimizing the cost function that defines the correlation between them. Thus, for the operational risks, the cost function is defined as in Equation 8.9, and for the affected operations the cost function is defined by Equation 8.10. The levels of significance for all of the above operational risks are also considered.

$$J((\delta, \gamma, c), \mathbf{b}_r) = \left[\frac{\sum_{j=1}^{(d+g+q)} cor((z_j^\delta, z_j^\gamma, z_j^c), \mathbf{b}_r)}{(d+g+q)} \right] \begin{bmatrix} SV\Delta \\ SV\Gamma \\ SVC \\ SVB \end{bmatrix} \tag{8.9}$$

$$J(\lambda, \mathbf{b}) = \left[\frac{\sum_{j=1}^{m} cor(\mathbf{z}_j^\lambda, \mathbf{z}^\mathbf{b})}{m} \right] \begin{bmatrix} SV\Lambda \\ SVB \end{bmatrix} \tag{8.10}$$

The aim in the above cost functions is to reach their minimal level by:

- Considering the value of the associated significance levels
- Minimizing the degree of exposure referring to operational risks and affected operations
- Minimizing the significance of the correlated parameters between the operational risks or between affected operations
- Minimizing significance of the correlated parameters between the operational risks or between affected operations with the associated risk equilibrium points or beta values

Furthermore, considering the trend analysis, an additional aim is to minimize the degree of accumulation RA and its trend RA_T referring to the operational risk or affected operations (see Chapter 6). In this case, the functions in Equation 8.6 and Equation 8.8 must also include the above two parameters.

The minimization of the degree of correlation implies isolation of the operational risks and the affected operations. Moreover, minimizing the exposure of the operational risks and affected operations means that the combination of operational risk probability and impact is at the minimal level. Note that isolation of the operational risks decreases their degree of exposure and significance. This combination of three elements, that is, significance–exposure–correlation (SEC), defines the "SEC methodology" for the operational risks optimization analysis proposed in this book.

The operational risk objective function J_{risk}, used in optimization analysis, is as defined in Equation 8.11:

$$J_{risk} = \min\left\{J(\delta,\gamma,c), J(\lambda), J(\mathbf{e}), J(\mathbf{b})\right\} \tag{8.11}$$

The operational risk's parameter matrix of the above cost functions is defined on a multidimensional space $\theta = [\theta_\delta, \theta_\gamma, \theta_c, \theta_\lambda, \theta_\mathbf{e}, \theta_\mathbf{b}]^T$. Each dimension determines the different types of the risk correlation analysis. Therefore, the primary concept is to find the point $\theta = \theta^*$ that minimizes the levels of operational risks and effects to operations, that is, $J_{risk}(\theta)$. The real values of the operational risks have to be minimized to the optimal points. The resulting overall risk will be set to the minimum possible level. Approaches that use optimization techniques in operational risk management analysis are presented in the following sections.

Optimization Techniques in Operational Risk Control and Management

In general, optimization problems are approached using derivative-based or derivative-free methodologies. Under these two main categories, a large number of different optimization techniques and methodologies can be found in literature. Full and detailed descriptions of the available optimization methods are beyond the scope of this book. However, and more importantly, this book aims to give guidance on the main principles of how and when to use optimization algorithms referring to the two different classes: derivative-based and derivative-free optimization. These algorithmic techniques and methodologies are used in optimizing operational risks that affect operational activities within different business lines.

Derivative-Based Optimization Methods for Operational Risks

When the models of operational risks are well defined, derivative-based optimization methods are suitable for implementation. The structure of such models is based on key indicators that include all the parameters that define the operational risks and their effects on operational performance(s). Thus, such types of methods can be used as a framework for designing optimal operational risk management systems.

The objective functions J_{risk} in Equation 8.11 have nonlinear formats with respect to an adjustable operational risk parameter θ. Due to the complexity and large amounts of information of J_{risk}, their minimization should be based on algorithmic approaches. Such algorithms must be iterative in nature and must be able to explore efficiently the input parameter space. In iterative methods, the next point θ_{next} is determined by a step-down approach from the current point, θ_{now}, in a direction vector $\mathbf{d}$ as illustrated in Equation 8.12:

$$\theta_{next} = \theta_{now} + \eta \mathbf{d} \tag{8.12}$$

where η is some positive "step size" (or in other words "learning rate") regulating to what extent the direction will proceed.

Alternatively, the formula defined in Equation 8.13 is used:

$$\theta_{k+1} = \theta_k + \eta_k \mathbf{d}_k \qquad (k = 1, 2, 3, \ldots) \tag{8.13}$$

where k denotes the current iteration number, and θ_k and θ_{k+1} represent two consecutive elements in a generated sequence of solution candidates $\{\theta_k\}$. θ_k is intended to converge to a (local) minimum θ^*. The next point θ_{k+1} should satisfy the inequality defined in Equation 8.14:

$$J(\theta_{k+1}) = J(\theta_k + \eta_k \mathbf{d}_k) < J(\theta_k) \tag{8.14}$$

The iteration method computes the kth step $\eta_\delta \mathbf{d}_k$ through two procedures:

1. Determining direction $\mathbf{d}$
2. Calculating step size η

In operational risk optimization analysis, the direction $\mathbf{d}$ is based mainly on the type of correlations between risks (i.e. positive or negative), their actual values, and their associations with their risk equilibriums and risk or performance set points.

All derivative-based algorithms call for movement toward a minimum point on the line determined by the current point $\boldsymbol{\theta}_k$ and the direction **d**. The optimum step size can be determined by line optimization defined in Equation 8.15:

$$\eta^* = \arg\min_{\eta>0} \phi(\eta) \tag{8.15}$$

where $\phi(\eta)$ is defined in Equation 8.16:

$$\phi(\eta) = J(\boldsymbol{\theta}_k + \eta\mathbf{d}) \tag{8.16}$$

The search of η^* is accomplished by line minimization search methods.[1]

The most popular and fundamental classes of derivative-based optimization techniques are the gradient-based optimization techniques that are capable of determining search direction according to the objective function's derivative information, as briefly presented next.

Gradient-Based Optimization

When the straight downhill direction **d** is determined on the basis of the gradient **g** of the risk objective function J_{risk}, such descent methods are called *gradient-based* methods. The gradient of the different operational risk correlations between $\{\delta, \gamma, c, \lambda, \mathbf{e}, \mathbf{b}\}$ defines the differentiable function J at $\boldsymbol{\theta}$. The vector of the first derivatives of J, is denoted as **g**. The mathematical formula of **g** is defined in Equation 8.17.

$$\mathbf{g} = \mathrm{g}(\boldsymbol{\theta}) = \nabla J(\boldsymbol{\theta}) \overset{def}{=} \left[\frac{\partial J(\boldsymbol{\theta})}{\partial\theta_1}, \frac{\partial J(\boldsymbol{\theta})}{\partial\theta_2}, \ldots, \frac{\partial J(\boldsymbol{\theta})}{\partial\theta_n}\right]^T \tag{8.17}$$

Based on a given gradient, the downhill directions follow the *condition for feasible descent directions* as shown in Equation 8.18:

$$\phi'(0) = \left.\frac{dJ\left(\boldsymbol{\theta}_{now} + \eta\mathbf{d}\right)}{\eta\mathbf{d}}\right|_{\eta=0} = \mathbf{g}^T\mathbf{d} = \left\|\mathbf{g}^T\right\|\left\|\mathbf{d}\right\|\cos\left(\xi\left(\boldsymbol{\theta}_{now}\right)\right) \tag{8.18}$$

where

ξ defines the angle between **g** and **d**.

$\xi(\boldsymbol{\theta}_{now})$ defines the angle between $\mathbf{g}_{now}$ and **d** at the current point $\boldsymbol{\theta}_{now}$.

Using the gradient-based descent method, the feasible descent direction is determined by deflecting the gradients through multiplication by a positive definite matrix **G** with some positive step size η as shown mathematically in Equation 8.19. This is a fundamental format in the gradient-based descent method.

$$\boldsymbol{\theta}_{next} = \boldsymbol{\theta}_{now} - \eta \mathbf{G}\mathbf{g} \tag{8.19}$$

Note that when $\mathbf{d} = -\mathbf{G}\mathbf{g}$, the descent direction condition (Equation 8.18) holds because $\mathbf{g}^T\mathbf{d} = -\mathbf{g}^T\mathbf{G}\mathbf{g} < 0$.

There are several variants of gradient-based methods, such as Newton's method and the Levenberg-Marguardt[2] method, that possess the aforementioned format to bias the negative gradient direction ($-\mathbf{g}$) for a better result.

The aim is to find a value of $\boldsymbol{\theta}_{next}$ that satisfies Equation 8.20:

$$\mathbf{g}\left(\boldsymbol{\theta}_{next}\right) = \left.\frac{\partial J\left(\boldsymbol{\theta}\right)}{\partial \boldsymbol{\theta}}\right|_{\boldsymbol{\theta}=\boldsymbol{\theta}_{next}} = 0 \tag{8.20}$$

In practice, Equation 8.20 will be almost impossible to minimize to zero.

Steepest Descent Method

"Steepest descent" is one of the oldest techniques for minimizing a given function defined in a multidimensional input space. This method forms the basis for many direct methods used in optimizing both "constrained" and "unconstrained" problems. Moreover, despite its slow convergence, the method is one of the most commonly used nonlinear optimization techniques due to its simplicity.

Considering Equation 8.19, when $\mathbf{G} = \eta\mathbf{I}$ for some positive value η and the identity matrix **I**, the steepest descent mathematical formula is defined as in Equation 8.21:

$$\boldsymbol{\theta}_{next} = \boldsymbol{\theta}_{now} - \eta^2 \mathbf{g} I \tag{8.21}$$

The minimum point η^* in the direction **d** is obtained by Equation 8.22:

$$\phi'(0) = \frac{dJ\left(\boldsymbol{\theta}_{now} + \eta \mathbf{g}_{now}\right)}{d\eta} = \nabla^T J(\boldsymbol{\theta}_{now} - \eta \mathbf{g}_{now})\mathbf{g}_{now} = \mathbf{g}_{next}^T \mathbf{g}_{now} = 0 \tag{8.22}$$

The steepest descent method[3] uses the gradient vector at each point as the search direction for each of the iterations. This method can be suitable in optimizing risk values where there is a high variation in the different types (i.e., positive or negative) or values of correlation between the operational risks. In that case, the gradient direction **d** may change as frequently as the parameters of the risk indicators and thus the risk correlation also changes.

Newton's Method

In Newton's method, the second derivative of the objective function J_{risk} (or second-order information) is used to determine the descent direction **d**. If the starting position $\boldsymbol{\theta}_{now}$ is sufficiently close to a local minimum, the objective function J can be approximated by the quadratic form (Equation 8.23):

$$J(\boldsymbol{\theta}) \approx J(\boldsymbol{\theta}_{now}) + \mathbf{g}^T(\boldsymbol{\theta} - \boldsymbol{\theta}_{now}) + \frac{1}{2}(\boldsymbol{\theta} - \boldsymbol{\theta}_{now})^T \mathbf{H}(\boldsymbol{\theta} - \boldsymbol{\theta}_{now}) \quad (8.23)$$

where **H** is the **Hessian** matrix, consisting of the second partial derivatives of $J(\boldsymbol{\theta})$.

Equation 8.23 is the Taylor series expansion of $J(\boldsymbol{\theta})$ up to the second-order terms. Higher-order terms are omitted due to the assumption that $\|\boldsymbol{\theta} - \boldsymbol{\theta}_{now}\|$ is sufficiently small.

By differentiating Equation 8.23 and setting it to zero, the quadratic function of $\boldsymbol{\theta}$ can define its minimum point $\hat{\boldsymbol{\theta}}$, that is, $0 = \mathbf{g} + \mathbf{H}(\hat{\boldsymbol{\theta}} - \boldsymbol{\theta}_{now})$.

If the inverse of **H** exists, there is a unique solution. Newton's method is defined when the use of the minimum point $\hat{\boldsymbol{\theta}}$ of the approximated quadratic function is chosen as the next point $\boldsymbol{\theta}_{now}$ (Equation 8.24):

$$\hat{\boldsymbol{\theta}} = \boldsymbol{\theta}_{now} - \mathbf{H}^{-1}\mathbf{g} \quad (8.24)$$

The step $\mathbf{H}^{-1}\mathbf{g}$ is called Newton's step and its direction is called Newton's direction.

Newton's method can be used for optimizing the parameters of complex operational risks models. Such operational risk models describe a multivariation of both its parameters and the type of correlation with high frequency. On the other hand, the main disadvantage of Newton's method is the computational time, which may cause numerical problems due to round-off errors.

There are many different optimization techniques and methodologies in the literature for financial and engineering mathematics. Advanced and extended approaches of the classical Newton's method such as modified Newton's methods and quasi-Newton methods are widely used in the implementation of derivative-based optimization methods. In most cases, hybrid optimization techniques are applied, primarily depending on the complexity of the problem (i.e., model, degree of parameters, correlation complexity and variation, amount of information data, etc.).

Rules in Designing Risk Optimization Techniques

The cases for selecting and applying optimization techniques and methodologies are numerous. However, there are some important steps that risk analysts, operators, or managers should consider during the optimization process in designing optimal operational risk management systems:

- The construction of the operational risk model should be clearly defined in terms of the parameters and operational risks under study.
- The operational risks and operational parameters that need to be optimized must be well defined. Note that most of the parameters are usually defined from the key risk indicators or any other risk measurement systems that are in use.
- The selection of the optimization algorithm should be driven by the complexity of the model that describes the operational risks or affected operations.
- The variation in the operational risks, if available, should be defined. Moreover, the upper and lower limits of operational risks acceptance should also be defined. This variation and upper/lower values indicate how dynamically the operational risks vary.
- Any constraints or limitations that are related to applying or adapting the optimal values of operational risks must be defined and considered in the optimization analysis.
- In some cases, the targeted values of risks are known and are desired by the operational managers. This helps the optimization algorithms move toward the "desirable" optimal values. Setting the operational risk values at their desirable levels helps such algorithmic techniques reach the optimal operational risks values much faster.

Termination Rules for Optimization Algorithms

Optimization algorithms are based on iteration processes. Thus, for minimizing the operational risk objective function, the descent method is typically repeated until one of the following termination criteria is satisfied:

1. The objective function for minimizing the overall operational risks value is sufficiently small.
2. The correlation functions defined in Equation 8.2 through Equation 8.10 are minimized to a sufficiently small value.

Considering the above two rules, it is important to note that due to the natural constraints in large organizations such as banks, the process for getting the operational risks to their optimal values is not always quick and easy. Thus, it is wise to tune the risk parameter values slightly to reach the optimal levels so that:

3. The length of the gradient vector **g** is smaller than a specific value.
4. The specified computation time is exceeded.
5. The step improvement of the minimization of the overall operational risks value is very small.

In Summary

Derivative-based optimization methods are structurally defined as straightforward algorithmic techniques, having low application complexity, and thus their optimization process is well understood. A main advantage of such methods is that the resulting optimal values can be reasonably explained through the applied optimization analytical process.

Derivative-Free Optimization Methods

In the design analysis of optimizing operational risks, there are some cases where the operational performances and risk models are not very well defined or the number of derivatives is too high. As a result, the calculation of their gradient vectors may be costly and unreliable. In these cases, derivative-free optimization schemes are preferable alternatives for operational optimization-based risk design. Derivative-free optimization methods are typically designed to solve optimization problems where the objective function is computed by a "black box"; hence, the gradient computation is unavailable.

The four most popular derivative-free optimization methods in these cases are simulated annealing,[4] genetic algorithms,[5] random search method,[6] and downhill simplex search.[7] To apply any of the above algorithms, an organization should consider the following three steps:

1. An operational risk model could be based on simple operational models based on linear or non-complex mathematical functions,

to more advanced ones by using functions with a high degree of complexity or even neural networks or fuzzy logic models. Because these derivative-free optimization methods are not relying on the gradient approaches, the model could even be nondifferentiable with respect to its parameters. Furthermore, control policies for managing the operational risks must be defined.

2. An objective function must be defined that is related to the management goals. In the design process of operational risk management systems, the objective function is defined by the operational risk parameters and the goal is to minimize the degree of the overall operational risk. Therefore, the main object that drives the algorithm is that the smaller the objective function, the better the optimization strategy for managing operational risks.
3. The objective function should be defined in such a way that its adjustment will minimize the overall degree of operational risks and update the operational parameters. The loop must be repeated until the objective function is below a given value or the analysis/computing time exceeds a specific upper boundary.

Some of the common characteristics that these methods have are described as follows:

- *Derivative "freeness."* These methods belong to the derivative-free optimization category and do not need functional derivative information to search for a set of correlation parameters that minimize (or maximize) the given objective function J_{risk}. However, they rely exclusively on repeated evaluations of the objective functions, and the subsequent search direction after each evaluation follows certain heuristic guidance. This is very important because in many cases in operational risk analysis, the objective function J_{risk} is not always well defined and available.
- *Intuitive guidelines.* Simple intuitive consents are the key drivers for designing and guide these search procedures for optimal risk values. Moreover, concepts motivated by so-called nature's wisdom are used, such as evolution and thermodynamics. Most of the main parts of the designing process for operational risk management systems are mainly driven by intuitive and natural concepts. Thus, derivative-free optimization methodologies are well suited for the overall operational risk management culture and practices.
- *Flexibility.* Derivative-free optimization methods relieve the requirement for differentiable objective functions J_{risk} of operational risk correlations. This is important in cases where objective functions of operations in banking organizations are difficult to construct based on their correlation derivatives. More important, based

on such methods, any complex objective function that may include many different types of correlations can be defined and optimized. In some cases, the objective function can even include the structure of a data-fitting model itself. Finally, not much more extra time in computation of the optimal values is needed.

- *Randomness.* Many of the derivative-free optimization methods use random number generators in determining subsequent search directions. This element of randomness usually gives rise to the overlay optimistic view that these methods are "global optimizers" that will find a global optimum given enough computation time. In theory, their random nature makes the probability of finding an optimal solution nonzero over a fixed amount of computation time. In practice, however, it might take a considerable amount of computation time, if not forever, to find the optimal solution of a given problem. In operational risk management, while analyzing a large number of risk parameters in operations, it is essential to look for their global optimal values.
- *Iteration and speed.* These techniques are iterative in nature and thus a stopping criterion needs to be set so it can terminate the optimization process in a reasonable amount of time.

In Summary

Derivative-free optimization methods give globally the best optimal values and can be very suitable in operational risk optimization analysis, especially when it is difficult to define the operational risk models. However, their applications need advanced knowledge of designing such algorithmic techniques from the analysts who design such operational risk management systems.

Without using derivatives, these methods are bound to be generally slower than derivative-based optimization methods. Another disadvantage of such optimization approaches is that, although the resulting optimal values are very close to the best global ones, it is not very easy to perform reasoning analysis. It is suggested that performance and risks analysts start the operational risk analysis with derivative-free optimization methods to have a good idea of the proximity of the optimal value; then by starting with these values and using derivative-based optimization methods, they can achieve the global optimal values with reasoning knowledge.

The Resulting Optimal Matrix

The optimal levels of the initial operational risk values form to construct the optimal risk matrix $\mathbf{\Theta}$ as defined in Equation 8.25:

$$\boldsymbol{\Theta} = \begin{bmatrix} \begin{bmatrix} \boldsymbol{\theta}^{\delta}_{11} & \boldsymbol{\theta}^{\delta}_{12} & \cdots & \boldsymbol{\theta}^{\delta}_{1d} \\ \boldsymbol{\theta}^{\delta}_{21} & \boldsymbol{\theta}^{\delta}_{22} & \cdots & \boldsymbol{\theta}^{\delta}_{2d} \\ \cdot & \cdot & \cdot & \cdot \\ \cdot & \cdot & \cdot & \cdot \\ \cdot & \cdot & \cdot & \cdot \\ \boldsymbol{\theta}^{\delta}_{n1} & \boldsymbol{\theta}^{\delta}_{n2} & \cdots & \boldsymbol{\theta}^{\delta}_{md} \end{bmatrix} \begin{bmatrix} \boldsymbol{\theta}^{\gamma}_{11} & \boldsymbol{\theta}^{\gamma}_{12} & \cdots & \boldsymbol{\theta}^{\gamma}_{1g} \\ \boldsymbol{\theta}^{\gamma}_{21} & \boldsymbol{\theta}^{\gamma}_{22} & \cdots & \boldsymbol{\theta}^{\gamma}_{2g} \\ \cdot & \cdot & \cdot & \cdot \\ \cdot & \cdot & \cdot & \cdot \\ \cdot & \cdot & \cdot & \cdot \\ \boldsymbol{\theta}^{\gamma}_{m1} & \boldsymbol{\theta}^{\gamma}_{m2} & \cdots & \boldsymbol{\theta}^{\gamma}_{mg} \end{bmatrix} \begin{bmatrix} \boldsymbol{\theta}^{c}_{11} & \boldsymbol{\theta}^{c}_{12} & \cdots & \boldsymbol{\theta}^{c}_{1q} \\ \boldsymbol{\theta}^{c}_{21} & \boldsymbol{\theta}^{c}_{22} & \cdots & \boldsymbol{\theta}^{c}_{2q} \\ \cdot & \cdot & \cdot & \cdot \\ \cdot & \cdot & \cdot & \cdot \\ \cdot & \cdot & \cdot & \cdot \\ \boldsymbol{\theta}^{c}_{n1} & \boldsymbol{\theta}^{c}_{n2} & \cdots & \boldsymbol{\theta}^{c}_{mq} \end{bmatrix} \end{bmatrix} \tag{8.25}$$

Note that

d, g, and q indicate the number operational risks defined as causes, events, or consequences, respectively.

m is the number of affected operations.

δ, γ, and c refer to causes, events, and consequences, respectively.

In operational risk optimization analysis, the cost functions aim to minimize the overall risk by optimizing the values of each of the underlying operational risks. The idea behind the operational risk optimization is that operational risks can be minimized to the optimal levels according to their correlation significance levels with the other risks, risk exposure, risk instability points, and set beta points that are known as risk drivers. This is a very efficient and transparent way of optimizing operational risks. Transparency in risk methodologies is a key issue in operational risk management. Moreover, it is a requirement from the Basel II Accord.[8] Note finally that the correlations analysis is based on proportional as well as inverse (opposite) interaction analysis.

Illustrating the Optimal Values of Operational Risks

In banking organizations, each of the operational activities is affected by a series of different operational risks. The degrees defined by the SEC methodology are used in operational risk optimization analysis. In Figure 8.2, the series of operational risks influencing the activities referring to "credit card" operations listed in Table 5.4 of Chapter 5. These operational risks levels need to be optimized for setting the overall operational risk impact to a minimal level. As can be seen from Figure 8.2, different operational risks, such as those referring to "missing transfers" and "account verification time," have different significant values and levels. Because it is almost impossible and very costly to minimize all these risks to zero, the aim is to balance them by defining their optimal levels. The results from the optimization analysis are illustrated in Figure 8.2, where each operational risk is defined by three bars; that is, the first bar refers

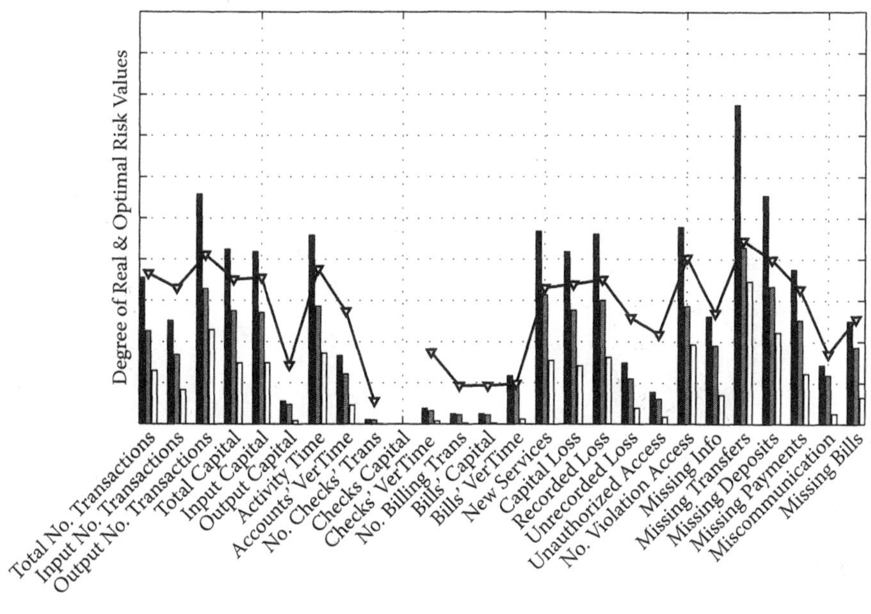

Figure 8.2 Bar chart that illustrates the actual (first bar) and optimal values (second bar), together with their differences (third bar), for all operational risks referring to "credit card" activities. The downward-pointing triangle indicates the percentage of variation.

to the actual level of operational risks, the second bar refers to the optimal operational risk level, and the third bar refers to the difference between the above two. Thus, the bar referring to the actual value of the "missing transfers" has the highest degree (i.e., 0.78), where in this case the optimal value should be around 45 percent less (i.e., 0.42). Note that due to the large measuring scale for the different operational activities, the illustrated values in Figure 8.2 are presented on a normalized scale. Note that normalization was discussed in Chapter 6. Similarly, in Figure 8.3 the different operational risks that are referring to ATM systems have different levels for their actual and optimal values. As can be seen in Figures 8.2 and 8.3, the variations of the operational risks from the initial, actual values, to the optimal points are different from one to the next. In both figures, the dotted lines with the downward-pointing triangles indicate the percentage of variation of each operational risk. There are therefore operational risks that exhibit a lot and those that exhibit very minor variations from their initial value to reach their optimal level. This variation indicates the effort needed for each operation to reach the optimal level.

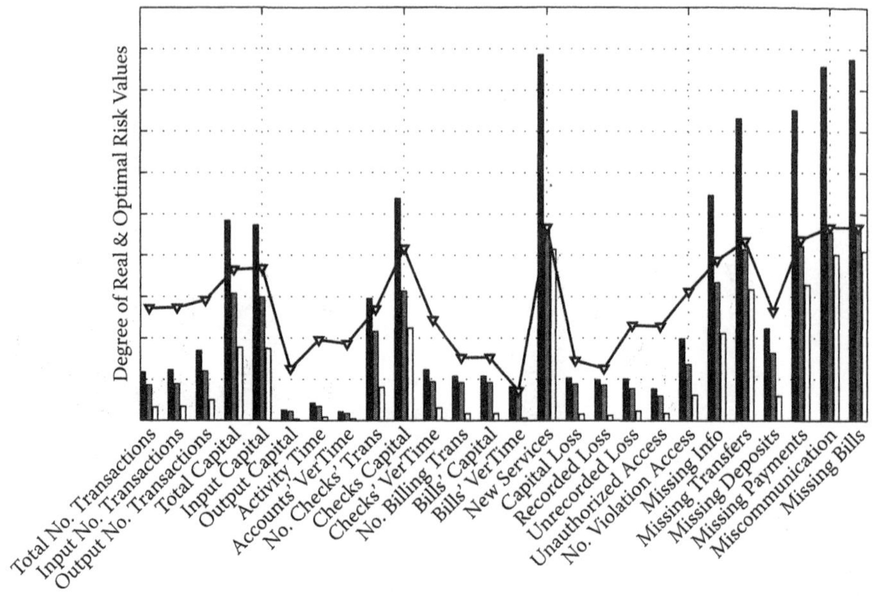

Figure 8.3 Bar chart that illustrates the actual (first bar) and optimal values (second bar), together with their differences (third bar), for all risks that refer to "ATM systems" operational activities. The downward-pointing triangle indicates the percentage of variation.

On the other hand, as illustrated in Figure 8.4, the bar plot illustrates the actual and optimal values for the operational risks referring to *unauthorized access*. This operational risk affects or refers to most of the operational activities (i.e., tellers, managers, transfer, IT, etc.). Such activities are driven and supported by different processes, people, and systems. However, the degree of implication for different operational activities varies. The aim is to identify the optimal degrees of the particular operational risks for each of the affected operations. The approaches of using optimization algorithms, as discussed in this chapter, can define the optimal levels for the particular operational risks, which affect different operations. Thus, Figure 8.4 illustrates the new "balanced optimal values" of the operational risk referring to "unauthorized access" for each of the operations.

Optimization algorithms are able to optimize the operational risk values so that they reach the desirable overall minimal operational risk levels. In some cases, the variation of the operational risk under study is very high, such as the one that refer to capital transfers in Figure 8.4. As will be discussed in later sections in this chapter, in this case the amount of effort needed to manage this operational risk is also very high. For some

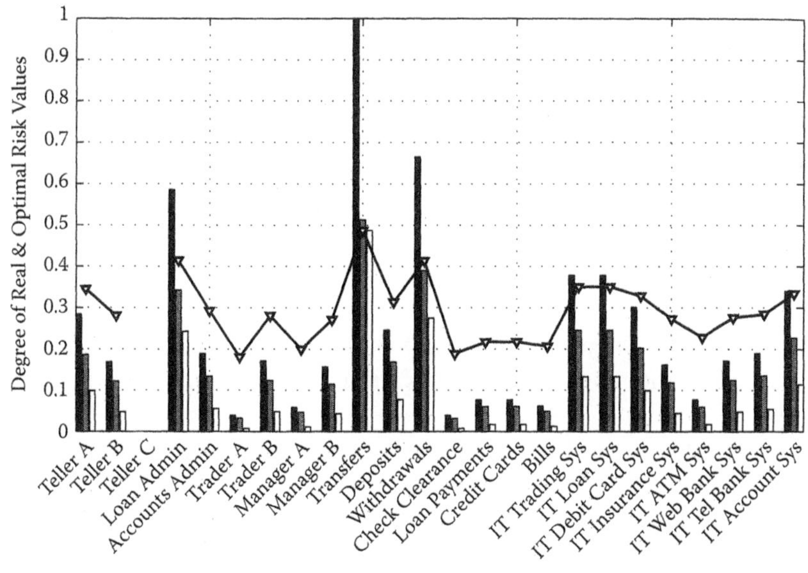

Figure 8.4 Bar chart that illustrates the actual (first bar) and optimal values (second bar), together with their differences (third bar), for the operational risk that refers to "unauthorized access."

other activities, however, the variation and thus the effort is very minor. Note finally that optimization algorithms are able to define the optimal values according to the set of constraints for the overall risk minimization to a desirable level. If, for instance, the banking organization has the aim to minimize the overall risk or the subrisks to no more than 30 percent, optimization algorithms will find the best balanced combination of the operational risks to fulfill the above desirable request.

Defining the Cost for Optimal Operational Risk Management

It is vital for risk managers to identify and decide how much to invest before the operational risks occur, as well as how much the acceptable cost is after the operational risks have taken place and affected the operations. In designing operational risk management systems, an actual budget should be estimated for each of the operational risk and for each affected operation.

This budget refers to the cost needed:

- For any changes or updates in the current processes/activities, systems, and people within the organization for preventing possible occurrences of the operational risks
- To activate the organization's operational risk polices in relation to acceptance, avoidance, or mitigation of the risks in operations
- To initiate recovery actions of the affected operations
- To initiate the business continuity or disaster recovery plan

In addition to the above, it should also consider any additional budget for managing the unexpected implications to the organization's performance for the above cases.

An example of the first case could be any budgeting cost for change management within the organization, such as applying internal auditing for the major trading activities. In such cases, the new additional processes could add cost to the organization in terms of investing or outsourcing in new activities. Initially, it may reduce the business performance as it may increase the bureaucracy as well as reduce the degree of business robustness, flexibility, and business reactivity. These may result in a slight diversion in the business path to reach its targets, such as a high rate of commission resulting from the trading, or it may even cause new operational risks. In general, changes in the processes, from minor to major, may cause a significant amount of implications and thus should be implemented very carefully based mostly on tuning them rather than on full reengineering. In case the latter is decided upon, the quality management system should be the main guidance in relation to operational risk polices. Moreover, modifications to the system for operational risk prevention are straightforward and their cost is well defined. However, where in some cases it is clear, in other cases it is difficult to estimate the cost of preventing operational risks that are due to people's activities and practices. For instance, the training cost to prevent unintentional mistakes that may cause serious impacts (to the organization or to the client) can be clearly defined. However, the cost for investing in driving employee attitude for being part of the risk management process by, for example, updating the loss event database is difficult to properly define and measure.

The budget for applying the policies that aim to avoid the risks in operations must also be well defined. Avoidance usually means to try to minimize the risk to the minimal possible level. The affected operations, once they are identified, must be recovered in the shortest time possible. That is mainly because an outstanding affected operation usually propagates undesirable affects to other operations and thus causes operational instability. Therefore, the budget that will eventually be spent for recovering the operations will increase exponentially. Thus, the cost for recovering after major or even minor losses may end up being very high, especially when the recovery time increases. Note also that the recovery process for a known risk occurrence and losses must be planned through scenarios that describe the steps of the process. Thus, the cost can be estimated based on these predefined scenario analyses.

In a disaster recovery process, people's actions, systems, and processes are involved to different degrees. Their reaction is predefined in disaster recovery scenarios and thus the cost and budget to be spent on them is already known fairly accurately. Finally, there are unexpected implications to the organization's performances resulting from all of the above cases. These are difficult to preidentify and thus it is very hard to assign the budget that should be spent on them.

It is very important to define the actual budgeting cost of the above operational risk control and management cases so as to evaluate whether and how much effort should be spent for each operation and operational risk during these processes. Moreover, a key aspect in operational risk management budgeting is to ensure that the summation of the overall effort for preventing the risks must be always less than the value of the overall potential loss Ψ, defined in the operational risk evaluation process in Chapter 6.

Equation 8.26 defines the formula for estimating the overall amount of budget Ξ needed for managing operational risks:

$$\Xi = \left[\sum_{i=1}^{v} \xi_i^V + \sum_{j=1}^{r} \xi_j^A + \sum_{l=1}^{p} \xi_l^R + \sum_{k=1}^{l} \xi_k^D \right] + \xi^I, \quad \Xi < \Psi \tag{8.26}$$

where

ξ^V is defined by the variation (var) of the v; that is, ξ^V = var (*processes, systems, people*).

ξ^A is defined by the cost from the differentiations between the initial and the optimal level of the r risks that need to be avoided.

ξ^R defines the budget for recovering the m number of affected operations, that is,

$$\xi^R = \left[\sum_{j=1}^{m} \xi_j^r \right] + \left[\sum_{j=1}^{n} \xi_j^r \right]^{\exp(d)}$$

n is the number of the additional affected operations resulting from the delay d of the predefined recovering time.
ξ^D defines the budget for the disaster recover of the k operations.
ξ^I defines the additional budget for the unexpected operational risks.

Note also that the budget for investing and controlling the operational risks is measured in periods of times, such as monthly, yearly, etc.

Optimizing Resource Allocation for Operational Risk Management

Every banking organization wants to achieve the highest levels of operational performance possible. Yet to do so almost always requires a delicate balancing act of "optimization" of all operational risks that affect performances. Managing optimally both the risks in operations and the required allocation of resources, which are associated to these risks, makes designing risk management systems very efficient and cost effective.

It is essential in designing optimal operational risks management systems to define how to distribute the investing resources for controlling and managing each of the risks in operations and for each of the budgeted cases listed in the previous section. This reinforces Principle 2 of Basel II, which refers to sufficient resources that must be allocated to operational risk management.[9]

The distribution of the available resources is estimated using mathematical optimization techniques and methodologies. Optimizing allocation of resources is an approach for defining the optimal distribution of resources needed. These resources refer to the control and management of the operational risks within the sites, departments, business lines, etc., to render operational risk management systems more efficient and cost effective. Note that in operational risk management, the term "resource" includes any type of business investment, that is, in personnel, systems, and processes. However, in most cases, the measurement definition of these resources is defined in terms of capital budgeting.

In the operational risk and resource allocation optimization analysis, all operational risks that result from processes/activities, people, and systems are considered at the same time to define their influences on the operational performances and business targets. This analysis is based on the following principles:

- Each operational risk affects a number of operations with different degrees of significance. Thus, each operation is affected by a number of different risks.

- Each operation is exposed and impacted by operational risks to various degrees. Operations with a high degree of exposure have a higher priority for attempting to minimize their operational risks.
- The optimal value of risks in operations indicates the degree of variation for each of the operational risks to minimize the overall degree of operational risks. Moreover, minimizing the overall degree of operational risks affects business performance and thus hinders reaching the business targets and objectives.
- People, processes, and systems affect the operations and create operational risks to different levels; they are linked to one another, which influences their interrelated performances.
- The cost needed to modify the operational risks from the current to the optimal value should be less than the losses caused by the risks.
- The effort needed for altering the risk effect is different for each operation that refers to people, processes, and systems.

Based on the above principles, the optimal allocation of resources needed for optimizing the levels of operational risks and the degree of effect on the operations is defined.

The elements in matrix $\mathbf{\Theta}$ of Equation 8.25 define the optimal values of operational risks that are defined using the SEC methodology. Additionally, the matrix $\mathbf{Z}$ defined in Equation 8.1 includes the initial values of the operational risks under study. The differences between the two matrices indicate the effort needed to reach the optimal level. Moreover, their correlations, (*cor*), and significance levels, *SV* defined in Chapter 6, together with their exposure levels, are also considered in the estimation of the effort that should be spent to shift the initial risk values to their optimal ones. Furthermore, the correlation degree between the operational cost and loss must also be considered in the estimation of the effort needed for controlling and managing the operational risks. Finally, the cost needed for modifying each operational risk from the current to the optimal degree is also considered in the estimation of the resource allocation. The cost Ξ needed for minimizing the overall operational risk is defined as in Equation 8.26. A high cost in minimizing operational risks indicates a higher amount of resources needed for their management. Moreover, the overall loss $\mathbf{\Psi}$ initiated from the operational risks must also be taken into consideration. Similar to the cost, the higher degree of losses resulting from the operational risks indicates that there is a higher need for resources to be spent on the control and management of these risks. Alternatively, the difference between cost and loss $[\Xi - \mathbf{\Psi}]$ can also be considered in the estimation of the resource allocation.

Matrix $\mathbf{\Phi}$ in Equation 8.27 defines the percentage analogy of the allocation of resources needed to reach the optimal levels:

$$\mathbf{\Phi} = \left[\left(\left[\mathbf{Z} \cdot SV_Z\right] - \mathbf{\Theta}\right) \cdot f\left(\Xi, \Psi\right)\right] \quad (8.27)$$

where, for calculating the $\mathbf{\Phi}$, it is important to consider the difference between the actual and optimal values as well as the losses and the cost needed to move from the actual to the optimal levels.

Illustrating the Optimal Allocation of Resources

The allocation of resources is a very significant task in designing operational risk management systems. The optimal allocation of resources, or, in other words, the effort needed to optimize the levels of operational risks, is illustrated by defining the percentage variation from the actual to the optimal values. There are four different cases that present these variations:

1. The operational risks that influence a particular operational activity
2. The affected operations that are affected by a particular operational risk
3. The operational risks that influence several operational activities
4. Each affected operational activity that is affected by several operational risks

Figure 8.5 shows a pie chart that illustrates the percentage effort needed to shift the operational risk values to the optimal levels, and the effects of a particular operation such as the one that refers to credit card activities (case 1). Similar to Figure 8.5, the pie chart in Figure 8.6 illustrates the percentage distribution in resources to shift the actual levels of operational risks referring to ATM systems to the optimal levels. In this case, operational risks referring to new services require a lot of resources to control and manage the operational risk faced by ATM systems.

The pie chart illustrated in Figure 8.7 defines the percentage of distributed effort that each affected operation needs to contribute for minimizing a particular operational risk, such as unauthorized access, into its optimal level (case 2). Thus, Figure 8.7 shows that the operations referring to transfers, loan administration, and withdrawals need to participate most for optimizing the levels of operational risks referring to unauthorized access.

Figure 8.8 illustrates the overall percentage distribution for each of the operational risks that affects all of their associated operations (case 3). For instance, in Figure 8.8 the operational risks that refer to missing transactions and billing transactions need 5.4 percent and 2.3 percent, respectively, of the overall budget to optimize their effect on all of its associated operations.

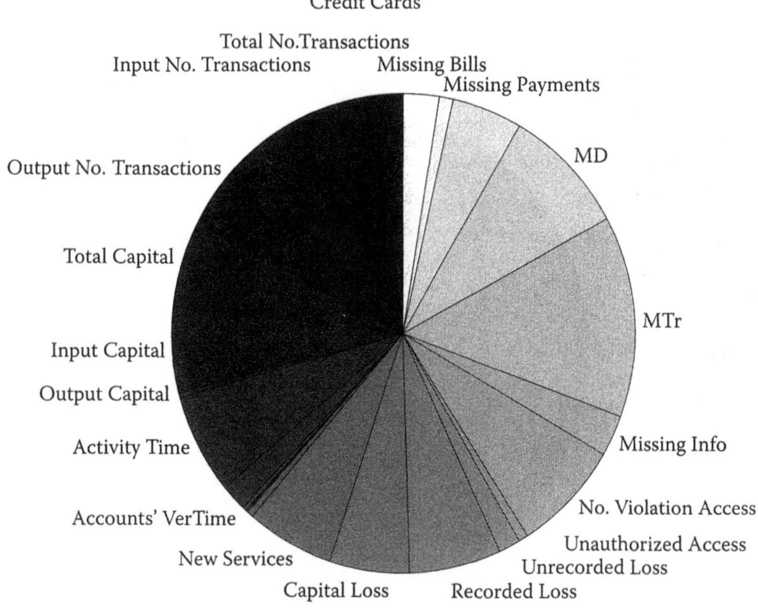

Figure 8.5 Pie chart that illustrates the percentage of effort needed to shift each of the operational risk values into the optimal ones for the "credit card" operational activities (case 1).

Finally, the pie chart in Figure 8.9 illustrates the overall percentage distribution of resources that each affected operation needs to minimize all its associated operational risks to their optimal levels (case 4). Thus in Figure 8.9, the percentage of the resources for the operation referring to check clearances is 5.7 percent. This is the amount of "effort" and resources that the organization must spend to optimize the levels of this risk.

Unconstrained and Constrained Optimization Analysis

Two types of techniques[10] can be used in operational risk optimization in relation to the algorithms' freedom to modify the values under study. These are called *unconstrained* and *constrained* optimization. In unconstrained optimization, any optimization algorithm used enables changes in the operational risk values toward any direction and to any level. On the other hand, in constrained optimization, the algorithms that can be used to try to optimize the operational risks are limited in their ability to change some of the risk values when they exceed a constrained set level.

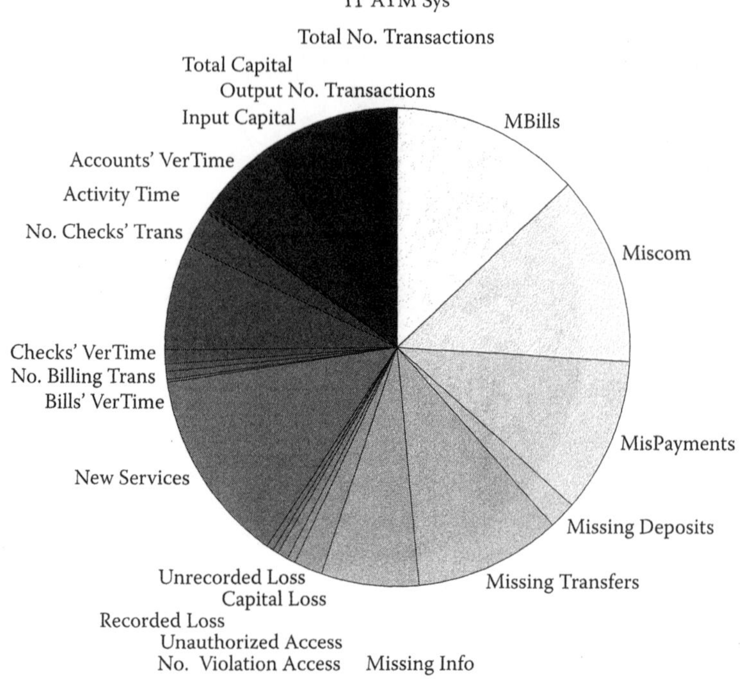

Figure 8.6 Pie chart that illustrates the percentage of effort needed to shift the operational risks, referring to the "ATM systems," to the optimal values (case 1).

Constraints can be specified for a particular operational risk or even for boundaries and zones that the risk values will not be allowed to surpass. When an unconstrained optimization method is used, the new optimal values of operational risks might differ considerably from their initial values. However, if constrained optimization is utilized, the new constrained optimal values of risks will be within the constrained boundaries. This means that if values of certain operational risks need to be changed to a certain amount but there is a limit on how much can be changed, then their optimal values will not exceed these levels. The cost function will try to reach its overall desirable level by attempting to "force" and optimize the rest of the levels of operational risks. The term "force" implies that these risks would not be modified to such degrees if unconstrained optimizations were to be used.

In the former case (unconstrained optimization), the overall operational risks will have higher possibilities for minimizing their values to the minimum possible levels. Note also that, in many cases of applying unconstrained optimization, only a few modifications to significant risks might be enough to minimize the cost function significantly.

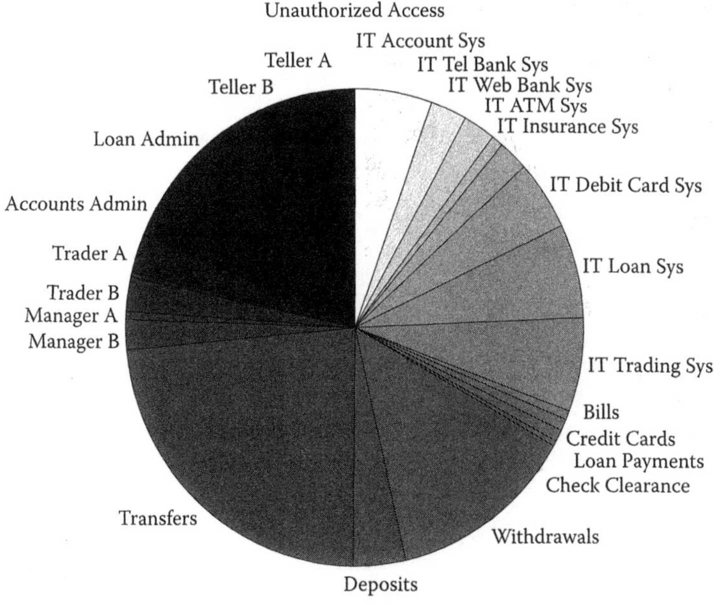

Figure 8.7 Pie chart that illustrates the percentage of effort that each affected operation from "unauthorized access" should invest to minimize the degree of affectation (case 2).

In the latter case, by using constrained optimization methods, there is the possibility of failing to minimize the cost function to a desirable level. Moreover, some of the operational risks that are not constrained may also need a higher degree of modifications. This is because these operational risks will be forced to minimize the overall degree of operational risks to the desirable minimal level.

If the cost of minimizing certain operational risk values is known, these operational risks could be set as constrained ones. In real business environments, constraints exist in operational management and thus in designing optimal operational risk management systems, constrained optimization methods are desirable. Thus, in combination with the identification of quantifiable parameters, risk tolerance levels (i.e., constraints) are established. These constraints should be clearly expressed to and approved by the managers or board of directors. It is important to note, however, that by setting many constraints, the optimization algorithms will probably not be allowed to drive the overall risk values to satisfy minimal levels.

Constraints related to financial and personnel (resources) issues, technical and systems performance limitations, and so forth are common in real business environments. Such examples include constraints in the

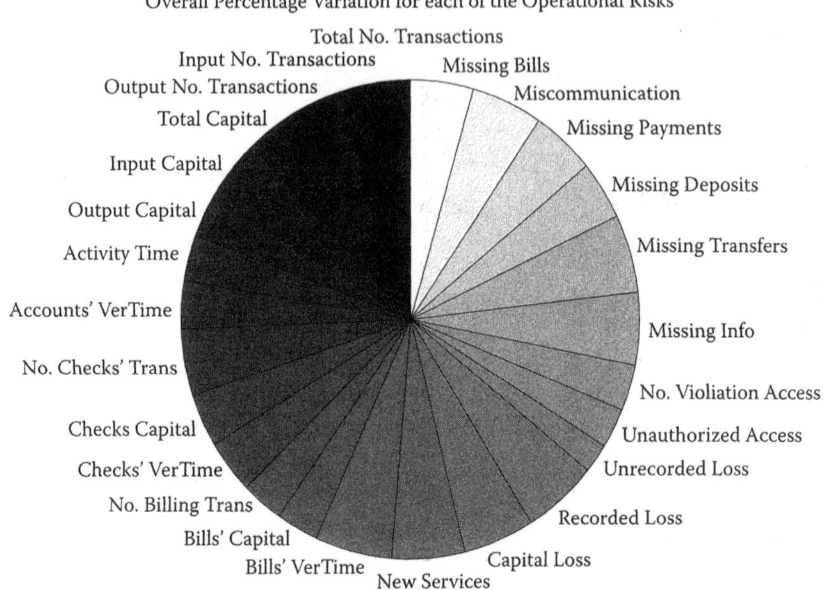

Figure 8.8 Pie chart that illustrates the overall percentage distribution effort, in resources, needed for each operational risk to shift its value into its optimal level (case 3).

amount of personnel there is on a team, such as less than five minutes system downtime. Thus, the optimization analysis must consider and integrate all the particular constraints to define the best minimum possible degree of the overall risk influences and effect on each operation. For instance, a technological limitation of Internet security that may result in a fraud during transaction operations must be evaluated and may be considered a constraint in the process of managing these risks to define their optimal degrees. Moreover, the optimal allocation of resources needed for managing the risks in operations also considers the available constrained resources. Furthermore, budgeting limitations for spending on different departments for operational risk management issues may be another constraint related to the optimization of resource allocation. The effect of these constraints on business targets and objectives should also be defined in relation to their resulting optimal risk values. Finally, it is important to note that most constraints are dynamically changing and thus must be frequently monitored because they may play critical roles in designing an effective and optimal risk management system. All optimal values should also be used in the distribution and risk profiling analysis to monitor, evaluate, and support the decision-management process.

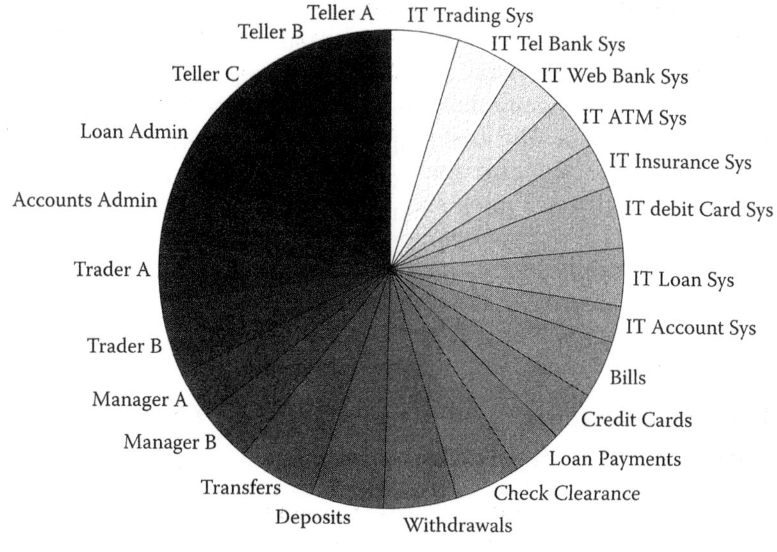

Figure 8.9 Pie chart that illustrates the overall percentage distribution effort, in resources, needed for each affected operation to shift its overall risk effect to their optimal levels (case 4).

Constraints to Modify Operational Risks Levels

In operational risk optimizing processes, the exposure and significance values of the operational risks must also be considered. During the optimization process, the modification of the operational risk values should be related to their exposure and significance values. In algorithmic optimization processes, the values of operational risks with high significance or exposure must be driven toward lower values. On the other hand, operational risks with a lower degree of exposure and or significance could accept higher variation during the optimization process. The above rules could be applied as constraints during the design of the optimization algorithms. In fact, such rules try to minimize the disturbances and losses initiated from the operational risks. Note that, in banking organizations, high modifications in operational risks having a high degree of exposures or significances (such as internal fraud), with potentially high impacts, cause high disturbances and losses. In such cases, minimizing the internal fraud that has a high correlation with the people, systems, and processes, their modification or tuning will need to be high. The "effort" needed from people, systems, and processes varies and mostly implies high cost and high expectations to apply these modifications practically. On the other hand, in the case of minor internal fraud, such as the ones that comes from the tellers, identifying the actual activities relating to such frauds will be costly. In general, a balance must exist between the expected modifications of the operational risk levels and their exposure as well as their significance levels. The best policy is to start the optimization process based on trying to minimize the cost function. The adaptation of the optimal operational risk values should be based on slow constant steps rather than on drastic reengineering actions. High modification carries the risk of not being applicable as well as causing a high degree of business disruptions.

Tuning, Adaptation, and Robustness of Optimal Operational Risk Systems

Because in the financial business environment both operational performances and business objectives are dynamically changing, the optimal operational risk values as well as the resources needed to control and manage them should be changing accordingly. The tuning of operational risk levels and allocation of resources enables the operational risk management system to be effectively adaptable. Efficient adaptation means that when setting the optimal degree of operational risks, there are only minimal implications to the operational performances and business objectives.

In the resulting operational risk control and management system, the optimal values of operational risks defined from the optimization analysis are also robust to support the business operational and financial stability. Operational robustness is a big issue because the tuning and adaptation process of the risks in operational performances have a financial/cost impact. The main purpose of designing a robust operational risk management system is to ensure that during the operational risk optimization process, operations have the minimum effect from operational risks. This will allow the operations to perform more effectively during the variation of underlying operational risks.

Summary

Optimizing the values of the operational risks renders their management very efficient and cost effective. Optimizing operational risks means defining the optimal levels of individual operational risks so that the overall magnitude of operational risks is minimized to the lowest possible and or desirable levels. Moreover, the allocation of resources required to reach this minimal level involves optimally distributing the resources needed for the operational risk management process within all business lines and operational activities. Optimization techniques and methodologies are based on algorithmic approaches that are able to combine large inhomogeneous and variable risk and performance information measurements. The main goal behind the optimization analysis is to optimize the operational risks to minimize the value of the operational risk cost function. This minimization is accomplished by considering the value of the associated significance levels, minimizing the degree of exposure referring to operational risks and affected operations between the operational risks or between affected operations. This combination of significance–exposure–correlation defines the SEC methodology introduced in this book, for the operational risks optimization analysis. Two main optimization methods can be used in designing optimal operational risks management systems. The first is based on derivative analysis of operational risk parameters and thus is very much applicable when the models of operational risks are well defined. Derivative-free is the second category of optimization approaches; it can be used when the operational risk models are difficult to define. The main principles together with rules and guidance for adopting the above optimization techniques and methodologies for the design of efficient operational risk management systems were presented in this chapter, and the resulting optimum matrix that illustrates the optimal values of operational risks was defined. This matrix is used as a basis to determine the cost for optimal operational risk management and the optimal resource allocation. Constraints referring to the operational activities of people, systems, and processes must also be considered during the operational risk optimization analysis. Furthermore, the exposure value and significance value must be considered in most of the steps for implementing the optimal operational risk management.

References

1. Beightler, C.S., Philips, D.T., and Wilde, D.J., *Foundations of Optimizations*, Prentice Hall, Upper Saddle River, NJ, 2nd edition, 1979.
2. More, J.J., The Levenberg-Marguardt Algorithm: Implementation and Theory. In G.A. Watson, Editor, *Numerical Analysis*, Springer-Verlag, London, 1977.
3. Curry, H.B., The Method for Steepest Descent for Non-Linear Minimization Problems, *Quant. Journal of Applied Mathematics*, 2:258–261, 1944.
4. Kirkpatrick, S., Gelatt, C.D., and Vecchi, M.P., Optimization by Simulating Annealing, Research Report 9335 IBM T.J. Watson Center, 1983.
5. Holland, J.H., *Adaptation in Natural and Artificial Systems,* University of Michigan Press, Ann Arbor, 1975.

6. Meisel, W.S., Computer Oriented Approaches to Pattern Recognition, volume 83 of *Mathematics in Science and Engineering,* Academic Press, New York, 1972.
7. Nelder, J.A. and Mead, R., A Simplex Method for Function Minimization, *Computer Journal,* 7:308–313, 1964.
8. Basel Committee on Banking Supervision International, Convergence of Capital Measurement and Capital Standards, A Revised Framework, June 2004. This paper is available free from their Web site (http://www.bis.org/bcbs/publ.htm).
9. Basel Committee on Banking Supervision, Sound Practices for the Management and Supervision of Operational Risk, February 2003.
10. Fletcher, R., *Practical Methods of Optimization: Unconstrained Optimization*, John Wiley & Sons, New York, 1980.

Chapter 9

Framework for Decision Making and Designing Optimal Risk Policies

Even a correct decision is wrong when it was taken too late.

—Lee Iacocca

Introduction

This chapter provides guidance on when and how banking organizations should plan and schedule their actions and policies used in designing the framework of operational risk management. The first sections of this chapter address planning actions and policies that should be applied for accepting, avoiding, or transferring/mitigating the operational risks. Aspects of scenario analysis, which is used extensively in this part of the operational risk analysis, are also presented. Moreover, guidelines for designing business continuity or contingency plans, which are widely used to deal with operational risks having a high degree of impact, are presented in this chapter. Business impact analysis referring to the design of "worst-case scenarios," as well as what operations and people are essential for the business to continue in as normal a fashion as possible, is discussed. Additionally, the establishment of alternate sites and the testing, maintenance,

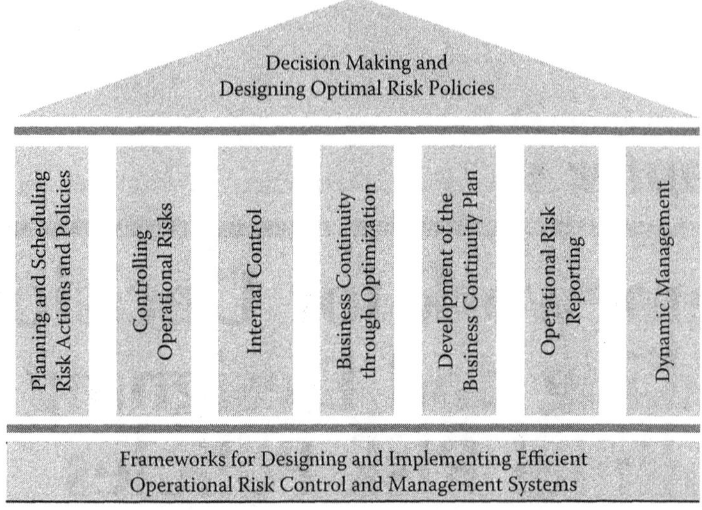

Figure 9.1 Main elements of Chapter 9.

and updating of the business continuity plan are explained in this chapter. Analysis referring to the thresholds in designing contingency plans and the time and frequency that should be set for their activation is also presented. The chapter also examines ways to control operational risks based on the planning and policies. Controlling for prevention and improvement, as well as controlling once thresholds have been reached and the importance of having the right people and systems in the right place with good communications, are some of the aspects discussed in this chapter. Moreover, the main guides for internal operational risk control in relation to Basel II requirements are presented. The importance of reporting systems for banking organizations is examined, and it is shown how organizations should be able to access and retrieve information from reporting systems to make intelligent decisions about controlling and managing their operational risks. Finally, the main aspects that should be included in operational risk management reports are illustrated. The layout of the chapter is illustrated in Figure 9.1.

Planning and Scheduling Operational Risk Actions and Policies

For each of the key operational risks identified, it is important not only to define its probability and impact, but also the decision that needs to be taken together with what method or ways the risk will be dealt with.

Based on the optimal levels of operational risks and the combination of the probability of an operational risk occurring and the impact it will have on the organization, a decision on whether to *accept*, *avoid*, *transfer*, or *mitigate* these risks needs to be made. These decisions depend heavily on the risk policies of the organization.

The estimation of operational risk probability, impact, and exposure, discussed in Chapter 7, is used in the risk profile analysis, whereas the optimal levels of the operational risks are defined as discussed in Chapter 8. The risk profiling and the optimal levels are used in defining the planning and scheduling of risk policies that the organization should set and actions that the organization should take before and after the operational risks occur. The planning process involves developing detailed strategies and actions for each of the risks in operation that have a high degree of probability, impact, or exposure. The planning process also prioritizes risk actions and creates an integrated operational risk management plan. Scheduling involves the integration of the tasks required to implement the operational risk action plans into day-to-day operational activities by assigning them to individuals and actively tracking their status.

The resulting optimal levels of operational risk probability and impact are used as the basis for constructing the operational risk action plans and policies referring to risk acceptance, avoidance, transfer, or mitigation (Figure 9.2). Thus, by defining and employing the optimal levels of risks in operations, organizations can derive more efficient and transparent strategic planning policies for operational risk management systems.

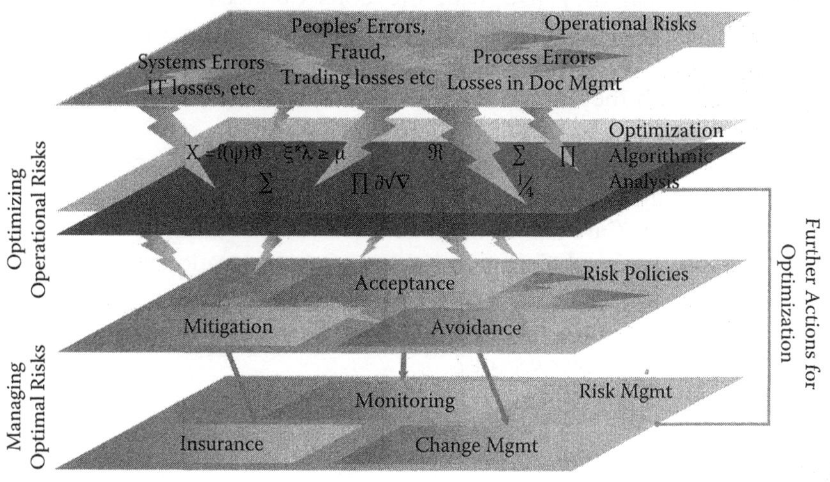

Figure 9.2 The optimal risk values can be the basis for constructing the risk actions as well as policies referring to risk acceptance, avoidance, transfer, and mitigation.

Planning Activities

When developing plans for reducing operational risk probability, impact, and exposure, risk analysts and managers should:

- Focus on the area of operational risks with high degree of exposure.
- Address the conditions to reduce the probability.
- Look for root causes as opposed to symptoms.
- Address the consequences to minimize the impact.
- Determine the root cause and then look for similar situations in other areas that may arise from the same cause.
- Be aware of dependencies and interactions among risks through the analysis of their significance values.

Scheduling Actions and Policies for Operational Risks

During operational risk action planning, risk analysts should define actions based on operational risk policies. First, when they are formulating operational risk action plans, they have to consider the following six issues:

1. *Research.* Does the operational staff know enough about this operational risk? Do they need to study the operational risk further to acquire more information and better determine the characteristics of the operational risk before deciding what actions to take?
2. *Accept.* Can they live with the consequences if the operational risks were actually to occur? Can they accept the operational risk and take no further action?
3. *Avoid.* Can they avoid the operational risks by changing the scope of business activities?
4. *Transfer.* Can they avoid the operational risk by transferring it to another group, organization, or individual?
5. *Mitigation.* Can the operational staff do anything to reduce and mitigate the probability or impact of the operational risk?
6. *Contingency.* Can the impact be reduced through a planned reaction? Can the organization get back to normal in minimal time in case of major disruptions?

Operational Risk Research

Much of the risk that is present in business operations is related to the uncertainties surrounding incomplete information. Operational risks that are related to lack of knowledge may often be resolved or managed most effectively by learning more before proceeding. Thorough research on the operational risk and its effect on operations is an efficient way to acquire this knowledge.

Operational Risk Acceptance

Some operational risks are such that it is simply not feasible to intervene with effective preventive or corrective measures. If that is the case, the organization should elect to simply "accept" such operational risks to realize the opportunities. In the case of operational risk "acceptance," a rationale for accepting the operational risks must be documented as the course of further actions. Moreover, a system of continuous *monitoring* should be developed in the event that changes occur in the probability, impact, or the ability to execute preventive or contingency measures related to the operational risks. Finally, when accepting the operational risks, banking organizations might make a mutual arrangement with another business or a business continuity supplier to ensure that they have help after an incident.

Although "acceptance" is not a "do-nothing" strategy, there is no need for developing mitigation or contingency plans. For instance, if an organization temporarily places its central information system servers in a basement room, flooding and heating could be probable operational risks with a high impact. However, mitigation of this risk would be too expensive and may cause too much disruption. Given that the probability of flooding and overheating is minimal at that particular place and period of year, it may be justifiable to accept this operational risk. However, steady monitoring of the heating as well as the condition of the basement must be the ongoing actions for avoiding these risks.

Note that documentation of the monitoring results must be available on request by the risk managers.

Operational Risk Avoidance

In case of "avoidance," the goal is to evade activities or situations that exhibit unacceptable operational risks and prevent an organization from taking more actions that may increase the operational risk exposure. Always have in mind that the actions taken must justify the benefit. The action, therefore, can be to reduce the level of business activities or withdraw from these activities completely. A further action is to define the implications on business performance of other related activities and business goals.

For instance, in dynamic banking business areas such as sales of new financial products, simultaneous updates of the software applications that support the associated business activities should be performed infrequently. This is because in most cases new software updates cause diversions that cannot be distinguished from the real benefits that may result from the sales activities. The frequency of updates/upgrades of processes or systems should also be done optimally.

Note that if an activity cannot be avoided, the level of the associated operational risks should be set to a minimum in the sets of constraints and reinitiate the optimization analysis.

Operational Risk Transfer

Whereas the avoidance strategy eliminates a risk, the transference strategy often leaves the risk intact but shifts responsibility for it elsewhere. Thus, for transferring their operational risks, banking organizations commonly use:

- Insurance companies
- Outsourcing service companies, etc.

An example of operational risk transfer is to outsource the credit verification for the E-commerce applications. In that case, although the operational risks still exist, the outsourced partner has the responsibility for them. Moreover, if the partner is better able to perform credit verification, then transferring the risks can also help to reduce them. The risks of implications due to natural disasters such as earthquakes are transferred to insurance companies. Finally, the actual values of operational risk significance resulting from the evaluation process, as well as the definition of the optimal levels of operational risks, can be used as a basis for designing "fair" risk transfer policies by the insurer or third party.

Note that:

- If the outsourced partner is more capable at eliminating particular operational risks, then transferring these risks can also reduce them.
- Operational risk transfer does not mean risk elimination. A risk transfer strategy may generate risks that still require proactive management.

Operational Risk Mitigation

In an effort to encourage better risk management practices, the Basel Committee is clearly interested in efforts by organizations to better mitigate and manage operational risks.[1] Such controls or programs have the potential to reduce the exposure, frequency, or severity of an event. Organizations must demonstrate that mitigation products are sufficiently capital-like to warrant inclusion in the adjustment to the operational risk exposure. There are many mechanisms to manage operational risk, including operational risk transfer through risk mitigation products.

Although the goal of risk avoidance is to evade activities or situations having unacceptable operational risk, risk mitigation planning involves performing actions and activities ahead of time to either prevent a risk from occurring altogether or to reduce the impact or consequences of it occurring. Operational risk profiling and optimization analysis are tools that can drive the operational risk mitigation process. Scenarios analysis of operational risk probability, impact, and exposure presents ways to show how to prevent risks from the stages of appearances to impact. The optimization process aims to minimize the impact of the risks in operations and the distance with their risk equilibrium point(s). An example of a risk-mitigating system is to use an optimal number of network connections to the intranet so as to reduce the probability of losing access and communication by eliminating the single point of failure. A well-designed data recovery plan, for example, can reduce the financial impact of a trading platform that breaks down, a low-frequency, high-impact operational risk. Operational risk mitigation can reduce losses triggered not only by external disasters, but also by internal practices. A further action in mitigation analysis is to "view" the optimal level as an identified constraint and reinitiate the optimization analysis. However, such constraints are not always known, and not every risk has a reasonable and cost-effective mitigation strategy. In cases where a mitigation strategy is not available, it is essential to consider effective contingency planning instead. A mitigation plan might have several actions, and the sequence might affect the mitigation's success for reducing, avoiding, or transferring the risk, so it is important to prioritize the steps in this plan.

Other questions of practical operational risk handling for any commercial financial undertaking include, for example, what can an organization do to avoid operational risks? How can it reduce the impact of operational risks? How can it transfer operational risks to a third party, such as an outsourcer or an insurer? How else can it finance business risks? Sometimes, the solutions are relatively straightforward. For example, if trading with a certain customer or country imposes unnecessary levels of risk, the simplest way to avoid that risk is to trade elsewhere. Similarly, it may be possible to reduce operational risks by modifying or tuning the processes by which transactions are handled. Losses arising from business disruptions due to electrical or telecommunications failures can be mitigated by establishing redundant backup facilities. Losses due to internal operational risks, such as employee fraud or product flaws, are harder to identify and insure against, but they can be mitigated with strong internal control and auditing procedures.

Note that a particular senior risk manager must be responsible for every mitigation plan. All milestones of the plan should be tracked in process, monitored, evaluated, and recorded.

Insurance as Operational Risk Mitigant

Currently, the primary risk mitigant used for operational risk is insurance. Insurance is a valuable instrument to transfer risks and to also complement operational risk management because it forces financial organizations to analyze their operational risks and to differentiate between their probability and impact. Referring to the existence and possible expansion of the use of such insurance products, representatives of both the banking and insurance organizations recommend that the risk-mitigating effects of insurance be recognized in the regulatory capital calculations for operational risk. It was partly in response to these comments that the Basel Committee decided to reduce the overall level of the operational risk capital charge. Because risk mitigation can be an important element in limiting or reducing operational risk exposures in an organization, an adjustment is being permitted that will directly impact the amount of regulatory capital that is held for operational risk. The adjustment is limited to 20 percent of the overall operational risk exposure result determined by the organization using its loss data, qualitative factors, and quantitative framework.[2] Insurance has been recognized by Basel II as an operational risk mitigant for those implementing the AMA.[3] Innovative insurance companies are developing more integrated risk cover products for operational risk. For insurance, Swiss Re New Markets has created a product labeled FIORI (Financial Institutions Operational Risk Insurance).[4]

Insurance is used to cover the losses initiated from high-impact and low-probability operational risks. For example, damages due to natural disasters can be insured against. More important, the degree of the operational risk exposure must be used to evaluate the actual risk severity. Based on the operational risk profiling analysis, the degree of the operational risk exposure is defined for such cases, that is, "low" probability and "high" impact. Thus, for insurance companies that have a clear view of the operational risk severity, their evaluation for mitigation cost will be based on the status of the actual operational risk.

There are long-standing types of insurance contracts (such as bankers blanket bonds) that have an extensive history of protecting banks against operational losses from events such as fraud and employee theft, and new insurance products intended to provide coverage of some of the emerging forms of operational risk. New types of insurance include finite risk insurance, insurance derivatives, and securitization[14] or "insuritization" based on bond products. The need for operational risk transfer solutions will increase as a result of such factors as complexity, globalization, new technology types of risks, regulators' requirements, and pressure for rational capital allocation.

There has been discussion that some security products may be developed to provide risk mitigation benefits; however, to date, no specific products have emerged that have characteristics sufficient to be considered capital-replacement for operational risk. As a result, security products may not be factored into the regulatory capital risk mitigation adjustment at this time.

The Basel Committee warns, however, that there is an important distinction between a genuine reduction of operational risk and merely transferring it to another business sector.[1] Noting the growing tendency to mitigate certain operational risks through insurance, it says that banks should recognize the possibility that they are replacing operational risk with a counterparty risk and perhaps leaving themselves open to further financial problems if the insurers are slow to pay out or if the loss is significantly adjusted. Insurance must not be a safety net for management failures. Insurance can help to mitigate economic and reputational consequences. It is not a substitute for sound operational risk management, but it complements risk management and is part of an integrated approach.

Scenario Analysis

Scenario analysis is extensively used in the design of the framework of strategies and policies for operational risks. Such scenarios include but are not limited to:

1. The bank's inability to reconcile a new settlement system with the original system, thereby preventing its implementation (such as in the case of the TAURUS system cancellation by the London Stock Exchange in 1993 resulting in a U.S.$700 million loss); recommendations resulting in a U.S.$100 million fine plus pending legal action)
2. A significant political event (such as the overthrow and reinstatement of Venezuela's president in 2002)
3. Massive technology failure
4. Nonauthorized trading (such as Barings Bank's losses of U.S.$1.6 billion in 1995[5]) and many others

The list of scenarios is only limited by management's past experiences and imagination. The primary advantage of scenario analysis is its incorporation of operational risk events that may not have become apparent yet. This is also the analysis' primary disadvantage. Scenario analysis is by its very nature subjective and highly dependent on management's subjective assessment of loss severity for each operational risk scenario. Moreover, it comprises a list of operational risk events without attaching a likelihood estimate to each event. Thus, scenario analysis is often used to sensitize management to risk possibilities, rather than strictly as an operational risk measure.

Two basic types of scenarios could be applied:

1. Historical
2. Hypothetical

Historical scenarios encompass the scenarios that reflect the changes in risk factors that occurred in specific historical episodes. On the other hand, hypothetical scenarios consider incidents that are thought to be plausible but have not yet occurred. Each type of scenario has its benefits. Depending on the operational risks, both approaches could be of value and should be used.

Controlling Operational Risks

The next step in the operational risk management framework is controlling operational risk. Control activities are designed to address operational risks that a bank has identified. During this step, all those who are involved with the operational risk management system should start carrying out activities according to the levels of the operational risks under study. In case no threshold levels have been activated, the control should be related to the prevention and improvement actions. In this case, the actions are related to how to set the optimal values as well as how to allocate the resources needed to manage the operational risks. However, in case the thresholds reach their limits, risk managers should implement corrective actions. The operational risk control is mainly driven by the implementations of the planning and scheduling of operational risk actions, policies, and contingency plans. Moreover, the controlling operational risk step ensures that the right people act at the right time.

Controlling Operational Risks for Prevention and Improvements

Controlling for prevention and improvements is based on the ongoing monitoring, evaluation, optimization, and operational risk profiling processes. During the monitoring process, controlling actions may take place when variations exist in the operational risk and performance indicators. Indicators that relate to operational risks having high significance values are initially under the "controlling/correcting" processes before reaching their threshold limits. This control policy can be very effective in terms of effort, time spent, and cost. Furthermore, it is a control action for "preventing" major losses. During the evaluation processes and operational risk profiling processes, the current and trend exposure of risk is defined and control actions on how to "prevent" the undesirable risk and performance can be set. Moreover, during the optimization analysis, the expected values of risk are identified so that the overall operational risk is minimized. This control action is aimed at "improving" the operational performances. All of the above corrective actions are based on small tunings of operational performance parameters to minimize operational risks. Some aspects that should be considered in the operational risk controlling process are listed in the following subsections.

Controlling Operational Risks after the Thresholds Have Been Activated

These control actions are based on the implementation of risk profiling and contingency plans. During the risk profiling process, the actual probability, impact, and risk exposure are illustrated before and after the threshold limits have been activated. Moreover, scenarios on how to shift the operational risks toward desirable areas within the space constructed by the axes of risk probability, impact, and exposure should be implemented.

Effective Communication to Control Operational Risks

The need for taking controlling actions is often detected by risk management automatic tools and systems, or by people. However, control actions must be taken by well-defined automatic systems or by authorized people with well-defined responsibilities as well as the expertise to react effectively. In both cases, all controlling actions must be reported (usually forming part of the risk reports). The operational risk control step ensures that the right tools, systems, and people act at the right time. The operational risk control step relies heavily on effective communication between systems and people. People need to receive notifications that certain operational risks and plans have changed, and to ensure that the right people take action at the right time. The operational risk control step cannot be effective unless communication between people and systems is also effective.

Internal Operational Risk Control

The Basel Committee, along with banking supervisors throughout the world, have focused increasingly on the importance of sound internal controls. This heightened interest in internal controls is, in part, a result of significant losses incurred by several banking organizations. An analysis of the problems related to these losses indicates that they could probably have been avoided had the banks maintained effective internal control systems.[6] Internal control systems would have prevented or enabled earlier detection of the problems that led to the losses, thereby limiting damage to the banking organizations.

When management considers its exposure to operational risk, it is necessary to assess:

- What aspects of operational risk the organization is exposed to
- How well the organization is managing this exposure to operational risk

When an organization has implemented controls to manage this exposure, the remaining residual risk is the level of risk to which the organization chooses to be exposed to in the course of its business. An organization will typically implement an operational risk management framework to monitor the effectiveness of these controls, the level of residual risk, and their compatibility with its operational risk management objectives and policies.

The Bank for International Settlements (BIS) mentions three main objectives and roles of the internal control framework:[6]

1. Efficiency and effectiveness of activities (performance objectives)
2. Reliability, completeness, and timeliness of financial and management information (information objectives)
3. Compliance with applicable laws and regulations (compliance objectives)

Banking organizations must incorporate a forward-looking element to operational risk control. In principle, an organization with strong internal controls in a stable business environment will have less exposure to operational risks than an organization with internal control weaknesses that are growing rapidly. In this regard, organizations will be required to assess and identify the levels and trends in operational risk in the organization. These assessments must be current and comprehensive across the organization, and must identify the critical operational risks facing the organization. The business environment and internal control factor assessments should reflect both the positive and negative trends in risk management within the organization as well as changes in an organization's business activities that increase or decrease operational risks. Because the results of the operational risk assessment, discussed in Chapters 5 and 6, are part of the capital methodology, management must ensure that the operational risk assessments are done appropriately and reflect the operational risks of the organization. Periodic comparisons by internal control should be made between actual loss exposure and the assessment results.

Internal operational risk control consists of five interrelated elements:

1. Management oversight and the control culture
2. Risk recognition and assessment
3. Control activities and segregation of duties
4. Information and communication
5. Monitoring activities and correcting deficiencies (tuning)

Special attention for internal control procedures should be paid to the following:

- New business/activity/product
- Internet activity, E-business
- Outsourcing
- Security, safety: access to infrastructure, internal data
- Client privacy protection, including data on clients
- Insider trading
- Money laundering
- Suitability of clients
- Branch/subsidiary offices, especially those that are far away from headquarters
- Overly profitable areas
- Internal communication/information flow
- Change management

An organization's analytical framework complements but does not substitute for prudent controls. Rather, with improved risk measurement, organizations are finding that they can make better-informed strategic decisions regarding enhancements to controls of processes, the desired scale and scope of the operations, and how insurance and other risk mitigation tools can be used to offset operational risk exposure. It is important that:

- Controls are effective and remain in place.
- Changes in the operation that require further operational risk management and control are identified.

- Actions are taken to correct ineffective operational risk controls and reinitiate the risk management steps in response to new hazards.
- Tools assisting in performing supervision include inspection, observation, and feedback programs.

Practical controls recognize that:

- There is some degree of risk associated with all operations. The goal of operational risk management is not to eliminate operational risk, but to control and manage these risks so that the objectives can be accomplished with the minimum amount of loss.
- Banking organizations should try to apply operational risk controls only in those activities and to those that are actually at risk. Too often risk controls are applied indiscriminately across an organization, leading to wasted resources and unnecessary irritation of busy operational personnel. It is necessary to apply redundant operational risk controls when practical and cost effective.

There is a recognition that internal operational risk control systems will differ among organizations due to the nature and complexity of an organization's products and services, organizational structure, and operational risk management culture. Assessing the internal operational risk control environment is clearly an area where the supervisory authorities already focus considerable attention. A number of standards cover topics relevant to the internal control. These include, for example, the Interagency Policy Statement on the Internal Audit Function and Its Outsourcing,[7] the Federal Financial Institution's Examination Council's (FFIEC's) Business Continuity Planning Booklet,[8] and the FFIEC's Information Security Booklet.[9]

Guidance for Internal Control

The Basel Committee has set some guidance for internal control:[10,11]

1. The board of directors should have responsibility for approving and periodically reviewing the overall business strategies and significant policies of the bank.
2. Senior management should have responsibility for implementing strategies and policies approved by the board, developing processes that identify, measure, monitor, and control risks incurred by the bank.
3. The board of directors and senior management are responsible for promoting high ethical standards to emphasize and demonstrate to all levels of personnel the importance of internal controls.
4. An effective internal control system requires that the operational risks that could adversely affect the achievement of the bank's goals are being recognized and continually assessed.

5. Control activities should be an integral part of the daily activities of a bank. An effective internal control system requires that an appropriate control structure be set up, with control activities defined at every business level.
6. An effective internal control system requires that there is appropriate segregation of duties and that personnel are not assigned conflicting responsibilities.
7. An effective internal control system requires that there are sufficient and full internal financial, operational, and compliance data, as well as external market information about events and conditions that are relevant to decision making.
8. An effective internal control system requires that there are reliable information systems in place that cover all significant activities of the bank.
9. An effective internal control system requires effective communication to ensure that all staff fully understand and comply with policies and procedures and that relevant information is reaching the appropriate personnel.
10. The overall effectiveness of the bank's internal controls should be monitored on an ongoing basis. Monitoring of key risks should be part of the daily activities of the bank as well as periodic evaluations by the business lines and internal audit.
11. There should be an effective and comprehensive internal audit of the internal control system carried out by operationally independent, appropriately trained and competent staff.
12. Internal control insufficiencies, whether identified by business line, internal audit, or other control personnel, should be reported immediately to the appropriate management level and addressed promptly.
13. Supervisors should require that all banks, regardless of size, have an effective system of internal controls that is consistent with the nature, complexity, and risk inherent in their business.

Business Continuity or Contingency Planning through Optimization

According to recommendations issued by the Basel Committee on Banking Supervision, continuity planning is a crucial element of operational risk management systems. Principle 7 of Basel II highlights that "banks should have in place contingency and business continuity plans to ensure their ability to operate on an ongoing basis and limit losses in the event of severe business disruption."[13]

Continuity plans address the "what to do" actions if a major operational risk occurs and focus on the consequences and how to minimize their impact. For this purpose, banks should identify critical business processes for which they ensure that the right people or systems act at the right time. Defining who is responsible for each of the steps of the recovery is very critical in the designing process of contingency planning. Apart from complying with Basel II requirements, all regulated financial organizations need to design effective business continuity planning. Disaster recovery focuses on the actions to recover from an unlikely event of a severe or catastrophic business disruption. On the other hand, business continuity planning addresses and plans various scenarios with different levels of severity and disruptive consequences before the disaster. Rather than focusing on full recovery following a major disaster, the business continuity plan addresses and plans various scenarios with different levels of severity and disruptive consequences. Business continuity planning is exactly that: keeping the business going. Business continuity planning is concerned with identifying critical business functions and ensuring that they can be restored in an appropriate timeframe. This includes both electronic and physical (paper-based) operations. Financial organizations are required to draw up continuity plans for each major area of business to protect operations from severe disruptions and emergencies and to reduce the adverse effects of any business disruptions. The objectives of business continuity planning are to minimize financial loss to the organization; to continue to serve customers and financial market participants; and to mitigate the negative effects disruptions can have on an organization's strategic plans, reputation, operations, liquidity, credit quality, market position, and ability to remain in compliance with applicable laws and regulations.

Business continuity planning basically refers to the advance planning and preparations that are necessary to identify the impact of potential losses arising from an emergency or a disaster. It then aims to recover all critical business operations; to formulate and implement viable recovery strategies; to develop recovery plans that ensure continuity of the services; and to administer a comprehensive testing and maintenance program.[12]

The objectives of business continuity planning are to:

- Minimize financial losses to the organization.
- Continue to serve customers and financial market participants.
- Mitigate the negative effects caused by operational risks.

Have in mind that banking organizations are operating in an environment where instant information access is expected 24 hours a day, seven days a week. System downtime is increasingly unacceptable. Banks have also awoken to the ruthless reality that natural and man-made disasters are a fact of life that they cannot escape from. Although banks cannot predict when operational risks may occur, they can take steps to be prepared and ensure their ability to respond rapidly to minimize the disruption. Clearly, the Y2K problem in the year 2000 and the events of September 11, 2001, were the most significant wake-up calls for business continuity and disaster recovery planning.

Building in business continuity, making it part of the way that a bank runs its business rather than having to "fire fight" any emergency, helps prepare banks to offer "business as usual" in the quickest possible time. How quickly and painlessly an organization manages to get back to business as usual in the event of a terrorist attack, fire, flood, or other disasters depends on how effectively it can devise, and put into action, its own business continuity management (BCM). Unlike operational risk, which is a relatively new branch of financial risk management (certainly in comparison to market and credit risk), BCM has been a part of "best practice" within the financial industry for some time. In today's global market, a major loss event in one market area could affect significantly the rest of the markets worldwide. The experiences gained from the terrorist attack in New York on September 11, 2001, have significantly increased organizations' ability to develop and apply their BCM policies. Thus, analogous terrorist attacks such as in Madrid on March 11, 2004 and in London on July 7, 2005, found financial organizations applying their BCM and the rest of the market having an exceptional behavioral maturity, that results, comparatively, in significantly less losses. Furthermore, it is important to note that it is the results of the market's knowledge that operational risk management is nowadays one of the demanding aspects in banking organizations and is also expected to extend in all business sectors.

Business continuity planning should be regarded as part of operational risk management. A systematic business continuity planning process is based on a risk and vulnerability analysis of operations. Most deficiencies detected through such risk and vulnerability analysis can be addressed, and need not be incorporated in the continuity plans. Business continuity planning may be regarded as a means of undertaking quality control of the operations. Business continuity plans should take into account different types of plausible scenarios to which the bank may be vulnerable, as well as the size and complexity of the bank's operations. The board of directors and senior management have the ultimate responsibility for business continuity planning and the effectiveness of their business continuity plan. Senior management should establish policies, standards, and processes for business continuity planning, which should be approved by the board of directors. Senior management should establish clearly which functions in the organization have the responsibility for managing the entire process of business continuity planning.

A process-oriented approach to business continuity planning involves and may not be limited to:

1. Risk assessment
2. Risk monitoring
3. Risk management
4. Business impact analysis (BIA)

The risk assessment for business continuity planning considers, in particular:

- The impact of various business disruption scenarios on both the organization and its customers
- The probability of occurrence based, for example, on a rating system of "high," "medium," and "low"
- The loss impact from both internal and external sources
- The safety of critical processing documents and vital records
- A broad range of possible business disruptions, including natural, technical, and human threats

In planning efficient business continuity, there are some key stages to consider:

- Business impact analysis
- Recovery strategy formulation
- Development of a business continuity plan
- Establishment of alternative sites
- Implementation and maintenance of the business continuity plan

These steps need constant board of directors and senior management oversight under the consideration of prolonged disruptions and catastrophic disasters. Figure 9.3 shows all these steps.

Business Impact Analysis

The objective of the BIA is to identify different kinds of risks to business continuity and to quantify the impact of disruptions. The quantification of impacts that are initiated from operational risks is defined in Chapter 7. The BIA helps to identify those critical business activities, banking services, and internal support functions, which, in the event of a disaster, must be consistently and effectively delivered. There is a need to analyze the business; therefore, the fullest possible picture of the complex interactions

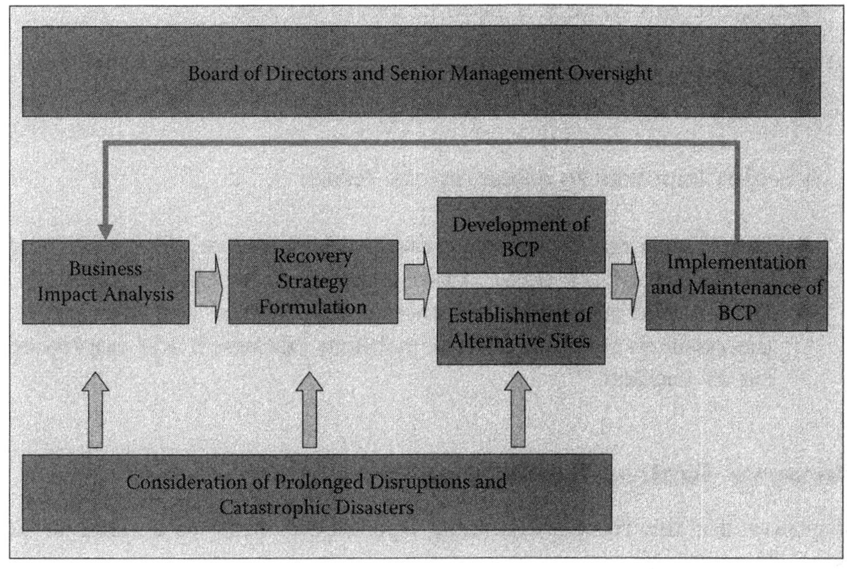

Figure 9.3 Key stages in business continuity planning.

inside the organization and between the organization and its customers and suppliers is needed.

The business impact analysis normally comprises two phases:

1. The first phase is to identify critical services that must be maintained and continued in the event of a disaster.
2. The second phase is a timeframe assessment. It aims to determine how quickly the organization needs to resume the critical functions or services identified (refer to Table 9.1).

Table 9.1 Business Continuity Plan Operations/Recovery Time Matrix

	Recovery Time			
Operations	*1 hour*	*1 day*	*1 week*	*1 month*
A	✓			
B			✓	
C				✓
D		✓		

During the BIA there is a need to assess the risk:

- How likely is it to happen?
- What effect will it have on the business?

It is also important to assess, in cost terms:

- How much could the organization afford to lose if an emergency prevented it from doing business for days, weeks, or months?
- How would suppliers, customers, and potential customers react if the business received adverse publicity because it was unprepared for an incident?

Recovery Strategy Formulation

Moreover, for the recovery strategy formulation there is a need to ask "what-if" questions:

- What is the worst-case scenario?
- What functions and people are essential, and when?

Here is a sample of these types of questions:

- What if the electricity supply failed?
- What if the IT networks went down?
- What if the customers could not contact the organization?
- What if the suppliers could not supply the organization?

What Is the Worst-Case Scenario?

Identify the worst-case scenario. If the plan enables the organization to cope with a worst-case scenario, it will also help it deal more easily with lower-impact incidents. Generally, the worst case will be something that completely stops the organization from carrying out its business.

What Operations and People Are Essential, and When?

To ensure effective business continuity planning, details of who needs to do what, when, and where immediately after an incident are required. It may be helpful to develop an operations/recovery time matrix as shown in Table 9.1 to show which important operations and processes need to be up and running after certain time intervals. However, in considering these operations and processes, it is very important to understand the relationship between them, that is, how the recovery or nonrecovery of one operation affects or is influenced by others.

Development of the Business Continuity Plan

The development of the business continuity plan (BCP) refers to a collection of procedures and information that needs to be developed, compiled, and maintained in readiness for use in the event of an emergency or disaster. BCPs should and will look different for different organizations. However, most good continuity plans share some important commonalities:

- Make it clear who needs to do what, and who takes responsibility for what.
- Include clear, direct instructions for the crucial first hour after an incident.
- Include a list of things that need to be thought about after the first hour.
- Agree how often, when, and how the organization will check its plan to ensure it is always a "dynamic" document.
- It is almost impossible to plan in detail for every possible event. Remember that people need to be able to react quickly in an emergency: reading lots of text may make that more difficult.
- Plan for worst-case scenarios. If the plan covers how to get back in business if a flood destroys the building, it will also work if one floor is flooded.

A good continuity plan will help the organization deal effectively with an incident, no matter what caused it. Banks do not have to be the target of terrorism for their power supply to be disrupted. Accidents such as workers cutting through a cable could produce the same result: the building will have no electrical power.

A variety of external parties may play key roles in the recovery process and therefore must be included in the planning stages. Roles and responsibilities of third parties (e.g., service providers, business partners, correspondent banks, etc.) must be defined in the plan and in written contracts, where possible. Contact information and notification requirements should also be specified.

BCPs are costly, and it may not be cost effective to have a fully developed and implemented plan for all the worst-case scenarios. It may be useful to consider two-level plans: one to deal with near-term problems, which would be fully developed with the physical capacity to put it into immediate effect, and the other to deal with a longer-term scenario. The longer-term plan may include plans on how to reconstruct the primary sites or to move to a new permanent work location. For example, this may require that duplicates of design documents, floor plans, and cabling diagrams should be kept off-site. An essential part of the BCP involves the backup of data, system redundancy, and plans for fail-over and restoration. Backup strategies must address both electronic and physical data. Every department and business line must have a continuity plan that is integrated with the overall plan of the banking organization. Note finally that in creating an effective BCP, financial organizations should not assume a reduced demand for services during the disruption. In fact, demand for some services (e.g., ATMs) may increase.

Establishment of Alternate Sites

There should be an examination of how key business functions are concentrated in the same or adjacent locations and how close the alternative sites are to the primary site. Basel II, in its Principle 7, Section 43,[13] highlights that relocation sites should be at an adequate distance from the impacted operations to minimize the operational risk that both primary and backup records and facilities will be unavailable simultaneously.

Testing, Maintenance, Updating, and Implementation of the BCP

Sometimes, any weaknesses in a plan are discovered when is put it into action. Testing helps confirm that a plan will be connected and robust if it is ever needed. Testing is also a good way to train staff who have business continuity responsibilities, and educate and make other employees aware of the plan. All employees need to be aware of the existence of the plan and how it affects them. Basel II, Principle 7, Section 44,[13] highlights that a bank should periodically review its disaster recovery plan and BCP so that they are consistent with the bank's current operations and business strategies. It also suggests that these plans should be tested periodically to ensure that the banking organization will be able to execute them. Major items like business impact analysis, disaster recovery strategies, and relevant service-level agreements related to the BCPs should be reviewed.

A formal testing plan must be built into the BCP. The objective of the testing plan is to ensure that all aspects of the BCP are reviewed at least annually. The testing plan should outline what types of tests will be used (full test, partial test, etc.) and their frequency. Formal testing documents should be produced.

The BCP should be updated and maintained to achieve the following:

- Reflect changes in the organization's personnel and in the operational risks it might face.
- Define schedules and budgets for updates and maintenance activities.
- Purchase tools and systems for update and maintenance.
- Define review criteria.
- Audit the BCP.

A formal annual statement should be submitted to the board on whether the recovery strategies adopted are still valid and whether the documented BCPs are properly tested and maintained.

Finally, in case of a disaster, the BCP should be implemented. The implementation of a BCP and restoration of business in the event of an emergency is dependent on the successful interaction of various components. The overall strength and effectiveness of a BCP can be decreased by its weakest component. An effective business continuity plan coordinates across its many components, identifies potential process or system dependencies, and mitigates the risks from interdependencies.

Thresholds in Designing Business Continuity Plans

An organization must define when and the level to which the BCP applies. To do this, thresholds should be established for the BCP based on the types of operational risks or the types of consequences and impact that will be encountered. Thresholds are like warning signals that light up while there is still time to avoid danger. These warning indicators should be able to notify when a condition is close to occuring or has occurred, expanding its stable level, and it is time to put the BCP into effect. Ideally, thresholds become true before the consequences occur. For example, if the condition is that the information data storage server runs out of hard disk space, the threshold might be that the server's disk has reached 80 percent of its capacity and is showing an upward trend.

In efficient operational risk management systems, thresholds become evident before the consequences and effects occurs. Thresholds must not be too low, because they will result in oversensitive business continuity planning systems, or too high, because they will not be able to prevent the negative effects. An optimal level of these thresholds must be identified. Fuzzy linguistic rules are most appropriate to incorporate in such warning systems. Note that as the risks' occurrence varies in business environment, the optimal level of thresholds should be able to readapt its values accordingly. Thus, in the example mentioned above, the threshold for the storage server may be reset at a value less than 80 percent if the upward trend increases its value; however, it may be reset to a higher level if the overall capacity of the storage has been increased significantly by adding new hard disks.

Time and Frequency of Threshold Activation

Thresholds should always be within the "loop" of the operational risk management process. The time and the frequency when the threshold should be activated may vary according to what is being monitored and controlled. For example, in the case of employee theft, thresholds should be activated on a daily basis. Moreover, thresholds should be activated on a frequency of minutes or even seconds for most processes related to capital trading; however, thresholds related to inadequacies in customer services could be activated on a monthly frequency. Nevertheless, risk managers must always be able to define and set activation for a threshold at any time.

Effectiveness of the Business Continuity Plan

It is important to capture as much information as possible about problems that occur concerning the effectiveness of the business continuity plan and thus to determine the effectiveness of such a plan or strategy for operational risk control. The results and lessons learned from execution of BCPs should be incorporated into a business continuity plan status and outcome report so that the information becomes part of the operational risk knowledge base.

An optimal operational risk management system should incorporate best-practice principles of business continuity planning, using a process approach to identify critical processes and operations. More important, there is a need to define the interdependencies that exist based on a risk analysis of the operations and detecting deficiencies to minimize impact on the continuity of the business. Such an approach ensures the effectiveness of the BCP such that the highest levels of business continuity are achieved.

Operational Risk Reporting

High-level operational risk reports must be produced periodically to be reviewed by the board and senior management. These reports must provide information regarding the operational risk profile of the organization, including the sources of operational risks both from an organization-wide and line-of-business perspective, versus established management expectations.

Operational risk reporting should work at two levels: internal and external. Internal reports are accessible to senior managers and the board of directors, and they should be able to receive, at a more corporate level, regular reports on financial, operational risk, and compliance data. External reports should include external market information about events and conditions that are relevant to operational risk management decision making. The results of monitoring activities should be included in regular management and board reports, and the reports should fully reflect identified problem areas and should motivate timely corrective actions on outstanding issues.

Operational risk management should ensure that information is received by the appropriate people, on a timely basis, and in a form and format that will aid in the monitoring and control of the business.

The reporting process should include information such as:

- The critical operational risks facing, or potentially facing, the organization
- Operational risk events and issues, together with intended remedial actions
- The effectiveness of actions taken
- Details of plans taken to address any exposures, where appropriate
- Areas of importance where certain operational risks are imminent
- The status of steps taken to address operational risks

The information provided in regular reports to the board of directors and senior management should be sufficient to allow:

- The board and executives to determine that the delegation of risk management duties have been effective and their requirements for operational risk management are being met
- The overall operational risk profile to be evaluated against the organization's risk strategy and appetite
- Key risk indicators to be monitored and the need for corrective or preventive actions to be assessed
- Business-line management to confirm that controls over key operational risks have been executed successfully and that failures and "near-misses" have been understood and assessed
- Evaluating the levels and trends of operational risks and their effect on business performances within business lines

- Understanding the effect on the business objectives and the financial and economic impact stemming from operational risks
- Evaluating the reasons for key assumptions in the capital planning process
- Determining the allocation of resources for managing the risks in operations
- Evaluating capital requirements based on the bank's evolving operational risk profile and whether any changes to the plan are necessary
- Proposing suggestions for operational risk management and decision making
- Having a clear picture concerning operational risk management issues

The reports should be generated from an automatic reporting system and thus available at any time. This helps in reviewing on a regular basis the status of operational management systems, the range of operational risks, as well as the number of times particular operational risks belonged to the top list. Note that risk managers and analysts should have the permission to add, but not to remove, relevant information to the operational risk reports.

Moreover, the report should also refer to the situations of operational risk management system regarding the following characteristics of the system:

- Consistencies, that is, there is consistency between assessment of the risks in operations and the actual operational risks faced, in which case the operational risk management system should proceed as planned.
- Variances, that is, there is a variation between the assessed operational risk with actual operational risks, in which case corrective actions in this area of risk control and management should be defined and implemented.
- Changeability, that is, the operational risk management cannot handle particular operational risks due to significant changes of those risks, in which case major corrective and preventive actions in this area of risk control and management should be defined and implemented.

Table 9.2 gives a sample of typical reports that need to be available to monitor and manage operational risk levels.

Table 9.2 Operational Risk Reports

Report	*Frequency*	*Address Following Issues*
Operational Risks	Depends on operational risk exposures	What major exposures does the bank have? How can the bank prioritize them? Where do they come from?
Risk Management Actions	Monthly/yearly Available at any time from the automatic risk reporting system	What can the bank do about the particular risk? How effective are any current risk initiatives?
Status of Operations	Daily/weekly Available at any time from the automatic risk reporting system	Is there a major change in some risk factors that could put operations at risk?
Events	After a major event	What happened? How did it happen? What did the bank do about it? What can the bank learn?
Executive Summary Reviews	Periodic At least annually	How effective is the bank's approach to operational risk management?

Basel II's Pillar 3 requires that the main approaches and results of the applied operational risk management system have to be available to the public. Therefore, stakeholders should be able to access reports on an external level that should show the major operational risks and the status of operational risk management actions. The purpose of a stakeholder or risk manager report is to communicate the overall operational risk to the organization. If operational risks as well as processes, systems, and people activity reviews are regularly scheduled (monthly or at major milestones), it helps to show the previous ranking of operational risks as well as the number of times an operational risk was in the top list of risks.

Main Aspects of an Operational Risk Management Report

An operational risk report should include the aspects discussed in this section.

Levels of Operational Risks and Performances

First, before any operational risk control actions are taken, it is important to identify the current status and significance of the risks in operations and how these risks affect the organization's performance. This information is a result of the evaluation process.

Operational Risk Trends

The knowledge of operational risk trends is also very important and thus any information referring to them should be included in the operational risk reports. This helps in decision making, especially for short-term action plans because trends give a clear view on future directions.

Operational Risk Distribution

There are two ways of viewing the operational risk distributions:

1. The distribution of operational risks within the operations
2. The distribution of the affected operations

Both of the above types of distributions should be reviewed and presented in the operational risk reports. This part of the operational risk reporting helps risk managers to have a better view of where and how the operational risk appears within the organization.

Operational Risk Probability, Impact, and Exposure

Operational risk reports should include the levels and distribution of an operational risk's probability, impact, and degree of exposure. The suggested scenarios of how to shift those values to lower levels should also be included in the operational risk report. The scenarios are defined by correlation analysis between each operational risk and the associated links with and causes to other risks.

Optimal Values of Operational Risks

The results from both constrained and unconstrained optimization analysis are used to extract the information on how to control and manage the operational risks. Both current and optimal values for each risk in operations should be represented graphically. Moreover, the results for optimal allocation of resources should also be illustrated graphically in reporting how much "effort" should be spent to control and manage each operational risk.

Operational Risk Management Actions

Reports are not made for only presenting statistical facts. They should also suggest actions to be taken for the risks with high significance values.

Ongoing Review of the Thresholds

The classification of thresholds is not always set correctly or cannot be automatically monitored. Any changes in the values of the current thresholds or any new set of thresholds must be reported. Forgetting to review thresholds means that if one of them has become true, it might have gone unnoticed, resulting in further delay on the business continuity plan and often escalating the consequences.

Reviews

Operational risk reporting and reviews must become a regular part of the workflow. For example, such a review should hold a place on the permanent agenda for any recurring meeting. The review can be highly effective without taking very much time. This is the key to continuously managing risks.

Decision and Dynamic Management

The operational risk management process is an iterative process. The operational risk management function should ensure that key operational risk management activities are revisited with appropriate frequency (e.g., annually or semiannually). Such activities include, but may not be limited to, determining that:

- Operational risk strategies and policies are still in line with the business objectives.
- Operational risks are identified and accountabilities remain current.
- Mitigation responses remain appropriate to the operational risk strategies and policies and are still valid based on a cost-benefit analysis.
- Lessons are learned from root-cause analysis and that these generate actions to improve the operational risk management processes.
- All actions arising are followed up in appropriate priority.

Improving the knowledge of the current operational risks by understanding their behavior and discovering new ones is an ongoing process for designing and implementing optimal operational risk management systems. This process should focus on the following key objectives:

- Improving the operational risk management system by capturing the knowledge fed back by the organization
- Providing quality assurance of the current risk management systems' activities and practices
- Capturing knowledge and best practices, especially surrounding operational risk identification and successful mitigation strategies

Capturing New Operational Risk Successfully

Operational risk classification is a powerful means for ensuring that knowledge from previous experiences is made available to the groups performing future operational risk assessments. Two key aspects of operational risk knowledge are often recorded using operational risk classifications:

1. *New risks.* Any new risk within the operations or a new operation that may be influenced by certain operational risks must be identified. Their significance and actual values should be derived and reviewed as explained in the corresponding sections of this book. The existing list of operational risks as well as any operational risk knowledge database must also be kept up-to-date.
2. *Successful (mitigation) strategies.* All experiences of operational risk management strategies that have been used successfully or even unsuccessfully must be captured and defined accordingly. Mitigation strategies are rather difficult but most critical for decision making. Their degree of success needs to be identified and evaluated after associated risks have occurred.

Operational Risk Review Meetings

The operational risk review process should be well managed to ensure all knowledge about operational risk management is captured. Operations management reviews as well as specific risk review meetings provide a forum for understanding about managing risks effectively. They should be held on a regular basis, and like other reviews, they benefit from advanced planning; development of a clear, published agenda; participation by all participants; and free, honest communication in a "blame-free" environment. Having many different perspectives on operational risks allows such meetings to be more productive, which helps effective decision making. Such meetings bring a feedback loop to the whole operational risk assessment, control, and management systems.

Operational Risk Knowledge Base

The operational risk knowledge base is a formal or informal mechanism by which an organization captures knowledge to assist in future operational risk control and management. Without some form of knowledge base, an organization may have difficulties adopting a proactive approach to operational risk management. The optimal levels of operational risks dynamically change as the operations and their associated risks are tuned and modified; this change must also be captured in the knowledge base.

Summary

The operational risk management framework provides overall operational risk strategic direction and ensures that an effective operational risk assessment, control, measurement system is adopted throughout the organization. The framework should provide for the consistent application of operational risk policies and procedures throughout the organization and address the roles of both the independent organizationwide operational risk management function and the lines of business. The planning actions and policies for managing the operational risks are based on their acceptance when their impact is very low or avoidance when their severity is high. Moreover, when the business implications initiated from operational risks are "high," banking organizations may need to transfer and mitigate such risks through insurance policies. Thus, the framework of risk policies should also provide for the consistent and comprehensive capture of data elements needed to measure and verify the organization's operational risk exposure, as well as appropriate operational risk analytical frameworks, reporting systems, and mitigation strategies. In addition, the framework of the operational risk policies should include a disaster recovery strategy that focuses on the actions that should be taken to recover from an unlikely event of a severe or catastrophic business disruption. More important, banking organizations must design a business continuity plan that helps banking organizations deal effectively with undesirable incidents. A contingency plan essentially describes how to restore normal operations when an adverse condition occurs. Operational risk contingency planning involves creating one or more fallback plans that can be activated in case efforts to prevent the adverse event fail. Contingency plans are required for all operational risks, including those that have mitigation plans. They address what to do if a high-impact operational risk occurs and focus on the consequences and how to minimize the impacts. Especially if the consequences disrupt many services, it may be valuable to bring some services back online first. It must be agreed beforehand on the order in which to restore the services, and it must be decided how long each part can be offline. In addition, contingency plans are based on risk policies of whether to accept, avoid, transfer, or mitigate the existing operational risks. The process and use of contingency plans was extensively discussed in this chapter.

Furthermore, control of operational risks based on the organization's policies, continuity plans, and scenarios must be well defined. Banking organizations must ensure that control actions refer to any operational risks with significant degrees of severity, and the people who are involved are well informed and ready to act accordingly. The framework must also include independent testing and verification to assess the effectiveness of implementation of the organization's operational risk framework, including compliance with policies, processes, and procedures. Finally, board and senior management must be able to have at any desirable time operational risk reports at any level of detail. These reports must provide information about the steps of the operational risk management framework, that is, from the identification, measurement, modeling, monitoring, and evaluation to operational risk profiling, optimization, and control actions. Because operational risks are dynamically changing, the planning actions and policies for managing them must be modified accordingly. Thus, this is an ongoing process. The choice of what planning actions and policies to choose mainly depends on a cost-benefit analysis. Inevitably, some operational risks are unavoidable or, from a cost-benefit standpoint, are worth taking. Capital should be set aside for such operational risks. Note finally that a bank that is able to show that it has prepared for various kinds of disruptions and that its services are reliable may gain a competitive edge over banks that have made no such plans.

References

1. Basel Committee on Banking Supervision, Consultative Document Operational Risk, Supporting Document to the New Basel Capital Accord, January 2001.
2. Federal Deposit Insurance Corporation (FDIC), Supervisory Guidance on Operational Risk AMA for Regulatory Capital, July 2003.
3. Basel Committee on Banking Supervision, Working Paper Regulatory Treatment of Operational Risks, September 2001.

4. Avery, R. and Milton, R., Insurers to the Rescue?, *Operational Risk Management Magazine*, p. 65, 2000.
5. Bank for International Settlements, Risk in Foreign Exchange Transactions, Basel, March 1996.
6. Basel Committee on Banking Supervision, Framework for Internal Control Systems in Banking Organizations, Basel, September 1998.
7. Internal Audit Function and Its Outsourcing, Board of Governors of the Federal Reserve System, Federal Deposit Insurance Corporation, March 2003.
8. Federal Financial Institution's Examination Council (FFIEC), Business Continuity Planning Booklet, May 2003.
9. FFIEC Information Security Booklet, January 2003.
10. Basel Committee on Banking Supervision, Framework for Internal Control Systems in Banking Organizations, Publication No. 40, September 1999, http://www.bis.org/publ.
11. Basel Committee on Banking Supervision, Framework for Evaluation of Internal Control Systems, Publication No. 33, January 1998, http://www.bis.org/publ.
12. Hong Kong Monetary Authority, Supervisory Policy Manual: Business Continuity Planning, TM-G-2, V.1, Hong Kong, 2002.
13. Basel Committee on Banking Supervision, Sound Practices for Management and Supervision of Operational Risk, Switzerland, February 2003.
14. Akkizidis N., Approach of Securitisation to Off-Balance Sheet Treatment, New Innovations and New Markets, 2000, MSc Thesis, Aberconway Libraries, Cardiff University, Business School, U.K.

Chapter 10

Concluding Remarks

The important thing is not to stop questioning.

—Albert Einstein

Operational risks are present and affect everyone across every business. In every operation undertaken in an organization, operational risks are involved. With the advent of the Basel II Accord, increasing attention is being given, and rightly so, to the assessment, control, and management of operational risks in financial organizations. The goal of operational risk management is to manage all those risks that are currently or potentially affecting operations so that business objectives can be accomplished with a minimum amount of loss. Managing does not necessarily mean eliminating but, more important, learning how to accept and minimize certain operational risks. The banking industry is by far the most advanced industry in attempting to manage credit, market, and operational risks in an integrated manner. Regulatory pressure has helped and motivated the banks to adopt a strategic approach to operational continuity and risk management. Banks are realizing that, by managing risks on the operational side, they can maximize returns through more efficient use of capital, thereby increasing shareholder value. The strong points for implementing Basel II stand out loud and clear. Apart from stakeholders increasing the pressure on their banks to adopt the Basel II Accord, regulators and analysts are clearly expecting banks to act on Basel II principles. Regulators will take this into account while issuing opinions and assessing the market.

Furthermore, credit rating agencies are also expecting banks to act on the accord. Fundamentally, the message is this: the greater the effort an organization adopts to understand, mitigate, and manage operational risks, the safer its business is considered to be, and the capital charge lowers accordingly. Whatever financial organizations intend to do, they must ensure that they fulfill regulatory requirements and observe all laws, financial or otherwise. A bank's reputation, its most valuable asset, is an issue of confidence and trust for which aspects of safety and security play a crucial role.

Basel II should not be seen as a burden on resources, but rather as a commercially practical option that will provide an opportunity to improve a financial organization's market position. More important, true competitive advantages arise from developing an organizational culture that proactively manages day-to-day operational risk, identifies new operational risks progressively, shares best practices in the organization and beyond, and systematically tracks operational risk exposures. Building the right culture for this begins with adopting a disciplined approach to operational risk management, starting with the board of directors and moving down through every level and business unit and across every major process in the organization. It needs to adopt a framework customized to peculiar needs for each organization and country of operation. Once the infrastructure is in place, the financial organization must learn to assess the type of its operational risks and its operational risk management frameworks, and assign monetary values to the operational risks it faces. As such, participants have already commenced work on putting in place procedures regarding operational risk management. Banks that have already started risk management programs view Basel II as a change agent. They use the new accord to focus bankwide attention on efforts to achieve operational risk management leadership. Basel II is also good news for banks whose risk management efforts began with the best of intentions but have disappeared gradually through lack of attention. Chief executive officers should recognize that moving so many parts of a bank — most business units as well as the treasury and other corporate center functions — to best practice involves a huge effort. If top management does not take the lead and ensure that benefits from a well-developed business case are captured, then the effort to put together an effective operational risk management program will fail. But the question is, will financial organizations be ready? How far have they reached, and what challenges are they facing?

In general, banks must first integrate an internal risk measurement methodology directly into their day-to-day operational procedures and major decision-making processes. With the advanced measurement approach (AMA), banks can use their own internal loss data to demonstrate to regulators that they should qualify for reduced capital reserves. The use of Basel II Advanced Management Approach (AMA) is subject to supervisory approval, and banks need to classify incidents according to their impact on business. It is essential to start collecting historical data for loss events now, using a data structure that cannot only gather and consolidate data from many sources, but also adapt to changes in the Basel II framework. Financial organizations with the most accurate, relevant, and timely data will be in the best position for acquiring regulatory approval, market validation, and reduced capital reserve. The challenges of implementing an advanced and effective operational risk management framework are therefore becoming increasingly significant.

Recognizing the rapid evolution in operational risk management practices, however, the Basel Committee is prepared to provide banks with an exceptional amount of flexibility to develop an advanced approach. This will allow banks to calculate operational risk capital that they believe is consistent with their types of activities and underlying operational risks. Although many of the details surrounding the AMA are still being worked out, it is assuredly of paramount interest to upper management. The banking services industry as a whole, notwithstanding the major differences among banks, has made considerable progress over the past two to three years in operational risk areas, such as definition, aspects of strategy and planning, structure, reporting tools, capital allocation, and operational risk transfer. Implementing Basel II necessitates that participating banks maintain a sophisticated quantitative and operational risk management infrastructure to ensure the integrity of their internal risk estimates. There is still a gap, though, to reach an effective, credible, and viable operational risk analytical framework. This book has attempted to present an efficient and optimal way to assess, manage, and control operational risks in banking organizations through efficiently evaluating and optimizing operational risks that impact the operational performances of banks' business lines. The same approach can be adopted for other financial organizations. It also showed that there is a need to optimize the distribution of resources, be it financial, systems related, or human, to manage the identified major operational risks.

Operational risk management solutions offer value far beyond an opportunity to reduce regulatory capital. Operational risk management solutions provide bankers with a comprehensive process that will enable them to understand, quantify, control, and manage operational risk in a structured manner, thus adding value to the bottom line. A comprehensive solution must include frameworks for identifying, measuring, modeling, monitoring, evaluating, controlling, and managing operational risks. It should also include a method of documenting, reviewing, and correcting the weaknesses in business processes and an efficient reporting tool that will deliver tailored relevant information to all levels throughout the organization. Best-practice operational risk management solutions demand a comprehensive structured approach with dedicated resources, both human and technical. Each organization's operational risk profile is unique and requires a tailored operational risk management approach appropriate for the scale and materiality of the operational risks present, and the size of the organization. One thing that financial organizations must keep in mind while selecting operational risk management solutions is that they must be flexible enough to accommodate any future regulatory and reporting requirement changes. Operational risks cannot be viewed in isolation. Any model developed by financial organizations to quantify accurately operational risk exposures should be able to "value" risk and relate risk to business processes and objectives, as well as to market and credit risks to form an enterprisewide risk management system.

This book has been written to guide the readers through the vast information surrounding operational risk and its management according to Basel II. More important, its aim is to guide the readers in designing and implementing effective and optimal operational risk management systems using a two-phase approach: assessment and control and management of operational risks. The assessment phase consists of identifying, measuring, modeling, monitoring, and evaluation of operational risks. The control and management phase includes operational risk profiling, optimization, reporting, and setting appropriate policies and decision making. The optimal levels of operational risks and the optimal allocation of resources to manage these risks are extremely important issues in achieving an effective and optimal operational risk management system.

This book introduced the concept of operational risks in financial organizations and highlighted the many aspects of operational risks via the various definitions found in industry and the literature on the subject. Furthermore, it illustrated where operational risks exist in financial organizations, together with the types of risk events that can affect them, with particular attention to people risks. It also addressed the main elements for managing operational risks and identifying the fundamentals of effective operational risk management frameworks. In addition, this book dealt with the efficacy of quantifying operational risks and the importance of loss events and operational risk data management.

The principles and guidelines set out in this book focused primarily on operational risk management. However, in developing their own frameworks, financial organizations will inevitably need to consider how their procedures and frameworks for managing different types of risk should be integrated in an enterprisewide risk management framework. This will ensure both consistency and completeness in their overall risk management approach. The operational risk management framework should therefore be developed within the parameters of, or to interface with, the organization's existing risk management culture, policies, and practices.

In addition, the book highlighted some benefits of complying with Basel II and what key people are needed to implement an effective operational risk management system. Some immediate actions that they should take to put them on the right path to effectively managing and controlling their inherent operational risks were also listed. The concepts of the Basel II Accord were highlighted, with various relevant references made to the numerous documents written by the Basel Committee on the subject. The three mutually reinforcing pillars, which together contribute to increasing the safety and soundness of the financial system, were also introduced, and factors in selecting a particular measurement approach were emphasized. Boards of directors and senior management of financial organizations as well as auditors are responsible for the integrity of operational risk management systems and processes, and this concept is emphasized in the ten principles that form the Basel II standard of operational risk management.

The AMA allows financial organizations to develop their own methodologies in measuring operational risks and the capital they need to set aside in accordance with certain guidelines proposed in Basel II. This approach is intended to be the most risk sensitive and to relate to the experiences of each financial organization. In this book, the AMA was explicitly discussed for efficiently assessing, controlling, and managing operational risks. In such approaches, steps should be taken to design and implement cost-effective solutions to reduce the operational risk to an acceptable and optimum level. Furthermore, the elements of an AMA framework, with emphasis on the internal operational risk loss event data and relevant external operational risk loss event data, were discussed. The book also highlighted the supervisory standards of the AMA and discussed the use of insurance under the AMA.

Operational risk identification is the first element in the process of designing the framework for an efficient and optimal operational risk management system in the AMA. Operational risk mapping and operational process mapping are used to define the general, high-level inputs and outputs and interactions between the operational risks and the operations. This mapping is used as the basis for the identification of the key operations and key risks indicators. The operational performance and operational risk effects, which are defined qualitatively, should somehow be converted to quantitative measurements. This can be achieved using key performance and risk indicators, which were discussed extensively in this book. Operations together with their associated operational risks were combined to construct the operational risk matrix. A loss event database also needs to be defined and considered in the operational risk identification process. The loss event database and the identified and measured key risk indicators are used to define and extract the information data related to operational risks and undesirable performances. Based on the correlation analysis of their information, the models referring to both operational risks and affected operations can be extracted. Three types of data that refer to causes, events, and consequences are used to define these measurement values. This information data is then used to estimate the degree of significance of operational risks by applying correlation analysis, which was discussed comprehensively in this book. The identified significant operational risk values are then used extensively in the design of operational risk assessment and management/control framework. Operational key risk indicators and significance values are used as fundamental aspects in the optimal operational risk monitoring and clustering analysis described in this book.

Modeling and monitoring the operational risks and affected operations illustrate a banking organization's current status in terms of operational risk hazards. The models of the operational risks as well as of the affected operations are defined through correlation analysis in this book. Managers of operational risks must be able to have a clear view of how the affected operations are linked to each other and how operational risks are related to each other. This helps banks to understand and control cascading effects of operational risks. Nonlinear three-dimensional surfaces were utilized in this book to graphically show this correlation effect and level of operational risk significance based on the correlation analysis. Such illustrations facilitate sophisticated monitoring of both operational risks and affected operations, which can serve as "warning signals" of present and future trends.

In the evaluation process, cluster analysis is a key tool that groups homogeneous operational risks or affected operations that have more similarities to one another than to members of other groups. Using such techniques and by introducing two methodologies, called CORE and CAOE, the equilibrium point(s) for both operational risk and affected operations were defined. Moreover, based on these methodologies, the corresponding trends and their accumulations were also defined. A method called MSE can be used to evaluate the severity of the operational risks and the affected operations. This method is based on distribution, significance, and trend analysis.

Moreover, in the evaluation process, a banking organization needs to estimate the economic capital it must reserve for covering potential losses initiated from operational risks. The unexpected losses resulting from people, systems, and processes can be defined by the degree of correlation between business activities referring to other people, systems, and processes.

The potential losses can be categorized according to their direct or indirect effect to operational risks. Their estimation is related to the expected and unexpected operational performances combined with their actual values. This book highlighted the use of operational VaR, determined by utilizing the extreme value theory (EVT), be used for estimating the capital needed to cover the potential losses resulting from operational risks.

The identification of the operational risk profile is based on probability, impact, and exposure analysis. The probability of operational risks refers to their causes, events, and consequences, which were defined in this book by considering the degree of correlations between the operational risks together with their actual values. Because the probability of one operational risk occurring might initiate other ones and thus increase the probability of new operational risks, a chain reaction may occur and may result in a higher impact of the initial operational risk. Therefore, understanding the correlations between the operational risks is a vital process in defining the actual probability and impact for each of the operational risks. By identifying the actual probability and by defining the impact through correlation and cluster analysis, financial organizations are also able to define the impact on the group of related operational risks. In this book, a methodology called "mountain operational risk profile" was adopted to model, evaluate, and analyze the operational risk profile. The operational risk modeling analysis can provide financial organizations with an overview of the actual probability and impact of operational risks, instead of relying only on assumptions. By representing the distribution of the probability, impact, and exposure of operational risks, the model of the operational risk profile was defined. This model can be used as a basis to construct the decision rule base for operational risk decision makers. Clustering analysis was utilized to define the linguistic terms of the rules. Moreover, fuzzy set theory was applied in this book to construct the rules and define how to estimate the values of their consequences. Examples were presented to show how defining the operational risk profile can be used as a powerful operational risk management tool. The analysis of the operational risk profile is a vital process in designing efficient operational risk management systems.

As introduced in this book, the need for designing optimal operational risk management systems originates from the fact that it is inefficient and expensive to try and minimize the values of operational risks to zero. Thus, optimizing the values of the operational risks makes their management very efficient and cost effective. This book defined optimization of operational risks as determining the optimal levels of risks so that the overall magnitude of operational risks is minimized to the lowest possible, or desirable, level. Moreover, the book examined the optimal distribution of the resources needed for the operational risk management process.

Optimization techniques and methodologies, with an approach called SEC methodology, were developed and used in this book. They are based on algorithmic approaches that are able to combine large inhomogeneous and variable operational risk and performance information measurements. The main principle behind the optimization analysis used in this book is to optimize the levels of operational risks to minimize the overall value of the operational risk cost function.

As discussed in this book, the operational risk management framework should provide for the consistent application of operational risk policies and procedures throughout the organization. The planning actions and policies for managing the operational risks are based on their acceptance when their impact and exposure is very low or avoidance when their severity is high. Moreover, when the business objectives are adversely affected by operational risks, banking organizations may need to transfer and mitigate such risks. Thus, the framework of effective decision making and setting optimal operational risk policies should also provide for the consistent and comprehensive capture of data elements needed to measure and verify an organization's operational risk exposure, reporting systems, and mitigation strategies. In addition, the framework of the operational risk policies should include a business continuity plan that focuses on how to deal effectively with undesirable incidents. Furthermore, controlling the operational risks based on the organization's policies, continuity plans, and scenarios must be well defined. Finally, the board of directors and senior management should have access to operational risk reports, which should provide information about the operational risk management steps, that is, from identification, measurement, and evaluation to operational risk profiling, optimization, and control actions. Because operational risks are dynamically changing, the actions and policies to manage them must be modified accordingly. The resulting optimal operational risk matrix that illustrates the optimal values of operational risks was also defined. This matrix can be used as a basis to define the cost of optimal operational risk management and the optimal resource allocation. Constraints referring to the operational activities of people, systems, and processes must be considered during the operational risk optimization analysis. The significance, exposure accumulation, and trend values of operational risks must also be considered in most of the steps for implementing the optimal operational risk management system.

The approaches introduced in this book for the evaluation, risk profiling, and optimization analysis enable banking organizations to minimize their capital requirements to the minimal possible levels, and, more importantly, achieve best practices in operational risk assessment, control, and management. It is important to note that these approaches are not

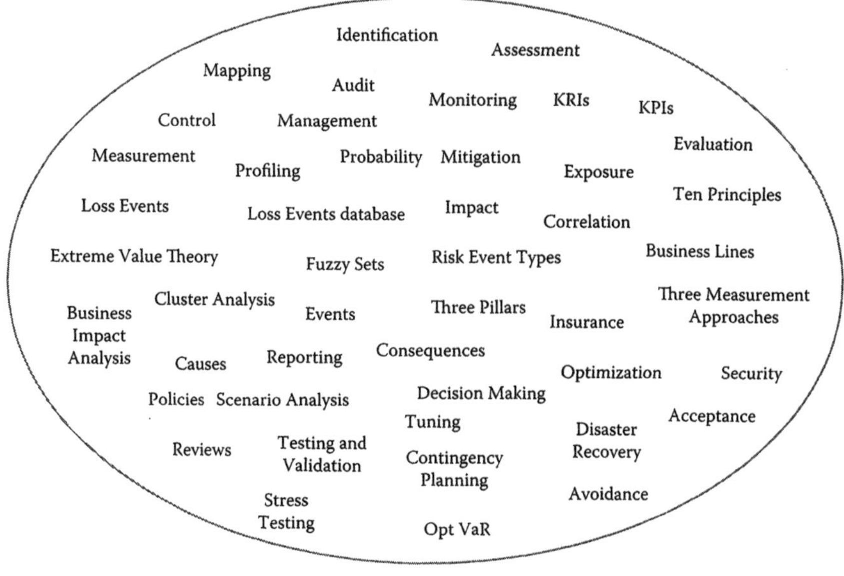

Figure 10.1 Key aspects of efficient and optimal operational risk management.

dependent on historical information, but rather are based on short-term information with a thorough coverage of the operational business activities within all business lines. The idea is based on designing a framework for efficient and optimal operational risk management system that relies on the information that comes from many daily operations covering all the business activities.

Some of the key points highlighted throughout this book are captured in Figure 10.1.

Many actions need to be taken by financial organizations to prepare them and put them on the right path to effectively deploying their operational risk management framework. Chapter 3 listed some action points to be taken under the three pillars of Basel II. Among some of the more general and immediate action points to be taken for the AMA are those listed below. Note that an attempt has been made to put them in order of urgency, but depending on the organization's objectives, a different sequence may be more suitable. Note also that some of these activities may be undertaken in parallel. They include but are not limited to:

- Identify the business goals and limits/constraints.
- Define what operational risks means for the organization and communicate this meaning throughout the organization.

- Identify key operations of the organization.
- Devise a strategy for how operational risks would be identified, assessed, monitored, and controlled or mitigated.
- Decide on external help if needed for implementation.
- Decide on the acceptance policies.
- Identify how to get the data (understand where and how to get the measurements) and consolidate that data into a single operational risk format/database and build loss event database and collect loss event data.
- Define and measure key risk indicators (KRIs) and key performance indicators (KPIs) (understand what to measure).
- Use internal loss data and KPIs for the identification of operational risks.
- Maintain a sophisticated quantitative infrastructure to ensure the integrity of internal/external risk estimates. This is a requirement for objective measurement.
- Map the performance of the operational risks in operations.
- Model the operational risks and affected operations; capture the interrelationships (correlation) between various risk types across departments and lines of business.
- Determine the potential causes, events, and consequences of operational risks.
- Monitor the operational risks.
- Evaluate the severity of the current and future operational risks and affected operations.
- Define the operational risk profile: probability, impact, exposure, and business impact analysis.
- Evaluate and classify the significance of the risks in operations.
- Determine how these risks affect performance and profitability, thus weaving a direct relationship between processes, products, and profit.
- Estimate and evaluate the capital reserves for covering potential losses that initiated from the operational risks.
- Identify the optimal levels of the risks in operations (acceptance management).
- Allocate optimally the resources to manage and control the operational risks.
- Allocate capital reserve based on the analysis of the organization's risk exposure.
- Tune the operational risks levels to reach the optimal levels.
- Where operational risks are evident and internal controls are inefficient, perform scenario analysis.
- Report on the operational risks.

- Design the contingency plan, business impact analysis, and scenario analysis.
- Test and validate the contingency plan.
- Decide on the necessity of insurance coverage based on the organization's exposure to operational risks.
- Review and audit the whole operational risk management system to understand its strong and weak points and implement corrective and preventive actions.

How much capital reserve is required depends on two key issues:

1. Inherent operational risk in the business
2. Operational risks related to people, processes, and systems or, stated another way, quality of the operational risk/control management system

Basel II should be approached as a major project with a number of working groups and several distinct phases (diagnostic, design, implementation, and testing), which may take several years. Operational risk management should be integrated with performance management, knowledge management, quality management, value-based management, integrated management, and enterprise risk management. Such integrations will prove that effective operational risk management improves performance and results and adds value.

The Basel Committee will continue to explore ways of improving the risk sensitivity of operational risks. It plans to work with the industry to identify techniques that result in operational risk reduction and transfer and possible operational risk mitigation techniques.

The upcoming test in the field of risk management is the integration between operational, credit, and market risks. Finally, the implementation of operational risk management frameworks in banking organizations is the forerunner of the enterprisewide risk management, the newest challenges in all financial business sectors worldwide.

The software named "*ButteRfLy*" ver 3.1 found on www.crcpress.com/e_products/downloads/download.asp?cat_no=AU3813 forms the backbone to all the approaches presented in this book. All graphical figures have resulted from the application of this software.

Appendix

Acronyms

Acronyms	*Meaning*
AMA	Advanced measurement approach
ASA	Alternative standardized approach
ATM	Automatic teller machine
BCM	Business continuity management
BCO	Business continuity officers
BCP	Business continuity plan
BIA	Business impact analysis
BIS	Bank for International Settlements
BM	Block Maxima
BNY	Bank of New York
CAOE	Clustering affected operations equilibrium
CEO	Chief executive officer
CIO	Chief information officer
ClORiP	Clustering operational risk profile
COO	Chief operational officer
CORE	Clustering operational risk equilibrium
Credit risk IRB	Credit risk internal rate base

CRM	Customer relationship management
CRO	Chief risk officers
CS	Credit Suisse
CSI	Customer satisfaction index
CSO	Chief security officer
DoMF	Degree of membership function
ECS	Exposure–Correlation–Significance
EI	Exposure indicator: represents a proxy for the size of a particular business line's operational risk exposure
EL	Expected loss
EVT	Extreme value theory
EWRM	Enterprisewide risk management
FCM	Fuzzy C means
FRG	Force of risk gravity
FS	Fuzzy set
FSA	Financial Services Authority
GAAP	Generally Accepted Accounting Principles
GDP	Gross domestic product
GEV	Generalized extreme value
GI	Gross income
GPD	Generalized Pareto distribution
HCM	Hard C mean
HW	Hardware
IAS	International Accounting Standards
IDS	Intrusion detection system
IID	Independently and identically distributed
IMA	Internal measurement approach
IRT	Internet-related technology
IT	Information technology
LDA	Loss distribution approach

LGE	Loss given event: represents the proportion of transaction or exposure that would be expensed as loss, given that event
MF	Membership function
MSE	Mountain surface evaluation
OR	Operational risk
ORM	Operational risk management
PE	Probability of loss event: represents the probability of occurrence of loss events
POT	Peaks over threshold
QAM	Quality assurance manager
RAROC	Risk adjusted return on capital
RE	Risk exposure
RMG	Risk Management Group of the Basel Committee
RPI	Risk profile index
SEC	Significance-Exposure-Correlation
SW	Software
UL	Unexpected loss
UPS	Uninterruptible power supply
VaR	Value at risk
VBM	Value-based management

Index

A

B

C

D

E

F

G

H

I

J

K

L

M

N

O

P

Q

R

U

V

W

For Product Safety Concerns and Information please contact our EU
representative GPSR@taylorandfrancis.com
Taylor & Francis Verlag GmbH, Kaufingerstraße 24, 80331 München, Germany

www.ingramcontent.com/pod-product-compliance
Ingram Content Group UK Ltd.
Pitfield, Milton Keynes, MK11 3LW, UK
UKHW021624240425
457818UK00018B/718

9780367391881